WAR OF THE WINDSORS

Dedication

This book is dedicated with many thanks to Jeffrey Simmons,
whose idea it was.

WAR OF THE WINDSORS

A Century of Unconstitutional Monarchy

Lynn Picknett, Clive Prince,
Stephen Prior and Robert Brydon

MAINSTREAM
PUBLISHING
EDINBURGH AND LONDON

First published in Great Britain in 2002 by
MAINSTREAM PUBLISHING COMPANY (EDINBURGH) LTD
7 Albany Street
Edinburgh EH1 3UG

ISBN 1 84018 631 3

A catalogue record for this book is available from the British Library

Typeset in Garamond
Printed and bound in Great Britain by
Creative Print and Design Wales

CONTENTS

	Acknowledgements	6
	Prologue	7
ONE	'A Kingly Caste of Germans'	11
TWO	'The People's Prince'	32
THREE	'Christ! What's Going to Happen Next?'	66
FOUR	'A Kind of English National Socialist'	100
FIVE	'The Most Unconstitutional Act'	133
SIX	'The End of Many Hopes'	159
SEVEN	'The House of Mountbatten Now Reigns!'	189
EIGHT	'That German Princeling'	222
NINE	'In Spite of Everything, He was a Great Man'	252
TEN	'After All I've Done for this F——ing Family'	278
EPILOGUE	'We the People'	308
	Notes and References	313
	Bibliography	326
	Index	333

ACKNOWLEDGEMENTS

We would like to thank the following people for their help, support and encouragement in the writing of this book.

Francesca, Michelle, Jo and Alice for, once again, putting up with us all and Lyndsay Brydon for putting up with some of us!

Our agents Lavinia Trevor and Jeffrey Simmons

For giving us their time, memories, experiences and information
Madeleine Masson, Yvan Cartwright, David Bews, Iain Gray, Willie Henderson, Charles Destrée, George Bethune, Barry Dunford, Niven Sinclair, Georgina Bruni, Margaret Laidlaw, Ralph de Toledano, Mohamed Al Fayed, Chapman Pincher, Michael 'Tim' Buckmaster, Richard Tomlinson, James C de C Scott, Jane Pelling, Marion Milne, Nicholas Gibb, Dr Hugh Thomas, Mike Wallington, Nicholas Sheetz, Anthony Cave-Brown, Walter Pforzheimer, John Taylor Cameron Simpson, Capt. Howard Sartori – USN, Trevor Poots, the late Kenneth de Courcey, the de Courcy family, Eric Taylor and Sir David Frost. Also 'Phoenix', and all those who have helped us but for various reasons prefer not to be named.

For their help in many different ways
Mary Neilson, Keith Prince, Debbie Benstead, Richard Taylor, Jim Naples, Sheila Taylor, Carly Beadle, Craig Oakley, Clementina Bentine, Lily and David Prince, and Sue and Tony Young

The staff of the following libraries and archives
British Library, London; Cambridge University Library; National Library of Scotland, Edinburgh; Georgetown University, Washington DC; House of Lords Record Office; Imperial War Museum; Public Record Office. Scottish Record Office; US National Archive, Washington, C.I.C. and C.I.E. archives at US National Archive, Maryland; Edinburgh City Library; St John's Wood Library, London

PROLOGUE

This book began as a sequel to *Double Standards: The Rudolf Hess Cover-Up* (2001), which presented the results of our ten-year investigation into the mystery of the flight of Hitler's Deputy to Britain during the Second World War. We concluded that – far from being the irrelevant sideshow it has been portrayed since 1945 – Hess's mission was a genuine attempt to negotiate an end to the war: indeed, it was enthusiastically supported by eminent figures in Britain, including members of the royal family. In particular, we uncovered evidence that George, Duke of Kent, the youngest brother of King George VI and the present queen's late uncle, had played a key role in the Hess plan. But once the Nazi's peace mission failed, the whole episode was quietly airbrushed out of history.

As *Double Standards* concentrated on the Duke of Kent's wartime activities, it only touched on the other, equally important, periods of his life. Our original intention for what became *War of the Windsors* was to write a book that examined this fascinating and influential figure in greater detail, for few today have even heard of the 'forgotten prince'. Kent's near-erasure from history followed his mysterious death in an air crash in August 1942, about which all the official documents have been withheld or 'lost'. It seems the campaign to make him a non-person in royal history was quite deliberate, because the royal family and their most loyal servants feared the consequences for their image should the truth about him ever be revealed. This complex and glamorous man also had the distinction of losing not one, but two, thrones. When Edward VIII abdicated in 1936 to become the much-reviled Duke of Windsor, it was Kent, rather than the next eldest brother the Duke of York (later George VI), who was initially considered as his successor: however, for reasons explained in these pages, this was an unacceptable option for the government of the time. After this, Kent was offered the crown of Poland, but first the onset of the war and then his untimely death in Scotland in 1942 prevented this plan from coming to fruition.

However, we soon realised that it was impossible to tell Kent's story without delving into other complex issues relating to Britain's royal family in the twentieth century, such as his relationships with the disgraced Edward VIII and his father, George V, for whom he acted as political advisor. Although much has been written about Edward's contact with Nazi Germany, few realise that it was maintained through the intermediary of the Duke of Kent – and that he had fulfilled the same role for the still-respected George V. As we will show, the old King's relationship with the Nazis went much further than most historians will admit: we were astounded to discover that Hitler's henchmen even influenced the composition of his government . . .

We were also fascinated by Kent's legacy for the post-war royal family, particularly the fact that his death paved the way for the rise of another incredibly influential figure in the history of the House of Windsor, Lord Louis Mountbatten, whose often ludicrous Baron-Münchausen-like self-aggrandisement concealed a deadly capacity for intrigue that occasionally tipped over into outright treachery. Eventually it was our agent, Jeffrey Simmons, who suggested that rather than try to untangle the Duke of Kent's story from its intricate royal background, perhaps it would serve us better if we wrote a 'secret history' of the House of Windsor from its creation in the middle of the First World War until the present day.

Researching the Rudolf Hess story also made us acutely aware of the problem of assessing the validity of history books that relied on official sources. In the case of the non-person Kent, all his personal papers and the official documents relating to him are kept in the Royal Archives at Windsor Castle, where they remain strictly out of bounds even to officially approved historians and biographers. This is a very unusual situation: it is customary for the private papers of members of the royal family to be opened after their death for the approved author of the 'official biography'. Not only does the embargo on Kent's papers reveal that there are aspects of his life that the royal family are not keen for us to know about – even 60 years after his death – but it also highlights a fundamental question about the way that history is written.

Academic historians rely for their sources on archives, diaries and collections of personal papers that are usually lodged with a recognised and respected institution, such as the Public Record Office, university libraries or the Royal Archives. It is accepted that there will be certain restrictions: for example, government records are subject to official secrecy legislation that withholds documents from public release for varying lengths of time, and prominent individuals who leave their personal papers to the nation may specify that they should not be made available for a certain period. But overall historians and biographers tend to assume that these – and only these – sources contain the truth, the whole truth and nothing but the truth. This, we discovered, is a great mistake.

However, assured of the lily-white veracity of their sources, royal writers and other historians rarely question either their completeness or accuracy. Our own experience has been a short sharp lesson in cynicism. Where the monarchy and government secrets are concerned, the 'official' sources are intended less as repositories of historical facts than an enticing framework for the story that they want written. This can be achieved in several ways, sometimes through the complete or partial restriction of archive material, as in the case of the Duke of Kent; or the withholding of a box of papers, as happened with a private collection that was scheduled for release in 2000, because they related to the Queen Mother (and in particular her true attitude to Nazi Germany on the eve of the war). In more extreme cases, history can literally be rewritten by destroying documents that would call the official version into question, or even by falsifying records that are passed on to posterity. We have uncovered several examples of such ruthless methods; now we realise that as far as archival material is concerned, nothing is sacred, and therefore no archive should be relied upon.

On the other hand, academic historians often reject controversial information because it does not originate in these officially endorsed repositories. One example is the 'China Dossier' compiled by MI5 on Wallis Simpson, which – as we shall show – played a crucial part in the abdication of Edward VIII, while its very existence is doubted by his biographers because they have never seen it in the official archives. This scepticism is quite unnecessary, for the dossier certainly existed, as we can prove from the testimony of people who saw it. Another example is the document brought by Rudolf Hess setting out in detail the peace terms offered by Hitler in 1941, which, according to our information, is locked away in the Royal Archives. With it are letters recovered from Germany at the end of the war by Anthony Blunt, which showed the true extent of contact between members of the British royal family and the Nazi Government. Because nobody has seen this correspondence since Blunt brought it back, of course it never existed – but we have uncovered evidence that the letters *have* been seen.

If an official biographer claims that he has been given complete and unrestricted access to the relevant files in the Royal Archives – as does, for example, Philip Ziegler, biographer of Edward VIII[1] – how can he tell that is the case? How can he be sure that the most sensitive documents have not been buried in some even deeper vault?

The royal family also operate a system of patronage – some might call it an elegant form of blackmail – where official biographers are concerned: their access to the Royal Archives (unlike the Public Record Office or the British Library) has to be approved, which means that the royal officials can select individuals who are considered a safe pair of hands.[2] Moreover, when access is granted for an official biography of a living or dead member of the royal family, part of the deal is that the finished manuscript is submitted to Buckingham Palace for approval. The Palace has the right – not infrequently exercised – to amend it. The manuscript of Ziegler's biography of Edward

VIII, published in 1990, was read personally by the Queen and Queen Mother[3] – which shows just how sensitive that subject still is.

The price of making any information public without going through these channels is being struck off the list of those permitted access to the archive, which, since most royal authors rely on such access for their career, spells the end of their livelihood. The British writer A.N. Wilson cites the case of a Palace-approved biographer who chanced across a letter in the Royal Archives written by Prince Albert to the Privy Council in 1861. The Prince Consort wrote that Queen Victoria was suffering from mental problems and that her behaviour was putting a strain on their marriage, and asked the Council whether, if the situation did not improve, he would be allowed to separate from her. Of course, this presents an entirely different image of their allegedly idyllic marriage, just as, over a century later, the crumbling relationship of Charles and Diana was still being projected as happy and secure, even up to the day of their official separation. Predictably, Wilson's informant begged him not to reveal his identity, since his professional future was at stake – he would be banned from the archive, and his career would be over. After Wilson wrote about the letter in his newspaper column (without mentioning his friend's name) he was told by another Palace-approved scholar that, given the way the Palace usually worked, the offending letter would almost certainly have been destroyed immediately.[4] Compared to some of the discoveries we made during the course of our research, this is a relatively innocuous example, but it shows the extent of royal control over the dissemination of both historical fact and official faction, and their abiding fear that the internal feuding – and sometimes all-out war – that has characterised the House of Windsor may become common knowledge.

There are also cases where writers have been pressurised by members of the royal family to suppress information, and – as we shall see – even where manuscripts have been altered to ensure that they conform to the accepted picture. And then, to add insult to injury, the amended manuscripts have been stolen, even from a secure bank vault.

It may come as no surprise that much of the information in this book clashes head-on with the generally accepted – and officially promoted – version of history, although it has been painstakingly pieced together from many different sources over several years. We consider that the dangers inherent in our producing such a book, while real and not inconsiderable, are – hopefully – outweighed by the satisfaction of uncovering the true story of the House of Windsor, despite a century of lies, obfuscation and fantasy. Surely by the twenty-first century, this famous democracy has earned the truth about the family that enjoys so many privileges as the representatives of the people of Britain.

ONE

'A KINGLY CASTE OF GERMANS'

H.G. Wells on the British royal family, 1917

George V may have echoed the traditional British xenophobia when he said, 'Abroad is awful. I know, I have been there,'[1] but in the days of over-heated anti-German feeling during the First World War – in which even innocent dachshunds were stoned in the street – his own pedigree was becoming not only an embarrassment but also a danger. With a name like Saxe-Coburg-Gotha – which was particularly unfortunate because the citizens of London had been bombed by Gotha aircraft – George was only too German. He and his wife, the formidably corseted Queen Mary – whose parents were also Teutonic – even spoke with a soft guttural accent, which came as something of a shock when his subjects heard him speak on the radio for the first time. So rather belatedly, as is so often the way when the British royal family react to the prevailing sentiments of the people, a new name was conjured out of nothing, like a magician's 'abracadabra', with which to banish the solid Teutonic air that surrounded the family. After rejecting a clutch of possibilities, King and Court finally settled on the name of 'Windsor': undoubtedly a stroke of genius, for that simple word had the power to summon up the image of the huge, solid castle with all its comforting associations of rock-like stability and timeless tenure. 'Windsor' instantly bestowed upon a stodgy and unstable German line a super-English aura. It was even, in its own way, rather romantic.

The association with age-old Windsor Castle immediately evoked dazzling golden eras of very British monarchs, with a suggestion here of Arthur and his questing knights, a touch there of Henry V and the glories of Agincourt and a top note of the ultimate royal icon, Elizabeth I, in her bejewelled carapace. Even set against such an illustrious background, the advent of the Windsors seems to have been on the whole a good thing, especially from the later perspective of Elizabeth II's unexpectedly successful Golden Jubilee. Today she rules with composure and confidence, if not noticeable panache and glamour, and to most ordinary Britons – and many others, across the old Empire in particular – she is the representative par excellence of a venerable and time-honoured royal house, which is perceived, despite the occasional wobble, never to have been less than noble and self-sacrificing.

The successive sovereigns of the House of Windsor are seen as the responsible, respectable – and unswervingly constitutional – upholders of the greatest surviving monarchy on earth. Although even in the twenty-first century we are not citizens of Britain, but still, quaintly – and to some offensively – *subjects* of the Queen, Britons on the whole tend to see the three kings and single queen of this relatively new royal house as the embodiment of the law, and fondly imagine that they have never so much as infringed it. Buried in the British psyche is the trusting notion that if the king or queen so much as thought about bending the law in any way we would somehow all know about it.

That, then, is the fairy tale . . .

WILKOMMEN TO THE WINDSORS

Far from being born in the mists of time, the House of Windsor leapt fully formed from mother necessity as recently as 17 July 1917 when the sailor King, bluff and bulging-eyed George V – who had acceded to the throne seven years earlier as a Saxe-Coburg-Gotha to his fingertips – issued a proclamation 'declaring that the Name of Windsor is to be borne by His Royal House and Family and relinquishing the use of all German Titles and Dignities', thus making for the first time the name of the family and royal house one and the same.[2] As Britain was now Germany's sworn enemy it was thought prudent for the royal family to distance itself from its German roots and continued dynastic links, particularly because the detested Kaiser Wilhelm II was the King's first cousin. Both men were grandsons of Queen Victoria and the German leader had been a frequent visitor to his British relatives.

It was all really rather embarrassing – and perhaps dangerous, too, for if harmless dachshunds could bear the brunt of anti-German feeling, might not the King himself be next in line for the attentions of a baying mob? But it seemed that the danger had passed, for the simple change of name turned this particular sausage dog into a greyhound waiting in the slips at one stroke: a tangible sign of the monarch's solidarity with his war-torn people.

Yet the Windsor initiative was not solely the result of a royal decision: pressure had been brought to bear. It had not escaped the notice of several well-placed critics that the royal family, and in particular the King himself, was distressingly Germanic. The Hanoverian legacy weighed heavily on the Crown as the war progressed, causing republicans such as the science-fiction writer H.G. Wells to write in exasperation: 'The British Empire is very near the limit of its endurance of a kingly caste of Germans.'[3]

Other names were also changed hurriedly. The brother of George's consort, Queen Mary, was transformed from Prince of Teck to the Marquess of Cambridge – another instantly evocative English name. And although Prince Louis of Battenberg, First Sea Lord at the outbreak of hostilities, was transmogrified into the Marquess of Milford Haven, his family name became Mountbatten – a direct anglicisation of 'Battenberg'. Unfortunately, although apparently sturdy and unflinchingly noble, there is no place in Britain that bears that name: in effect, it was as flimsily fictitious as that of any Ruritanian hero. As a name it could be said to be all drawbridge and no keep – a description that also fitted to perfection its most famous bearer, Prince Louis's second son, later Earl Mountbatten of Burma, who will feature prominently in this story.

However, the 'rebranding' of the royal house was not merely a hasty reaction to the war, a pragmatic decision to address a very embarrassing situation: the conflict brought to a head issues that had been hovering over the royal family for decades. Ever since the advent of the House of Hanover in 1714 the royal family had never succeeded in shaking off the feeling that they were foreigners, that despite their elevated position and tenuous connection to great English ancestors, there was something not quite British about them, a feeling that the ancient aristocratic families delighted in exacerbating.

There is no doubt that the House of Windsor had a very German background. Since the House of Hanover became the ruling dynasty of Britain, the royal family had certainly flaunted its German origins and connections. Because Parliament had passed a law decreeing that no Catholic could accede to the throne, when the last of the Stuart monarchs, Queen Anne, died, the Crown passed to the person who would have otherwise been 52nd in line, George Guelph, the Elector of the small German state of Hanover.

George I (reigned 1714–27) was German by birth – and never let anyone forget it. He showed little interest in England and its culture, never mastered the language and spent half of the rest of his life in Hanover, where he died and was buried. George III (reigned 1760–1820) was the first of the line to be born in England.

Proud of their roots, the Hanoverians made a point of taking spouses from other German royal families, most famously when Victoria (reigned 1837–1901) married Prince Albert of Saxe-Coburg-Gotha. Queen Mary was the first royal spouse since the advent of the House of Hanover to speak English as a first language – but even this was largely an accident: she was born at her parents' London home, but they came from Teck in Germany.

The Hanoverians were not simply foreigners imposing themselves on the British: until Victoria came to the throne, the King of England was also the ruler of Hanover. (The Hanoverian rules of succession forbade a woman from being ruler, so when Victoria became Queen, her uncle, the Duke of

Cumberland, took the throne of Hanover.) Even so, Queen Victoria declared that 'the German element must be cherished and kept up in our beloved home'.[4] Indeed, she and Albert chose to live at Balmoral because the landscape reminded them of Germany.

All of George V and Queen Mary's children were brought up bilingual in English and German. Even as late as the 1930s, the future Edward VIII declared, 'I have not one drop of blood in my veins which is not German.'[5]

As a result of Victoria and Albert's union – unlike the present queen, she took her husband's name when they married – on the accession of her son as Edward VII in 1901 the British royal house became Saxe-Coburg-Gotha. Edward was, however, the one and only monarch to reign under this name.

With the added pressure of war with the Fatherland, in 1917 the royal family suddenly stood out like lederhosen at an investiture. Something had to be done. The new name of Windsor was intended to reinforce the family's adopted Englishness (as 'Britishness' was then termed in those far-off, politically incorrect days) and also to extinguish, once and for all, the impertinent idea that the country was reigned over by a foreign dynasty.

However, the reality was somewhat different: in fact, the German connection was only part of the reason for the change of name – and even then not the most important part. Another event had rocked the old order in Europe in the months before the King's proclamation, prompting all royal and aristocratic houses to cast around for ways of shoring up their defences. The Russian Revolution had dramatically marked the end of Tsar Nicholas II's reign and he had abdicated in March 1917. Although at that time he and his family still lived, it was a shocking and profoundly worrying event for all other royal families. Suddenly no royal family felt safe. Could the unthinkable happen even in Britain?

Now that republicans like H.G. Wells were playing on anti-German feeling unleashed by the war to try to turn the people against the monarchy, George V had no other option but to publicly deny his Teutonic roots. Undoubtedly, it was the Russian Revolution, rather than the war itself, that inspired George's change of name – after all, the war had already lasted for three years when he finally took the step of becoming the first Windsor.

MAKER OF THE WINDSORS

George may have proclaimed his overnight transformation into a Windsor, but unsurprisingly – being as remarkable for his lack of imagination as he was for his deficiencies of intellect – he had not thought of it for himself. The honour for creating today's dynasty goes to the King's Private Secretary, Lord Stamfordham, who, following the death of Queen Victoria in 1901, had emerged as the most powerful figure in a group of courtiers and royal officials which took on the role of protecting the ruling family and preserving the monarchy at all costs.

As Sir Arthur Bigge, Stamfordham had been Queen Victoria's last Private Secretary and her son, Edward VII, continued to make the most of his undoubted talents by appointing him as Private Secretary to his own heir, then the Duke of York. The title 'King's Private Secretary' sounds innocuous enough, but it is one of the most important positions in the country: indeed, at the end of the nineteenth century, Prime Minister Lord Rosebery called it 'the most important in public office'.[6] Modern constitutional historian Vernon Bogdanor describes it as a 'crucial constitutional role'.[7]

The Private Secretary is the sovereign's personal adviser whose primary function is to guard the sovereign's constitutional position, ensuring that the king or queen is properly informed about the issues on which their government is advising and assisting them in exercising the royal prerogative. More than that, he is the link between Crown and Parliament and between the sovereign and prime minister. And yet, as far as is practicable, he 'always remains anonymous'.[8] (This was easier to achieve before the present queen's reign, but even today the title gives the public the impression that the Private Secretary is basically a personal assistant.)

On his accession George V elevated his loyal servant and kingmaker to the peerage and assiduously kept him by his side as chief informant and advisor on political and social issues. After Stamfordham's death in 1931, George was to write that he 'taught me how to be a King'.[9] It is largely due to Stamfordham and his network of advisers and informants that the British monarchy survives to this day, having successfully muddled through the great crises they brought upon themselves and the upheavals caused by the wind of change.

A key figure in this 'Palace mafia' was Lord Esher, effectively the King's image consultant – a function he had also performed for his predecessor, Edward VII. Esher was a true believer in the monarchy and as such swore to dedicate his life to preserving it – if necessary, even through the medium of judicious change. It was he who instituted the policy of – to use his own term – 'democratisation' of the monarchy, although this may seem strange coming from one who wrote of the 'curious superstition which men call democracy'.[10] However, he was realistic enough to acknowledge that if the monarchy were to survive in the turbulent twentieth century, the institution would at least have to adopt the semblance of becoming more democratic. It was cynical and typically tough-minded: in those days the Palace mafia was not known for timidity or weakness in issues that really mattered. And neither is its modern counterpart.

There was also the pervasive feeling that the machinations of public relations were required as Britain struggled to assert itself in the early years of a new and uniquely demanding age. This was the province of George V's Press Secretary, Clive (later Lord) Wigram, who declared: 'The press is a powerful weapon in the twentieth century!'[11] Wigram had effectively created his own job when he had proposed that the Palace should employ 'a well-paid press representative, with an office and sufficient sums for propaganda purposes',[12] and after the person he originally proposed for the post declined the honour.

Astonishingly for such a reactionary cabal, Buckingham Palace became one of the first great institutions to recognise the importance of the media in public relations: the first royal Press Secretary had been appointed by Queen Victoria as far back as the 1860s, but Wigram was to change the role from simply informing the press about the daily toings and froings of the family to creating a very specific image of the ruling dynasty. News reports were to be carefully controlled in order to maintain that image and influence public opinion – a considerably easier task in Wigram's day than in today's scandal-hungry and less deferential age where 'leaks' generally do not serve the royal family well.

The tight little coterie of Stamfordham, Esher and Wigram essentially created 'the Palace' in the sense that we understand it today, the non-military bodyguard of courtiers and officials that protects the family, as much from itself as from baleful outside influences. In particular, Stamfordham's self-appointed task was to monitor the opinions of all sections of the British public about the royal family – with especial emphasis on the all-important working classes – and to analyse the implications for the monarchy, to formulate policies and suggest courses of action that would be advantageous to the new Windsor dynasty.

A particularly valuable source of information came from clergymen with parishes in working-class areas and who were therefore in day-to-day contact with the 'ordinary people' – for example, the Bishop of Chelmsford, John Watts-Ditchfield, who had made his reputation as a vicar in London's poverty-stricken Bethnal Green, and Clifford Woodward, the Canon of Southwark. It was they and their like who would be among the first to note any groundswell of Bolshevik tendency among the 'great unwashed', or indeed any less dramatic grumblings and murmurings about George as King.

Wise counsellors know that it is always an excellent idea to keep an eye on the potential opposition and Stamfordham's royal mafia even infiltrated organisations that appeared to present some threat to the monarchy, real or imagined. This sort of vigilance has remained a major function of the royal mafia, although of course the individuals have changed over the years. The problem as Stamfordham saw it was that the institution of the monarchy had emerged from the nineteenth century in deep trouble and the crisis had been exacerbated by the First World War.

THE GREAT WAR

Despite playing up to the role of the quintessential Englishman, George V only accepted the change of name to Windsor reluctantly, after Lord Stamfordham – ever the smooth tactician – persuaded him of its necessity. Like other royals, George believed that dynastic ties were above politics, even those of war: indeed, European – especially German – royals and aristocrats were appalled at the abrupt emergence of the 'Windsors', one registering his disgust that royal tradition should be sacrificed for 'a mere war'. When told of the change of name, the Kaiser quipped that he was going to see a performance of Shakespeare's *The Merry Wives of Saxe-Coburg-Gotha*. (As he was not known for his wit, it is possible that this quip originated with one of his image makers.)

Up until the middle of the First World War, George seems to have been blissfully oblivious to the dangers of his Germanic ties. Presaging the royal family's attitude two decades later to the gathering storm of the second great global conflict, George thought it best that Britain kept out of the coming hostilities that seemed increasingly certain to engulf all the nations of Europe. A matter of days before Britain declared war on Germany on 4 August 1914 (as it happened, on the future Queen Mother's 14th birthday), he told the Kaiser's brother, Prince Henry of Prussia, that he hoped Britain would remain neutral.[13]

The outbreak of war was somewhat awkward for the British King. He held the honorary rank of Field Marshal in the German Army and was godfather to one of Kaiser Wilhelm's sons. For his part, the Kaiser was removed as Knight of the Garter, largely because of the popular demand that his and other Germans' banners be removed from St George's Chapel, Windsor. George had resisted this move, to no avail. (Ironically, Wilhelm II, who was something of an anglophile, had been criticised in Germany for being too English in his ways.)

The Anglo-German chumminess continued during the war: while the shells screamed down on British and German trenches, the Kaiser sent his 'loyal and devoted' good wishes – through neutral Sweden – for the golden wedding celebrations of Victoria's oldest surviving daughter, Princess Helena, and her husband Prince Christian of Schleswig-Holstein, George V's cousin.[14] George V argued with the Prime Minister, Herbert Asquith, that one of his cousins could not really be considered as an enemy because he was merely in charge of a prisoner-of-war camp.[15] But even George was finally persuaded that ties had to be severed – and be seen to be severed – especially after the onslaught of criticism from the likes of thinkers such as H.G. Wells, who wrote in *The Times* in 1917: 'The security of the British monarchy lies in . . . a courageous severance of its destinies from the inevitable collapse of the Teutonic dynastic system upon the continent of Europe.'[16]

It was small comfort that the British royals were not alone in their difficulties: before the war, hereditary rule had been the norm in Europe. Before the first shot was fired there were only three republics – France, Switzerland and San Marino – but by the time the dust had settled after the Armistice of 1918, there were 14. Not only had the most powerful royal house in Europe, the Romanovs, fallen to the Bolsheviks, but also the apparently indestructible Hapsburgs' Austro-Hungarian Empire had been swept away.

Germany itself was a mess. It had been a confederation of nearly 40 states of varying sizes, including four kingdoms and many other forms of hereditary rule (duchies, principalities and so on), all united under the Kaiser (or Emperor) as the King of Prussia had become in 1871. This glittering edifice had completely crumbled by the end of the war: all of these kings and princes had been forced to abdicate and republics were established. In Bavaria, the last king was forcibly deposed by a communist uprising and a short-lived Soviet republic was proclaimed – to the outrage of the German nationalists and even one apparently insignificant Austrian, who was determined to rid the country of the Bolsheviks. But although Adolf Hitler succeeded in trouncing the communists, of course he did not restore the monarchy to the land, perceiving the concept of the German Führer to be greater than any king or emperor.

Although Stamfordham had long recognised the threat posed by the rise of republicanism and of the Labour movement, the situation was now much worse than he had anticipated. He had assumed that any challenge to the monarchy would come through the ballot box, with the election of a Labour government. Indeed, the British people had undoubtedly moved to the Left as a direct consequence of the war. The Bishop of Chelmsford told Stamfordham in July 1917 that, in his estimation, the advent of a Labour government in the wake of war was 'probable'.[17] In fact, the first Labour government was elected just seven years later. But now there was the additional threat of a Russian-style revolution and the wary Stamfordham knew that any form of political agitation – or 'direct action' in today's terminology – could be the spark to set it off, just as the Russian Revolution began with food riots in St Petersburg. This was seen as a very real danger.

In June 1917, a conference of left-wingers was held in Leeds to mark the Russian Revolution. It was attended by over a thousand delegates. A secret report of the speeches and resolutions was drawn up for the War Cabinet and a copy passed to the King, who was appalled to discover that there had been repeated calls for a British version of the Revolution. The future Labour Prime Minister, Ramsay MacDonald, had not only congratulated the Russian people on the overthrow of the Tsar and the old order but added to the Leeds audience: 'Now the war is on, now is your chance.' The War Cabinet report pulled no punches, concluding that the Leeds conference 'intended to lead, if possible, a revolution in this country'.[18] It was no coincidence that despite being in the middle of a great war, 1917 was a record year for strikes.

The King was a worried man: his advisers could offer little in the way of hope. Lord Esher reflected the fears of the War Cabinet report when he wrote: 'We shall be lucky if we escape a revolution in which the monarchy, the Church and all our Victorian institutions will founder. I have met no one who, speaking in his innermost mind, differs from this conclusion.'[19]

From her Windsor eyrie, Victoria herself had predicted that the British Crown would not last beyond the 1930s, and Edward VII believed that his son and heir would be the last King of Great Britain. They were nearly right.

ABANDONING THE TSAR

Concern over the possibility of a revolution in Britain led George V to commit a grave act against his wider family – indeed, against normal humanity itself. A few days after Tsar Nicholas's deposition, the new Russian Government made a formal request to the British Government for asylum for their royal family, stressing the danger they faced from the extremist element.[20] A meeting of Stamfordham, representing the King, Prime Minister David Lloyd George and other political leaders, agreed (it was even proposed that the Romanovs be accommodated at Balmoral) and the Russian Government was informed of this decision.

However, after analysing the possible reaction of the Labour movement to having the Russian royals on British soil, Stamfordham changed his mind and advised the King that giving them asylum would only inflame revolutionary tendencies: the only sensible course was to retract the offer. Eight days after the first meeting he wrote to the Foreign Secretary, Arthur Balfour, expressing the King's doubts 'on the grounds of expediency'. Balfour replied that it was too late – the offer sent to the Russian Government could not be withdrawn. However, the King and Stamfordham kept up the pressure – Stamfordham writing that the move would 'undoubtedly compromise the King and Queen' and that it would work to the benefit of anti-monarchists. Eventually the Prime Minister agreed and the promise of a safe haven was withdrawn.[21]

Not only was this act immoral, but it was unconstitutional. As we will see, the cornerstone of Britain's constitutional government is that the monarch must abide by the advice of his ministers. The minister in question, the Foreign Secretary, had advised George V that the offer of asylum could not be withdrawn, and that should have been the end of the matter. Instead, the King and Palace kept up the pressure on the Government until it changed its mind. A little over a year later, Tsar Nicholas, his wife (George V's cousin) and their children were executed by bullet and – for those who stubbornly clung to life – also by bayonet.

It was recognised that such apparent heartlessness on the part of the King would do him no good with the people, so it was decided that the Prime Minister, Lloyd George, would take the blame. At the time, and for decades afterwards, the official explanation was that it was he who had retracted the offer of asylum for the desperate Romanovs – which was technically true, but omitted the fact that he had only done so after sustained pressure from the King. This royal whitewash splashed yet wider when it was later claimed – most stridently by the mendacious Lord Mountbatten[22] – that George V had pleaded with Lloyd George to rescue the Russian royals. For example, George's son, as Duke of Windsor, was to write that 'my father had personally planned to rescue him [the Tsar] with a British cruiser, but in some way the plan was blocked' and that 'it hurt my father that Britain had not raised a hand to save his Cousin Nicky'.[23] However, when state papers relating to the affair, which included Stamfordham's notes to the Government, were finally released in 1986 – having been withheld for 50 years after the King's death – it was conclusively shown that this was a lie.

Although it is beyond the scope of this book, there is also a question over the fate of that portion of the Romanov fortune which was held in London and whether it ended up in the coffers of the House of Windsor.[24]

NEW BLOOD

Changing the name of the royal house was only part of a swathe of moves designed to make the monarchy appear more acceptably English and democratic. It was also announced that, in future, descendants of the royal family who were not in the immediate line of succession would lose their royal status,[25] and George V finally bowed to pressure to agree to end the custom of marrying royal princes exclusively to royal brides (i.e. foreigners), and – although this was not actually effected for some years – accepted that they might begin to marry British ladies. The essayist Cecil Battine summed up this groundswell of opinion when he wrote that 'princes must marry British subjects or lose their rights'.[26] (As things turned out, this extremely timely move was to save the monarchy in the dark days of 1936.)

The King's advisers were supportive: the Bishop of Chelmsford opined that 'the stability of the Throne would be strengthened if the Prince of Wales married an English lady' (in retrospect a particularly astute remark). The Canon of Southwark also advised that the Prince of Wales should marry a daughter of 'one of the great English families' – and so much the better if she was from one with an excellent war record.[27] The politicians, too, realised the wisdom of marrying the royal family into the British aristocracy. Queen Mary told one of her ladies-in-waiting, Lady Airlie, that Lloyd George had informed the King that the British public would not tolerate any more marriages to foreign brides.[28]

Stamfordham's overwhelming raison d'être was to enable the monarchy to edge closer to the British people: indeed, he believed they failed to do so at their peril. Curiously, however, this democratisation was easier than might be thought – and certainly easier than it would have been in other countries – because of the age-old notion that the King was the ally of the common people against the rapacious nobility, a concept that romantically smacked of Arthurian mythology. This idea fostered a peculiarly paradoxical attitude towards royalty on behalf of the people that was summed up during George III's reign by the poet Samuel Taylor Coleridge as: 'If Monarchs would behave like republicans, all their subjects would act as royalists.' Stamfordham decided to exploit this historical lesson.

Projecting the image of a king at one with his people against the aristocracy was helped by the fact that since the advent of the House of Hanover, the royals and the nobility had never been close. Given to marrying foreigners – especially fellow Germans – the Hanovers were seen to snub good British stock and there was resentment that the Crown was no longer in the hands of a British family. None of the upper crust really trusted the German upstarts and, in terms of breeding, the old British families considered that they were far superior to the Crown.

Besides, the continued transfer of executive power from the monarch to ministers and Parliament meant that the upper classes were actually more powerful than the King, for they had control of Parliament itself. This was obvious in the House of Lords, where peers of the realm sat by right of birth, but in the eighteenth and nineteenth centuries the majority of elected members of the House of Commons also came from a noble background – either younger sons of titled families or related to them by marriage.[29]

As a result, the royal family had become increasingly isolated from the upper classes, which came to regard it as merely symbolic, even irrelevant. Indeed, any noble who made a royal union would be seen to be marrying beneath him- or herself. (This attitude clearly died hard: in 1981 the late Earl Spencer, when asked if his daughter Diana might feel she was not good enough for the royal family, sniffed that on the contrary, *they* were not good enough for *her*.) In fact, there were no marriages between the House of Hanover and aristocracy until 1871, when Princess Louise, Victoria's fourth daughter, married the Duke of Argyll. After this there were five marriages to *Scottish* families, but it was not until George V's only daughter, Mary, married Viscount Lascelles in 1922 that an *English* family penetrated the hallowed royal circle. Even then, this was the choice of the aristocracy, not the royal family: when Queen Victoria cast around for a husband for one of her daughters she found no takers among the English nobility.[30]

The rift between the nominal rulers and the ruling class can be detected in the image deliberately projected by the royals. Victoria and Albert, for example, were the embodiment of middle-class values and standards, although many of them could be more properly ascribed to the German bourgeoisie than to the mores of upright – and uptight – middle England. However, whether by accident or design, this had a distinct political advantage: shortly before Victoria's accession, the Great Reform Bill of 1832 had extended the vote to middle-class men over 21 who could identify with the new Queen and her ultra-respectable husband. Now that the vote had been extended to all men and women over 30, was it possible for George V to convince the working classes, too, that he was 'one of us'?

THE POWER AND THE GLORY

When Elizabeth II, who was lunching with her mother, asked if she may have a second glass of wine, the Queen Mother responded swiftly: 'Oh darling, do you think you should? After all, you have to reign all afternoon.' Reigning is an odd occupation at the best of times, and the role of the monarch is frequently the subject of confusion, partly because there is no written British constitution and partly because the age-old role is still obscured with the cobwebs of a very lengthy – and often thoroughly bloody – history.

Perhaps strangely, it was not part of Stamfordham's – or the Palace's – strategy to convince the people that the King played a vital function in the government of the country, for two reasons. First, although the monarch does have an important constitutional role and *is* central to the orderly running of the country, the rise of republics had made it much harder to argue that these jobs could only be carried out by a hereditary sovereign.

Secondly, to a large extent the monarch's very *lack* of hands-on political power had protected the institution of the Crown, particularly through the radical years of the nineteenth century. Unlike the more autocratic regimes, the British royal system offered nothing specific to rebel against – although political ideologues have often tried to argue that doing nothing much should be no guarantee of a particularly highly paid position. In Britain, because the monarchy had so little political power, it could only be held up as an example of social inequality, not as its cause.

The Palace also believed the general populace had no idea about the subtleties of the British constitution, and in this they were not alone. Lord Stamfordham himself complained that of the three monarchs he served, only Queen Victoria properly understood her constitutional role.[31] But what is this elusive and passing strange monster, the constitutional monarchy? Although an oft-quoted phrase is that the King or Queen 'reigns but does not rule', the royal family's official website[32] defines the present Queen's role in these words:

> As well as carrying out significant constitutional functions, the Queen also acts as a focus for national unity, presiding at ceremonial occasions, visiting local communities and representing Britain around the world.

As Britain has no written constitution, the 'significant constitutional functions' are based on custom and precedent. Unfortunately, this hallowed vagueness tends to resist clarification of certain issues, particularly when situations arise for which there is no precedent. There is help at hand, however, in the form of the 'bible' for British monarchs, the economist and journalist Walter Bagehot's *The English Constitution*, written in 1867. He is still regarded as the authority in all matters constitutional and his work was the present queen's textbook when she was tutored as Princess Elizabeth.

The constitution is a strange organic animal that has evolved steadily over the course of three centuries, producing certain principles that now underpin the whole system. In the days of absolute monarchy, the king was the only individual invested with certain powers – for example, the authority to make laws, summon or dissolve Parliament, have money minted, raise an army and declare war. In principle, nothing has changed: Elizabeth II is still the only person in the land with the authority to make these things happen. However, there is now a mutual understanding with her government whereby she will only use her powers when they ask her to do so. In effect, as the concept of the constitutional monarchy evolved the sovereign agreed to hand over their powers in practice while retaining them in theory.

While only the Queen can make a law, in reality she no longer does so on her own initiative, but gives the Royal Assent to laws that have been agreed by the Houses of Parliament. In theory she – or any of her predecessors – could decide not to give their Assent, but in reality this has never happened since the United Kingdom's Parliament was established in 1707.

This principle also applies in the appointment of the prime minister. In the past, monarchs appointed their own ministers and were free to choose whomever they wished. Technically it is still 'Her Majesty's Government' that actually rules. But these days, by custom, the monarch appoints as prime minister the leader of the political party that has the majority (the most MPs) in the House of Commons, and appoints as Cabinet ministers those whom the prime minister selects. Ultimately this means that the 'Queen's' choice of the political make-up of the government is in the hands of the voters, and all she really does is rubber-stamp the people's decision.

As we shall see, there are still circumstances in which the monarch can use – and has used – their prerogative to appoint a prime minister, particularly in times of crisis or emergency. As the royal website puts it: 'There could be exceptional circumstances when the Queen might need to exercise the discretion she still retains to ensure that her Government is carried on.'

The most crucial component of the constitutional system is the innocuous-sounding word 'advice' – the Queen is obliged to act upon the advice of her ministers (i.e. the Prime Minister and the Cabinet). In every practical sense, 'advice' actually means 'instruction', although of course it would be undignified for the Crown to admit it. It is unthinkable for Her Majesty to receive *orders*. Once the government has given its advice, either to pursue a particular course of action or indeed *not* to pursue a course of action, the monarch has no option but to acquiesce. The implicit sanction is that if the king or queen disregards the advice, then the government would have no option but to resign, as they would no longer enjoy the sovereign's confidence. What would happen in such a situation is unknown because it has never arisen, although, as we shall see, on occasion in the twentieth century it has come much closer than most people realise. This is what is meant by 'constitutional crisis', a situation that can only be resolved by the abdication of the monarch or the resignation of the government and its replacement by a new administration.

However, at the beginning of the twentieth century the King had not yet explored the potential loopholes in this arrangement. The monarchs wanted to see just how far they could go in getting their own way when their ministers opposed them. In theory, if one government opposes the monarch he or she could always dismiss it and appoint another one that was more to their satisfaction. But could the monarch really do that in practice? Certainly, Edward VII and George V believed they might have been able to get away with it.

Another course of action that allowed the King to stay within the letter of the constitution while undoubtedly being against its spirit depends on the nature of the relationship with the prime minister. If they were on good terms, it was always possible to discuss a matter informally and – incredibly – actually agree between them what advice the prime minister would give. This was a strategy that George V used to great advantage.

Monarchy and government are like two inebriated men leaning against each other: if one should lose his footing, the other comes crashing down too. The relationship between sovereign and government comes down to self-interest: both have deterrents, the *threat* of which can be used to put pressure on the other, but actually carrying them out would involve their own demise. The prime minister and government can threaten to resign if the monarch ignores their advice; the monarch can threaten to abdicate if he or she seriously disagrees with the government's policies. And, because of the ramifications for the country, a government would have to feel very strongly about a particular issue to call the sovereign's bluff in such a situation.

In fact, the threat of abdication was used fairly regularly in the eighteenth and nineteenth centuries in order to assert the monarch's authority – sometimes getting their own way, sometimes backing down when their bluff was called. George III used it three times, George IV made the threat (unsuccessfully) over Catholic emancipation, and even Queen Victoria used it successfully in 1877 to get Disraeli to change his policy on the war between Russia and Turkey. However, as we will see, the threat of abdication has also been used in the twentieth century – in very dramatic ways.

It may be used more frequently than we know, because if a monarch did threaten to abdicate over a particular issue we would be unlikely to hear about it. It would be done at the prime minister's audience with the sovereign, today held weekly but in previous reigns far less regularly – at times only once a month. It is the strictest rule of government that nothing discussed in these audiences – of which no record is made and no third party is allowed to be present – is ever made public. (In fact, any communication between sovereign and prime minister in any form is kept an eternal secret.) The monarch is allowed to brief their Private Secretary afterwards on what has been discussed, but that is all.[33]

The constitutional monarchy, therefore, works by mutual agreement and understanding between the sovereign and government over the limits of their powers, held together by the threat of 'mutually assured destruction' if the arrangement breaks down. But the system is not entirely based on voluntary understanding: certain of the monarch's powers are also limited by law – laws that the sovereign has had to agree to and perhaps even sign personally. For example, he or she is forbidden by law from being, or marrying, a Roman Catholic.

Similarly, although the sovereign alone has the power to declare war, in 1701 it was enshrined in law that they could not do so without Parliament's agreement. The law also restricts the monarch's control of the armed forces, a clause that was carefully included in the 1689 Bill of Rights, only 40 years after the end of the English Civil War that had pitted King against Parliament. The future generations of Parliamentarians wanted no more cavalier charges against the forces of democracy.

This was thought necessary because of another aspect of the sovereign's power that if misused and unchecked could result in tyranny at the top. The king or queen has remained the head of the armed forces, which in theory are loyal to the Crown: all servicemen and women swear allegiance to the reigning monarch, not to the Government, or even to the country (although this only applies to the army, Royal Air Force and Royal Marines; for historical reasons the Royal Navy does not take any similar oath). In the event of a civil war, the armed forces would be compelled to take their orders not from Parliament but from the monarch.

However, the Bill of Rights declared that 'the raising or keeping of a standing army within the Kingdom in time of peace, unless it be with the consent of Parliament, is against the law'. Even today, Parliament must pass an annual Continuation Order to confirm that the Army and RAF can continue to exist. Although the armed forces serve the Crown, Parliament has the power to disband them.

Another group – major players in the hidden world of government – is also nominally loyal to the Crown, although employed to put into practice the policies of the elected government. This is the Civil Service, part of which comprises the intelligence and security services such as MI5 and MI6. And as we shall see, there have been times when those organisations have put their loyalty to the monarch above that due to the Government . . .

Constitutionally, the sovereign must remain above party politics and politically neutral because he or she is required to work with a government that could be formed by any party – which has to feel it has the monarch's confidence. Famously, Bagehot defined the monarch's role in government as consisting of three basic rights: to be consulted (and by implication, also informed) by the government, to encourage and to warn. Of course the monarch will have personal views about *policies* and it is actually not merely their right but also their constitutional duty to express them to their Government through the prime minister ('encouraging' the policies they approve of and 'warning' of the consequences of those they don't). Every Tuesday evening the Prime Minister visits the Queen for an informal – and secret – chat, during which she speaks freely and listens intently. But having heard her views through the Prime Minister, the Government is not obliged to act on them.

In this way, the constitutional machine is a finely balanced and highly sensitive instrument, which has steadily evolved as the balance of power has been tested in the fires of rebellion and the deep waters of debate.

THE GREATEST SHOW ON EARTH

Even in her lengthy period of seclusion, the 'Widow of Windsor', Victoria, continued to fulfil her constitutional duties – giving her royal assent to laws and so on – which is the main purpose of a constitutional monarch. Yet to the public, to whom these daily chores were invisible and unknown, she was neglecting her country. This was an important lesson for the likes of Stamfordham.

For all the tradition behind the constitutional system, by George V's day the monarch had become merely, in his father's words, a 'signing machine'[34] and 'doing the boxes' went on behind closed doors. On the other hand, when the Sovereign is *seen* to do something – such as opening Parliament (which Victoria did neglect, fulfilling this function only eight times in the last 40 years of her reign) or appearing amid the martial splendour of Trooping the Colour – the public is reminded of how much they mean to them. This wave of sentiment escalates during the more spectacular celebrations such as coronations and jubilees – as was made abundantly clear in June 2002 when, against all expectation, Elizabeth II's Golden Jubilee was a smash hit with the people, rather incongruously culminating with millions of voices (although the monarch's was not one of them) belting out 'All You Need is Love'.

Even in George V's day, the need for pageantry and ritual was obvious, and Stamfordham and his colleagues recognised that the continuation of the monarchy depended not so much on tedious day-to-day constitutional chores as on their symbolic and ceremonial role – and the more visible the better.

This aspect of the sovereign's role was also addressed by Bagehot, but is less easy to define – and therefore control – than their constitutional duties and privileges. It is the *myth* of kingship, the monarch as embodiment and custodian of the traditions and heritage of the country, as expressed in the ritual and pageantry of the Crown; perfectly expressed by the Palace website in their description of the Queen as the 'focus for national unity'. Bagehot cautioned that this intangible but almost mystical aura should go untarnished by familiarity, declaring in one of his most famous phrases that 'We must not let daylight in on magic': easy enough in the days when the media were largely obsequious and therefore deaf, dumb and blind to royal misdeeds, but easier said than done in the era of telescopic lenses and endemic lack of respect. In any case there are distinct dangers in not letting daylight in on magic: this is the principle that has allowed the Palace mafia to cover up the more dubious aspects of the family's behaviour.

After Victoria's death there was a conscious decision to use the ceremonial and ritual aspects of monarchy to increase its popularity (even to the extent of inventing 'age-old' traditions that had never existed). Immediately after his accession, Edward VII (urged by his advisers) took steps to restore some of the high-profile ceremonies that had languished into disuse due to his mother's pathological grieving process. It was no hardship for this imposing figure, for he loved ostentation and theatricality. He insisted that the Gold State Coach (although hideously uncomfortable and liable to induce sea-sickness, as the present queen will testify) be brought back into service for the State Opening of Parliament for the first time in 40 years, and sat in it, larger than life, in his field marshal's uniform, enjoying the enthusiasm of the crowds. If the people had someone to cheer, it was good news for both King and Parliament. His son, George V, although very different temperamentally, went further and began to wear his Crown to the State Opening, looking like a child's idea of a King – the ultimate awe-inspiring spectacle.

Another example of active myth-making was David Lloyd George's invention of the ceremony for the investiture of the heir, Edward, as Prince of Wales at Caernavon Castle in 1910. It appealed to the 'Welsh Wizard', Lloyd George, who was then not only Chancellor of the Exchequer but also Constable of the castle, for it would be mutually advantageous. As the Prince's official biographer, Philip Zeigler, puts it, 'some time-honoured traditions were hurriedly invented' for the occasion.[35]

PARAGONS OF VIRTUE

In George V's day, such ceremonial occasions were, however, few and far between: the royal family could not be permanently on display as Stamfordham and the Palace group thought desirable. The answer was for the whole of the royal family to take on social roles, to be held up as custodians and personifications of moral values – for example, by shamelessly promoting theirs as an example of the archetypal, perfect family life. They were to launch a charm offensive on the working class, going out and meeting them face to face and adopting a philanthropic role.

When George and Mary threw themselves into an orgy of foundation-stone laying, ribbon cutting and gracious waving to malodorous crowds, there was the underlying implication that these were such upright and moral beings as to be the exemplars for all lesser mortals. As Stamfordham and his like had intended, it was understood that the royal family values were there to be emulated – but of course this was seriously tempting fate. Of all families, the royals have a particularly dismal history in this respect.

Indeed, the high-profile affairs of the present generation of young royals are nothing new – though today, thanks to a ubiquitous and ever-hungry media, we get to know about them almost as soon as the first bed has been rumpled. But the level of sordid intrigue was considerably worse in previous centuries. In writer Karl Shaw's words, compared to past royal standards, 'Prince Charles's devotion to his mistress, Camilla Parker Bowles, probably qualifies as fidelity'.[36]

Royal marriages have been arranged for dynastic, political and financial reasons. It was tacitly understood that kings and princes would enjoy mistresses and – to a lesser extent, thanks to the prevailing double standards in matters of sexuality – that queens and princesses would also take lovers. So ingrained is this idea that when Princess Diana threw the fact of Camilla in her husband's face, he responded with hurt innocence that if she did not exist in his life, he would be the only Prince of Wales in history not to have had a mistress. (The outside world, for all its promiscuity, had moved on into sexual accountability, but Charles in his traditional royal hothouse, had genuinely not noticed it – or if he had, considered himself to be above such middle-class values.)

Victoria herself was of course a byword for respectability and dutiful dullness, although the same could hardly be said of certain members of her family. Her grandson and heir, Prince Albert Victor, Duke of Clarence, was an infamous libertine who was implicated in a raid on a homosexual brothel – and even, although very improbably, suggested as a candidate for Jack the Ripper. His father, the obese but genial Edward VII, is said to have slept with some 1,500 women, being denounced when Prince of Wales by crusading journalist W.T. Stead as 'a wastrel, a gambler and a whoremonger'.[37]

His most famous mistress was the intelligent and dignified Alice Keppel who, by an extraordinary stroke of fate, was the great-grandmother of Camilla Parker Bowles and who was even allowed by the ever-gracious Queen Alexandra to attend the King's deathbed. His other paramours included the famous French actress Sarah Bernhardt and Oscar Wilde's protégée, Lillie Langtry. All of London – indeed, all of English society – knew of the King's mistresses, but it was of paramount importance to prevent the ordinary people from hearing about them. As ever, they must believe in a morally impeccable royal family.

Even the famously uxorious George V kept mistresses, one of whom he shared with his notorious brother, the Duke of Clarence.[38] George later enjoyed the services of prostitutes during his frequent sojourns at the seaside resort of Bognor Regis.

Of course the danger of such profligate sowing of the royal seed was a bumper crop of illegitimate offspring. Indeed, having so many illicit relationships, many of them extremely well established – and in the days before contraception was either reliable or acceptable – was virtually guaranteed to produce some children on the wrong side of the blanket. In the past this was not considered a problem: George IV had cheerfully acknowledged three of his bastards, but is known to have had at least one more, while William IV fathered 11 such children. One of Alice Keppel's daughters, Sonia, who was born in 1900, is rumoured to have been fathered by Edward VII – although both royal family and Alice's husband George always denied this. In the eminently respectable early years of the twentieth century, however, such matters were shameful and were to be hushed up at all costs. It was of prime importance to the Palace that such mishaps should never be made public – especially as at least one of these children was to prove a real threat to national security . . .

Yet as the royal family entered into the brave new world of the twentieth century, with new and nobler ideals and an image that must, above all, be kept untarnished as far as the vast mass of the people was concerned, it soon became obvious that they had to be protected as much from themselves as from any foreign threat or republican uprising.

As the then Chancellor of the Exchequer (soon to be Prime Minister), David Lloyd George, said of the new king shortly after his accession: 'The King is a jolly chap, but thank God there's not much in his head',[39] echoing the feeling of the real movers and shakers, to whom a thinking monarch would have been a disastrous threat. Even the King's official biographer, John Gore, described his subject (though carefully not in his book) as 'a profoundly ignorant and rather stupid man'.[40] The neurotically ordered George had spent most of his life killing birds and sticking stamps in his albums – the latter hobby at least furnished his successors with assets worth about two million pounds in today's money.

Although portrayed as fair-minded by his apologists, George V shared the class-based prejudices of his milieu and era. When told about the furore caused by the fact that, when the *Titanic* sank in 1912, first-class male passengers were allowed into the lifeboats ahead of third-class women and children, he failed to see what the fuss was about, declaring that 'if a man pays first-class fare he is entitled to preference'.[41]

Although George shared a mistress with his brother Albert Victor, keeping her in the leafy north London suburb of St John's Wood where many rich men kept their 'other' women, the two men also shared another, very different, female, though this one was a byword for upright virtue. George's queen, Princess Victoria Mary of Teck (known as 'May' in the family) had, in fact, been brought to London as the intended bride of Albert Victor. There was nothing odd in this, for all royal unions then were arranged marriages (unlike the late twentieth century, when only some were). The engagement was announced in December 1891, after both future bride and groom announced bravely that this was a love match. Fortunately for Mary, her uncontrollable and more than half mad fiancé considerably fell ill within a matter of days and died on 14 January 1892, officially of the influenza that was ravaging the ranks of his fellow army officers. Some commentators[42] believe that his symptoms sounded more like terminal syphilis, which would hardly have been surprising given his promiscuous lifestyle. Others have gone further, suggesting that he was murdered because of his unsuitability to inherit the throne, but although his death was remarkably timely, no evidence has ever been produced to support this theory.

Still judged by Victoria to be a suitable bride for the heir to the throne, Mary's betrothal was seamlessly switched to the next in line, George, and they married 18 months later. As far as can be ascertained from the written record, she never mentioned Prince Albert Victor again.

George and Mary had their honeymoon at York Cottage, Sandringham – a curious and somewhat macabre setting, considering it was where her first intended had died. Although never palatial and badly designed, York Cottage remained their home until George was crowned King in 1910, becoming increasingly crowded as each new child was added to the nest.

As the daughter of Prince Franz and the voluminous Princess Mary Adelaide of Teck, a granddaughter of George III, Mary's status had been less than secure because her father was the issue of a morganatic marriage between Duke Alexander of Württemburg and a Hungarian Countess – not without some irony in the dark days of the abdication, as we shall see in a later chapter.

The quiet and shy Mary, who tried never to laugh in public because she believed, with some justification, that it made her look like a horse, bore up with dignity. Her husband only confessed his emotion in the form of letters to her, and even then it was cautious, expressed in the language of slightly sentimental friendship rather than a grand or even lukewarm passion. Mary was not one to complain, certainly not after making such a good marriage, and especially with her background of genteel poverty and the ignominy of having a huge mother who was known as 'Fat Mary'.

Although the future Queen Mary hated the indignities of pregnancy and childbirth (and very possibly conception, too), she dutifully produced a brood of Windsors and then set about more or less ignoring them, thus helping to create the new generation of utterly dysfunctional and neurotic royals – and arguably sowing the seeds for the greatest royal crisis for many years. The heir to the throne, Prince Edward ('David') was born in 1894, becoming Prince of Wales in 1910, at the age of 16. Prince Albert ('Bertie') was born in 1895, followed by the only girl, Princess Mary, in 1897. With the new century came Prince Henry, two years later Prince George, and the youngest and most vulnerable, the epileptic Prince John, arrived in a cold-hearted world in 1905, only to die 13 years later, having had no opportunity to make his mark on life, royal or otherwise.

When he was 11, John was removed from the family and taken to a secluded cottage on the Sandringham estate, where he was cared for by one of the royal nurses, Charlotte 'Lalla' Bill, and two menservants. He was never visited by his mother or most of his family. Although it was common for epileptics to lead relatively isolated lives, the royal family's banishment of little John was cruel in its extremity. He died after an epileptic fit in January 1919 and was buried 'very privately' (so wrote Queen Mary) three days later in the churchyard at Sandringham (not Windsor, where members of the royal family are usually laid to rest). His separation from the family was not reported in the press, not even in his obituaries, which also failed to mention his epilepsy. (One must not let daylight in on magic . . .)

Their mother's mantra being 'I must always remember that their father is also their King', Mary herself rarely showed anything other than distant condescension towards her offspring, although she did occasionally read to them, which was a thrilling departure from a world peopled almost exclusively by servants. Her coldness even strayed beyond the fashionable neglect of their offspring by aristocratic mothers: whatever she felt towards them remained as tightly bound inside as the formidable whalebone restricting her imposing Germanic figure.

The long-term plan of Stamfordham and the Palace mafia to ensure the survival of the monarchy was intimately bound up with the character and actions of the heir to the throne, but ironically that was nearly the Crown's undoing.

TWO

'THE PEOPLE'S PRINCE'

The newspapers' title for Edward, Prince of Wales, 1926

After the Armistice, and the uneasy first months of peace, Lord Stamfordham's plans for the democratisation of the royal family could be properly implemented – mainly through the heir to the throne, Edward (who was known to his family as 'David'), Prince of Wales. In him rested the future, and the responsibility also fell, to a certain extent, on the next brother in line, Prince Albert ('Bertie') – a prospect that neither the young man himself nor his father viewed with any great enthusiasm. Bertie was unsuited for public life, being afflicted with a terrible stammer that caused unnaturally long pauses as he fought to spit out his words, growing increasingly more humiliated and frustrated as they stuck in his throat.

The two younger brothers, Henry ('Harry') and George were not really considered for major royal roles immediately after the First World War because of their youth, and Princess Mary was never considered, being a woman. Later, when the King and Queen realised that their son George was surprisingly bright – by far the most intelligent of the Windsor brood – they also began to hand over some of the royal duties to him. Henry, however, was a different matter, being unrelentingly dim – like an aristocratic airhead straight from the pages of a P.G. Wodehouse novel – and is distinguished by making no real impact on this story whatsoever.

According to Stamfordham and the Palace mafia's grand plan, after the First World War the King and Queen increased their social and philanthropic activities enormously, visiting hospitals and child welfare centres, and lending their support and patronage to charities. It is no coincidence that the overwhelming majority of their visits were to the most militant areas.

Like today's immediate royal family, the children of George and Mary came into the world in two waves, which meant that Edward and Bertie were brought up together, although the heir later formed his closest sibling alliance with the youngest surviving brother, George.

The nature of their upbringing ensured that the 'heir' and first 'spare' were both highly strung, although this manifested itself in different ways. The older boy became reckless, with a marked rebellious streak, not at all what his parents hoped of him. Bertie became withdrawn and neurotic, and unassertive to an almost unbelievable degree: he once sat for hours in a darkened room rather than dare ask a servant to switch on a light (although it seems incredible that it never occurred to him to do it himself, custom would not have permitted a royal prince to carry out such a demeaning task). He was by nature a conformist and his nervousness reinforced his desire to fit in, not to draw attention to himself in any way.

These traits can be traced back to the boys' upbringing, for not only were they denied parental love and encouragement, but their first nanny, Mrs Green, was little short of a madwoman. Kirsty McLeod, author of *Battle Royal* (1999), the joint biography of Edward VIII and George VI, describes her as 'a sadist who showed a perverted affection for David and almost total disregard for Bertie'.[1] Eventually, her interesting little ways were noticed – she would pinch Edward's arms when he was in his parents' presence so that he screamed and was sent away, back to her care – and she was replaced by Charlotte 'Lalla' Bill, who was much more like a surrogate mother. But by then too much harm had already been done. Bertie, in particular, had suffered by being fed too little and very irregularly, which meant that his digestive system was wrecked and the comfort that most young children associate with mealtimes was not a noticeable part of his childhood. He also suffered from being forced to write with his right hand – which may well have contributed to, or even caused, his stammer – and from having to sleep in metal leg braces in an effort to cure his knock knees. Bertie was a mess, but to his credit he tried hard not to be.

THE HEIR

Edward Albert Christian George Andrew Patrick David was a golden-haired, blue-eyed boy who grew up to be confused, spoilt and wilful – as the family and the Government were to discover, this was a dangerous combination. Today, analyses of his life are inevitably coloured by the later drama of his abdication and the rather bogus and pathetic figure he cut as the Duke of Windsor, trailing pointlessly around the world in the shadow of the chic and dominant Duchess. As a result he is mostly regarded as an immature playboy who always put personal pleasure before duty. But was this always so? What were Edward's real motivations?

Many believe that, lured away by long years of nightclubbing and partying, Edward came to detest the formality of Court life and to recoil from the idea of being king, seeking (if only subconsciously) a reason to escape the manacles of the throne. Some even believe that he decided against becoming king in his youth. Certainly, after he abdicated, Charlotte

Bill wrote to Queen Mary that even as a teenager he had never wanted to ascend the throne.

As a young man, Edward appears to have been beset by a lack of self-worth, which led to alternating periods of black despair and the determination to prove himself. These cyclical moods shaped both his behaviour as Prince of Wales and his attitude to his destined role as King Emperor. Biographer Frances Donaldson summarises the prevailing picture of the young Prince of Wales: '. . . an exceptionally attractive young man, eager to succeed at his job, spoiled and moody and of small intellectual capacity, but quick, imaginative, and responsive.'[2]

For generations a naval career had been considered a fitting way for royal princes to occupy their youth and early adult life before taking on their more onerous royal duties, and George V decided that his two eldest sons should be no exception. Both attended the Naval College at Osborne on the Isle of Wight, then going on to the Royal Naval College at Dartmouth.

It was at Dartmouth at the beginning of 1911 that an event occurred that may well have had a major impact on Edward, not to mention the monarchy and the course of British history: both princes succumbed to an outbreak of mumps. Edward in particular was seriously ill for two weeks. The boys were 16 and 15 respectively at the time, a dangerous age to contract mumps, which can cause sterility (by preventing the normal development of one or both testicles). Many commentators believe that this is what happened to Edward. Harold Nicolson, George V's official biographer who was privy to certain royal secrets, wrote in his diary that 'something went wrong with his [Edward's] gland on reaching puberty'.[3] The evidence includes his lack of children[4] and the fact of his strangely youthful appearance, which was so extreme as to constitute a case of arrested development. He was a real Peter Pan, always looking years younger than he was – even until almost the end of his days – and a later aide during his wartime governorship of the Bahamas (Frank Giles, who went on to become editor of the *Sunday Times*) recalls seeing the Duke of Windsor in the shower, noting with astonishment that his body was completely hairless 'even in the place where one would most expect [hair] to be'.[5] Windsor would have been in his mid to late 40s at the time. If he was sterile, or afraid that he was, this could be another reason for his despair about being cut out for the job of the heir to the throne, seeing that the Prince of Wales' primary function is to marry and produce an 'heir and a spare'. Was this also a reason – perhaps at an unconscious level – for his avoiding marriage until he was in his 40s? If he was sterile, this would explain a great deal about his personal torment, sense of inadequacy and black moods, not to mention the nature of his relationships. After all, there was no sure way of knowing the truth about being infertile in those days apart from failing to father children.

EDWARD'S WAR

After three months as a midshipman on the battleship HMS *Hindustan*, Edward left the navy, going to Magdalen College, Oxford, where he became the first royal prince to live in rooms at a university. He was despatched to Paris in the spring of 1912 on his first foreign visit – hardly a trip made in heaven for he hated France and the French (ironic for one who was to spend the long years of his exile based there). Much more congenial to him were the Easter and summer holidays of 1913 that he spent with relatives in Germany, the first with King Wilhelm and Queen Charlotte of Württemburg, the second with his uncle and aunt, the Grand Duke and Duchess of Mecklenburg-Strelitz. He was greatly looking forward to a return visit the following year, but the increasingly tense European situation in the summer of 1914 prevented it.

It was at this time that he discovered a particularly alluring way of killing time – the glitter and fizz of grand balls and dancing. He attended his first ball on 7 July 1914, and three days later triumphantly recorded in his diary that he had only had 8 hours sleep in the last 72 hours.[6] Of course dancing involves that other implicit rite of passage – meeting women. But he had barely started on an almost uniquely promising career as a charmer when the First World War interrupted the social scene.

His attitude to the conflict provides an interesting insight into his character. Ordered by his father to stay in London while it was decided what he should do, Edward pleaded for an active role in the fighting – and in this, against all the odds, he was at least partly successful, being given a commission in the Grenadier Guards. But he was never to fire a shot himself.

He served in France, Egypt and Italy but – to his enormous frustration – he was employed in a non-combative role, doing clerical duties and carrying despatches. Throughout the war he tried relentlessly to be allowed into the trenches, while the Palace and military command kept him as far away from them as possible. Especially after 1917, Stamfordham made repeated efforts to have him recalled out of harm's way to London so that he could start being groomed for his official duties.[7]

However, the action he did see, if only from a safe distance, with its concomitant loss of friends and colleagues, brought the horrors of war home to him. Even this immature royal lad with his almost Churchillian *Boys' Own* attitude was faced with terrible mutilations and the bloodiest slaughter the world had ever seen. Several of his fellow students from Oxford were killed in the trenches, and his first equerry, Major William Cadogan, was killed in the early stages of the war. In France he saw battlefields littered with unburied and decomposing bodies and bits of bodies, and on one occasion in September 1915, after coming under bombardment from shells, returned to his car to find his driver had been killed by shrapnel. In his letters to friends and in his diary he ranted against the 'fucking Boche' and 'German buggers', saying that if he had his way the British would take no prisoners – literally.[8]

In August 1916, after yet once more being kept away from visiting the front line, he wrote in his diary of his 'misery', saying: 'I feel quite ready to commit suicide and would if I didn't think it unfair on Papa'.[9] Most of the men at the time who were committing suicide did so because they saw no way *out* of the trenches.

The prince came home in February 1919 to begin the new role decided for him by Stamfordham, and his first engagement under the new regime took place within a few weeks – after he had been given advice on public speaking by one Winston Churchill.

THE FAIR SEX

Edward found women delectable, especially older, preferably married ladies who were a cross between Mother and Nanny. His first love was Lady Coke, a married woman 12 years his senior – no small age difference when he was only 21. Beginning in the summer of 1915 this passionate but apparently sexless relationship lasted for three years.

Edward's quest for true love took a quite different turn in the spring of 1918, when he fell in love with Lady Rosemary Leveson-Gower, daughter of the Duke of Sutherland, to whom he proposed marriage. Even now, it is impossible to be certain whether she turned him down or his parents refused to give their permission for the union, although it would have suited the new policy to have had their heir marry into an English family. However, Queen Mary wrote that the family of Rosemary's mother had 'a taint of blood'.[10] But by the time Rosemary's star had waned, Edward had already embarked on the first long-term affair of his life, with Winifred 'Freda' Dudley Ward, the wife of a Liberal Whip.

The romance had a quirky start: in February 1918 the Prince of Wales had been a guest at a party thrown by Maud Kerr-Smiley in Belgrave Square, when the air raid siren sounded. Freda and a gentleman friend took shelter in the doorway and Mrs Kerr-Smiley invited them in to take refuge – and meet the Prince of Wales. (With one of those nice touches of irony that tend to beset historical figures, the hostess was the sister of Ernest Simpson, second husband of the infamous Wallis.) The very next day the smitten Edward called on Freda, beginning a close relationship that was to last for 16 years, to the point when Wallis took over. With sincere affection on both sides it should have been the making of him, but quite clearly it wasn't. There was a certain amount of strain involved, for once again his family seriously disapproved – although in dating a married woman he was merely carrying on a well-established royal tradition.

In the summer of 1919 Edward left home, setting himself up in apartments in York House, part of St James' Palace, not far from Buckingham Palace in terms of hundreds of yards, but with his new-found freedom, light-years from the parental constraints. Financially, too, he was not only independent but also very rich. When he became Prince of Wales in 1910 he had inherited the Duchy of Cornwall and its revenues, but could not touch them until he reached his majority – then 21. At that age he came into the then huge sum of £400,000, in the region of £20 million today. And although he often pleaded poverty throughout his tumultuous life, he was never less than a very wealthy man.

BEING BERTIE

The second son of King George V and Queen Mary was born in 1895 and was christened Albert Frederick Arthur George, known to the family as Bertie. Unlike Edward, he was still serving with the Royal Navy when the First World War broke out, although he missed most of the fighting through illness, which took the form of various stomach complaints that were due to a duodenal ulcer that went undiagnosed for three years of agony and shame. He also suffered from chronic debilitating seasickness – all in all, hardly the ideal son of the sea. At the outbreak of hostilities his ship, HMS *Collingwood*, was sent with the fleet to Scapa Flow, but once again – just three weeks into the war – he was invalided out, this time with acute appendicitis. However, he did manage to return, if intermittently, to his ship, and no doubt to his great relief and joy saw action at the Battle of Jutland in 1916 in which he acquitted himself well.

But even this was the exception rather than the rule: in 1917 he was finally declared unfit for service at sea and was transferred to a new branch of the navy, the Royal Naval Air Service, then to the Royal Air Force (RAF) when it was formed in 1918. Ironically for a prince with such a wimpish image, he was the first member of the royal family to earn a pilot's licence, thus becoming – in theory at least – one of the dashing new knights of the air.

It was at this time that Bertie found support in the form of a deep friendship with Louis Greig, whom he had met at Osborne where the latter, a Surgeon-Lieutenant who was working as Assistant Medical Officer, treated him for his stomach complaint. A Glaswegian, his full name was Louis Leisler Greig, but as Leisler – the name of his father's business partner – is German, it was dropped after the war. A bond grew between the two young men, which George V viewed with such favour that he gave Greig the considerable responsibility of looking after Bertie's health. Greig was seen to be good for his confidence, and so after the war he became one of the Prince's equerries. In the words of his grandson, Geordie Greig, he became 'mentor, physician and friend' to Bertie.[11]

After the war, Bertie was sent to Cambridge, but of course with no serious expectation of any kind of academic success. There is no sign he showed any enthusiasm for the place.

While all eyes were on the 'heir' and 'spare', the two other boys were relatively unknown and therefore enjoyed somewhat greater freedom. Unlike

Edward and Bertie, George and Henry went away to school – St Peter's Court Preparatory School in Kent – which marked another small step in making them appear more ordinary, although it did little for the grand plan of the democratisation of the royal family.

One of their teachers at St Peter's noted the contrast between the two brothers in a letter to their former tutor, Henry Hansell: 'Judged by the performance in the classroom of Prince Henry, we were not expecting too much of the younger brother [George], but he turns out to be a clever little boy who is already showing himself more advanced than his contemporaries – and his brother.'[12]

While Harry moved on to more years of academic bafflement, this time at Eton in September 1913, the intelligent and witty Prince George followed the customary naval path, which – it was decided for him – was to become a real career. This was bad news for him: he had an artistic nature (Edward called him 'Bohemian', which covered a multitude of sins) and hated navy life, taking every opportunity to escape.

THE CHARM OFFENSIVE

From 1919 the Prince of Wales began to carry out the role that had been carefully crafted for him by Stamfordham and the Palace – charming the working classes. Modern historian Frank Prochaska writes, 'Palace policy prompted the Prince of Wales to initiate his goodwill tours to mining and industrial sectors, which were to do so much for his reputation.'[13] He also became the President of the Royal Society for the Prevention of Cruelty to Animals (RSPCA) and Royal National Lifeboat Institute (RNLI), and was made a fellow of the Royal Society.

However, he made the greatest impact in the gritty mining areas, touring the communities of South Wales in 1919, where he went down a coal mine and made speeches that adroitly included declarations of his commitment to 'the welfare of our ex-servicemen and the improvement of housing conditions, both of which I have very much at heart'.[14] Of course his First World War service also helped create a sense of solidarity with the ordinary men, and his role as 'soldier Prince' was deliberately emphasised by his publicists, although it was not all 'spin'. If nothing else, the Prince certainly had the common touch. Indeed, from the very outset of his public life, he made a point of meeting Labour politicians and local councillors, whom he almost always managed to charm.[15]

The others may have been famous and dutiful to their well-manicured fingertips, but no other member of the royal family set the pulse racing like the blue-eyed Prince of Wales with his golden presence. However, despite his sympathy for the downtrodden and unemployed, it should be realised that here was no champagne socialist. At the time of the post-war election of 1918 he wrote: 'One dreads to think of the Labour people returning a greater number of members . . . and then all these crazy women candidates . . .'[16] As Philip Zeigler notes, 'His radicalism and disapproval of social injustice were real enough, but he was still to the right politically.'[17]

But was his professed concern for the working class genuine, or was he just obeying orders? Was it a cynical ploy to preserve the monarchy, or was it for real? On the one hand, there is no doubt that Edward was falling in with directives from the Palace, but on the other he had discovered a real talent in himself for communicating with ordinary people and there is every indication that he revelled in it. And many of the sentiments he expressed about social welfare – particularly of ex-servicemen – appear to have been from the heart. But his harder edge comes through in a letter to Freda Dudley Ward after his tour of Glasgow in 1920: 'To TOI, and TOI only, I say that I do feel I've been able to do a little good propaganda up there and given communism a knock.'[18]

The tone suggests the sharing of a secret, which is the propaganda aspect of his tour of the Glaswegian tenements, with the underlying agenda of slowing the spread of communism among the workers. These are exactly the intentions set out by Stamfordham and his team in 1917.

The probability is that Edward was determined to throw himself into the task in hand because he thought he could excel in it and was genuinely concerned – *and* because he was told to get involved for cynical PR purposes. It seemed to suit everyone, and Edward was winning the approval of the Palace mafia. This was not to last.

However, having seized the role of charmer of the underclass perhaps in order to prove himself to his father as much as the masses, Edward was determined to do it *his* way. Soon after embarking on his public life in 1919 he confided to Mabell, Countess of Airlie – one of Queen Mary's ladies-in-waiting who had become a confidante – that he was frustrated at his job 'because they won't let me have a free hand'.[19] Inevitably this brought him into confrontation with the Old Guard, together with his increasingly dissolute and louche lifestyle. The King was horrified by his son's consorting with the 'fast set' – suspiciously debonair young men who wore wristwatches and women with red fingernails, all capering furiously to a savage jazz rhythm as if to obliterate the memory of torn and bloody soldiers hanging on barbed wire in No Man's Land. They slept around, they drank, they doped. Even the King, a man of no imagination and virtually zero grasp of psychology, could only see squalor, indignity and probably ruin for his eldest son.

Edward was wearing himself out trying to be all things to all people: the dutiful son, the mass charmer, the attentive lover, the party animal, the reckless action man, the heir to the throne. Inwardly, he felt he was failing in most, if not all, of them. He rapidly became short-tempered and frustrated with his job, writing to Freda in June 1919: 'Gud [sic] how thine E. does loathe palace & court life . . . given he was never intended for that sort of existence.'[20] He often wrote to his mistress of his bouts of grim depression – 'the black, black mist', as he called it.[21] The black mist thickened and its stranglehold grew. On Christmas Day 1919 he wrote to his Private Secretary Godfrey Thomas (who had been head-hunted for him by Stamfordham) in a letter that was obviously kept far from confidential:

> A sort of hopelessly lost feeling has come over me and I think I'm going kind of mad!! . . . I've never felt like this in my life before, and I'm rather worried about it and feel incapable of pulling myself together . . . I feel faint at the thought of next year's trip [his second Empire tour, to Australia] – Christ, how I loathe my job now and all this press 'puffed' empty 'succés'. I feel I'm through with it and long to die. For God's sake don't breathe a word of this to a soul. No one else must know how I feel about my life, and everything. I tell you as my greatest friend and the one man I can trust and who really understands me. You probably think from this that I ought to be in the madhouse already . . . I do feel such a bloody little shit.[22]

But somehow he did pull himself together, although the black mists were to return from time to time. Following the grand plan, he became ambassador to the Empire, successfully building on his first Empire tour, to Canada in August 1919, which was greatly acclaimed – again, he seems to have genuinely charmed the crowds and the people he met. During this tour he was invited to Washington to meet President Woodrow Wilson, which also led to his first taste of New York. He loved it, the brashness, the energy, the intoxicating sense of youth and daring – and, of course, he became enslaved by its vibrant night life. The tour was to spark off his lifelong love of America and all things American, and he cultivated, deliberately or unconsciously, a slight but perceptible American accent, which was further to inflame his parents' view of him. He also appreciated the great open spaces of the North American continent: on his tour of Canada he bought a ranch.

Then came the eight-month tour of Australia and New Zealand, but although he had been dreading it, at least he had a new playmate. This tour marked the first appearance of a young man who was to become a major player in the fortunes and future of the House of Windsor, the young Lord Louis Mountbatten, then a gangly 20-year-old with a hearty manner and ringing laugh. There was little about him to suggest his astonishing powers of manipulation, although in fact they had already been employed to get him on the tour, as aide to the prince.

RISE OF THE POWER BEHIND THE THRONE

Although becoming a quintessentially English figure, Mountbatten was firmly of German royal stock, albeit slightly tainted. His pedigree came from the House of Hesse, an important Grand Duchy of Germany. Louis's grandfather, Prince Alexander of Hesse–Darmstadt, was the second son of Grand Duke

Louis II – or at least that is the official version. In fact, Alexander was the illegitimate son of the Grand Duke's wife and a court chamberlain, and therefore Mountbatten should have had no right to the title of Prince.[23] To compound this problem, Prince Alexander made an unwise marriage to one of his sister's, the Tsarina's, ladies-in-waiting, Julie Hauke, with whom he eloped in 1851. Although she was the daughter of a Polish count, the rules of marriage of the Russian and Hesse royal families were strict and unyielding, and for marrying beneath his station Alexander was deprived of some of his status and any claim to the throne of Hesse. His title was changed to Prince Alexander of Battenberg (a small town in the Grand Duchy of Hesse).

However, the eldest son of the tainted union, Prince Louis of Battenberg – Louis Mountbatten's father – got himself back into the main line of the Hesse-Darmstadt family by marrying his cousin, Princess Victoria Alberta, who was also the granddaughter of Queen Victoria (as indeed her names make abundantly clear). Prince Louis wanted a naval career, so he settled in England at the age of just 14 where he became a member of the expatriate 'court' of German royalty and nobility that included the Tecks. However, although he became a British subject, he always regarded Germany as his home. Prince Louis enjoyed a spectacular career in the Royal Navy – including a period as Director of Naval Intelligence – and in 1911 was appointed First Sea Lord by Winston Churchill, then First Lord of the Admiralty.

The future Earl Mountbatten of Burma was the youngest of four children, born in 1900 at Frogmore House, Windsor. Although christened Louis Francis Albert Victor Nicholas, he was always known as 'Dickie'. (He was 'Uncle Dickie' to the present queen.) He could boast an illustrious pedigree – and, being him, he did so, repeatedly: his great-grandmother was Queen Victoria, his great-grandfather, grandfather and uncle were Grand Dukes of Hesse, while his aunt was the Tsarina, the wife of Nicholas II, who was to die with her family at the hands of the Bolsheviks. His elder sister would marry the heir to the Swedish throne.

Bilingual in English and German, Louis attended Locker's School in Hertfordshire where he emerged as a natural leader – for example, being captain of the school cricket team. In May 1913, he too went to Osborne Naval College, acquitting himself rather better than Edward and Bertie. That summer he holidayed in Hesse, where the Tsar, Tsarina and family were also guests. But his distinguished background was suddenly to prove a double-edged sword: when war broke out the other cadets thought Mountbatten was a German spy.

The First World War was considerably more traumatic for the family name. His father, Prince Louis, resigned as First Sea Lord in October 1914. It is often claimed that he dutifully offered his resignation, realising the possible embarrassment he might cause the Government. However, the truth is that he had to be forced out of office.[24] The compromise at which the Establishment and Battenberg arrived was that the powers that be for their part gave him the title of Marquess of Milford Haven, while he changed the family name to Mountbatten: in this way Prince Louis Francis of Battenberg became Lord Louis Mountbatten, although the 'Lord' was in fact a courtesy title only. And so, at the age of 17, he lost his royal status and was forced to change his family name.

His father's fall from grace, coupled with his dubious ancestry, was probably one of the major factors that fuelled the young man's immense ambition and desire to prove his superiority in every endeavour and aspect of life. Another formative factor was the contrast between his royal blood and his relative poverty (he had only his naval pay and income from dividends that brought in around £300 a year). Indeed, the young Mountbatten considered that his family, being related to so many royal houses, was superior to the British royal family. (In later life he became obsessed with royal genealogies and particularly with demonstrating how he was related to the most illustrious sovereigns throughout the course of European history.)[25]

The living embodiment of the old order of royal dynastic Europe – at least the German and Russian houses – that was swept away during or as a result of the First World War, the young Mountbatten was, if nothing else, one of the few truly larger than life characters associated with the House of Windsor. Ruthlessly ambitious, staggeringly vain and arrogant, he truly believed himself incapable of making a mistake. One commentator wrote in the 1980s of Mountbatten's 'combination of gargantuan vanity with cockily unlimited self-assurance and conceit'.[26] To him everyone and everything was a means to an end – the fulfilment of his own glorious destiny. Writing of his time as Chief of Combined Operations in the Second World War, historian Nigel Hamilton calls him 'a master of intrigue, jealousy and ineptitude', going on: 'Like a spoiled child he toyed with men's lives with an indifference to casualties that can only be explained by his insatiable, even psychopathic, ambition.'[27] Adding his voice to the chorus of disapproval, leading political historian Andrew Roberts describes him as a 'mendacious, intellectually limited hustler, whose negligence and incompetence resulted in many unnecessary deaths – the numbers of which increased exponentially as his meteoric career progressed'.[28]

The Queen's Uncle Dickie was completely immoral and unprincipled, with an absolute disregard for the truth. He did nothing that was not to his own advantage, becoming adept at smoothly switching sides as it suited him. Shortly before his death in 1979 – in an explosion on board his boat in Ireland – according to his biographer Richard Hough, he said: 'It is a curious thing, but a fact, that I have been right in everything I have done and said in my life.'[29] Of course, this was said without a flicker of irony.

Few would agree with Mountbatten's bombastic remark, but it is entirely in keeping with his great gift for rewriting history to suit himself, a process that began in his early years and – as we shall see – grew to astonishing proportions. An example of this can be seen in a letter he wrote to his mother during his overseas tour with the Prince of Wales in July 1920. In this he writes about Freda Dudley Ward as 'the Prince's great friend' and 'about whom you have probably heard – Oh, such wicked lies'.[30] Again, one would suspect irony or humour, but it would be out of character.

Sometimes his talent for invention and reinvention earns a mild rebuke even from the more Establishment-minded biographers and historians. For example, Philip Ziegler declares, 'Mountbatten was apt to recall what he wished had happened rather than the less colourful reality.'[31] However, others were considerably more blunt. The later Prime Minister Anthony Eden branded him 'a congenital liar',[32] and Field Marshal Sir Gerald Templer told Mountbatten directly in the 1960s: 'You're so crooked, Dicky, if you swallowed a nail you'd shit a corkscrew.'[33] These were the views of the people who knew him; to millions who saw him as the very distinguished war hero and uncle of the Sovereign, such opinions would smack almost of sacrilege – and Mountbatten himself worked assiduously throughout his long life to foster precisely that image. This was a skill he also brought to bear on behalf of the monarchy itself, although there was nothing altruistic or idealistic in it. To him, the preservation of the Crown was inextricably linked with self-preservation.

SEXUAL SECRETS

Mountbatten's cavalier attitude to the little matter of the truth was symptomatic of his profound personal belief that whatever he wanted to do was justified because he wanted to do it. This amorality (to be kind) was also a feature of his private life – although of course in any case the upper classes were notorious for their unbridled promiscuity, something that his own family had developed into a fine art.

Mountbatten's elder brother George (eight years his senior), who inherited the Milford Haven title when their father died in 1921, was a promiscuous bisexual who was married to another promiscuous bisexual – but according to most reports, mostly lesbian – Nadeja ('Nada'), Countess of Torby, the granddaughter of Tsar Alexander III and niece of the murdered Nicholas II. But George Milford Haven's greatest claim to fame was his collection of pornography, on which he lavished over £500,000 in today's money, lovingly binding it into volumes emblazoned with the family crest. This was hardly run-of-the-mill titillation, as it even included photographs of – horrors! – aristocrats having sex with their servants. But far more distasteful to those with active and normal consciences were the photographs of bestiality and family orgies in which even children took part. On George's death in 1938 this was inherited by his son David, who in turn donated part of the collection to the British Museum (surely one of the odder contributions to the national heritage). The existence of this cache of perversion was no secret in London society, and it was to feature in a US Supreme Court hearing – a child custody case – in 1934, although of course none of this appeared in the British press.[34]

Mountbatten very largely followed this 'anything goes' attitude to sex, becoming a promiscuous bisexual in the family tradition, as was his wife, the fabulously rich heiress Edwina Ashley, whom he married in 1922. Mountbatten later admitted, 'Edwina and I spent all our married lives getting into other people's beds,'[35] which is of course taken to refer to heterosexual flings, as some of them were. But it is well established that Mountbatten also indulged in sexual relationships with men, although he is vehemently defended on this issue by his friends, staff and official biographers.[36]

However, we have evidence of Mountbatten's bisexuality from Edwina Mountbatten's friend and biographer, Madeleine Masson. It was totally accepted by Edwina and her circle that, like many of his time and class, Mountbatten was actively bisexual, although of course this was strictly not for public knowledge in the days that sex between men was a criminal offence.[37] His proclivities were sufficiently well known when he accompanied the Prince of Wales on his Empire tours that rumours flew about the true nature of their relationship.[38]

The plot thickened when, after serving with the Royal Navy in the First World War, Mountbatten went up to Cambridge (in October 1919), where he met and befriended Bertie. But it was while at Cambridge that Mountbatten made another friend who was to prove highly significant both personally and politically. This was James Jeremiah Victor Fitzwilliam Murphy – who was known as Peter – a gifted Irish student who was fluent in French, German, Russian and Italian. He was also homosexual and very left-wing – that special Cambridge blend – and a leading light of the communist undergraduate scene. Murphy was to become Mountbatten's constant companion until his death in 1966, and seemed to have been accepted totally by Edwina. Although without an official role on Mountbatten's staff, Murphy's relationship with both the Mountbattens was so intimate that many people describe it as a *menage à trois*.[39]

It was probably under Murphy's influence that Mountbatten, although a staunch upholder of the old European royal dynasties, later became convinced that socialism and communism would eventually triumph, taking steps to ensure that if they did, he would still come out on top. Mountbatten evinced a lifelong talent for being on the winning side, even if this meant backing all possible sides until one looked likely to triumph conclusively over the others – then changing his allegiance accordingly.

It was around this time that Mountbatten heard the Prince of Wales was to visit Australia and determined to accompany him as part of his long-term plan to ingratiate himself with the royal family. Philip Zeigler writes: 'At once he began to pull every string that might secure him a place in the party.'[40] This included enlisting Bertie's aid, a ploy that was so successful that at Christmas 1919 he was asked if he would like to accompany him on the tour.

They sailed on the HMS *Renown* in March 1920: officially Mountbatten was part of the staff of the head of the tour, Rear-Admiral Halsey – unofficially he was the ADC to the Prince of Wales. Mountbatten's glittering career was under way.

As the tour progressed, Mountbatten wrote home to his mother:

> . . . you've no idea what a friend David is to me – he may be six years older but in some respects he's the same age as me. How I wish he wasn't the Prince of Wales, then it would be so much easier to see lots and lots of him. He's such a marvellous person and I suppose the best friend I've ever had.[41]

There was a telling addendum: 'He does so want to meet Papa and you away from his – as he calls them – "rotten" family.'[42] By this time Edward had spread his disloyal feelings for the royal family all over London and was now continuing the process abroad. Meanwhile, he was writing to his mother that Mountbatten was 'such a charming boy, and he cheers me up'.[43] Indeed, someone had to do it. Mountbatten wrote home about the Prince's 'deep depressions' and that '. . . it is very difficult to keep David cheerful. At times he gets so depressed, and says he'd give anything to change places with me.'[44] Things went so badly with the Prince of Wales that by July 1920 there were real fears that he was heading for a complete breakdown, his strained behaviour beginning to cause comment in the press – but only the foreign press, of course.[45]

Edward returned from the tour of Australia and New Zealand in October 1920, and although scheduled to leave on another to India almost immediately, argued that he was too exhausted. He and his father had serious differences of opinion on the matter, but in the end the Prince won the day and it was agreed to delay that tour for another year. But while Edward recuperated, Mountbatten was not going to let him stray out of his influence for too long, managing to get himself invited to York House, where he stayed until his marriage in 1922.

In between the Australian and Indian tours, Edward undertook another series of hectic provincial trips: three days in Glasgow, ten in Devon and Cornwall, four in South Wales and five days touring twenty-seven towns in Lancashire alone. Large and wildly enthusiastic crowds had greeted all his appearances wherever he went.[46] Indeed, these and the foreign tours, together with Edward's mixing with the stars of the British and American stage and screen, ensured that he became the first true royal celebrity of the modern age, a male Diana, whose very presence seemed to bestow a sort of magical glow on even the most prosaic of surroundings.

Back in London, however, he threw himself with renewed vigour into the glitzy nightlife, being seen on most nights throughout the 1920s in the Embassy Club, often with his brother George (who appears to have had exceptionally generous leave from the navy). They mixed with the richest and brightest young things, the most glamorous men and women. But Edward was largely absorbed with his mistress, Freda Dudley Ward: their affair continued throughout the 1920s in a way reminiscent of Edward VII and Alice Keppel. Edward visited her nearly every day and became a beloved avuncular figure to her children. The whole affair was quite open – even the cuckolded Mr Dudley Ward knew and tacitly approved of it, although it simply wasn't talked about.

Even so, the Prince of Wales indulged himself in several brief affairs and innumerable one-night stands, perhaps more in an effort to prove himself a man than any innate love for women or addiction to the sex act. In any case, he won few points as a lover: one woman who slept with him on a liner to New York said afterwards: 'He wasn't much good, but it's not every night that one sleeps with the future King of England.'[47]

Meanwhile the hideously shy, stammering Bertie was still hiding in the shadows, so the Prince of Wales decided to initiate him into the joys of sex, which he did with accustomed *brio*. Having chosen leading musical dancer Phyllis Monkman for this historic task, Edward himself arranged their encounter, getting Louis Greig to summon her from the Comedy Theatre to dine with Bertie in private rooms in Mayfair's Half Moon Street – 'dine' being the customary euphemism.[48] And astoundingly, without any outside help, Bertie proposed to vivacious socialite Helen 'Poppy' Baring, a Conservative MP's daughter, only to have the whole thing quashed by Queen Mary. Poor Poppy did not fit the new Stamfordham mould for royal brides, not being from the family of a duke, marquess or earl.

In October 1921 duty called Edward away from the London fleshpots and the quasi-domestic bliss with his mistress. He set off on a tour of India and Burma, which also included a visit to Emperor Hirohito in Japan, and was again accompanied by Dickie Mountbatten, the most ambitious limpet in the navy. During this tour, which lasted until July 1922, Mountbatten noted that 'David goes through his "black" phases more often than ever now, poor chap'.[49]

It was during this tour that Edward forged another lasting friendship with the officer assigned to assist him in organising his polo-playing schedule, Captain Edward Dudley ('Fruity') Metcalfe, who was to work for the prince in various capacities for many years. Metcalfe also became his regular companion on his excursions into London's nightclub scene.

A LITTLE MATTER OF TAX

Although Edward may seem to have been developing a concern for the plight of the working man, he also shared the Windsors' finely honed talent for personal avarice and acquisitiveness. Never was this more pronounced than in the Prince of Wales' tax arrangements, an astonishing case in which there was blatant collusion between the royal family, senior civil servants and even the judiciary, where the servants of the Crown obeyed the royals just when they knew it to be constitutionally or legally questionable – or even plain wrong. Having committed the deed, they then engaged in a cover-up to prevent the flag-waving public from finding out about it.

In 1921 the Prince of Wales pleaded that as a member of the royal family he should be exempt from paying income tax on the lucrative revenue from the Duchy of Cornwall (this land, some of which is actually in south London, automatically passes to each succeeding Prince of Wales). This arrangement harked back to a situation that had arisen eight years previously, when the Duchy was still being held in trust for him until he reached the age of 21. The Duchy and the Inland Revenue had been at loggerheads on this issue: the Duchy claiming that royals are exempt from paying tax, and invoking Crown immunity – the principle that unless an Act of Parliament specifically includes the monarch, the law does not apply to him or her. To resolve the dispute, an appeal was made to the Law Officers for a ruling.

The Law Officers duly decided that Crown immunity did indeed apply and so income from the Duchy of Cornwall was not liable to taxation – an astonishing verdict that was certainly wrong on both legal and constitutional grounds.[50] As we shall see in a later chapter, the idea that the monarch should be exempt from tax on their *personal* income is a serious distortion of the constitutional rules. (Indeed, both Queen Victoria and Edward VII had paid income tax – and even George V was doing so at the time.) But more obviously, of course, Crown immunity only applies to the reigning monarch and by no stretch of the imagination to their children. Even more bizarre was the fact that George V was *not* claiming Crown immunity on his own income.

However, it is clear that the Law Officers had little faith in their own argument but were simply twisting the law to satisfy the heir to the throne. This is revealed by the curious fact that, uncertain that their ruling would be upheld if the Inland Revenue challenged it in court, they recommended that the Duchy should continue to pay tax anyway, but on a voluntary basis. In 1921, however, Edward rejected this arrangement and again the Law Officers were asked for a ruling, and once again they agreed with the Prince on the same grounds – Crown immunity. In return, Edward agreed to make a 'voluntary contribution' to the Treasury – of less than half of his putative tax bill. This is the origin of Prince Charles's voluntary arrangement of today.[51]

To prevent the shadiness of this astonishingly unconstitutional favouritism from becoming known, the whole arrangement was shrouded in such successful secrecy that it was not until the 1990s that it was uncovered by writer-researcher Phillip Hall, who unearthed a Treasury file on the matter, marked 'Secret', from the Public Record Office.[52] This explosive file revealed that a series of measures were taken to prevent the fact of the tax-free Duchy income from being known by either Parliament or the public. It makes one wonder who the Inland Revenue works for.

The tenants of the Duchy of Cornwall continued to deduct tax from their rents and pay it to the Inland Revenue – who secretly paid it back to the Duchy. And the Duchy stopped publishing annual accounts – or more precisely, produced only two copies: to comply with the law one was lodged in the library of the House of Commons and one in the House of Lords' Record Office (this practice continued until 1982). However, the smokescreen continued, as the accounts listed the voluntary payments as 'tax' in order to cover the fact that the Duchy was no longer paying it. In fact, until 1969 when Charles inherited the title, the Palace routinely stated that the Duchy profits were liable to tax and that it was being paid.[53] These statements were knowingly untrue.

A ROMANTIC REVELATION

At this time, the Palace had not yet put into practice the idea of marrying the new generation of royals into British, rather than foreign, families. Although this new idea particularly applied to the Prince of Wales, as time passed he still showed no inclination towards marriage. Despite his crippling shyness, Bertie was a better prospect, and by this time, as we have seen, he had also had affairs. And like Edward, Bertie had taken an older married woman as his mistress – Sheila, Lady Loughborough – but unlike his dashing elder brother, when pressed by his father into giving her up, Bertie meekly obeyed.

Then Lady Elizabeth Bowes-Lyon arrived on the scene, his future Queen Consort and, as his widow, the world-famous and extremely long-lived Queen Mother. However, the true story of her involvement with the royal family is somewhat different from the one that is so lovingly trotted out by the saccharin-sweet school of royal writing that takes all Palace PR as the gospel truth.

The youngest daughter of the 13th Earl of Strathmore and Kinghorne, she grew up in Glamis (pronounced 'Glahms') Castle in Scotland, famous for its ghosts and background role in Shakespeare's *Macbeth*. She was the eighth of nine children, born after a seven-year gap. Her much beloved brother David (of whom more later) was born two years later: because they were the babies of the family they became particularly close.

Despite her father's elevated position in society, as the youngest daughter of a large family she had little money of her own, so it was hoped that she would make a good marriage – a hope that she fervently shared. Yet all seemed set for a glittering future: in those days she was slim and although notably old-fashioned in dress and hairstyle she had a quiet elegance and grace, and a winning way with men, which she never completely lost in all her 101 years. There was always something pretty, fluffy and flirty about Elizabeth, without in the least seeming to be improper or 'fast'. It was an image she cultivated assiduously.

It was at the first RAF Ball at the Ritz Hotel in the summer of 1920 that she first met Bertie, the guest of honour. With her quiet manner and huge blue eyes that seemed to adore every man she met, the tiny Scottish aristocrat was an instant success with the gawky second-in-line to the throne, and in his own quiet but determined way he began to pursue her.

This, then, was the beginning of the now-fabled love match, but it was not quite as it is usually told. When they met she was actually in love with Bertie's equerry, James Stuart, known as Jamie, who was her escort at the RAF Ball. He introduced her to his prince and instantly his own fortunes took a turn for the worse, in the time-honoured way of those who put obstacles in the path of royalty. Queen Mary, together with Lady Strathmore and Jamie's own mother, Lady Moray, arranged for Jamie to be despatched to Oklahoma to work in the oilfields.[54] (He later became a Conservative MP and, in the 1950s, Secretary of State for Scotland.)

Clearly, Elizabeth got over the loss of Jamie rather quickly. Always shrewd and hugely ambitious, she set her sights on quite another young man – and it wasn't Bertie. Astonishingly – at least when compared to the usual story – she decided to become Queen by marrying the heir to the throne, the Prince of Wales. And it appears that both George V and Queen Mary seriously considered her for this role. As British author A.N. Wilson writes: 'From her early twenties, Lady Elizabeth Bowes-Lyon showed ambition to be Queen of England.'[55] Indeed, many years later, as Duke of Windsor Edward told biographer Michael Thornton, author of *Royal Feud* (1984), that 'Elizabeth Bowes-Lyon was determined to marry into the royal family, so after his third proposal, she settled for the runt of the litter'.[56] This line is generally put down to Windsor's bitterness at the way the royal family had treated him and his wife, but the evidence does bear it out.

As Windsor said, Elizabeth did turn Bertie down at least twice: some researchers put the number of Bertie's proposals at four.[57] He first proposed to her in the spring of 1921, but Elizabeth refused him. He also proposed at least once more in 1922 and got the same response. It was not until nearly two years after his first proposal that she accepted.[58]

In August 1921 Queen Mary travelled to Glamis Castle – according to today's official version to assess Lady Elizabeth's suitability as a bride for Bertie. But even Palace-approved biographer David Duff, author of three books on the Queen Mother, acknowledges that she was not checking her as potential as a bride for *Bertie* – but for *Edward*.[59] While at Glamis, Queen Mary invited Elizabeth to be one of the bridesmaids at the forthcoming wedding of Princess Mary to Henry, Viscount Lascelles.[60]

So what had happened to change Elizabeth's mind about the Prince of Wales? Why did she suddenly decide to marry Bertie? If the King and Queen had wanted her as a bride for the heir to the throne they would have virtually *ordered* the Strathmores to provide their daughter for the role. Under the circumstances it can only be because *Edward* rejected the plan. It was only then, after Bertie proposed a third time, that she settled for second best, but as biographer Kirsty McLeod notes: 'Elizabeth was not good at coming second.'[61] This was something that Edward, and his future wife, were to discover the hard way.

Many years later, as Queen Mother, Elizabeth said, 'It was my duty to marry him, and I fell in love with Bertie afterward.'[62] But if she were really persuaded it was her 'duty', why did it take two years and at least three proposals? And if no less than Queen Mary had persuaded her of that duty, why did she turn Bertie down again the following year? Elizabeth's statement contrasts with one she is reported to have made to a friend, when she admitted that like many other girls of her time and place she *had* been in love with the Prince of Wales, adding: 'He was such fun – then.'[63]

Interestingly, she did discuss Bertie's proposals with Edward, who told her rather bluntly: 'You had better take him and go in the end to Buck House.'[64] Does this reveal that – as early as 1922 – Edward had decided he would never be King, or was it simply one of his 'black moods' in which he regularly despaired of ever matching up to his father's great expectations? There is another angle to this conversation between the heir to the throne and the ambitious little Scots girl. If Edward had told her he would never be King, had this finally swung her in favour of the lovelorn Bertie, the second-in-line?

In the coming tumultuous years, the new Queen was to find flexing her muscles vis-à-vis Edward and his grand passion, the erstwhile Mrs Simpson, almost addictive. Whenever she could, she arranged for obstacles to be put in their path, and later even blamed them for her husband's premature death (despite the fact that he was a heavy smoker and virtually an alcoholic). But perhaps there was more than a suggestion of 'hell hath no fury like a woman scorned' in the behaviour of Elizabeth towards her former love – and potentially greatest prize.

BERTIE TRIUMPHANT

In the light of this information about Elizabeth, it is significant that on 5 January 1923 the *Daily News* carried the story headlined 'Scottish Bride for Prince of Wales', which was picked up by other newspapers. Although the story failed to mention the bride's name, the Palace swiftly issued a denial. Eight days later, on 13 January, Bertie made his third (or possibly even fifth) proposal, and this time Elizabeth accepted. Coming so soon after the press stories and the official denial, the timing is suspicious to say the least. There was no going back, no hope now of ever marrying Edward: she knew where her destiny lay.

The official announcement of the engagement between Lady Elizabeth and Bertie was made two days later. The announcement of a royal betrothal to a British lady was considered, in the words of David Duff, to be 'revolutionary',[65] despite the fact that the King had made his intentions on this matter known as far back as 1917.

It was just after the announcement that Elizabeth made a bad mistake that brought her up sharp, but which she never repeated in eight decades. She broke one of the great taboos of the royal family and gave interviews to the *Daily Mail* and the *Star*, for which she was reprimanded by the King himself. After that she restricted her public announcements to set speeches and occasional responses to questions from the crowd, always anodyne and always upbeat, along the lines of 'How lovely' or 'Absolutely marvellous'. Said with a heartbreaking smile and a twinkle in her amazing blue eyes it passed almost for wit.

Yet the interviews she so ill-advisedly gave in the early days of her royal betrothal are very revealing, for Elizabeth was already rewriting history. She told the *Star*'s reporter on the subject of her relationship with Bertie: 'The story that he asked me two or three times amused me . . . Now look at me. Do you think I am the sort of person Bertie would have to ask twice?'[66] This was chutzpah.

The marriage took place on 26 April 1923, at Westminster Abbey. The Prince of Wales (no doubt feeling very relieved) was his brother's 'supporter', the royal equivalent of best man. Photographs of the newly-weds in their carriage reveal both of them to look triumphant, but for rather different reasons: he because despite his personal shortcomings he had finally secured the hand of a much-sought-after aristocratic woman that even his father approved of, and she because she had married the second-in-line, who might even become the heir. Three years before, Bertie had been created the Duke of York, and now she was a royal duchess, who had begun to look as if born to the part.

By royal standards, the Yorks were relatively poor. They bought their townhouse at 145 Piccadilly with a bank loan and filled it with second-hand furniture. However, in 1931 the King offered them Royal Lodge in Windsor Great Park, which became their country seat and the later Queen Mother's much loved retreat.

The marriage was a time of great change for both partners, but perhaps especially for the shy and introverted Bertie. Louis Greig, his favourite companion, adviser and mentor since the First World War, who had become Comptroller of the Duke of York's household, was to depart. The two men were so close that Bertie even sent him a gauche note after his wedding night, which included the following: 'It is now 12.45 and I have not had a bath yet!! Everything was plain sailing, which was a relief. You know what I mean. I was very good!!'[67] 'Plain sailing' is not quite a description of wild passion, but it is to be hoped that Elizabeth shared his assessment of his own performance.

Greig resigned as Comptroller in October 1924. He had tense relationships with certain courtiers, but according to the son of Sir Clive Wigram, the King's Assistant Private Secretary, it was the new Duchess of York who finally sealed Greig's fate. Apparently the King had told Wigram: 'I don't care what the little duchess says but he is not going to go.'[68] The fact that, despite even the King's word on the subject, Greig did go says much about the steely determination of the fluffy little duchess. However, the two men did manage to remain friends.

The Yorks' first daughter – today's internationally respected Elizabeth II – was born in April 1926, and was duly christened Elizabeth Alexandra Mary, after her mother, great-grandmother and grandmother respectively. Her birth caused a sensation in the press: indeed, later that year Bertie remarked that his only claim to fame was that he was the father of Princess Elizabeth.[69] Margaret Rose followed four years later, in 1930. According to some accounts, the reason for the three-year delay in having their first child and the four-year delay in producing their second was that the Duchess had difficulty conceiving. Perhaps Bertie's teenage mumps were to blame, as they were with Edward's fertility.

Bertie and Elizabeth settled into domestic life which, if the usual stories are correct, was little short of blissful, although it is admitted that the Duke of York suffered from incapacitating rages, called his 'gnashes', during which anyone in his path would receive the full brunt. From time to time Elizabeth found herself in that unfortunate position – according to Palace servants, he was even seen to hit her on occasion[70] – but she possessed a perfect technique for calming him, holding his wrist gently and saying 'tick-tock' as she counted his pulse, while looking into his eyes with an encouraging smile. But while private life was making a man of him, his public duties remained onerous and embarrassing, although he always made a game enough stab at them.

Because of his stammer and general awkwardness, especially when compared to his glamorous older brother, the Duke of York had largely been kept out of the public eye. He had become patron of some organisations that fitted nicely with the post-war policy, most significantly as President of the Industrial Welfare Society (which grew out of an organisation concerned with the health, housing and welfare of munitions workers in the First World War). Stamfordham had noted that Bertie seemed to have a genuine social conscience, while the Prince of Wales merely spoke of possessing such a thing.[71] Bertie also represented his father on foreign state visits – most of them to Yugoslavia for some reason.

Now his profile had risen considerably with his marriage and the birth of a golden-haired heiress, he had to take on a more public role, if only deputising for his brother when he was out of the country. The prospect of being publicly compared to the dazzling Prince of Wales was a nightmare come true for Bertie, even given his new-found confidence through the gently encouraging Elizabeth. He was in a complete panic over his first public address – giving the closing speech of the Empire Exhibition at Wembley in October 1925. As if to rub salt in the wound, one of the major exhibits that he could hardly miss was a life-sized sculpture of the Prince of Wales made out of butter. Film footage of the speech is excruciatingly embarrassing: the Duke of York grasps his notes desperately while waiting for the words to find their way out. The stadium was packed and the event was broadcast around the

Empire – worse, among the millions who tuned in was his father, who later wrote to Prince George about it, saying: 'Bertie got through his speech all right but there were some rather long pauses',[72] which was remarkably low-key considering the scale of the debacle. To make matters much, much worse, Bertie was due to be sent on his first Empire tour, of Australia, in January 1927. It was imperative to deal with his stammer, which although never completely cured was rendered more manageable by the speech therapist Lionel Logue, with the support and encouragement of the Duchess of York. More than anything else, the breathing exercises gave him a sense of control and of growing confidence.

MOUNTBATTEN AND HIS HEIRESS

Meanwhile Mountbatten fretted about his relative poverty. Despite his royal ancestry and being regarded as the second most eligible bachelor in England after the Prince of Wales, he had no real capital. He earned £310 a year from the navy and dividends brought in about another £300 – hardly enough to provide him with the lavish lifestyle he believed he deserved as by divine right. Suddenly, the way forward revealed itself in the glamorous form of Edwina Ashley, heiress to a vast fortune, whom he met in 1920. He was instantly smitten, both by her personal charms and her fabulous wealth. Apparently genuinely in love, he decided to marry her and, as in most things, he got his way. Their relationship started in August 1921.

Edwina, then just 19, was the daughter of the right-wing Conservative MP Wilfrid Ashley, the later Lord Mount Temple. More importantly, Edwina was the granddaughter of Sir Ernest Cassel, a German-born Jewish financier who had built himself up from nothing to be one of the richest men in Europe, becoming Edward VII's personal financial adviser. (Edward VII was Edwina's godfather.) She was heiress to Cassel's fortune – £2.3 million, a phenomenal sum at that time, the equivalent of over £80 million today, which she inherited when Sir Ernest died a month after Edwina and Louis' relationship began.

Edwina followed Louis to India, inviting herself to stay with the Viceroy (an old friend of her grandfather's). Mountbatten proposed to her on St Valentine's Day 1922: on their engagement, in another example of his rewriting history, Mountbatten wrote to his mother, 'I have never really sown any wild oats, and as I never intend to, I haven't got to get over that stage which some men have to.'[73] As a descendant of George II, by law Mountbatten had to secure the King's permission to marry, but this was not a problem. The Prince of Wales agreed to be his best man. He was created a Knight Commander of the Victorian Order (KCVO) as a mark of honour. (Membership is awarded by the monarch to those who have rendered particular service to the royal family.) They were married in London in July, a month after their return. It was the society wedding of the century, according to the *Star*, even eclipsing Princess Mary's royal wedding of six months before. There were 1,400 guests, including the whole of the royal family, and a crowd of 8,000 gathered outside the society church, St Margaret's in Westminster, to throw confetti and go wild with vicarious joy.

The newly-weds spent their wedding night at Broadlands, Hampshire (Edwina's father's country house) and their honeymoon was something of a grand tour, taking in Paris, Spain and (to the disapproval of some sections of the British press) Hesse in Germany. In September they sailed off to the USA, first to New York then to Hollywood, where they mixed with film stars such as Douglas Fairbanks Jr. and Charlie Chaplin (whose wedding present was to direct them in a one-reeler, which revealed – surprisingly perhaps – that they had no noticeable theatrical talent).

Back home, they moved into Brook House – which Edwina had inherited – on the corner of prestigious Park Lane in central London, not far from Buckingham Palace. However, it was obvious from the beginning that theirs was no domestic idyll in the style of the Yorks up the road in Piccadilly. Before long the Mountbattens both embarked on extramarital affairs, although it is not clear who strayed first. Within a year, on a visit to New York with his brother George (the porn collector), who had inherited the Milford Haven title, and his wife Nada, the Mountbattens were arguing ferociously in public, although they continued to adore each other. At the end of the scheduled trip Edwina announced that she was going to stay in the States for a while with Nada: those who knew of Nada's lesbian proclivities (which included most members of society) began to wonder . . .

Mountbatten was not to be outdone. On his solo voyage home aboard the liner *Berengaria*, Noël Coward booked himself the next door cabin and the two struck up a 'friendship' during the crossing.[74] In fact, according to Madeleine Masson, the two men had a torrid affair.[75] (This was shortly after Coward had also begun a two-year affair with Prince George.)

For the rest of their long married life Louis and Edwina settled into a loose arrangement that suited them both – affairs with whoever they pleased, often going for months without even seeing each other, but still more or less content to remain a couple. If nothing else, it was good for their respective reputations. Biographer Brian Hoey writes: 'The Mountbattens' was arguably the most open marriage of their generation.'[76] That is, open to the knowledge of their social circle: to the press and more moral-minded lower classes there was never a hint of their goings on. And in any case, Mountbatten was now a very wealthy man: the first part of his long-term plan was in place.

A complex man emotionally – although undoubtedly he was the greatest love of his life, there were significant others – one of his lifelong relationships began in 1926. The lady in question was Yola Letellier, the wife of a French newspaper proprietor, who knew about the relationship, as did Edwina – and the royal family.[77] Mountbatten and Yola became long-term lovers. Edwina, too, embarked on extramarital affairs: in the words of biographer Richard

Hough, 'She loved having affairs and hearing of the affairs of others, travelling and relaxing with women friends, experimenting with drugs and from time to time with gambling and drinking too much.'[78]

Her long-term lover was Lieutenant-Colonel Harold 'Bunny' Phillips, who was married to Gina, daughter of Sir Harold and Lady Zia Wernher (Nada's sister). Edwina's intimacy with that family opened the way for Mountbatten, too. When in his 60s he openly embarked on a relationship with Bunny's daughter – Sacha, the Duchess of Abercorn, his own goddaughter. Once again, however, the affair was kept well away from the public gaze. By that time Mountbatten's image was well established as the crusty old hero of the sea, the stalwart widower of an impeccable wife. But Sacha said after his death, 'He actually preferred married women as they were safer. He knew it could only go so far and that's what he wanted. No permanent commitment.'[79]

For the remainder of the 1920s, Mountbatten concentrated on his career in the Royal Navy, but his scheming to establish himself as an indispensable friend of the royal family was by no means quiescent. It was during this period that he homed in on yet another Windsor son – this time it was the outrageous and attractive Prince George.

SECRETS OF THE PLAYBOY PRINCE

Throughout the 1920s, George reluctantly continued to serve with the navy, but there are few official records of his career because – for reasons that will become obvious – there is a continuing embargo on all his papers. But details can be pieced together: according to researcher Robin Macwhirter he spent a period with Naval Intelligence at Rosyth in Scotland,[80] and in other postings he served in the Mediterranean and China. He also studied languages, for which he had a marked, and very un-Windsor-like aptitude – even managing to get his tongue around the notoriously difficult Dutch language – at Greenwich. But despite the riotous sailor traditions of shore leave, of which he made the most, George was intensely frustrated by navy life. He had 'an artistic temperament', a phrase that was as true as it was occasionally euphemistic and, like Bertie, suffered badly from seasickness, which made him view the long weeks at sea with utter dread.

In the 1920s he was given little in the way of royal duties or honours, although his father did make him a Knight of the Garter in 1923. But while his royal life seemed to have stalled temporarily, his private life was quite another matter. During his leave and frequent absences from the navy on the grounds of ill health (both real and fictitious) he joined Edward on London's glittering social circuit, becoming very close to his glamorous elder brother, with whom he had more in common than he had with the gauche Bertie or almost retarded Harry. As diarist Chips Channon put it delicately, Edward and George 'drank deeply from life'.[81]

Although a devoted cocktail and jazz man, there was more to George than wild Charleston parties. He had a fine appreciation of art and antiques, which he collected – under his mother's watchful and admiring eye – and loved the theatre, opera and ballet. He was also very dashing: he was to qualify as a pilot in 1930 and loved fast cars. (He was one of the first to fit his car with a radio.) But only too often it seemed that the attraction of the endless round of parties had him firmly in its grasp: he was often spotted at the Embassy and other clubs, sometimes playing the banjolele on stage. George put his dazzling good looks and massive reserves of charm to good use on the social scene, having a string of affairs with society girls. He had a particular penchant for black women, such as the American singer Florence Mills, with whom he had an affair. He also loved mixing with the stars of stage and screen – for example, being a friend of the great light comedy and dance star Fred Astaire, who managed to keep his own bisexuality very largely a secret for most of his long life. And it was George's own affairs with men that were to bring him, and the royal family, to the very brink of appalling scandal.

Christopher Warwick, author of *George and Marina* (the nearest there is to a biography of Prince George), writes that the Prince's 'appetite for sexual adventures was voracious . . . as much with men as with women, with aristocrats, show business personalities or with strangers'.[82] And the academic Steven Runciman, a friend of George's wife Marina, said to her, 'I was told no one – of either sex – was safe with him in a taxi.'[83] Perhaps it says just as much for the Kaiser's grandson as Prince George when the former described the latter – approvingly – as 'artistic and effeminate' and noted that he 'used a strong perfume'.[84]

Probably George's most famous homosexual liaison was with the celebrated British playwright and songwriter Noël Coward – he of the silk dressing-gown, long cigarette holder and peculiar, clipped accent that has given rise to countless spoof impersonations. They met during the run of Coward's review *London Calling* in early 1923.[85] (Coward's co-star Gertrude Lawrence, herself rumoured to be bisexual, found Prince George in her dressing-room, trying on one of her wigs.) The two men became lovers, and although their sexual affair petered out after just two years, they remained close friends until the Prince's death in 1942. Their relationship was an open secret among London's glitterati.[86]

More sensationally, Coward also hinted strongly that the Prince of Wales had nervously experimented with homosexual affairs, saying: 'He pretends not to hate me but he does, and it's because I'm queer and he's queer but, unlike him, I don't pretend not to be.'[87] In later years, as the Duke of Windsor, Edward was famous for his apparent homophobia, often saying, 'I can't stand those fellas who fly in under the transom,' while making little camp flapping gestures with his hands.

George had no such qualms. He had many high-profile gay affairs, including one with the female impersonator Douglas Byng and another with the son of the Argentinian ambassador, Jose Evaristo Uriburu, then studying at Cambridge. The relationship was broken up by the boy's outraged father.

Meanwhile, the Prince continued to visit clubs and pubs where guardsmen could be picked up – the most notorious being the Packenham, near the Household Cavalry barracks in bohemian Chelsea. According to those who also frequented the Packenham, George was often accompanied on these excursions by Mountbatten (his marriage to Edwina having settled into the convenient upper-class 'anything goes' pattern) and the Duchess of York's younger brother, David Bowes-Lyon.[88] Some even claim that the Prince of Wales occasionally dallied in this gay underworld.

Of course there were dangers in such behaviour, particularly at a time when sex between two men was still a criminal offence (indeed, its decriminalisation was still 40 years away). Prince George was even arrested on at least one occasion, when he was caught in a police raid on a gay club called the Nut House, where he was blithely dancing the night away, his face caked in full 'slap', and was taken to Bow Street police station.[89] Of course he was released as soon as the police discovered his identity: his fellow clubbers were not so lucky.

At that time a gay man could still be sentenced to several years' hard labour, his life ruined forever. Many found they could face neither the disgrace nor the future in prison and took their own lives: indeed, George V was known to have remarked that he thought such men normally killed themselves. His youngest son failed to comply with that unwritten rule, while the Palace mafia nervously waited in the wings to extricate him from his every latest indiscretion and crime. Similarly the Prince of Wales and Mountbatten were also protected from scandal and ruin by the very fact of their birth and status. In those days the press would not have dreamt of revealing the content of the royal family's skeleton-packed cupboards to the world. The lower classes had to be kept admiring at all costs, so the royal image makers oiled the machine of public relations with lies and cover-ups.

In any case, George had a stalwart protector in his brother Edward, who regularly came to his aid when he got himself into trouble. For example, in 1932 an architect in Paris – a former gay fling – attempted blackmail with George's ill-advised love letters. It was Edward who paid up.[90]

Oblivious to the mores of the public and bent on enjoying himself hugely, George continued his chosen lifestyle, embarking on a gay affair that was to have some serious and significant repercussions in later years. Around 1927 he forged an alliance with a young Cambridge student, Anthony Blunt, later the Surveyor of the Queen's Pictures and, of course, still later revealed to be a Soviet spy. The relationship between George and Blunt was noted by several of Blunt's 'intimates'.[91]

The affair probably began through the introduction by the flamboyant Prince Chula Chakrabongse, a half-Russian member of the Thai royal family who was a friend of Blunt at Trinity College and part of George's London set.[92] Part of the attraction was that the two were passionate about art and art history, Blunt's speciality. It was only in the late 1970s that he was publicly unmasked as a Soviet spy. According to the account given to his MI5 interrogators and later in a public interview, the attraction to communism that led to his recruitment by the Soviet NKVD (forerunner of the KGB) did not begin until the early or mid-1930s, a few years after his liaison with Prince George.[93] More important for this story, however, was the fact that it brought Blunt into contact with Mountbatten – and through Kent and Murphy they kept in touch for many years.[94]

George had another, more deadly, secret at this time. During 1928 he became addicted to cocaine and morphine, having been introduced to the drug scene by one of his female lovers, an American named Kiki Whitney Preston ('the girl with the silver syringe'). But once again, the Prince of Wales came to the rescue. Despite his own love of nightclubs and the party circuit, Edward seemed more in control and detested drugs. By all accounts, and despite claims to the contrary, the evidence suggests that he was not even much of a drinker at this time – although George remained a heavy drinker for the rest of his relatively short life. In the summer of the following year, Edward confronted the seductive addict Kiki, forcing her to leave the country.[95] Indeed, according to biographer Sophia Watson, Scotland Yard chased several other girls, and presumably also young men, out of the country to protect George's reputation.[96]

The Prince of Wales then set about carefully and intelligently curing George of his addiction, shutting him away in a house in the country and staying with him during the traumatic time of going 'cold turkey'. He even abandoned his holiday plans with Freda Dudley Ward, to whom he described his role as 'doctor, gaoler and detective combined'.[97] This terrible phase lasted from the summer of 1929 until January 1930, when George seemed to be cured, although his brother continued to worry about him reverting to his bad habits until his marriage four years later. Even George V was impressed by Edward's devotion, writing: 'Looking after him for all those months must have been a great strain on you & I think it was wonderful all you did for him.'[98] So in one way at least, George's wild ways brought the Windsor family closer together, if only temporarily. Much, much worse was in store . . .

POLITICAL MANOEUVRES

By the early 1920s the Palace mafia under Lord Stamfordham – who was very much still in control, despite being in his 70s – was no longer simply monitoring and sounding out different shades of opinion about the royal family, but had begun to act in ways that would normally be deemed the province of the police or security services.

Scotland Yard and branches of the Government kept the Palace informed of the surveillance and monitoring of potentially subversive groups and movements that posed a threat to the monarchy. For example, the War Office drew up a report on the Leeds meeting to back the Russian Revolution referred to in Chapter One. When the British Communist Party was formed in 1920 the Palace was not only sent reports on its activities by the Metropolitan Police, but also infiltrated its own agents into the Party, under the direction of Sir Henry Thornton, an American who was General Manager of the Great Eastern Railway, using his own employees for the undercover work. The reports were handled on the King's behalf by his Assistant Private Secretary, Sir Clive Wigram, and copies were duly passed on to Scotland Yard because the intelligence gathered by this route tended to be of a higher standard than their own.[99]

Stamfordham's informants included Ethel Snowden, the wife of Philip Snowden, the Chancellor in the 1924 Labour Government, who kept up a secret correspondence with Stamfordham and the King.[100] And the Palace and the King personally were provided with secret police reports, as in February 1925 when George V was shown the police's file on the spread of communism among Cambridge undergraduates.[101]

However, although the Sovereign's political power had been steadily eroded by Parliament, the royal prerogative was still a force to be reckoned with. George V was keen to exercise it whenever he could, sometimes as a direct challenge to his ministers and Parliament, in a show of bravado, flexing his constitutional muscles to show the politicians that the monarchy was not entirely impotent. The events of May 1923 demonstrated this often tense relationship between King and Parliament, and also brought to power one of the major players in the later drama of the abdication, Stanley Baldwin.

Andrew Bonar Law had been Prime Minister of a Conservative Government for only six months when he was diagnosed with incurable throat cancer. Everyone agreed that the obvious choice of successor was Lord Curzon. However, George V – and, we can guess, his Palace advisers – decided that it was no longer wise for the Prime Minister to be a member of the House of Lords. He therefore 'sent for' Stanley Baldwin, then Chancellor of the Exchequer, and asked him to form a government. This was a shock to everyone, including Curzon, who had travelled from his country seat to London on the King's summons fully expecting to be told he was the new Prime Minister, only to have Stamfordham break the news that he had been passed over for the top post.

The reason for the King's decision was that, as the Labour Party was now emerging as a political force to be reckoned with, but had no peers and therefore no representation in the House of Lords, appointing a prime minister from that House would appear to be showing favour to Labour's opponents. (A prime minister in the Lords could not be questioned by Labour MPs.) Although this seems remarkably fair and constitutionally impartial, it is clear that George V's true motive was to preserve the monarchy in the event of a future Labour Government.[102] The fact that the King disliked Curzon but liked Baldwin was also probably a major part of the equation.

Baldwin's first period as premier only lasted a few months, as a general election in October 1923 resulted in the Conservatives losing their overall majority, although still the largest party in the Commons. Despite the King's pleas, Baldwin resigned. Labour had won the second largest share of the seats, so George V asked Labour leader Ramsay MacDonald to form the Government – the first Labour administration, which was in fact a pact with the Liberals. The day dreaded by the King and Stamfordham had finally arrived.

By all accounts, the King genuinely liked MacDonald, although their first audience was somewhat sticky. The new Prime Minister was keen to show the King that he represented no threat to the monarchy, declaring that 'his earnest desire was to serve his King and Country'.[103] The King complained about a number of inflammatory republican speeches made by some key Labour figures and about the singing of 'The Red Flag'. To appease the King, MacDonald did not include one of the leading republican MPs, George Lansbury, in his Cabinet. George V seemed to be won over, writing in his diary wonderingly:

> He impressed me very much, he wishes to do the right thing. Today 23 years after dear Grandmamma [Queen Victoria] died, I wonder what she would have thought of a Labour Government?[104]

Human nature being what it so often is, it was perhaps predictable that the new Labour ministers, MPs and their wives rushed to mix with the upper crust at royal garden parties and other regal functions. Much as it went against the grain, George V even dropped the dress code for court events – a simple levée coat would now suffice instead of the old knee breeches. (This represented an enormous sacrifice for the King, who was almost pathologically obsessed with 'correct' dress, as his sons often found out the hard way.) Lord Stamfordham even arranged a cut-price deal on levée coats at the gentlemen's outfitters Moss Bros., duly informing the Labour Chief Whip about the bargain.[105]

Astonishing though it may seem, through the judicious use of flattery and charm, the King and the Palace drew the teeth of Labour. Indeed, they were largely responsible for the character of the Labour Party as we know it – after all, the first Labour Government was a totally unknown quantity and could easily have been much more radical. As we will see, George V also later engaged in other machinations to neutralise further what he saw as the Labour menace.

Despite all the compromises, the first Labour Government was short-lived, lacking an overall majority and being only sustained by a deal with the Liberals that collapsed in just under a year. The resultant general election returned Baldwin and the Conservatives to power.

THE BRINK OF REVOLUTION

The General Strike of May 1926 was the most serious threat faced by the Government – and the monarchy – between the wars. It began with a strike by the coal miners, but escalated when the Trades Union Congress (TUC) called all union members out on strike indefinitely to show their support. It was a massive display of working-class solidarity: public transport stopped, newspapers were not printed and factories and power stations were closed. It was an unprecedented event – or series of events – and struck terror into the heart of the old order. Was this the beginning of a Russian-style revolution, the beginning of the end for the House of Windsor?

Baldwin and his Government – like the King – regarded the General Strike not as an industrial dispute but as a challenge to the very foundations of the constitution, and consequently refused to negotiate or compromise with the strikers. Non-union volunteers, predominantly from the middle and upper classes, stepped in to keep the country running, driving buses and lorries, manning switchboards and acting as messengers. It was surprising how many of the idle hedonistic set rushed to get their hands dirty during that peculiar episode: even Edwina Mountbatten threw herself into helping out, which probably gave her a taste for the obsessive charity work that characterised her much later life. Yet the class system was not so easily overthrown: even the massed pickets outside the great newspaper buildings in Fleet Street touched their caps deferentially when the top-hatted newspaper barons strode through. It was a very British strike.

It was also an exceptionally delicate time. The Government's reaction to the strikers had to be carefully judged: too weak and the country could be brought to its knees, too strong and the situation could escalate into full-blown riots. Winston Churchill, who was Chancellor of the Exchequer in Baldwin's government, was of course one of those who urged that the most stringent measures be taken against the strikers, characteristically calling for the army to be brought in. Baldwin made him editor of the short-lived Government newspaper, the *British Gazette*, published in place of the other dailies, in order to 'stop him doing worse things'.[106]

The situation was very tense as far as the King was concerned. There was great nerviness at the Palace – would this end with a Bolshevik uprising and all that that implied for the royal family? In the event, however, the General Strike fizzled out after just eight days, but there was great uncertainty during that time about which way it would go.

How should the King react? Stamfordham and his advisers insisted that he should not be seen to take either side, and should do nothing that would either encourage or (more likely) condemn the strikers, but to sit it out and, when it was resolved, to take the line of moderation and compromise. Ironically, this was not the view of the allegedly reformist and more egalitarian Prince of Wales, who thought a more active role should be taken in support of the Government. Hurrying back from lotus-eater land in Biarritz on the eve of the Strike, he saw it as a direct threat to the royal family, writing in his later memoirs (1951):

> Along with many of his thoughtful subjects my father was plainly confused in his own mind as to whether the strike ought to be classed as party politics in the accepted meaning of the term or whether it smacked of revolution. However, because of the deep split that had been produced within classes he counselled me and my brothers to abstain from all public or private comment on the issues and to remain more or less out of sight until the trouble blew over. But that was like asking a man in a burning building to retire to his room while the firemen coped with the blaze.[107]

Edward kept abreast of the developments each day by visiting Government departments and going to the House of Commons every afternoon. In the evenings he went around London checking on the situation with 'friends in the Metropolitan Police' (his words).[108] We do not know what influence he succeeded in bringing to bear during his self-imposed rounds of the capital. But in one clear breach of royal neutrality he lent his car and chauffeur for the delivery of Churchill's *British Gazette* to Wales. It seems the Prince of Wales was spoiling for a fight with what he saw as Soviet-backed union leaders.

Yet he was still a useful card in Stamfordham's winning hand. His years of promoting Edward as having the 'common touch' paid off. Edward's hurried return to Britain to face the crisis, coupled with his by now well-established caring image, led the newspapers to dub him the 'People's Prince'.[109] Stamfordham must have been ecstatic.

'STUNTING'

Edward continued his role as the compassionate royal face throughout the 1920s, contributing to miners' relief funds and supporting charities concerned with the welfare of ex-servicemen, such as the British Legion and Toc H. In 1928 he became patron of the National Council of Social Service and under his influence it began to focus on work with the unemployed. He continued his hugely successful tours of working-class towns in the provinces and outside England – Tyneside, Lancashire, the Midlands, Wales and Scotland. But while he was always cheered to the rafters wherever he went, he was becoming disillusioned with 'princing' as he called it. He had been princing for ten years and the strain was showing. In 1925 Chips Channon recorded that the Prince's friends were saying that he was unhappy and would cheerfully renounce the succession.[110] In 1927 he wrote a letter to Godfrey Thomas that summed up his confused feelings towards his job:

> It's just the *chronic state* of being the P of W – of which I'm so heartily

and genuinely fed up . . . I've got a lot older lately and don't look for excitement the way I used to. And I believe I'm more conscientious over the less artificial side of my stunting than I was. But I have to go through with too many artificial 'bulls'. I suppose some of it is inevitable, still I rebel against it and I find it tricky.[111]

It is interesting that he acknowledges that the endless crowd-pleasing is mere 'stunting', but still realises that there is a 'less artificial' side to it all. However, the rift with his father about his lifestyle and irresponsible conduct continued to escalate. Edward escaped from 'princing' to his Bertie Woosterish life of clubbing, drinking and amorous exploits during country weekends.

Concern about the attitude of the Prince of Wales was to spread beyond the confines of his family. In September 1927 he, Prince George and Prime Minister Stanley Baldwin travelled to Canada for its Diamond Jubilee celebrations. During that trip, according to his biographers, Keith Middlemass and John Barnes, '. . . even then Baldwin was preoccupied with the problems which the Prince's behaviour and attitude suggested would become acute when he became King'.[112] The Prime Minister regarded Edward as worryingly irresponsible and immature – a time bomb waiting to explode among the foundations of the constitutional monarchy.

Those closest to the Prince shared this pessimism – if anything they saw the problem as being even more acute. Captain Alan 'Tommy' Lascelles had been the Prince's Assistant Private Secretary since 1921, and a significant exchange is reported to have taken place between him and Baldwin on this matter during the Canada tour as they watched the Prince riding. Lascelles remarked that he 'couldn't help thinking that the best thing that could happen to him, and to the country, would be for him to break his neck'. Baldwin replied, 'God forgive me. I have often thought the same.'[113]

A CLOSE CALL

In October 1928 the Prince of Wales and Prince Henry embarked on a 'semi-private' visit to East Africa: although there were some official engagements the trip mostly consisted of big game hunting and yet more amorous exploits among the expatriates. Both brothers became lovers of the adventurous and sexually aggressive – not to mention married, of course – Beryl Markham, who was to become the first woman to fly solo east-west across the Atlantic. She was five months' pregnant at the time she began her liaisons with the royal princes, and continued the affairs back in London.[114] (Later, her husband Mansfield Markham and his brother Charles used Henry's love letters to blackmail the royal family. As a result Henry put £15,000 in a trust fund for her, on which she continued to draw until her death in 1986. When *would* the royal boys ever learn?)

The fun and games in Kenya were not to last, being interrupted by the news that George V was seriously ill. Edward's reaction to the news was almost the last straw as far as his Assistant Private Secretary, 'Tommy' Lascelles, was concerned. Becoming increasingly appalled by the Prince's behaviour, he had written a few days earlier: 'I am thoroughly and permanently out of sympathy with him . . . His personal charm has vanished irretrievably so far as I am concerned, and I always feel as if I were working, not for the next King of England, but for the son of the latest American millionaire.'[115]

Although Stanley Baldwin cabled the Prince with the news, by then he had no illusions about Edward's capacity for wrong-headed behaviour, and felt compelled to add that should the King die and 'you have made no attempt to return, it will profoundly shock public opinion'.[116]

Both Baldwin and Lascelles seem to have got Edward's measure perfectly. According to Lascelles, on reading the cable from London, the Prince said, 'I don't believe a word of it. It's just some election dodge of Baldwin's. It doesn't mean anything.'[117] Boiling over with fury, Lascelles replied: 'Sir, the King of England is dying, and if that means nothing to you, it means a great deal to us.' The Prince's only immediate reaction was to go out and seduce the wife of the local commissioner.[118]

Not surprisingly, on their return to Britain, the disgusted Lascelles resigned. But once persuaded of the urgency, Edward sped back to England with utmost haste – taking a cruiser to Brindisi in Italy, where Mussolini had laid on his own private train and ordered the track to be cleared as far as the Swiss border. Despite all the dash and fuss, Edward was inwardly quaking. Was this the end of his freedom? He might have despised 'princing' but that was nothing compared to being constrained by the role of King.

The Prince of Wales was met at Folkestone by Stanley Baldwin, who accompanied him by train to Buckingham Palace. During the journey the Prince – who might very shortly be King – told Baldwin that he could always talk frankly to him on any subject. Baldwin later recalled: ' . . . a most curious impression came over me, a feeling of certainty that one day I most certainly *should* have to "say something to him" – and that it would be about a woman.'[119]

Coincidentally, his arrival back in Britain and this conversation with Baldwin happened on 11 December 1928 – eight years to the day before his abdication.

Having made his headlong dash back to his father's bedside, the heir was greeted by the old King characteristically: 'Damn you, what the devil are you doing here?'[120] The following day he was operated on for a streptococcal infection – while Edward went through agonies in case it all went wrong – which was a success, although he took many months to recover. During this time Edward was part of a Council of State, set up to perform the Sovereign's duties while he was incapable. This was his first taste of the actual duties of a king and it confirmed his worst suspicions about the job.

THE TURNING POINT

By the time of the June 1929 general election British society had changed forever. This election was the first in which men and women of all classes voted on an equal footing (although women over 30 had had the vote since 1918). This brave new political world led Stamfordham to observe (in very idiosyncratic grammar): 'We must recognise that democracy is no longer a meaningless shibboleth; with the enormous increase of voters by the women's franchise it is the actual voice, for better or worse, the political voice of the state.'[121]

That watershed election returned a Labour Government – and Ramsay MacDonald was Prime Minister once more. But his timing could not have been worse. The Wall Street Crash would soon bring economic disaster and spiralling unemployment, not just in the USA and Britain but across much of the world, with far-reaching consequences for history, and specifically for the fate of the Prince of Wales.

THREE

'CHRIST! WHAT'S GOING TO HAPPEN NEXT?'

Edward VIII at the funeral of George V

When George V's *eminence gris* Lord Stamfordham died, still in office, at the age of 81 in March 1931, Queen Mary wrote to the Prince of Wales that the King was 'quite knocked over by the blow' and described his 'depression & grief' at his adviser's death.[1] Stamfordham was replaced by his assistant of many years, Sir Clive (later Lord) Wigram, a devoted disciple of Stamfordham who was well trained in his methods and philosophy: another champion in the cause of preserving the monarchy at all costs.

Ironically, Stamfordham did not live to see George V's greatest political triumphs. Within a few months of his mentor's death – undoubtedly under Wigram's guidance – the King made a series of brilliantly shrewd moves that did much to re-establish the political influence of the Sovereign. Unfortunately this also entailed some blatantly unconstitutional and often unethical manoeuvrings, which in the long term have only served to tarnish the image of the monarchy.

Constitutional monarchs favour coalition governments, because the major check on their political influence is the 'rule' that they must avoid any hint of favouritism for a particular party. This effectively prevents the King from making any statement or taking any course of action with the remotest suggestion of a political sub-text. In a coalition government, in which all the parties participate and agree on policy, matters are much easier: the Government either agrees with the King's proposed move (in which case he can do it) or the ministers disapprove of it (in which case he can't). For this reason, Stamfordham had advocated the idea of a National Government – a coalition consisting of all three main parties – which was enthusiastically embraced by the Palace, including Stamfordham's successor, Sir Clive Wigram.[2]

In 1931 the first proper Labour Government, led by Ramsay MacDonald, was into its second year in office. George V personally liked and got on well with the Prime Minister – as well as several of his ministers from working-class backgrounds, whose company suited the no-nonsense King – but that was not synonymous with admiring the Labour movement as a whole. Indeed, he saw MacDonald as a moderating influence to keep the excesses of the Left at bay. As far as George was concerned, the perfect government would be a coalition (ideally with the Conservatives in the majority) which excluded Labour but at the same time – somehow – still with Ramsay MacDonald as Prime Minister. This may appear like a fantasy government dreamt up after rather too many brandies. But, incredibly, that is precisely what he got.

By August 1931 MacDonald's Government was struggling to cope with the economic and social effects of the Depression, which had sent unemployment soaring, shattering the nation's economic stability. The Bank of England was pressing the Government to make drastic reductions in public spending – including, most controversially, a ten per cent cut in unemployment benefit, which for obvious reasons a socialist government was set against. Such a measure would also present grave dangers to the old order, for might it not result in pro-Bolshevik riots? The nightmare of the fate of the Romanovs raised its ugly head once more, but given the extreme economic situation, what else could the Government do?

Britain's economy depended on a massive short-term loan from American banks, which had promised to communicate their decision to the Government on Sunday, 23 August. An emergency Cabinet meeting was called for that day to deal with the decision. It was all set to be a vitally important 24 hours for Britain: indeed, in the words of Phillip Hall, it was 'probably the most crucial day of his [George V's] reign'.[3] (So crucial, in fact, that he abandoned his summer break at Balmoral and returned to London specially.)

While the massed British Establishment waited with bated breath, the American banks pronounced that they would be pleased to grant the loan – provided that the Bank of England assured them that they were satisfied with the Government's programme of spending cuts. Of course, as the Americans well knew, the Bank would only be satisfied if the measures they urged – including that dangerous cut in unemployment benefit – were put into practice. What to do? The future of the British economy hung on this decision. In the event, the Cabinet was split: MacDonald had no option but to resign. He asked the King for a dissolution of Parliament, to call a general election.

Ramsay MacDonald had reckoned without the almost unprecedented input of the King. When he went to Buckingham Palace to tender his resignation, George V refused to accept it, declaring that it was a time of national emergency and MacDonald was the best person to lead the country. Instead of calling a general election, the King argued for a coalition with the Conservatives and Liberals. At the audience, MacDonald (as confirmed by a note he wrote at the time[4]) made the King aware of the precise consequences of such an astonishingly radical act. If the other leaders agreed to participate in a coalition in order to push through the spending cuts, most of his Cabinet would resign. He would lose the support of his party – and that would be the end of him as leader. Did the King really want to provoke such a response?

Nevertheless, George summoned the leaders of those parties, Stanley Baldwin and Sir Herbert Samuel (acting Liberal leader while Lloyd George recovered from an operation), and asked them if they would be willing to co-operate in a National Emergency Government led by MacDonald. Of course it was difficult for a party leader in those deferential days to refuse the King, so they agreed in principle but, as there were some reservations, George offered to chair a meeting between the three leaders at the Palace the next day (Monday, 24 August).

At the meeting – MacDonald with the Cabinet's collective letter of resignation in his pocket – the Conservative and Liberal leaders made it clear that they were not totally happy with the proposition, so it was agreed that the National Emergency Government would be a temporary administration with the sole purpose of pushing through the spending cuts. The King agreed that once they had done this he would dissolve Parliament and that the ensuing general election would be fought on the usual party lines.

This was not merely a gentleman's agreement, but was actually put in writing and signed by the King and MacDonald, Baldwin and Samuel: indeed, this was the arrangement that MacDonald reported to his Cabinet. It was the King's responsibility, as he had called and chaired the meeting, to guarantee that the agreement was kept.[5] However, as we will see, George V himself broke it.

Despite MacDonald's warnings about what it would mean for his position in the Labour Party, George V appointed him as Prime Minister of the National Government, on his personal prerogative and based on his own political judgement.[6] Unsurprisingly, when MacDonald reported the agreement to his Cabinet and Party there was outrage. All but three of the Cabinet ministers resigned, and the backbenchers expelled MacDonald and his handful of supporters from the Party. The second Labour Government fell, to be replaced by what was intended – indeed agreed – to be a temporary coalition, which now did not include the Labour Party.

It is also abundantly clear that during the crisis weekend George V was taking advice on the economic situation from others – particularly on the possible consequences of the American banks refusing the loan. Before his audience with MacDonald on the Sunday, he had lunched with Sir Edward Peacock, the Canadian head of Baring's Bank and a director of the Bank of England who acted as the King's personal financial adviser.[7] (Indeed, Peacock had just been invested as a member of the Royal Victorian Order.) George V's official biographers insist that the lunch meeting had nothing to do with the economic crisis, but it is hard to believe that the subject was ignored, especially when later in the same day the King took steps to ensure that the economic measures urged by the Bank became a reality.

If George had discussed the crisis over lunch, in itself this was an unconstitutional act: although the sovereign can take advice on political matters from people other than his ministers, he or she is not permitted to do so without informing the Prime Minister of such a step.[8]

The spending cuts – including the all-important 10 per cent decrease in unemployment benefit – were duly passed. According to the Buckingham Palace agreement the temporary Government was now redundant. However, at the end of September, MacDonald discussed the return to normal party politics with the King, who remarked with astonishing lack of tact to a Labour leader: 'If a Socialist Government came into power and carried out their extravagant promises to the electorate, this country would be finished . . .'[9]

On 3 October 1931 the King had told MacDonald that he would not accept his resignation, although he did agree to a dissolution of Parliament. However, matters become even more murkily unconstitutional – not to say downright bizarre – for then it was declared that the election would be fought by the National Government (a Conservative–Liberal coalition), led by former Labour leader MacDonald *against* the Labour Party.

The National Government triumphed, while Labour suffered a trouncing (from which they did not recover until 1945), winning just 52 seats against 554. Astoundingly, George had succeeded in getting his dream Government: the new National Government was largely Conservative.

The coalition under MacDonald – surreally a Prime Minister without a party – was to continue for four years, enduring in one form or another until the Second World War. It was solely the King's creation, the end result of a series of blatantly unconstitutional moves. Unsurprisingly, the details of George V's role did not emerge into the public domain for decades, but even now the full implication of his unconstitutional behaviour is rarely understood. Yet the facts are unequivocal: in the third decade of the twentieth century, George V had effectively elected his own government. Constitutional historian Vernon Bogdanor says that George V was 'not merely the facilitator of the new Government . . . but the instigator of it. Three times he had made it clear to MacDonald that he did not wish to accept his resignation . . .'[10]

The constitutional propriety or otherwise of the King's actions has been debated ever since his role in the events of 1931 became known. Some defend him on the grounds that, technically, he did not exceed his constitutional powers. However, historian and former Conservative MP Sir Robert Rhodes James shows that while maintaining the illusion of keeping within their limits, George V had in reality far exceeded them. The King argued that when he called the other party leaders to the Palace to request that they join an emergency coalition, he had acted on his Prime Minister's advice, but ignored the fact that he had told MacDonald what he wanted that advice to be – in James's words, 'he had accepted what was in fact his own advice'.[11] James goes on to explain George V's motives: 'He had, at long last, found a Prime Minister he could manipulate and employ for his own purposes.'[12]

The King now had exactly the bizarre hybrid Government he wanted: a Conservative-dominated coalition in which the Labour Party was not even included, led by his preferred Prime Minister – who, although Labour, was no longer a member of his own party. And the King had actively caused Labour to be banished to the political wilderness. Sir Robert Rhodes James writes: 'If the shattered Labour Party, now doomed to temporary extinction in the forthcoming general election, had fully realised the King's role in its demise, the consequences could have been grave for his reputation as a politically disinterested monarch.'[13]

James does not mince words, referring to George V's 'blatant political bias' and his 'crucial part in [Labour's] destruction'.[14] Whatever else he may or may not have been, the King was determined not to be a political cipher. George also compounded his unconstitutional – not to say unethical – behaviour by ignoring the agreement that had been signed at Buckingham Palace at the end of August. Although MacDonald and the other party leaders decided to change the agreement, the King should have refused them permission to do so. As he had called and chaired the meeting, he was effectively its guarantor.[15]

The choreography and nature of George's moves in this unedifying episode were obviously far too clever for him to have thought them up for himself. In fact, they bore the distinct fingerprints of his Private Secretary, Sir Clive Wigram, one of whose main functions was to advise the King on what he could and could not do within his prerogative and who therefore should have prevented George from sailing so close to the wind.

The King did not control the new Government, although MacDonald – now dependent on him for the continuation of his political career, as there was no way back to the Labour Party – was very acquiescent and the National Government pursued policies of which George approved. But the creation of the National Government was highly significant because it set the scene for later events that had a profound effect on Britain's preparedness for the Second World War.

ECONOMY WITH THE TRUTH

Naturally, the 10 per cent cut in unemployment benefit was not very popular. Bearing his image in mind and to show solidarity with the people, George V volunteered to reduce his Civil List payment by a matching 10 per cent. (In addition, an outraged Prince of Wales was asked by his father to donate £10,000 a year to the Treasury.) Superficially, this seemed to be a magnanimous gesture – but was it quite what it seemed?

First, it must be remembered that the monarch's Civil List is not for personal expenditure, but to pay for official expenses as Head of State such as the upkeep of Buckingham Palace and Windsor Castle, and staff salaries (although the Windsors are notoriously parsimonious). Unlike the unemployed, who now had 10 per cent less money with which to feed and clothe their families, George V was only volunteering to cut his *outgoings*, not his income, by a similar proportion. While the backstreets of Newcastle and Birmingham saw an exponential rise in malnutrition, there was never any threat that the King's family might starve.

George's initial idea – of which later Windsors would have been proud – was to cut the wages of the Royal Household and the staff at his official residences (paid from the Civil List) by 10 per cent, but MacDonald hastily pointed out that this would not be a particularly popular move. However, in the end savings to the Civil List were made through economies in running the Royal Household, and had little impact on the King himself.[16] When it comes to money, the Windsors are uncharacteristically knife-sharp – and not given to self-sacrifice.

All George's instincts for self-preservation were called into being when the Depression began taking its toll on his private income. If nothing else, this succeeded in making an impact on him. Something had to be done to prevent the Government getting its hands on his personal wealth, but if cutting his servants' salaries was not a good move, what could he do? It was difficult, but he had a brainwave. He stopped paying income tax.

He did this simply by exercising his royal prerogative, decreeing that he would no longer pay tax on his income from his hereditary revenues from the Duchy of Lancaster[17] – a move to which the Chancellor of the Exchequer, Neville Chamberlain, agreed. He did so not only without making this arrangement public, but without even disclosing it to Parliament.

At the time of George's accession in 1910, the Palace had assured the House of Commons that the King would continue to pay tax on income from the Duchy. Now that this had changed, the House should have been informed – it remained ignorant of the move.[18] But something else makes it constitutionally questionable. Although George's two predecessors (Victoria and Edward VII) had paid income tax (an innovation of Victoria's reign), the justification for its cessation under George was that the previous monarchs had only paid up voluntarily. However, the fact that two monarchs had paid tax and George had done so over a period of 90 years *should* have created a constitutional precedent. In any other sphere of the monarch's life it would have done so unquestionably. The other justification used was Crown immunity – the principle that the Sovereign is not bound by any Act of Parliament unless it specifically says he is. Legally, it is highly questionable if this applies to the king or queen in their capacity as private individuals, although no judge or court has ever been called on to give a ruling on the issue.

The exemption from tax saved George about £20,000 a year (over £500,000 today). This was an increase on his *personal* income – the Civil List cut of £50,000 a year represented a reduction in his official expenses – so in the end the King was up on the deal. But while the 10 per cent reduction in the Civil List was made public, his giving up paying tax was kept secret. In addition, the cut in the Civil List stopped in 1935, when the economic situation had improved, but the exemption from tax continued until 1992, when the present Queen 'volunteered' to pay it.

George V's decree prevented him having to pay tax on his revenue from the Duchy of Lancaster, but he still paid up on his other sources of private income: rents from his private estates at Sandringham and Balmoral, and investments in stocks and shares. In 1933, however, the King's advisers discovered a convenient loophole in the system. Although most dividend payments were taxed at source, he had invested heavily in Government war loan stock that was *not* taxed at source, being intended to attract foreign investors – who were not liable for income tax in Britain. British taxpayers had to declare the income from this source on their tax return – but the monarch has never been required to complete one. When the Duchy of Lancaster switched its holdings to this type of stock in 1933 George V was the direct beneficiary of a double whammy.[19] As the Duchy no longer paid tax on its investments, its profits soared. When that money was paid over to the King's Privy Purse he paid no personal income tax on it.

THE STATUTE OF WESTMINSTER

The King ended 1931 with another advance in his political influence, this time where the Empire was concerned. In December, Parliament passed the Statute of Westminster, which recognised the independence and autonomy of the 'Dominions' – Canada, Australia, New Zealand, South Africa and what was then the Irish Free State – as distinct from the rest of Britain's overseas colonies. Until then these possessions had been subordinate to the British Parliament, but the Statute of Westminster made their parliaments equal to the Mother Parliament (i.e. they could now enact laws of their own), together with a similar constitutional arrangement as far as the Sovereign was concerned.

This meant that the British Government no longer had any control over these five nations, while the King remained their Head of State. Although this arrangement now compelled George to accept the advice of six Prime Ministers on their respective countries' affairs instead of just one, the overall effect was to increase his political power.

Earlier in 1931, George V had proposed the Duke of York as the new Governor-General of Canada, but the Labour Government had rejected this as unconstitutional. Now, however, the British Cabinet would have no say in the matter. (Indeed, Prince Henry was later appointed as Governor-General of Australia, as was Prince George, although the war prevented him taking up the post.)

This shift in emphasis vis-à-vis the Empire led to the situation where two foreign policies effectively came into being: the British Government's and that of the King/Palace.

THE RISE OF ADOLF HITLER

The economic recession caused by the Wall Street Crash of 1929 had another far-reaching consequence. It revived the fortunes of one particular struggling German political party – Adolf Hitler's National Socialist German Workers' Party (Nationalsozialistische Deutsche Arbeiterpartei, or NSDAP) or 'Nazi' for short.

The Nazis exploited the widespread discontent resulting from the galloping Crash-fuelled inflation in Germany, seizing hearts, minds and votes. In the elections of 1932 they emerged as the largest party in the Reichstag and in January 1933 Hitler was appointed Chancellor. Further consolidation of their power followed and in March he was granted dictatorial powers, declaring himself Führer (Leader) of Germany. (Curiously, one of his first moves was to exempt himself from income tax.)

Hitler had campaigned on the understanding that should he achieve power through the ballot box, he would declare himself a dictator and dispense with democracy (although he did promise to submit to regular referenda to ensure that the German people were content with this arrangement).

The Nazi Party had been formed in 1920 with one overriding objective: to restore German dignity by redressing the humiliations heaped on the nation by the Treaty of Versailles following their defeat in the First World War. The Treaty had excised territories from Germany and allocated them – and their predominantly German-speaking populations – to new nations created in the wake of the Great War, Czechoslovakia and Poland. Hitler promised to retrieve these lost slices of the old German map. He also pledged that Germany and Austria would be united in accordance with the wishes of the majority of the people in those two countries, but which the victorious Allies had forbidden.[20]

The Treaty had also severely restricted the German armed forces, ostensibly to prevent them from waging another aggressive war: of course this also meant that Germany was no longer capable of defending itself. This was the final humiliation. Hitler and the Nazis promised to rebuild the army, navy and air force – to restore Germany to its 'glorious' greatness and prepare it for its undoubtedly golden destiny.

Other objectives had been added to the Nazi agenda, which had been set out in the 'bible' of Nazism, Hitler's *Mein Kampf* (*My Struggle*), published in 1925. As we revealed in our previous book, *Double Standards: The Rudolf Hess Cover-Up* (2001), *Mein Kampf* was actually co-authored by Rudolf Hess – in particular the chapters dealing with geopolitics and economics – who became Hitler's Deputy Führer.[21]

Having united with Austria and clawed back the territories lost through the

Versailles Treaty – creating the 'Greater Germany' – Hitler planned that Germany would expand eastwards, colonising the Slavic countries that lay between it and Russia. For years he had made no secret of wishing to destroy communism in Germany and its source in the Soviet Union – as he revealed in a 1928 newspaper interview 'to the applause of the whole civilised world'.[22] Of course, there were many among the British upper classes who strongly sympathised with such an ambition.

NAZIS: THE BRITISH PERSPECTIVE

Reactions in Britain to the rise of Nazi Germany were mixed, but it was clear that one way or another the brutal new regime was set to have a significant impact on the political and economic future of Europe. Many – from all political persuasions – thought that Germany *had* been unfairly treated after the First World War and that it should be allowed to reclaim its stolen territories, provided that the people living in those areas wanted it. Seeing Hitler's massing forces and noting his characteristic modus operandi, others were worried that these territorial ambitions would inevitably bring Germany into conflict with Britain. And there were some, of course – most notably Sir Oswald Mosley, founder of the British Union of Fascists – who actively approved of the Nazi ideology and saw Hitler's bully boys as laudable role models.

Several leading British political and financial figures were invited to Germany and came back impressed by what they saw. One of the first to visit was Lord Rothermere, owner of the *Daily Mail*, whose pages praised the Nazis for their confrontational attitude towards communism, urging Britain and France to adopt a friendly attitude to the new regime. Even that great Liberal, David Lloyd George, was openly impressed after being invited to meet the Führer.

Whatever the attitude, from 1934 all eyes were on Germany, trying to gauge which way fortunes would go. The most noticeable result of the Nazi regime was an apparent economic miracle taking place in the Fatherland. When the party first came to power, unemployment stood at seven million yet within a mere five years – virtually overnight – the figure had plummeted to precisely zero. From being the European nation most destabilised and demoralised by the Depression, the new Germany came to have the highest standard of living of any country apart perhaps from Switzerland, and was even beginning to approach that of the United States. Great public building projects, such as the network of autobahns, underscored Germany's burgeoning sense of self-confidence. In response to these startling changes, foreign investment poured into the country, especially from the United States.

Excited by such a boom, many in Britain sought to tap into this vibrant new economy. Several major Anglo-German banking projects leapt into being during this period, with the City of London happy to invest heavily in

German industry. And if such a turnaround could happen so quickly in Germany, might it not also happen here in Britain? It was an intriguing thought, shared by many eminent people in the country.

On the other hand, it soon became apparent that Germany was committing much new capital to building up its armed forces: a business opportunity that many British companies enthusiastically embraced. (Ironically, until the outbreak of the war, Stuka dive-bombers and Spitfires were both powered by Rolls-Royce engines.) Others, however, were alarmed at Germany's massive military build-up – particularly Winston Churchill, then in his 'wilderness years', largely regarded as a political has-been whose heyday was long past. He began to issue warnings about the dangers of allowing Germany's militarisation to go unchecked or unmatched. The lone voice in the wilderness at first, Churchill began to call on Britain to rearm.

Since the First World War the country had steadily cut back on its armed forces, the navy being particularly affected by cutbacks in shipbuilding and personnel in the early 1920s. (Because it was Admiralty policy to shed those with private means, one of the officers who was to have been axed was Lord Louis Mountbatten, shortly after his marriage to Edwina. Of course he pulled strings, persuading the King and Prince of Wales to intervene with the Admiralty on his behalf.)[23] Only at the beginning of 1935 did the Government agree to a very limited rearmament programme: some believed that this would act as a deterrent to Germany or any other aggressor, while others thought that Britain should be following Germany's martial lead. Britain's military power had also declined sharply since the Great War.

THE ROYAL FAMILY AND THE NAZIS

In recent years much has been made of Edward's pro-Nazi views, from his time as Prince of Wales through his brief kingship to his wartime activities as the Duke of Windsor. However, he was not the only royal to have a keen interest in the ideals and methods of National Socialism, or to oppose a war with Nazi Germany – but his later disgrace made him a convenient scapegoat, neatly deflecting the public's attention from the unacceptable fact that his father and brothers were also somewhat sympathetic towards the Nazis, at least for a time.

As the 1930s progressed the possibility of war with Germany became the subject of escalating political discussion, bringing with it one of the royal family's nightmares. As we have seen, the First World War had decimated the old order of royal dynasties in Europe, and in Britain it had pushed the population further to the Left. The monarchy had survived, but at the cost of some hasty fancy footwork and reluctant compromise with its traditional values. The King and the Palace feared that another war – whatever the cause – would finish off all monarchies altogether, either directly or by causing another big shift to the Left. (This analysis, if not the consequences, proved correct: Labour came back to power with a landslide in the first elections after the end of the Second World War, and during the war itself trade union membership increased by 30 per cent.)[24]

It was imperative for the royal family that another war in Europe was avoided, particularly another conflict with Germany that would inevitably resurrect the unpalatable reflection on the royal family's true origins. While Queen Mary's accent was only slightly guttural, her outlook on life was certainly Teutonic. The family still had relatives in Germany. Even the Prince of Wales is reported to have boasted in the 1930s, 'I have not one drop of blood in my veins which is not German.'[25]

Faced with the increasingly tense international situation, in 1935 George V declared to Lloyd George: 'I will not have another war. *I will not.* The last one was none of my doing and if there is another one and we are threatened with being brought into it, I will go to Trafalgar Square and wave a red flag myself sooner than allow this country to be brought in.'[26] The King's choice of imagery is telling. It harks back to an event of September 1870, when – following the declaration of the Third Republic in France – 10,000 people wearing red caps and singing the 'Marseillaise' met in London's Trafalgar Square, flying a red flag next to Nelson's Column. Clearly, George V saw a new European war as inseparable from republicanism, but boldly asserted that he would rather voluntarily declare Britain a republic than have one forced on the country by war.

However, it is significant that his negative feelings were about the consequences of war: of the rise of the Nazi party he said not a word. How did he and his family really view Hitler's regime? After decades of careful public relations and a few judicious omissions, the answer is unexpected – and somewhat disturbing.

George V's serious illness in 1928 had forced his heir to consider what he would do when he *did* become King. What kind of King did he want to be? Clearly, he had no intention of being a merely passive constitutional monarch. The thought of being an ineffectual King, unable to take sides over political issues, was all the more unpalatable because he did have his own, very strong, political views. Perhaps the clearest statement of his political attitudes – or rather attitude to politics – is his own, made many years later as the disgraced Duke of Windsor:

> Like the Parliamentary system, the constitutional Monarch who stands aloof from and above politics is a British invention. As a device for preserving the Crown as a symbol of national unity while divesting itself of abhorrent forms of absolutism it is a remarkable example of the British genius for accommodation. But one effect of / this system, which is perhaps not so well understood by the public, is the handicap imposed upon a Prince, who, while obliged to live and work within one of the most intensely political societies on the

earth, is expected to remain not merely above party and faction, but a-political.[27]

We have seen that his politics – and his image – centred on the need for the monarchy to build stronger links with the working classes, particularly as the Depression continued to bite. On the other hand, he naturally loathed communism. To reiterate Philip Ziegler's words, 'His radicalism and disapproval of social injustice were real enough, but he was still to the right politically.'[28] His political views were shared by Prince George – indeed, George, as the most intelligent of the brothers, was able to formulate his political ideas on a more intellectual level and turn Edward's instinctive and emotional ideas into a more structured political philosophy.

Although the charismatic George had always been his parents' favourite son – particularly his mother's – it was only around this time that the King and Queen realised what a potential asset they had in him. Soon he began to fulfil a larger quota of public engagements, both at home and abroad, such as acting as the King's representative at King Haakon of Norway's Silver Jubilee in 1930. George had even managed to overcome his father's objections to him having a career, becoming a Foreign Office employee, the only royal Civil Servant in history. Of course a member of the royal family in Government service is constitutionally questionable: probably the only reason the Prime Minister allowed it was the fact that George was the youngest of the brothers, effectively an 'also-ran'.

Because of the continued wall of silence around all matters concerning Prince George, his time at the Foreign Office remains mysterious, although it is known that he found his duties frustratingly 'too undemanding',[29] so in April 1932 he transferred to the Home Office – where he worked as a very unglamorous factory inspector, covering the working-class areas of Southwark, Woolwich and south Essex. This was a most unexpected side to the playboy prince.

George shared Edward's interest in social matters and perhaps found inspecting factory floors a good way of educating himself about the circumstances of the working class. Delighted to be able to report something new and quirky about the royals, the press were to dub him the 'Democratic Duke', a fitting title for the brother of the 'People's Prince'. With his charm and incisive intellect, George was emerging as a force to be reckoned with in the royal family. Soon he was also being described as the King's political adviser.

While Edward and George may have been enjoying a new sense of direction and purpose, this departure from the usual protocol was viewed with caution by the politicians. Although George V had managed to create a Government that was to his liking, he was still careful not to interfere in its policies. And the last thing the politicians wanted was an heir to the throne with strong political views or ambitions. It is hardly surprising that both

Edward and George would be interested in Nazism: indeed, it could be said that their political views succinctly defined the term 'national socialism'. Hitler's movement seemed to have found solutions to the same problems that concerned them: the Führer and his party had turned round their country's economy while at the same time successfully suppressing communism. This was exactly what the Prince of Wales wanted and, like many others, he wondered if the same methods could work in Britain, even establishing an informal study group in 1935 to analyse events in Germany.[30]

However, even at that time it was abundantly clear that the Nazis had no truck with parliamentary democracy, achieving their extraordinary social turnaround through a dictatorship that boasted of disregarding the civil rights of others. This is what is so disconcerting now when questions of Nazi sympathies in the 1930s are raised, particularly among the soi-disant great and the good. How far did Edward himself embrace the more disturbing aspects of these ideas?

Many people in that era believed that democracy was a spent force and that the future belonged to the strong, dictatorial leader who combined sweeping autocratic powers with immense popularity. The success of Mussolini's Italy and Hitler's Germany, while parliamentary democracies such as Britain and France still struggled with economic and social deprivation, only seemed to confirm this line of thinking. It may seem a naïve view now, but then we have the benefit of hindsight.

Before the Second World War, the concept of the strong dictator was not regarded with particular anxiety by the British Establishment. Mussolini had been in power in Italy since 1922 without ruffling too many feathers. If anything, his style of government was admired – even by Churchill, who also favoured dictatorial leadership, and who called Mussolini the 'Roman genius . . . the greatest lawgiver among men'.[31]

The concept of the all-powerful head of state appealed to the Prince of Wales, as he made clear as the Duke of Windsor in 1940 in Madrid, telling the Spanish Count Nava de Tajo that he believed the age of constitutional monarchy had passed and that the future lay in the hands of the dictators.[32] The other aspect of Nazi policy with which Edward, Prince George and the King were at one was the branding of the Soviet Union as the real enemy. They believed implicitly that Britain and Germany should stand together against the Red Menace.

In private conversations, Edward made no secret of his agreement with the ideals and methods of Hitler and Mussolini.[33] (In 1970, as Duke of Windsor, he said to Lord Kinross, 'I never thought Hitler was such a bad chap.')[34] Therefore it is hardly surprising that he sought out those with similar views – or that fellow believers should have seized on such an opportunity to influence the future King.

One like-minded individual was Edwina Mountbatten's father, Lord Mount Temple, the right-wing former MP and founder of the Anglo-German

Fellowship, which worked for friendship and understanding between the two nations and whose membership featured some of the most prominent in the land. It is known that Edward enjoyed frequent discussions with him. (Ironically, Edwina herself was inclined to the Left.) Another member of the extreme right-wing circle that the Prince favoured was the soon-to-be-notorious Sir Oswald Mosley, who also believed that dictatorship would become the norm. At the beginning of the 1930s the former Labour MP founded the New Party, which performed dismally in the 1931 general election, but he went on to found the British Union of Fascists a year later, a much more blatantly quasi-Nazi organisation.

The Prince of Wales was extremely interested in Mosley's ideas and the two men became firm friends, remaining so after the war; Mosley and his second wife Diana, also 'in exile' in France, were frequent guests of the Windsors. The Duke is reported as often saying, 'Tom [as Mosley was known to his friends] would have made a first-rate Prime Minister.'[35] (Diana Mosley, one of the literary Mitford family, wrote a biography of the Duchess of Windsor in 1980.) And his sister-in-law, Lady Alexandra Curzon, married Edward's best friend, 'Fruity' Metcalfe: both of them were very interested in Nazism.[36] (Lady Alexandra's nickname was 'Ba-ba' – within a few years her detractors were calling her 'Ba-ba Blackshirt'.)

AN ALTERNATIVE STRATEGY

Another important influence on Edward's political views was the Imperial Policy Group, a right-wing political 'think tank' and pressure group chaired by the Earl of Mansfield, which consisted mainly of Conservative MPs. Its aim was to influence Government policy in directions that the Group considered would protect and further the interests of the British Empire. Staunchly anti-communist, it regarded Stalin's Russia as the greatest threat to Britain.

In 1935 the Imperial Policy Group appointed as its Secretary 26-year-old Kenneth de Courcy, one of the most controversial and complex characters in the behind-the-scenes world of politics, foreign affairs and intelligence. He had been born into relatively humble circumstances in Oldham, Lancashire, the son of a clergyman and a mother of German and Belgian descent, but in his 20s he made a fortune from property investments in the north of England.

Despite his relative youth, de Courcy's intelligence and astuteness made him the lynchpin of the Imperial Policy Group. Travelling widely, particularly in Europe and the USA, he discovered everything he could about the international situation and established a network of contacts and informants throughout the world. With a marked talent for gathering and analysing information, his work provided an entrée into the secret circles of politics, diplomacy and intelligence.

The ubiquitous de Courcy also ran his own private intelligence network, called the Special Office, which even penetrated the highest levels of the Nazi regime, providing extremely useful information for MI6. He boasted of having 'a spy in every embassy' and was himself an MI6 agent, recruited personally by its wartime chief, Sir Stewart Menzies, who became a close personal friend.[37] They shared many of the same views about Britain's interests, in particular that the Soviet Union posed a far greater threat to Britain than Nazi Germany.

Shortly before his death in 1999, de Courcy contacted us as a result of our research into Rudolf Hess's 1941 peace mission – although not personally involved, he knew many of the main players at the time and after. Since de Courcy's death we have been allowed access to his papers, particularly those that dealt with his friendship with Edward as Prince of Wales, King and Duke of Windsor.

Edward was both courted by and interested in the Imperial Policy Group: undoubtedly he was heavily influenced by it. Perhaps incongruously, he and de Courcy – the Lancashire clergyman's son – became close friends. De Courcy was with him during the abdication crisis, and after the war became the Duke of Windsor's representative in discussions with the British Government.

The situation in Europe becoming increasingly more tense as the 1930s progressed, the Imperial Policy Group and de Courcy realised that eventually Britain would be faced with a stark choice between Nazi Germany and Stalinist Russia: one the enemy, the other an ally. De Courcy (who, despite his right-wing bias, was firmly anti-Nazi) and the Group considered an alliance with Russia was the worst choice for Britain, believing that a war with Germany should be avoided, as it would irretrievably damage both nation and Empire.

De Courcy's view was that Britain's interests were best served by staying out of any war in Europe. Since it was inevitable that Germany and the Soviet Union would come into conflict, they should be allowed to weaken themselves irretrievably by fighting each other – to Britain's advantage. De Courcy and the Imperial Policy Group therefore worked to prevent Britain going to war with Germany (and once war had been declared they worked just as hard to end it as soon as possible).

De Courcy managed to persuade some influential individuals that this would be the correct course of action for Britain. They included Sir Stewart Menzies of MI6 – the implications of which are staggering: despite the prevalent Churchillian ethos of fighting them on the beaches if necessary, the fact is that during the war Britain's major foreign intelligence service was resolutely working to negotiate peace with Germany.[38] Edward agreed with this strategy, saying in 1966: 'I thought that the rest of us could be fence-sitters while the Nazis and the Reds slugged it out.'[39] He had expressed a similar view in September 1939 when he was informed that Britain and France had finally declared war on Germany: 'I'm afraid this may open the way for world communism.'[40]

'THANK GOD HE HATES THE JEWS'

Of course, Germany's economic revival took place against the backdrop of the scapegoating of Germany's Jewish population and increasingly stringent measures to deprive them of their civil rights. Hitler had made no secret about wanting Germany free of Jews, although at that stage the Nazi strategy was to make life so uncomfortable for them that they would leave of their own volition. Only later was this supplemented by enforced emigration, and later still by the atrocities of the Final Solution.

Sad to say, although some voices were raised against these measures in Britain, from both inside and outside the Jewish community, they were very much in a minority: the plight of Germany's Jews failed to be seen as particularly important either by pro-Nazis or those who viewed the regime with alarm. (On the whole, the latter were more worried about what Hitler's rise would mean for Britain's interests.)

Germany was not the only nation in which the Jewish population was suffering prejudice and persecution at the hands of their fellow countrymen, nor the only one in which institutionalised anti-Semitism deprived Jews of their civil liberties. Ironically, a very similar situation existed in Poland at that time. The fact that it was happening elsewhere made it all too easy to turn a blind eye to this aspect of Nazism at a time when the future horrors of the Final Solution were unimaginable.

Neither did Nazi anti-Semitism bother the royal family. Lady Diana Cooper wrote of George V shortly after his accession that she disliked everything about him 'except that I thank God he hates the Jews'.[41] And, as we will see, as late as 1938 George VI urged the Government to put pressure on Germany to *prevent* Jews from emigrating.

Anti-Semitism was as rife in the royal family as elsewhere in the upper classes. The Duchess of York once remarked about Edwina Mountbatten, 'She's only partly English, you know. Her mother was half-Jewish.'[42] None, though, were as crass as the Duke of Gloucester's reported remark, 'You can say what you like about this Hitler Johnny, but he's got the right idea about the nosey boys.' The only problem Queen Mary had with Hitler was his rustic Austrian accent, declaring: 'He never did learn to speak the language properly.'[43]

WAR BETWEEN THE WINDSORS

All this took place against the backdrop of an increasing rift between the Prince of Wales and his father. What little relationship they had ever enjoyed had irretrievably broken down: they communicated infrequently and saw each other even less. The King was particularly bothered by his son's reluctance to get married, together with his continued preference for married women. Modern to his fingertips where his own interests were concerned, Edward insisted that *he* would choose his wife.[44]

Prince George's star, however, was in the ascendant. He maintained good relations with both George V and the Prince of Wales, and managed to influence both of them with his political thinking. And because of his glamorous good looks, charm and concern for the workers, he was becoming increasingly popular with the public, which was further expanded by his marriage in 1934 to the equally glamorous Princess Marina of Greece.

Until he married Marina, George had continued his wildly hedonistic double life. His friendship with Mountbatten became firmer at this time – as it did with Edwina. She and her favourite lover, the Earl of Sefton, used to go out on double dates with Prince George and whichever lady he was seeing at the time. Because George and Edwina were seen on the town together so often rumours flew that *they* were having an affair,[45] but according to Edwina's biographer and friend Madeleine Masson, George and *Mountbatten* were also lovers.[46] Given their extraordinarily hedonistic and abandoned life this sort of uninhibited musical beds should not be surprising.

The royal family were greatly relieved when he met Marina and, after a whirlwind romance, married this intriguing foreign royal. Princess Marina of Greece and Denmark was born in 1906, the youngest of three daughters of Prince Nicholas of Greece (son of King William George I of the Hellenes) and the Russian Grand Duchess Helen Vladimirovna. Being of German descent but also with her fair share of Romanov blood – both her parents were great-grandchildren of Tsar Nicholas I – she literally embodied the old European dynasties.

In fact, the Greek royal family was almost entirely of German descent. Towards the end of the nineteenth century, the other nations of Europe had decided that Greece should have its own monarchy, appointing one of the sons of Christian IX of Denmark (Queen Alexandra's brother), William George I, as its first King. The solid German roots of the Danish royal house are evidenced by Marina's characteristically cumbersome family name of Schleswig-Holstein-Sonderburg-Glücksburg.

The Greek monarchy had a turbulent history. William George I was assassinated in 1913. Then in 1917 Constantine I and the rest of the royal house – including Marina's immediate family – fled into exile, to be restored by a popular vote three years later.[47] The convoluted family trees did not end there: Prince Philip – the future irascible husband of Elizabeth II – was Marina's cousin (his father was her uncle, Prince Andrew of Greece, and mother Princess Alice of Battenberg – Louis Mountbatten's sister). Based in Switzerland, the young Marina was a guest at Princess Mary's wedding in 1922 before coming to England for the London 'season' a year later.

As with Elizabeth Bowes-Lyon, Marina was first considered as a suitable wife for the Prince of Wales,[48] though she too ended up with one of his brothers. In fact, in 1927, at the age of 21, she had an affair with Edward that according to Chips Channon 'might well have led to marriage and was progressing very well, but Freda Dudley Ward, at the last moment, interfered and stopped it'.[49] Poor Freda was soon to receive a dose of her own medicine.

Prince George and Marina met in September 1933 at a house party given by the eccentric society hostess Lady Emerald Cunard. He was overwhelmed by the Greek princess's beauty and willowy chic that she enhanced with Parisian couture, even if some of it was copies only: especially when compared to the 'dowdy duchess', as certain society critics called Elizabeth, and the solidly worthy Princess Mary, she was the *denier cri* in modern glamour. George was entranced by her: unsurprisingly, their affair began soon after. He said at the time, 'She is the one woman with whom I could be happy to spend the rest of my life.'[50] (The 'could' suggests he was unsure that he could spend the rest of his life with *any* one individual.)

In summer 1934 Marina travelled to Yugoslavia for a three-month holiday at Bohinj, the summer home of her sister Olga and her husband Prince Paul of Yugoslavia. With typical Bond-like style, the dashing George borrowed a plane and flew to Bohinj to propose to her. The engagement was announced by the Palace on 28 August, and in October 1934 George was created Duke of Kent (a title last held by Queen Victoria's father), shortly before their marriage amid great pomp and fanfare on 29 November 1934. (With no trace of irony, the official Palace catalogue of wedding gifts lists the silver cigarette box from the British Union of Fascists just before *A Book of Jewish Thought* from the Chief Rabbi.) The deliriously happy Duke and Duchess of Kent honeymooned in the Caribbean before moving into their townhouse at 3 Belgrave Square in central London. In October 1935 Marina gave birth to their first son, Edward (there were to be two other children, Princess Alexandra and Prince Michael of Kent). That December George's aunt, Princess Victoria, died, and in her will she left him her house, the Coppins, in Iver, Buckinghamshire, which is still the Duke of Kent's country seat.

The new addition to the family injected another uncomfortable element into the already turbulent royal atmosphere. Because of Marina's impeccably royal lineage she considered herself a cut above the other members of the royal family – and was not afraid to show it. As biographer Christopher Warwick writes: 'Her acute awareness of who she was, not just as Duchess of Kent, but as a thoroughbred princess of both royal and *imperial* descent in her own right, meant that she exuded a distinct air of superiority. As a result, she was never properly absorbed into the British royal family . . .'[51]

Kenneth Rose writes that the British royals 'did not share her consciousness of royalty as a caste apart, or of a Europe composed more of dynasties than of nations'.[52] Indeed, Marina saw herself not merely as royal, but as *imperial*. As Donald Spoto notes: '. . . she regarded herself as the inheritor of true Imperial Royalty, of far more ancient and genuine blue blood than the Teutonic Windsors.'[53] For this reason, there was a distinct coolness between Marina and Queen Mary (who was not even an upstart Windsor, but an even more obscure Teck). Even more chilly was the Duchess of Kent's attitude to her sisters-in-law, the Scottish aristocrats the Duchesses of York and Gloucester

(Henry, now the Duke of Gloucester, married Lady Alice Montagu-Douglas-Scott, daughter of the Duke of Buccleuch, in November 1935), whom she famously described as 'common little Scotch girls'.[54] (According to some even this is a sanitised version, her actual word being 'tarts'.) Marina's self-assessed superiority was something else to be filed away in Elizabeth's grudge box until she came into a true position of power on her husband's death.

A few months before Marina's wedding to Prince George, her sister Elizabeth had married the German Count Charles zu Törring-Jettenbach (known as 'Toto') who lived in Munich. The Kents' frequent visits allowed them to see at first hand what was going on in Nazi Germany – perhaps sometimes even providing a convenient smokescreen for George's undercover political work. Indeed, the Duke and Duchess of Kent were at the forefront of the movement for Anglo-German co-operation, through Count Toto and others, in particular Prince Philip of Hesse-Cassel, to whom Marina was also related by marriage. Her cousin, Princess Sophie of Greece, was married to his brother, the ardent Nazi and SS Colonel Prince Christopher of Hesse-Cassel. (Princess Sophie was the sister of the future Elizabeth II's husband, the more famous Prince Philip, a fact that was to become very embarrassing for the royal family, especially after the war.)

A BLOND VIKING PRINCE

A much younger member of the Greek royal family who was to become an important addition to the British royal circle appeared on the scene at this time: Prince Philip of Greece. Like Princess Marina he was a member of the German–Danish Greek royal family. Christened Philippos (which, appropriately for a talented polo player, means 'horse'), he bore the family name of Schleswig-Holstein-Sonderburg-Glücksburg. His title was simply Prince Philip of Greece.

Philip's father was Marina's uncle, who was married to Lord Mountbatten's sister, Princess Alice of Battenberg. Profoundly deaf since birth, she could lip-read in several languages and was extremely intelligent, like her son, but also highly sensitive and artistic – qualities that she did not pass on to him in abundance. Like Marina's family, they went into exile in Switzerland between 1917 and 1920. Philip was born on the island of Corfu in the incongruously named family home, Mon Repos, after the restoration of the Greek monarchy in 1921. The only boy, there was a seven-year gap between him and the next sister. He was raised to be fluent in English, German and French, although he only began to learn Greek towards the end of the twentieth century when he reacquainted himself with the Greek Orthodox religion.

Before Philip was a year old, revolution broke out again in Greece. King Constantine I (Philip and Marina's uncle) was packed off into exile, and – after Alice's appeal to both George V and the Pope – Philip's family were rescued from Corfu by a British battleship in December 1922. It was a huge drama, which Philip later played down, but seems to have secretly relished. HMS *Calypso* was despatched to Corfu on the personal instructions of George V, but because questions were raised in Parliament about what the Royal Navy were doing rescuing Greek royals from a civil war (not to mention who was footing the bill), the whole episode was covered up. A memorandum written by a Foreign Office official states:

> The original source of the instructions (the King) cannot be quoted. Perhaps the Prime Minister will be prepared to say that he instructed the Admiralty to issue the necessary orders.[55]

(As it turned out, Prime Minister Bonar Law refused to comply with this telling example of mendacity, with the result that Parliament was left in the dark about who had actually taken the decision.)

Virtually penniless, the Greek Prince Andrew and his family were housed secretly in Kensington Palace for a while (the King and Bonar Law having agreed that the presence of exiled Greek royals in Britain should be kept from the public) before settling in Paris. Once his four daughters had been married off, Prince Andrew abandoned his family, blithely going off to Monte Carlo to live with his mistress, spending the rest of his life gambling and drinking.

Philip's mother, Princess Alice, suffered a severe nervous breakdown, which eventually manifested itself as religious mania (she believed she was engaged in a sexual relationship with Jesus) and was institutionalised in a Swiss clinic. She later returned to Greece and founded a charitable religious order called the Sisterhood of Martha and Mary, in which she played a very active part. Accounts of her mental state differ. According to some she was quite mad for the rest of her life – but it is significant that when Greece was occupied by the Nazis during the Second World War she sheltered Jewish families, and some believe she feigned madness when questioned by the Gestapo. After living in seclusion in Buckingham Palace following the exile of the Greek royal family in 1967 – incongruously dressed in a simple nun-like habit of her own design – she died in 1969. But it was not her alleged madness nor her relationship to the Queen's husband that earned her lasting recognition: 20 years after her death her body was reburied in Jerusalem in accordance with her wishes, and honoured by Israel as a 'Righteous Gentile' for her selfless work with the Jewish victims of Nazism.

Now effectively an orphan, blond and blue-eyed little Philip – his Danish genes manifested at an early age – was shuffled around between relatives, spending time in Paris, Romania (particularly Transylvania) and, of course, England. It was a rootless, mostly poverty-stricken life that had little to recommend it for an energetic and bright youngster, except perhaps for a rapid change of scene and the knowledge that however irritating people might be, they would soon be left behind.

Eventually, by some weird family logic it was agreed that he should be brought up by his uncle, George, Marquess of Milford Haven, Louis Mountbatten's brother: in 1930, at the tender age of nine, he went to live in his country seat, Lynden Manor in Berkshire. As we have seen, Milford Haven's main claim to fame was his massive collection of extreme pornography, which included photographs of whole families in sexual contortions. George and his wife Nada could also have given master classes in what may euphemistically be called an uninhibited lifestyle. Nada's main female lover, Gloria Morgan Vanderbilt, was virtually living at Lynden Manor at this time. It was in this environment that Philip spent his formative years when he was home from his boarding school at Cheam in Surrey.

However, he was not to stay there long – perhaps his unmissable presence threatened to cramp their lifestyle. The Milford Havens/Mountbattens decided that Philip should be educated in Germany, and at the age of 13 in 1934 he was sent to a famous school at Schloss Salem (a thirteenth-century Cistercian monastery), by Lake Constance, a militaristic regime that advocated a Spartan outdoor life. The school had been founded by Prince Max von Baden – father-in-law of Philip's sister Théodora – together with the famous educationalist Kurt Hahn. The year before Philip's arrival, the Jewish Hahn fled the Nazi regime and founded Gordonstoun in the wilds of northern Scotland. (Hahn later converted to Christianity.) By the time of Philip's arrival at Schloss Salem, it is reported that the Hitler Youth was in full swing among the students.[56]

Philip only attended Salem for a few months, after which it was decided to transfer him to Hahn's new school, Gordonstoun. He was there for five years, blossoming in the hearty atmosphere of practical jokes and cold showers – a return to the old Empire ethos of a healthy mind in a healthy body. But his Gordonstoun days were remarkable for a more disquieting reason: during the entire time he spent there he was never once visited by his immediate family.

Between Philip's return from Salem and his arrival at Gordonstoun, Nada Milford Haven's lover Gloria Morgan Vanderbilt was embroiled in a sensational case in the US Supreme Court. Gloria was the widow of one of the stupendously rich Vanderbilts, by whom she had a ten-year-old daughter, also named Gloria (later the famous fashion designer). Gertrude Vanderbilt Whitney, sister of the deceased husband, successfully sought custody of little Gloria on the grounds that her mother's decadent lifestyle made her an unfit parent. (It was at this trial that details of the Milford Haven pornography collection were revealed: one of the questions raised by Whitney's lawyers was whether the Milford Havens had ever shown it to little Gloria. One could ask the same about Philip.)

The court heard graphic details of Gloria Morgan Vanderbilt's lesbian relationship with Nada and her affair with Prince Gottfried of Hohenlohe-Langenburg (with whom she had cohabited for a year). Prince Gottfried was now married to Prince Philip's eldest sister Margarita, and she and her husband sailed to America to testify on Gloria's behalf, but to no avail.

The trial, with lurid testimony from maids and other servants about what they had seen Gloria and Nada – and Gloria and Prince Gottfried – get up to in the bedroom was an absolute sensation in America. But it was reported only briefly in the British press, and then without the juiciest bits, because of the Milford Havens' close relationship to the royal family.

All four of Philip's sisters married Germans from important dynasties. As we have seen, Margarita was the wife of Gottfried of Hohenlohe-Langenburg. The next, Théodora, was married to Bertholdt, the hereditary Landgrave of Baden, and Cecile to George Donatus, the titular Grand Duke of Hesse and the Rhine. (Although the German monarchies had been abolished at the end of the First World War, the families still retained much of their property and prestige, continuing to hold the titles, if only nominally.) However, it was the youngest sister, Sophie, who had made the most potentially compromising marriage. In 1930, she wed Prince Christopher of Hesse-Cassel (Christof von Hessen-Kassel), the son of the Landgrave of Hesse.[57] Prince Christopher of Hesse-Cassel was an SS Colonel (Standartenführer) attached to Himmler's personal staff, becoming head of the Forschungamt – a security service under Hermann Göring's command that carried out surveillance on potential 'subversives' (i.e. anti-Nazis) in Germany – in 1935. Sophie and Christopher named their eldest son Karl Adolf, partly in Hitler's honour.[58] Christopher's eldest brother, Prince Philip of Hesse-Cassel (who succeeded to the title of Landgrave in 1945) had joined the Nazi party in 1930, becoming the Nazi governor of Hesse in 1933 and, later, the liaison between Hitler and Mussolini.

THE IRRESISTIBLE RISE

Meanwhile, the major player in young Philip's future life was making good progress in his all-out determination to become the most important man in the land. Mountbatten's naval career continued its inexorable rise, but he also thought it prudent to maintain his valuable friendships with the Prince of Wales and the Duke of Kent, with especial emphasis on increasing his influence over the heir to the throne. As Edward was showing no signs of doing the decent thing and marrying some appropriate future mother of the next heir, Mountbatten took it upon himself to draw up a list of 18 suitable brides – significantly, all European royalty – which he submitted to the Prince of Wales, only to have the whole idea of marriage rejected out of hand.[59]

The Mountbattens continued in their open marriage, often being compelled to take steps to avoid public scandals, especially where Edwina was concerned (Louis was much more discreet). At the end of May 1932 *The People*'s gossip column included a story under the headline 'Society Shaken by Terrible Scandal'. No names were mentioned but the story said that a 'highly connected and immensely rich' society woman was having an 'association with a coloured man' and that 'a quarter which cannot be ignored' – an accepted euphemism for the King – had ordered her to leave the country until the scandal had died down. In those days, interracial intercourse was seen as obscene and immoral, an unnatural act that provoked widespread repugnance. (Indeed, it was illegal in many American states until long after the Second World War.)

The King and Queen required Edwina to sue Odhams Newspapers, publishers of *The People*, because of the implication that they had ordered Edwina out of the country. Although the King and Queen did regularly intervene to protect the reputation of the family (witness the fate of the many young women who had been forced abroad to protect Prince George) it was felt that it was not in their interest that such behind-the-scenes manoeuvring should become public knowledge.

The Mountbattens obediently filed for libel, returning to London in July for the hearing, at which the identity of the 'coloured man' was revealed as Paul Robeson, the black American actor who had appeared on the London stage to great acclaim. Edwina not only denied having an affair with Robeson, but stated she had never met him. She won her case and *The People* apologised and retracted the story. Edwina made a point of refusing to accept any damages. The next day the Mountbattens lunched with the King and Queen at Buckingham Palace – an event that was carefully brought to the attention of the press as evidence of their continued favour.

Researchers differ on this episode. Richard Hough, biographer of both Louis and Edwina, states that she simply lied under oath on the King and Queen's instruction – if true, with very grave implications for both herself and the Windsors – and that she had been amorously involved with Robeson, who had attended several parties at her London home.[60] Others, such as Philip Ziegler and Janet Morgan, state that Edwina's diaries and correspondence (in which she was not noted for her discretion) do not mention Robeson at all.

Faced with this confusion, we asked Madeleine Masson – not only a biographer but a close friend of Edwina and her sister Mary, Lady Delamere – for clarification. According to Madeleine, the story is both true and false. Edwina *was* having a passionate affair with a black entertainer but it was *not* Robeson. (In fact, *The People* had not named the man concerned.) Her real lover was the jazz musician Leslie 'Hutch' Hutchinson and it was a serious love affair, not merely a sexual fling. It was all very clever: Robeson's name had been used so that she could truthfully deny the affair under oath.[61]

Technically that may not have constituted perjury under oath on the orders of the King, as claimed by others, but it comes close. After all, Edwina was saying that *The People*'s claim about her relationship with an unnamed 'coloured man' was untrue. However, one consequence of the case is certain. Edwina, who was open about her affairs and liaisons, was staggered by the hypocrisy of the royal family and the fact that they had forced her into a witness box to protect *their* reputation, not hers. In Hough's words, it turned her from 'a soft republican' into a 'strong and vocal anti-monarchist'.[62]

THE NAZIS AND THE KING

We know what the Windsors thought about the Nazis, but what was the Nazis' opinion of the Windsors? From the beginning – in fact, even before they came into power – Hitler, Hess and the other Nazi leaders were keen to cultivate important friends in Britain, especially when they turned their attention east towards Russia. If an alliance could be forged with Britain – or even if Britain could be persuaded towards neutrality – this would substantially increase the Nazis' chances of success.

Mein Kampf had set out Hitler's hugely respectful attitude towards Britain, which he echoed in other writings that were to have comprised a 'sequel', but which were not published in Hitler's lifetime. (Found by the Americans after the Second World War, the manuscript was published in 1961 under the title *Hitler's Secret Book*. One of the chapters is actually entitled 'England as an Ally'.) But Hitler made no secret of his abiding hatred of France and the French – at least one thing that he had in common with Edward, Prince of Wales.

As both Edward and the Duke of Kent had expressed a serious interest in National Socialism – indeed, their political thinking and the Nazis' long-term strategy ran in very much the same direction – it was both natural and easy for the German regime to establish good relations with them. Joachim von Ribbentrop, Germany's wartime Foreign Minister and previously Hitler's roving emissary, dined with the Duke and Duchess of Kent in London. The Nazi regime was particularly keen to cultivate the Prince of Wales, knowing that he must soon accede to the British throne. For his part, the Prince began to do what he could to encourage friendship with Germany.

In June 1935 he gave a speech to the British Legion – the ex-servicemen's organisation that attempted to broker peace and foster understanding with Germany (its chief, the retired General Sir Ian Hamilton, was a fervent admirer of Hitler) – in which he encouraged them to 'stretch forth the hand of friendship' with Germany and even spoke of a 'spiritual alliance' with that nation.[63] It was not a popular pronouncement: his speech angered both the King and the Government who saw Edward to be wilfully interfering in foreign policy matters. It was neither the first nor the last time he would do so.

The Prince of Wales' sympathies for certain extreme-right ideals will not come as a surprise today to many people, for whom he may be the black sheep anyway. However, few realise that George V himself was not only favourable towards Hitler's regime, but also may have actually allowed the Nazis to influence his own political moves – astoundingly, *even when it came to creating a government*.

As early as 1929 Nazi ideologue Alfred Rosenberg was entrusted with the task of making contacts with the right people in London. One of his foremost agents in this project was a former pilot named Baron William de Ropp. Born into a noble Baltic family, he settled in Britain in 1910, becoming a naturalised British citizen and marrying an Englishwoman. In the First World War he served as a pilot in the Royal Flying Corps, under the command of Squadron Leader Frederick Winterbotham. In 1920 Baron de Ropp and his wife moved to Berlin, becoming a close friend of Rosenberg, through whom he met Hitler, Hess and other Nazi leaders.

The first contacts between the Nazis on the one side and British political and aristocratic circles on the other were managed by Rosenberg using de Ropp and other intermediaries, but the Baron's proved to be the most successful. De Ropp reactivated his friendship with his former commanding officer, Frederick Winterbotham. This contact finally paid off in 1931 when the de Ropp–Winterbotham link allowed Rosenberg himself to travel to London and be introduced to people sympathetic to closer Anglo-German co-operation once the Nazis had attained power. The stridently anti-Semitic Rosenberg made several trips to London, becoming a popular figure in society circles. His report for Hitler's personal attention in 1935 explains:

> There it was possible to make a number of contacts which worked out well for Anglo-German understanding. In the forefront here was Squadron Leader W. [Winterbotham], a member of the Air General Staff, who was entirely convinced that Germany and England must move together to ward off the Bolshevik danger.[64]

(Note the theme of Britain and Germany working together against the 'greater threat' – in other words, communist Russia.)

The de Ropp–Winterbotham connection worked in two directions. In 1930 Winterbotham had been appointed to the newly formed Air Intelligence Section of MI6. As de Ropp was using him to open channels for Rosenberg in London, so Winterbotham was using de Ropp to make contacts in Germany in order to gather intelligence on German aircraft production and the Luftwaffe. So was Winterbotham simply pretending to believe that the two countries should form an alliance against Bolshevism? The unfolding story suggests that this was improbable, particularly because the channel he opened was also used by the royal family to pursue behind-the-scenes contacts with the Nazis. (Of the three armed services, it was the leadership of the RAF that in the 1930s was the most opposed to war with Germany.)[65]

According to Rosenberg's diary, in January 1935 de Ropp requested an urgent private meeting with himself and Hitler, as a most delicate situation had developed. Squadron Leader Winterbotham had telephoned from London to say that he had been approached by an individual whom Rosenberg cautiously described as George V's 'political adviser'. He was told that the King was concerned about the way the situation in Germany was being presented in the British press and had asked his 'political adviser' to establish a discreet contact with the German Government to see how this could be rectified. Clearly, this mysterious individual knew that a direct channel to Rosenberg could be opened through Winterbotham.

De Ropp needed to know whether Hitler would authorise this clandestine contact with the British Head of State, even through an intermediary. Rosenberg's diary records that 'De Ropp is going to meet with the King's Adviser in a club in London to inform him about what is going on. Yesterday [20 January] he left.'[66] It is unclear whether the identity of the King's Adviser was known to de Ropp and Rosenberg at this stage – but was too sensitive to record in a diary – or whether they genuinely had no idea who he was. But later reports clarify the matter: the King's 'political adviser' was *the Duke of Kent*. Clearly Kent knew that Winterbotham could be used to establish contact with the Nazi hierarchy. (Having acquired his pilot's licence in 1930, Kent was part of the international aviation fraternity that included Rudolf Hess and other leading Nazis.)

De Ropp met the Duke at the RAF Club and spent several hours briefing him on the developments in Germany – and the ideals and objectives of the Nazi Party.[67] This was in order that Kent in turn could brief the King. It transpired that George and Marina had visited Count zu Törring-Jettenbach and Marina's sister in Munich towards the end of 1934, and on their return the Duke had briefed his father on the situation in Germany. This had convinced the King that the British press was misreporting what was happening in the country under the Nazis, and as a result – undoubtedly under Kent's guidance – George V had requested the briefing by de Ropp, not only on the subject of what was happening in Germany but also on the Nazis' political ideas. Rosenberg's report for Hitler in October 1935 tells the story in more detail:

> At the end of last year we were notified that the King of England pronounced himself dissatisfied with the official press reports. The Duke of Kent's visit to Munich had only worsened the English King's opinion regarding the official news reporting, and so one day we received the request from London to explain about National Socialism down to the last detail to the Duke of Kent for the purpose of informing the King of England. After careful consultation with me, de Ropp travelled to London where he unobtrusively had a three-hour conversation with the Duke of Kent, who then reported to the King of England. It may be accepted that this meeting contributed greatly in strengthening the pressure for a reconstruction of the Cabinet and mainly towards beginning the movement in the direction of Germany.[68]

This is astounding. Through intermediaries (including his own son), George V had opened a secret line of communication to the heart of the Nazi regime. Making this kind of contact with any foreign government without the knowledge and acquiescence of his Prime Minister, Cabinet and Foreign Office is profoundly unconstitutional. It is strictly against the rules for the sovereign to take advice on political matters without informing his Prime Minister. But for the British monarch to take such advice from the *Nazis*, a foreign government with the worst reputation for human rights, even then – and especially one with which Britain may soon be at war – is an unimaginable transgression. The fact that the intermediary was another member of the royal family may have made the contact less likely to leak, but it only makes the conduct worse.

While it is true that at that time Rosenberg held no official position in the Nazi Government, his role as influential ideologue and Hitler's adviser – particularly on racial matters – was no secret. (Indeed, after Hitler's brief imprisonment following the attempted coup in Munich in 1924, Rosenberg had been temporarily leader of the Nazi Party.) And, although it was de Ropp – who was not a member of the Nazi Party – who was sent to give the briefing, it is inconceivable that the King and the Duke of Kent did not know that he was a Nazi agent. Certainly Winterbotham was aware of it and undoubtedly would have told the Duke of Kent.

Astoundingly, Rosenberg's report to Hitler ends by saying that de Ropp's briefing contributed to the 'reconstruction of the Cabinet'. At the beginning of 1935, the National Government headed by Ramsay MacDonald – which had been unconstitutionally created by George V – was still in power. However, it was becoming increasingly clear that the Prime Minister was rapidly succumbing to senility. Fortunately he resigned in May and the King appointed Stanley Baldwin as Prime Minister, still in charge of the coalition Government. Although Baldwin was the leader of the Conservative Party, the largest party in the coalition, the King choosing him as Prime Minister was something of a surprise. Baldwin, too, was getting on and had let it be known that he intended that he and MacDonald would retire together, handing over the reins of Government to Neville Chamberlain. This was also the wish of the majority of the Cabinet and Conservative MPs. But the King, in the words of Roy Jenkins (in his 1987 biography of Baldwin), appointed Baldwin 'without question or consultation'.[69] Undoubtedly this was largely because he felt he could work with Baldwin, whereas Chamberlain had never held the office of Prime Minister and was an unknown quantity. But could George also have been influenced by the fact that Baldwin was opposed to Churchill's demand for rearmament and believed that there should be no war with Germany? Baldwin obviously had the same view as Edward, Kent and the Imperial Policy Group, as can be seen from his words: 'If there is any fighting in Europe, I should like to see the Bolshies and Nazis doing it.'[70]

As Prime Minister, Baldwin naturally wanted to appoint his own Cabinet. According to Roy Jenkins: 'The King then saw Baldwin on 20 May, and engaged in an active discussion of the shape of the new Cabinet. King George

V always had strong views as to who was suitable for which office, and did not hesitate to express them to his Prime Ministers.'[71]

One of the most important appointments over which the King was able to influence his new Prime Minister was that of Sir Samuel Hoare as Foreign Secretary. Baldwin wanted to appoint Hoare as Viceroy of India but George V, in Jenkins's words, 'effectively vetoed' it.[72] Instead Hoare became Foreign Secretary, a much more important position, largely because he was one of the most ardently pro-peace politicians of the time – and as a former British intelligence officer who had been stationed in Russia at the time of the 1917 Revolution, also vehemently anti-Bolshevik. Hoare worked hard to avert the war with Germany, and indeed continued to labour clandestinely to extricate Britain from the war after hostilities began. As we discussed in *Double Standards*, he was intimately involved with organising Rudolf Hess's peace mission to Britain in 1941. (Baldwin gave Hoare his brief as Foreign Secretary in the terse words: 'Keep us out of war; we are not ready for it.')[73]

Within months of his appointment, Hoare was embroiled in the first of the major 'appeasement' controversies when Italy invaded Abyssinia (Ethiopia). Together with the French Foreign Minister, he attempted to end the crisis by making an agreement with Mussolini that he could keep a large part of the territory he had invaded. There was widespread outrage, both in the country and in Parliament, and the explosive furore forced Hoare to resign.

The new Government of 1935 was fundamentally comprised of 'appeasers', to use the modern term, and there is no doubt that George V had a significant – and unconstitutional – input into its formation. The King's political judgements were shaped by his views on Nazi Germany and his desire to prevent a war, but it is equally clear that his views on Germany had been shaped by the secret briefing, brokered by the Duke of Kent, four months before – by an agent sent to London by Alfred Rosenberg *with the sanction of Adolf Hitler*.

Incredibly, there is no other interpretation: in effect, through the King himself the Nazi leadership had exerted a degree of influence over the creation of a British Government – which through its stance on rearmament and desire to avoid a confrontation with Germany (and Italy) was music to Hitler's ears.

WOOING WALLIS

The rumblings of an imminent war in Europe were almost nothing compared to the increasing upheaval at the Palace over the conduct of the Prince of Wales. Always in love with love and almost masochistically devoted for a short time to the object of his affections, he had now met *the* woman – but as far as the Old Guard were concerned, she was the *end*. This was the now legendary Wallis Simpson, to whom the Prince had been introduced in late 1930 or early 1931. Although it led nowhere at the time, three and a half years later it was quite another story.

Originally Bessiewallis Warfield, one of the poorer relatives of a Baltimore society family, the later Duchess of Windsor was probably born in 1896 – although some suggest that it was two years earlier, before her parents had married, which is perhaps supported by the fact that her birth was never registered.[74]

In 1916 she married a naval pilot (and heir to a family fortune), Lieutenant Earl Winfield Spencer, who turned out to be a violent alcoholic. As a result, and because he was frequently posted away, Wallis began to have affairs in Washington's diplomatic circles. Her first was with the Italian ambassador, Prince Caetini; another lover was an Argentinian official. She was already getting a taste for movers and shakers, no doubt savouring their power vicariously. It was a man's world, but she was rapidly learning how to overcome such obstacles.

When Spencer was posted to China in 1922 Wallis joined him there, but when civil war broke out she spent most of her time in Hong Kong, until another break-up with her husband, after which she lived in Shanghai and for a while with friends in Peking. As she was an integral part of the diplomatic social circle, it has been suggested – but never proven – that she acted as courier on behalf of US intelligence at this time. (It has also been alleged that she passed information to the Russians.)

Wallis returned to Washington in 1926 to divorce her husband, soon becoming seriously involved with Ernest Aldrich Simpson (half-British on his father's side) who ran a shipping business with offices in New York and London. In the summer of 1928 Ernest moved to London, where he and Wallis were married. If it seems to have been a passionless relationship, it was – at least for a time – a good friendship and Wallis began to thrive in her newly assumed role as society hostess, for which she rapidly became justly famed. Soon, though, her talents for serving imaginative – and very un-British – food and brittle after-dinner conversation were to be completely eclipsed by an unsought notoriety. This strangely angular woman with the rat-trap mouth but exquisite taste in the most chic and unfussy clothes was to take the world by storm, for all the wrong reasons.

She met the Prince of Wales at Lynden Manor, home of the louche Milford Havens. George Milford Haven threw a weekend party to which he invited Lady Thelma Furness, a long-term lover of Edward's and the sister of Gloria Morgan Vanderbilt – Nada's lesbian lover – and to which Thelma invited her friends, the Simpsons, and of course the Prince of Wales. Soon Ernest and Wallis became a constant sight in the Prince's social circle: by 1932 he was a regular dinner-guest at their cosy central London flat in Bryanston Court. Wallis and Ernest also became frequent weekend guests at the Prince's beloved country retreat, Fort Belvedere, near Windsor.

In January 1934 Thelma went back to the States for a few months, asking Wallis to 'look after him while I'm away' and to make sure he 'doesn't get into any mischief'.[75] Fate duly tempted, it obliged by having Wallis succeed her as royal mistress almost seamlessly.

By the time Thelma returned, Edward and Wallis were clearly more than just friends, and she found herself frozen out. Even worse was the Prince's treatment of Freda Dudley Ward (who had been out of circulation for some months because one of her daughters was seriously ill). In the summer of 1934 she telephoned the Prince at York House – only to be pole-axed by the revelation that he had given instructions that she should not be put through ever again. (Freda is not mentioned once in Edward's memoirs, which were published in 1951. It is as if she had never existed, yet she and her family had provided him with a second-hand experience of happy domesticity for some time. Her daughters were also devastated by his sudden silence.) Not least because of Freda's cruel banishment after 16 years, it became apparent that Wallis was no passing fancy. This was serious, both romantically and constitutionally.

At the beginning of 1935 Edward ordered that two rooms at Fort Belvedere should be kept permanently for the Simpsons, although it was Wallis alone who made most use of them. As it became clear what was happening, the Duchess of York refused to visit the Fort and put pressure on Bertie not to mix with the couple. (Elizabeth's famous repugnance at Edward and Wallis's relationship may have been less a righteous reaction to the choice of royal mistress than the bitter response of a woman scorned.) His affair also caused his relationship with his father to break down even further.

The problem was not that he was having a relationship with another man's wife: his family should have been used to the situation by then, as that had been his emotional modus operandi for 16 years. Possibly the horrified reaction was because she was American. But most likely it was because he was utterly besotted with the peculiar Wallis (whom they naturally assumed was a gold-digger) and that, unlike with Freda, he was being wildly indiscreet about it. (Clearly the heir could be indiscreet with short-term affairs, but had to keep serious, long-term relationships quiet.) It was also a question of timing. The King was now 70 and had suffered poor health for some years: when Edward could become King at any moment, it was almost the worst time to embark on such a clearly unsuitable liaison.

In April 1935 Lord Wigram had a meeting with the Prince at Fort Belvedere to discuss the possibility of his imminent accession and also to broach the subject of Mrs Simpson. Wigram explained that sooner or later the press and the country would get to hear about it. Edward told Wigram that his friendship with Wallis was innocent and, in any case, it was nobody's business but his own.

Perhaps it was innocent: some researchers believe that Wallis was a life-long virgin, perhaps because of some physical deformity, even technical hermaphroditism. (However, this is strenuously denied by the Parisian physician who attended her in her last illness.) From time to time Wallis herself dropped intriguing hints about the unusual nature of her close relationships, at one point declaring that she had never let a man touch her 'below the Mason–Dixon line',[76] although of course this could have been a joke. Conversely, there are those who think Wallis was a sexual predator, employing exotic or even deviant erotic arts with which to ensnare her victims – indeed, more than half of London society seemed to belong to this camp in the months before the abdication, but it is hard to pinpoint any documentary justification for this view.

As rumours spread about Wallis's closeness to the besotted future King – whose painting of her toenails at a poolside drinks party was undignified, to say the least – and even her apparent control of him, George V became increasingly distraught. In 1934 he asked MI5 to prepare a dossier on Wallis for his 'private and confidential attention'.[77] The King's use of the security service for such matters raises questions of propriety, not so much because the King was using MI5 (after all, the private lives of the royal family obviously have implications for the nation) but that the service reported direct to him and not to the Government. In any case, the King does appear to have been using MI5 as a private detective agency.

The MI5 file on Wallis that became known as the 'China Dossier' (or 'China Report') – it was, in fact, three separate reports – was to have significant consequences. (One of its contributors was Roger Hollis, who had been based in Shanghai at the same time as Wallis. He later became the Director of MI5.) But the China Dossier is hugely controversial: Philip Ziegler doubts it even existed on the grounds that nobody has found a copy of it in any official archive.[78] Perhaps naively, he says that it is 'inconceivable' that George V would have requested MI5 to produce such a report, although other royal biographers such as David Duff accept that it was the King's routine practice to ask for his sons' girlfriends to be investigated.[79]

The existence of the China Dossier – although not its contents – was known in royal and Government circles during the abdication crisis of 1936. (Although Kenneth de Courcy was to have its existence confirmed by no less than Queen Mary's equerry some years later.)[80]

The China Dossier gave a very lurid account of Wallis's past, particularly the period she had spent in Hong Kong and China. It said that she had been introduced by her first husband to the 'Singing Houses' of Shanghai and Hong Kong – brothels that boasted girls who were highly trained in the more imaginative and esoteric of the sexual arts. The Dossier claimed that not only did Wallis indulge in all manner of erotic variations – with differing combinations of both male and female partners – but she also had herself trained in some of the girls' techniques. According to the report, she was nothing less than a nymphomaniac. The file also noted her close associations and possible love affairs with Nazi and Italian Fascist diplomats, and suggested that she may be spying for one or both of these potentially hostile nations.

The truth or otherwise of the China Dossier's allegations is hard to establish. Although there are some tantalising gaps in Wallis's story during her period in the Far East – and undoubtedly she enjoyed some interesting times there – the allegations are so extreme that it is hard to take them seriously. Almost certainly a deliberate attempt to portray Wallis in the worst possible light, they were at least exaggerated, if not wholly invented.

However, the China Dossier succeeded because King George and Queen Mary believed it. No doubt this contributed further to the King's disdain for his son and heir, and ensured that after his death and Edward's accession to the throne, Queen Mary would be set against Wallis.

THE MURDER OF GEORGE V

The Prince of Wales's frustration with his position was such that he was known to talk about renouncing his rights to the throne on several occasions during this period.[81] In view of his abdication, is this evidence that he never really wanted to be King and took the first opportunity to parachute out of the hated situation? Although this will be discussed more fully in the next chapter, it does reveal that the thought of abdication or renunciation had at least crossed his mind.

George V himself made several references to the possibility of his son's abdication. In the summer of 1935 one of Edward's officials, Sir Lionel Halsey, recorded that the King had remarked that perhaps it would be better if the Prince abdicated.[82] At the end of the year, ill and depressed, he told a courtier, 'My eldest son will never succeed me. He will abdicate.'[83] Significantly, he had written in his diary, 'When I am gone, he will ruin himself within a year.'[84] But his most famous comment on the subject came just a few weeks before his death: 'I pray to God my eldest son will never marry and have children, and that nothing will come between Bertie and Lilibet and the throne.'[85] (The steady and unimaginative Princess Elizabeth was his favourite, not least because their characters were so similar.)

The King had not enjoyed good health since the winter of 1934–35. A lifelong heavy smoker, at Sandringham for the Christmas and New Year break in 1935 he developed a chest infection and began to weaken dramatically. His physician, Lord Dawson, realised that the King's heart was failing, so the family members who were not at Sandringham – including the Prince of Wales, who was at the Fort – were summoned there on 16 January 1936. It was clear that the King had only a few days to live.

On the afternoon of Monday, 20 June, Lord Dawson wrote what has become a classic royal announcement, for broadcast on the BBC that evening: 'The King's life is moving peacefully towards its close.' Soon afterwards George slipped into his final coma and a few minutes before midnight he was declared dead. It is the stuff of which royal legends are made. In fact, there was a somewhat different twist: his death had been aided and abetted, stage-managed for greater effect. The truth came out 50 years later when Dawson's notebooks were released to the public, revealing that the King had been the victim of euthanasia. In fact, the story had already been recounted privately by the Duke of Windsor in a letter to Kenneth de Courcy:

> Later that evening, after dinner, Dawson came in to see my mother and myself and said to both of us, 'You would not wish him to endure any undue suffering?' My mother said that we did not and I concurred; only very much later, as I reflected upon the situation, did it occur to me that Dawson intended to ease my father's departure from this earth. I was truly horrified when I discovered that Dawson had administered not one but two lethal injections. It was certainly not my intention to give him such authorisation when I agreed that my father should not be subjected to a great deal of suffering . . . Effectively, Dawson murdered my father.[86]

Curiously however, in Dawson's notebook, he says that it was the Prince who had conveyed Queen Mary's wish to the physician that her husband should not suffer unduly – with which he agreed.[87]

The reason for the decision to hasten the King's death was not out of compassion for the old monarch, but – in Dawson's own words – due to 'the importance of the death receiving its first announcement in the morning papers rather than the less appropriate evening journal',[88] most specifically *The Times*. (Dawson telephoned his wife to ask her to request its editor to hold the front pages pending an announcement.)

Dawson injected first morphine and then cocaine into the King's jugular vein. He would usually have asked his nurse to administer the injections, but noted that 'it was obvious that she was disturbed by this procedure'.[89] He was aided in his grim task by the fact that it was unlikely he would be found out, at least in the immediate future, as no death certificate was issued.

Although it is improbable that George V would have lasted the night anyway, the unpalatable fact remains that euthanasia was illegal then and still is now, when several high-profile legal cases reveal the law's continued repugnance for helping even the sickest loved ones out of this life. Indeed, even in twenty-first century Britain, men and women are given custodial sentences for helping those close to them to die with dignity. It appears that most authors regard the anomaly of George V's death as nothing more than an unusual turn of events – worth a posthumous rap over the knuckles for Dawson – but such complacency conceals the extreme seriousness of the act. While ordinary people continue to suffer the full weight of the law for playing God, the royal family of nearly 70 years ago got away with what was technically murder – after all, the euthanasia had been sanctioned by the Queen and the Prince of Wales. And, although Dawson wrote that he was motivated by the King's need for the 'dignity and serenity which he so richly merited and which demanded a brief final scene',[90] he also acknowledged that the more immediate factor was the 'importance' of the King's passing being announced in *The Times*. (In any case, the comatose King was beyond suffering.)

The family (excluding Henry, who was also ill) were called in for the old King's final moments. When Dawson pronounced him dead, the Queen kissed his forehead, then bowed to her son and kissed his hand as the new King. Prince George did the same. According to Wigram, who was also present, 'The Prince of Wales [*sic*] became hysterical, cried loudly, and kept on embracing the Queen.'[91] This touching scene was unlikely to be a natural outpouring of a son's grief. More probably it was due to the sudden realisation that he was King and the golden days of boyish irresponsibility were finally, and terribly, over. The brief and traumatic reign of Edward VIII had begun.

After the lying in state in Westminster Abbey, George V's funeral procession through London took place on 28 January (with Wallis Simpson watching from St James's Palace, as arranged specially by the new King). George V's coffin was borne through the streets on a gun carriage on which rested the Imperial crown. During the procession the diamond-and-sapphire-encrusted Maltese cross on top fell off – to be smoothly scooped up by one of the guard of honour without so much as breaking step. King Edward VIII was heard to mutter, 'Christ! What's going to happen next?' One of those who overheard this, Cabinet minister Walter Elliott, muttered to his neighbour, '*That* will be the motto of the new reign.'[92]

FOUR

'A KIND OF ENGLISH NATIONAL SOCIALIST'

Joachim von Ribbentrop on Edward VIII, 1936

When Edward VIII abdicated after less than a year as King not only was the drama intense, but the danger for the monarchy – even the stability of the country – was acute for a tense few months. Yet seen from the perspective of the early twenty-first century, it seems almost a footnote of history; interesting, colourful, but essentially non-important where the big issues of politics and world affairs are concerned. However, that view is not borne out by the facts.

The abdication is either regarded as the act of an over-privileged and selfish royal who placed his personal life above duty to the country, the result of failed scheming by an American divorcee who set her sights on becoming Queen of England, or, of course, one of history's greatest romantic gestures. But all these views see Edward VIII's actions primarily as an intensely personal drama, failing to note the true extent of its serious political ramifications.

In fact, the King's abdication was actually of immense significance, not only for the constitution – where it represented a turning point in the centuries-long power struggle between the monarchy and politicians – but also for the international community. With new insights, it is a revelation to discover that Edward VIII's abdication was actually one of the most pivotal events of the twentieth century, its shock waves even being felt today. Indeed, it is not too much of an exaggeration to claim that if Edward VIII had not abdicated, the country, and even the wider world, would probably be a very different place nearly 70 years on.

Although there is no doubt that Edward adored Wallis Simpson to the point of masochistic prostration, behind the love affair was a complex interplay of opposing political movements (both in Parliament and on the street), conflicting factions within the royal family and an orgy of scheming to achieve personal and political ambitions.

Later, as Duke of Windsor, Edward was to drop hints about a plot by Prime Minister Stanley Baldwin to exploit the King's desire to marry Wallis Simpson to expel him from the throne – although this sort of comment is usually blamed on the Duke's lifelong bitterness about the way that he and his wife were treated. However, others who were close to him during his brief reign and members of his entourage have made the same claim: in Brian Inglis's words, 'Baldwin realized even before the summer holidays that the King would have to be brought under control or compelled to leave the throne.'[1] This is consistent with the comments that Baldwin made to Alan Lascelles during their Canada tour in 1927, which suggest that long before Mrs Simpson came on the scene Baldwin realised that he was going to be a particularly troublesome king.

Significantly, two of the earliest commentators on the abdication suggested that Baldwin had made good use of the opportunity afforded by the Wallis Simpson affair to get rid of the King. Compton Mackenzie, in *The Windsor Tapestry*, published in July 1938, pointed to contradictions, discrepancies and deliberately misleading comments in Baldwin's statements to the House of Commons that suggested that the real issues behind the abdication were being deliberately concealed.

In 1939, the respected political and royal historian Phillip Guedalla's book *The Hundredth Day* – about the key events of 1936, including the abdication – came out, only for the British Government to attempt to ban it.[2] In the event, they were unsuccessful. The author sent a copy to the Duke of Windsor, who in 1940 wrote to him praising the book and saying:

> I am only now beginning to realise the virrulence [*sic*] of the campaign that Official England launched against me the day I ascended the throne, and how, with Machiavellian cunning, it used the fertile soil of the American press in the fabrication of sufficient evidence against me to justify its ultimate aim of having me out.[3]

Guedalla analysed Baldwin's actions during the crisis (on which he had inside information that has since proved correct), noting a curious thing about the Prime Minister's behaviour at the time: he missed many obvious opportunities and ignored courses of action that might have brought about a satisfactory solution. Guedalla concluded that this could only be explained if Baldwin had no intention of finding a solution. He *wanted* Edward VIII to abdicate.

THE NEW KING

As soon as he ascended to the throne, it became very obvious that the new King would be a very different animal from his father. Expressing his loyalty in the Commons on Edward's accession, Stanley Baldwin said that Edward had 'a wider and more intimate knowledge of all classes of his subjects . . . than any of his predecessors'.[4] Of course, as far as the people were concerned this was a good thing. But to the politicians, a popular sovereign, particularly one as independent-minded and rebellious as Edward, could only spell trouble. It was clear that this King refused to be a mere figurehead whose opinions could only be expressed in secret audiences with his Prime Minister.

Although George V (or more likely his Palace advisers) had proved adept at manipulating the Government from behind the scenes, using subtle chess moves was neither Edward's style nor within his capabilities – he was far too easily bored for the exquisite intricacies of chess-playing. He wanted to be a 'hands on' king, but whether he had the necessary long-term commitment and stamina is another matter.

This view is shared by J. Bryan and Charles Murphy, the American writers of *The Windsor Story* (1979), close friends of the Duke and Duchess of Windsor after the war. (Murphy was the ghost writer of both their memoirs.) Writing of Edward's attitude when he was still the Prince of Wales, they conclude, 'The strongest possibility is that Wales wanted to be King, but on his own terms, which he knew that the Court, moulded by his father in his own uncompromising image, would almost certainly reject.'[5]

Those who moved in his immediate circle during his brief reign accused Edward of two apparently mutually exclusive flaws: neglecting his duty and interfering in state affairs. However, as Brian Inglis pointed out in his *Abdication* (1966), both failings are consistent with his personality, which was evident right from the First World War: he was desperate to make his mark in grand schemes but bored by the detail and the routine demands of working towards the goal.[6]

From the outset, Edward sent signals to his Government of how he would conduct himself in his reign. Incredibly, on St David's Day Edward refused point-blank to show the Home Secretary a proposed radio speech.[7] As his Private Secretary Sir Clive Wigram repeatedly pointed out, radio broadcasts by the monarch have to be vetted by the Home Secretary: Edward was seriously challenging both the Government and his own Private Secretary. As it happened, the speech was innocuous enough, but his refusal to bow to custom sent a warning salvo across the Government's bows. Clearly, the new King was potentially a very dangerous man.

Later in March, Edward gave a speech in which he wanted to express his support for greater Indian self-determination. The Home Secretary had no hesitation in removing this passage – but not without resistance on Edward's part.[8] Already he was threatening to be uncontrollable, apparently having no thought as to what the consequences of his words might be. But what would Gandhi and his supporters – not to mention apopleptic ex-Indian Army colonels – have made of such encouragement from India's King Emperor?

Alarm bells really sounded when, at the beginning of July, it was reported that he proposed to call a conference to try to resolve the situation in Ireland.[9] However well intentioned this might have been, it was certainly not the kind of move that sat comfortably with the idea of a constitutional monarch: it simply was not acceptable for the King to take the initiative on such matters. If he wanted to be personally involved in the Irish question, he should have taken his father's example. George V had made a public appeal for unity and understanding in Ireland after the 1922 settlement, but had left the issue to the politicians. Surely, they muttered, that was how to play it. The Government was becoming increasingly anxious about the glamorous and popular loose cannon in the big house at the top of the Mall.

Even his method of dealing with the day-to-day business of his job left much to be desired. The King's slipshod attitude to the mass of paperwork that came his way caused raised eyebrows among his staff and the Cabinet. It was not unusual for him to leave papers lying about, often neglected for days, then return them covered in tell-tale cocktail stains. Any of his many guests could have taken the opportunity to read highly confidential Government documents. For this reason – and because of ministerial mistrust of his pro-German feelings – the Foreign Office began to practise the breathtakingly drastic step of withholding the most sensitive documents from him.[10]

As the 'People's Prince', Edward had established a reputation for sharing the problems and concerns of ordinary folk but, as we have seen, he was certainly no democrat. This was the era of the dictatorial 'man of the people', as Hitler and Mussolini were perceived to be. They believed that the interests of the masses were best served by dictatorship, not by allowing them a say in running the country. Tellingly, diarist Chips Channon noted in November 1936 – just as the abdication crisis was about to break: 'The King . . . is going the mild dictator way, and is pro-German, against Russia and against too much slip-shod democracy. I shouldn't be surprised if he aimed at making himself a mild dictator, a difficult enough task for an English King.'[11] Given Edward's personal friendship with the likes of Oswald Mosley, this was indeed a dangerous state of affairs.

Typically, there was an element of double standards – or, more accurately, blindness to the contradictions – in Edward's championing of the poor and unemployed. Like most Windsors, he was always obsessed by money and apparently suffered from the lifelong illusion that he was hard up. As soon as his reign began he tried to increase his wealth by various means, including cutting the costs of the private estates he inherited. (At the same time he continued to lavish costly jewels on his beloved, who described herself deliriously as 'Wallis in Wonderland'.) This entailed making the Sandringham and Balmoral workers redundant, a particularly savage move as most had live-in jobs in areas with little alternative employment. This saved about £7,500 (about £180,000 today), almost pocket money compared to the vast fortune spent on Wallis.[12] In addition, he made redundancies at Buckingham Palace and cut wages by 10 per cent – as his father had threatened but never put into practice. Although the wages were actually paid out of the Civil List, Edward simply pocketed the savings.[13]

In June 1936 the King wanted to divert £250,000 (over £7 million today) of the Duchy of Lancaster's capital into his private funds, but the Chancellor of the Duchy stopped him as it was against the law (although the Duchy is the monarch's hereditary source of revenue, making up the major part of the Privy Purse, an Act of Parliament prevents the monarch from touching the capital). He did, however, transfer to his own account the entire contents of the Duchy's No Kin Investment Fund – £38,000, or the equivalent of about £900,000 today.[14] This fund arose from an ancient right dating back to the fourteenth century, by which the Duchy takes the personal money, property and land of anyone who dies intestate in the county of Lancashire.

INTERNATIONAL TENSION

The Government was also concerned that Edward was far too free in his conversation. Traditionally, if the monarch had a particular view on domestic or foreign policy he would only express it in private to his ministers or Palace officials. Worse, Edward talked openly to friends about some of the most sensitive aspects of the international situation – concerning Germany, Italy and the threat of Bolshevik Russia. Even at the time of his father's funeral, Edward expressed his views on Nazism and communism, without any sense of discernment or self-censorship, to the Finnish representative.[15]

Like many before the war whose views suffered a miraculous sea-change afterwards, Edward believed that communism, both at home and in the Soviet Union, was the greatest menace Britain faced. To him and his ilk, the Nazis and Italian Fascists had not only shown how it could be successfully suppressed in their own countries, but were vital in preventing Russian expansion. This was a view he repeatedly stressed in conversations with friends – and to Government ministers.[16]

Undoubtedly, one of Edward's top priorities was fostering closer ties with Germany. Even during George V's last illness, he spoke to the German ambassador, Leopold von Hoesch, on this issue and stated his intention of visiting the Berlin Olympics in the summer of 1936.[17] At his first official reception for diplomats in February, it was remarked that he gave considerably more time to von Hoesch than anyone else.[18] Equally, on the German side it was clear that getting the new King on side – or rather, even more on side – was one of their top priorities. Although, as we have seen, the Nazis had been able to exert some influence over George V, the old King was basically a Conservative of the old school, his main points of agreement with the Nazis being the menace of communism and the avoidance of a war between Britain and Germany. Edward had a much more obviously national socialist cast of mind and also seemed more willing than his father to try to exert direct influence over his Government.

Even before his accession this was a major worry. In 1934, the German Ambassador in Washington reported that Edward had declared that he failed to share his father's view of the relationship between the Sovereign and his ministers and that he 'felt it to be his duty to intervene if the Cabinet were to plan a policy which in his view was detrimental to British interests'.[19] Therefore Hitler realised that it was important for Edward to have regular contact with a Nazi representative, although, as he was now King, it was imperative that this contact did not seem in any way official.

Accordingly, Charles, Duke of Saxe-Coburg-Gotha, one of the German noblemen who had been removed from the Order of the Garter during the First World War and had since embraced the Nazi ideology, was sent as the regime's unofficial envoy to the King. He joined the Nazi Party in 1935, becoming a Gruppenführer in the SA (Brownshirts) and was to become a member of the Reichstag between 1937 and 1945. Saxe-Coburg-Gotha dutifully sent Berlin many reports on his meetings with the new King: during one discussion about the Prime Minister's attitude to Germany, he reported that the King asked defiantly, 'Who is King here, Baldwin or I? I wish to talk to Hitler and will do so here or in Germany. Tell him that, please.'[20] (This reveals that he unquestionably knew full well that Charles was representing Hitler.) Charles also reported that Edward regarded an alliance between Britain and Germany as being 'an urgent necessity and a guiding principle for British foreign policy'.[21] Another of his reports significantly echoes Channon's words about his dictatorial ambitions:

> The King is resolved to concentrate the business of Government on himself . . . The general political situation, especially the situation of England herself, will perhaps give him a chance. His sincere resolve to bring Germany and England together would be made more difficult if it were made public too early. For this reason, I regard it as most important to respect the King's wish that the non-official policy of Germany towards England should be firmly concentrated in one hand and at the same time brought into relations of confidence with the official policy.
>
> The King asked me to visit him frequently in order that confidential matters might be more speedily clarified in this way. I promised – subject to the Führer's approval – to fly to London at any time he wished.[22]

Von Ribbentrop, who became Ambassador to Britain during Edward's reign, described him to a Bulgarian prince as 'a kind of English national socialist'.[23] At the time von Ribbentrop's appointment was greeted with puzzlement in diplomatic circles. Up to then, he had been Hitler's roving envoy, a very powerful and important position. Assigning him to an ambassadorial post was seen as a definite demotion, prompting the widespread belief that he had fallen from favour. However, after his tour of duty in London von Ribbentrop became Foreign Minister, so clearly Hitler harboured no doubts about his abilities. It seems that good diplomatic relations with Britain were regarded as such a priority that the best man had to be sent.

THE KING'S THREAT

The most serious of Edward's pro-German moves occurred just three months after his accession – when he used the time-honoured threat of abdication to influence the Government in a direction that played into Hitler's hands. The Nazis had spent their first years in power rebuilding Germany's economy and feverishly rearming. But now Hitler began to put his territorial ambitions into operation, initially by reclaiming the areas taken from Germany by the Treaty of Versailles. In this, the reactions of Britain and France were all-important. Would they threaten war at the first sign of Germany breaking the Treaty? Or was it simply too great a risk?

The first test of how far Hitler could go occurred in March 1936. As a result of the 1925 Treaty of Locarno Germany was not allowed to keep any military forces in the industrially and strategically important area of the Rhineland around Cologne. This was to prevent Germany using it as a base for attacking France or Belgium, and to allow France rapid access to Germany in the event of a war. On 7 March Hitler called in the British, French, Belgian and Italian ambassadors and told them he had repudiated the treaty and ordered his troops to reoccupy the Rhineland. It was a gamble – as Hitler later acknowledged, had the French responded militarily, his forces would have easily been defeated, being nowhere near strong enough at the time. Indeed, Hitler had given orders to his generals to retreat at the first sign of opposition. For the next few days Hitler was on tenterhooks as he waited to see how Britain and France would react. Eventually, neither nation did any more than condemn Germany for contravening the Locarno Treaty: a mere slap on the wrist.

Albert Speer, Hitler's architect who was to become Minister of Armaments in the Second World War, records that the crisis passed after four days when Hitler received a message from London, which he greeted with great relief before telling Speer, 'At last! The King of England will not intervene. He is keeping his promise. That means it can all go well.'[24]

More details about Edward's actions were revealed by Fritz Hesse, a press attaché to the German Embassy in London who claimed that von Hoesch had met the King and appealed to him to use his influence to ensure that the Government did not act over the reoccupation of the Rhineland. The next day, Hesse was present during a telephone conversation between von Hoesch and the King, in which Edward said that he had sent for Baldwin and told him that if the Government decided on a military response *he would abdicate*.[25] This was presumably what had so relieved Hitler, the meaning of the message about the King 'keeping his promise'.

This is astounding. Edward had used the 'nuclear deterrent' of abdication as a threat to ensure his Government did what he wanted. (As far as history records, this was the first time such a threat had been used since Queen Victoria 60 years before.) Except in the most dire emergency, no Prime Minister would be responsible for the abdication of a sovereign because of a disagreement over policy – the resultant crisis would split the nation and could well cause the Government to fall. Perhaps more to the point, Edward had blatantly used his threat of abdication to get what the *Nazi* Government wanted . . .

Published in his book *Hitler and the English* in 1954, Fritz Hesse's account is dismissed by most mainstream historians as a sensational invention, largely on the grounds that it is surely inconceivable that any British monarch, even Edward VIII, could do such a thing, and because of the lack of official confirmation. But audiences between the Sovereign and Prime Minister are kept absolutely secret – no minutes are taken and no third person is present – so there would be no record of Edward making such a threat. Even so, the fact remains that Hesse's story is supported by Speer's account of the message received by Hitler. Anthony Eden also told the Czech Ambassador seven months later that Edward had interfered over the Rhineland affair.[26]

This episode was a revelation – if it were still needed – to Baldwin of exactly what kind of King he was dealing with. It also reveals that Edward's thoughts revolved around abdication as a threat. But if Baldwin decided that the King had to be forced into abdication, it could not be because of a constitutional crisis over Government policy. That was too dangerous: after all, the country might agree with the King. This incident also showed the benefits as far as Nazi Germany was concerned of keeping Edward on the throne.

A TIME BOMB CALLED MRS SIMPSON

Edward's relationship with Wallis Simpson – although kept out of the press – was only too well known to Queen Mary, now the matriarch of the royal family, and to the Prime Minister. This was cause enough for concern, but the crisis was precipitated when Edward made it known that he wanted to marry his American amour, which meant a swift divorce from Ernest. Brooking no denial from any quarter, within a month of his accession Edward resolved to marry Wallis, and it was not long before this came to Baldwin's attention.

However, there was more to the Prime Minister's opposition to the match than his horror at the scandal of the King wishing to marry a double divorcee – and an American at that. According to John Parker, Baldwin had received a security report on her association with von Ribbentrop, as well as her link with 'German monarchist circles' with which she fostered independent contact.[27] This may refer to her friendship with Prince Otto von Bismarck, who was attached to the German Embassy in London, and his wife Princess Anne-Marie. (No one seems to have spotted the irony: if maintaining contact with 'German monarchist circles' made one a security risk, the entire royal family should have been put under surveillance.) Prior to his appointment as Ambassador, as Hitler's roving envoy, von Ribbentrop had been a familiar face at London's social events, often attending the same dinner parties as Mr and Mrs Simpson, where the increasingly besotted Edward was also a guest.

In June 2002, the FBI's files on Wallis – originally the result of an investigation ordered by President Roosevelt in 1941 and obtained by *The Guardian* through the US Freedom of Information Act – were made public. According to these files she and von Ribbentrop were more than fellow diners: they were lovers. The information came from two sources: Duke Charles Alexander of Württemburg, a former von Ribbentrop aide (who later settled in the USA as a monk) told the FBI that while he was in London, von Ribbentrop sent Wallis 17 carnations every day – representing the number of times they had slept together. A second, unidentified, source claimed that she had maintained contact with the Nazi when she decamped to Cannes during the height of the abdication crisis.

It must be said that the reliability of these sources is uncertain – the FBI at that time had a tendency to record gossip as fact. While Wallis may have had an affair with von Ribbentrop, she was unlikely to be a Nazi spy. As we shall see, because it was of vital importance to Hitler personally that Edward VIII should not abdicate, as a Nazi agent she would hardly have precipitated the crisis. He was much more useful to them as monarch than as ex-King in exile. However, even an innocent association with von Ribbentrop was cause enough for the Government's disquiet.

Another headache for Baldwin was that Wallis was a foreigner: would she feed British state secrets to intelligence agencies at home? The US Ambassador to France, William C. Bullitt, was a friend who often visited the Simpsons in London – just one of many diplomats from the Embassy who frequently dropped by, some of whom were known to work for US Intelligence. One of these was the Military Attaché for Air, Major Martin F. Scanlon: he and his wife were particularly close friends of the Simpsons and, through Wallis, also of the King. (The Scanlons were among the five guests, all Americans, that Edward invited to dinner on the day of his abdication.) One particularly scandalous episode rang alarm bells in Whitehall and the Palace: after the Scanlons had celebrated the 4 July weekend with Edward and Wallis at Fort Belvedere, Scanlon recorded in his diary: 'I was taken aback when, as we were starting back to town, the King asked me to take his "Boxes" to Buckingham Palace and deliver them to Hardinge [the King's Private Secretary]. I had a feeling that Hardinge did not approve of the King's practice of confiding State papers to the care of an American intelligence officer.'[28]

Although Britain was on friendly terms with the USA – even before the era of the 'special relationship' – the possibility that *any* foreign government may have access to state papers was a serious cause for concern. Even if Wallis was not actively an agent for the German, Italian or American Government her very position and circle of friends made her an appalling security risk. And this was compounded by Edward's infamous carelessness with state papers, which he left lying around when Wallis, and others, were weekending at Fort Belvedere.

THE DIVORCE

If Edward wanted to marry Wallis by the set date of his coronation on 12 May 1937, in order for her to be crowned beside him, she had to obtain a divorce from Ernest. The matter was increasingly urgent, especially as the process took at least six months. It was agreed between all the parties that to avoid (or at least minimise) the scandal, Wallis would have to divorce Ernest on the grounds of *his* adultery. This was not too difficult – by then he was deeply involved with Mary Raffray (Wallis's old school chum) whom he subsequently married.

At that time the British divorce laws were more than a little quaint. In order to establish adultery, a husband or wife had to be seen in bed with their lover by a third party. This was stage-managed by Ernest and Mary by booking into a country hotel (she under the assumed name of Buttercup Kennedy), and then, having 'accidentally' left the bedroom door unlocked, being discovered by the chambermaid in bed together – chatting.

Another potentially difficult aspect to the divorce laws was that if a woman petitioned for divorce on the grounds of her husband's adultery, and it could be shown that *she* was also committing adultery, then the divorce would be refused. This is why Edward and Wallis had to insist that theirs was a chaste relationship and continue to maintain that they had not slept together before their wedding night. (Edward later successfully sued people who had insinuated that they had.)

Undoubtedly, under the law as it stood in 1936, the Simpsons' divorce was illegal because it was arranged in collusion between the couple and Wallis's intended next husband – the Sovereign and the 'fount of law' himself – with the connivance of royal officials. If anyone had challenged it, the divorce could have been stopped.

The King then asked lawyer Walter Monckton to take care of the divorce and obtained the services of a solicitor, Theodore Goddard, and the country's best courtroom advocate, Norman Birkett (who had represented the Mountbattens in the 'Robeson' case). He had first brought Monckton in as his legal adviser when it seemed likely that he would soon become King, in 1928. When Edward's elevation failed to materialise at that time, he appointed him Attorney-General of the Duchy of Cornwall. Both Edward and Wallis repeatedly assured Monckton and Goddard that she was not divorcing Ernest so that they could marry – it was just that discretion was necessary because of their 'friendship'.

Following this Edward and Wallis went off on their summer holiday, the celebrated Mediterranean cruise on the yacht *Nahlin*. Although this features prominently in most reconstructions of the abdication affair, in fact, it is something of a red herring. After all, the cruise was by no means the start of the affair. However, it attracted a lot of attention in the American and European media, but little in the British press: at this time the public at home were unfamiliar with the name Wallis Simpson – incredibly, a situation that would last for another four months. But it was not all moonlit dinners and cosy twosome pedaloes: the King did carry out some official visits during the cruise, visiting a colourful cast of potentates including the King of Bulgaria, the Regent of Yugoslavia, Kemal Atatürk, President of Turkey, in Istanbul and, during his return journey, the Austrian President.

In the middle of September, not long after their return from holiday and as her divorce trial came nearer, Wallis was in the throes of panic about the magnitude and implications of their affair, writing to Edward from Paris that she had decided to return to Ernest as she was 'better with him than with you' and that she was sure that, if they continued, it would all end in disaster because of his new responsibilities.[29] According to Alan Lascelles (who was now back in Edward's service, having been 'inherited' from George V's staff), when he got this letter he telephoned Wallis and threatened to kill himself if she failed to return to him. It is perhaps significant that her apparently genuine willingness to reject her royal lover is at odds with her image as gold-digging harpy who never passed up an opportunity to claw her scarlet nails into Edward's wealth. And this is not the only departure from the accepted story.

THE KING'S ENEMIES

During his first months in office, Edward had stirred up a great deal of opposition for various reasons, including his casual and irresponsible attitude to state business, scandalous behaviour with Wallis and his often brash efforts to carve out a hands-on political role for himself.

By October, with the divorce hearing rapidly approaching, Edward had powerful enemies arrayed against him. Not only was Baldwin determined to see him go (for all the reasons outlined above), but he had incurred the displeasure of the Court and the latest incarnation of the 'Palace mafia', in particular the all-powerful Private Secretary. The Court was opposed to Edward both on principle (because of his flaunting of age-old customs, not to mention his cocky and casual attitude) and simply because of his unacceptably immature character. Paradoxically, the Old Guard came to regard the King as a real threat to the monarchy. They noted with alarm and rage that early in his reign he had sacked two officials, including the Comptroller Admiral Sir Lionel Halsey, because they had dared to criticise his relationship with Wallis.[30]

The old King's Private Secretary, Sir Clive Wigram, rapidly became disenchanted with Edward VIII. To ensure continuity, it is the custom at the start of a new reign that the Private Secretary should remain in office for at least six months. As soon as this period was over, it suited both parties that Wigram should go. Edward wanted his long-term Private Secretary as Prince of Wales, Godfrey Thomas, to take his place but he declined, so Wigram's assistant, Major Alexander ('Alec') Hardinge, was appointed to this all-powerful position. As was the custom, Hardinge received a knighthood soon after the appointment. However, even this honour failed to mollify him: Hardinge regarded the King as irresponsible and was deeply unhappy about his differences with the Government's foreign policy, particularly where Germany and Italy were concerned. Seriously at odds with his master from the start, Hardinge was to play a pivotal behind-the-scenes role in the abdication.

The King also unwisely fell foul of another major cabal within the Establishment. Almost immediately after acceding to the throne Edward – a Freemason since 1919 – sponsored Ernest Simpson's membership of an important Masonic Lodge in the City of London, whose Grand Master was former Lord Mayor Sir Maurice Jenks. However, Simpson's candidacy had been opposed by other members of the Lodge on the grounds that it violated Masonic law because Edward was involved in an adulterous relationship with Ernest's wife. Jenks had to ask the King whether he was, in fact, engaged in a sexual relationship with Wallis – and Edward denied it. On this basis, Ernest was allowed in.[31] However, many in the Masonic world simply refused to accept Edward's word, believing that he had blatantly committed the heinous crime of lying to a fellow Freemason. The outrage grew when they discovered that Edward intended to marry Ernest's wife. It was also suggested that Simpson, who wanted to join the Lodge because of its promised business advantages, had effectively blackmailed the King into sponsoring him. By the time of the abdication crisis, therefore, Edward was regarded by Freemasons as untrustworthy, to say the least. It was not an enviable – or even a safe – position in which the King found himself.

Interestingly, it was Jenks, because of his position as Ernest's Grand Master, who seems to have been the first outsider to know of Edward's intention to marry Wallis. When Simpson told him about it at the beginning of February 1936, Jenks immediately informed the Prime Minister, who in turn sent for Sir Clive Wigram so they could discuss the matter. At this stage Baldwin and Wigram refused to take it particularly seriously, the consensus being that Simpson was attempting to use his wife to blackmail the King. They even considered deporting him.[32] The Prime Minister declined Wigram's suggestion that he should talk to Edward about it, as Baldwin – at least so it is claimed – thought the affair would soon blow over.

The antipathy of Freemasonry towards the King is very significant because it spelt the end of Establishment support: its loyalties were already beginning to shift. At the end of November – as the crisis was breaking – the Duke of York was installed as Grand Master Mason of Scotland. All the indications suggest that he took his Masonic oath and duties most seriously (as George VI, he was to establish a precedent of the King being directly involved in English Freemasonry), which may explain the emphasis of his diary entry about Edward's departure after the abdication: 'When D. & I said goodbye we kissed, parted as freemasons, & he bowed to me as his King.'[33]

The Masons were not the only representatives of the Establishment massing against the King. Another highly influential individual who was determined that he should go was Geoffrey Dawson, editor of *The Times*. In regular contact with Baldwin throughout the crisis, the two men co-ordinated their actions to undermine the King's position. So effective was this in sealing Edward's fate that Lord Beaverbrook later wrote of Dawson, 'But for him, Edward VIII would still be on the throne.'[34]

Putting her sacred duty before maternal loyalty, Queen Mary, too, was concerned that her son's behaviour – marriage or not – would damage the standing of the monarchy. However, as we shall see, another factor tipped the Queen Dowager against Wallis, making her adamant that Edward should never marry her while he was King.

To this burgeoning list should be added the Church of England, then firmly opposed to the remarriage of divorcees, especially in church, no matter which partner had been to blame.

THE DRAMA UNFOLDS

Today we follow every twist and turn of major events through newspapers, television and radio, rapidly becoming au fait with even the smallest detail, sometimes even before the leading players themselves know about it. But in 1936 nothing about the crisis appeared in the British press until a little over a week before the abdication. As A.N. Wilson asks, what about the much-vaunted public's right to know (the press's usual justification for delving into the private lives of public figures)?[35] Clearly, the Establishment in those days was both contemptuous and fearful of the public's opinion in such a critical and divisive drama.

With Wallis's divorce hearing set for 27 October, Walter Monckton arranged for it to be heard at Ipswich, on the East Anglian coast – conveniently a long way from London and Fleet Street. The imminence of the hearing effectively brought matters to a head: if successful, a decree nisi would be granted, and after a further six months a decree absolute. By the end of April Wallis would be free to marry – in time for the coronation.

Edward was concerned that even with the Ipswich venue, the press might still get wind of the story. Astonishingly, he summoned the press baron, Lord Beaverbrook, owner of the *Daily Express*, to Buckingham Palace, to ask him to use his influence to prevent any hint of Wallis's divorce appearing in the British press. (Beaverbrook delayed going to the Palace for two days, pleading severe dental problems. However, his diary for that time, while innocent of dental appointments, does record a meeting with Ernest Simpson.[36])

Beaverbrook, together with Monckton, then went to see Esmond Harmsworth, the Chairman of the Newspaper Proprietors' Association, who also happened to be *Daily Mail* owner Lord Rothermere's son. Harmsworth called a meeting of the newspaper editors who made a gentlemen's agreement not to cover the Simpson divorce case in their pages (an unimaginable scenario today). Incredibly, this voluntary embargo was even agreed by the left-wing *Daily Worker*!

Beyond the shores, however, there was no such gentleman's agreement: indeed, the foreign press was plunged into a feeding frenzy. The American press in particular had a field day with the divorce story. *The New York Journal* of 26 October gleefully headlined: 'King Will Wed Wally'. By today's standards official British reactions were little short of surreal – importers of American newspapers and magazines even began feverishly cutting out the pages that referred to Wallis. Of course newspapers with pages missing were unlikely to deflect attention from the matter in hand, leading to the pertinent Parliamentary Question: 'What is this thing that the British public are not allowed to see?'[37]

Canadian-born newspaper baron Lord Beaverbrook – one of the most powerful men of the twentieth century, who could and did make and break governments[38] – became one of Edward's advisers as the crisis deepened. He hated Stanley Baldwin and, though he had no strong feelings about Edward personally or the monarchy generally, delighted in intrigue and power struggles for their own sake. When Churchill's son Randolph later asked Beaverbrook why he got involved in the abdication affair, he replied 'To bugger Baldwin!' Clearly, Beaverbrook hoped to use Wallis to bring down a government he despised.

The final thrust came from an unexpected source – the King's own Private Secretary, Alec Hardinge. In his regular meetings with the Prime Minister, Hardinge had attempted to persuade Baldwin to intervene with the King over Wallis, but he was reluctant to do so. On 15 October, without Edward's knowledge, Hardinge took it upon himself to write to Baldwin asking him to stop the divorce.[39]

The following weekend there was a meeting at Cumberland Lodge, Windsor, the home of Lord FitzAlan, Viceroy of Ireland and a former Conservative Whip, which was attended by Hardinge, Baldwin, the Duke of Norfolk and Lords Salisbury and Kemsley.[40] This gathering persuaded Baldwin that he should see the King about Mrs Simpson. The Prime Minister asked for an audience with the King, which took place on 20 October. Following Hardinge's urging, Baldwin asked Edward to persuade Wallis to delay her divorce, to which the King replied shortly that it was her private business.

When it became clear that Edward refused to intervene in the matter of the divorce, Hardinge visited the Duke of York – the next in line – to warn him that it was possible that his brother might abdicate.[41] At this stage in the proceedings, Hardinge appears not only to have exceeded his authority but also markedly jumped the gun. Of course his visit had the effect of putting the fear of God into Bertie.

THE IMPORTANCE OF LOSING ERNEST

Wallis's petition was duly heard in Ipswich on 27 October 1936. Perhaps it was not entirely a coincidence that the judge, Mr Justice Hawke, had been Walter Monckton's predecessor as Attorney-General of the Duchy of Cornwall.[42] The police were out in force, enthusiastic about their special orders – the result of behind-the-scenes arrangements between Edward and the Chief Constable of Suffolk.[43] They efficiently prevented reporters from following Wallis as she left court, following this up by smashing press cameras, no doubt as much to make a point as just for the fun of it.[44]

On 13 November, Hardinge wrote an 'Urgent and Confidential' letter to the King setting out the position and his feelings on the matter – one of the most candid letters ever written from a Private Secretary to his monarch. However, although this is usually seen as the expression of his profound personal dilemma between his duty to the Crown and loyalty to the King, if that were the case, why did he show this highly personal and confidential letter to Dawson of *The Times* first?[45]

After pointing out that the press silence was not going to last forever, he told him that the Cabinet was meeting that day to discuss the situation:

> As Your Majesty no doubt knows, the resignation of the Government – an eventuality which can by no means be excluded – would result in Your Majesty having to find someone else capable of forming a Government which would receive the support of the present House of Commons. I have reason to know that, in view of the feeling prevalent among members of the House of Commons of all parties, this is hardly within the bounds of possibility. The only alternative remaining is a dissolution and a General Election, in which Your Majesty's personal affairs would be the chief issue – and I cannot help feeling that even those who would sympathise with Your Majesty as an individual would deeply resent the damage which would inevitably be done to the Crown, the corner-stone on which the whole Empire rests.
>
> If Your Majesty will permit me to say so, there is only one step which holds out any prospect of avoiding this dangerous situation, and that is for Mrs Simpson to go abroad *without further delay*, and I would *beg* Your Majesty to give this proposal your urgent consideration.[46]

Taking this as an ultimatum, Edward furiously by-passed Hardinge and used Walter Monckton as his liaison with the Prime Minister throughout the rest of the crisis – in Monckton's words, 'thus temporarily taking over Hardinge's principal duty as the constitutional link with the Prime Minister and Cabinet'.[47] Yet Hardinge's letter is important for several reasons. It is the first mention of the possibility that the Government might resign over the issue, just as Hardinge had also been the first to mention that it might provoke the King's abdication.

Perhaps he was merely acting within his primary role as the King's adviser on the constitution, anticipating possible outcomes. On the other hand, it could be that he was guilefully telling each side what they wanted to hear – Baldwin that he had an opportunity to force the King to abdicate, and the King that he had a chance to overturn the Government. In any case, if Hardinge's letter was supposed to help the situation, as it turned out, it was a grave miscalculation – Edward was in no mood to be swayed by its more-in-sorrow-than-in-anger, remonstrating tone. Indeed, in his neurotic and increasingly traumatised state, if anything, it pushed him in the opposite direction.

Baldwin had another audience with the King on 16 November, this time bringing up the subject of his marriage to Mrs Simpson. Edward told Baldwin that this was not negotiable, he intended to marry her and that was all there was to it. Baldwin expressed his surprise and shock at the news (although, as we have seen, Ernest's Grand Master had told him about it nine months before), responding that the marriage would not meet with the approval of his subjects. (Phillip Guedalla points out that throughout the crisis Baldwin repeatedly told the King that both Parliament and the people did not want Wallis to be Queen – but never provided any evidence to back this up. He certainly never asked Parliament or put it to the people.)[48] For the first time the word 'abdication' was used, though the two men's accounts differ on the context. Baldwin's wrote that Edward simply stated that he intended to abdicate in order to marry Mrs Simpson; Edward's version was that he said that although he did not believe that the people were against the marriage, he would abdicate if the Government opposed him.[49] The difference is vital: Edward said he used the *threat* of abdication – as he and his predecessors had in order to get their own way – whereas Baldwin's version is that Edward had announced that he was actually going to abdicate.

'SOMETHING MUST BE DONE'

Two days later the King paid a two-day visit to the mining communities of the Rhondda and Monmouth valleys in south Wales, areas particularly hard hit by the Depression. In a hectic schedule, he visited closed mines, squalid housing estates and a Labour Exchange in which lines of shabby and hopeless unemployed propped up the wall. He also made an unscheduled stop at a defunct steel works in Dowlais, where the former workforce of some 9,000 men gathered to see him – most of them still without jobs. It was here that he made his famous remark that 'Something must be done to find them work'.

He repeated this phrase more emphatically the next day, when he told the Chairman of an Unemployed Men's Committee that 'Something will be done about unemployment'.[50] A quotable soundbite, it received widespread publicity. It was a calculated and shrewd move: Edward was throwing down the gauntlet, building support with the public while daring the Government to oppose him.

Edward was priming the people before the crisis broke – but in doing so also reminding the politicians why he was so dangerous. A king might show his sympathy with the unemployed, but never promise to get something done for them. That was politics; taboo for a monarch.

After his return from Wales a way out of the crisis was suggested: a morganatic marriage, whereby Wallis would not take the status and titles of Queen, and neither would her children inherit royal titles. She would simply be the King's wife. Although fairly common among European royalty, morganatic marriage was unfamiliar ground to the British monarchy, and would therefore require Parliament to pass a special Act.

The morganatic suggestion was put to the King and Baldwin by Lord Rothermere, but via the intermediary of his son Esmond Harmsworth, who had lunch with Wallis to sound her out on the idea. Interestingly, she agreed to it in principle, perhaps an unlikely response for an ambitious woman with her sights on a right royal future. He then saw the King who agreed that Harmsworth should put the idea to the Prime Minister. Baldwin was summoned for an audience on 25 November, at which Edward asked him what he thought of it. The Prime Minister gave his informal opinion that Parliament would refuse to pass the necessary legislation – a very revealing reaction: originally, he had told the King that his only objection was to Wallis becoming Queen. But now that a way around this had been suggested, in Guedalla's words, Baldwin 'appeared reluctant to consider means by which the consequences that he feared might be avoided'.[51]

In response, Edward made the formal request that the proposal should be put to Cabinet and the Dominions' Parliaments, effectively entrusting his future to Prime Minister Stanley Baldwin. Brian Inglis writes, 'Now, indeed, the King's head was on Baldwin's block.'[52] By asking for the Cabinet to give *formal* advice on the morganatic marriage proposal Edward had bound himself to accept that advice – and that of the Dominion Governments. He had made the fatal error of making the matter official. Indeed, it is regarded as his big tactical blunder, but had someone advised him to take this line of action – and if so, who was it? Could it have been the Machiavellian Alec Hardinge?

The King also instructed Baldwin to act as his intermediary with the Governments of the Dominions. Again, this was unnecessary as well as unconstitutional on both the part of the King and the Prime Minister: since 1931 the Dominion Parliaments had been completely independent of Westminster. This irregularity was recognised by the Cabinet who, in case the matter was raised in the Commons (although in the event it never was), had already decided to lie and announce that the Dominions were communicating directly with the King.[53]

Edward's ill-advised instruction also handed the initiative over to Baldwin – which he exploited for all it was worth. Most authorities agree that the Prime Minister gave the Dominions biased and loaded information to ensure a negative answer: for example, telling them that in his opinion the British Parliament would never pass the necessary legislation. It almost seems like an act of suicide: Edward appeared to give Baldwin every advantage to precipitate a constitutional crisis.

The popular impression today is that Edward was forced into a position where he was compelled to abdicate because the Government objected to him marrying a divorced woman. This is not the case. The Government rejected the idea of putting through the required legislation to allow him to marry morganatically. It was as simple as that. In fact, Baldwin consistently refused to be drawn into giving his formal advice on the subject of the marriage or Wallis as Queen. When he put the morganatic idea to his Cabinet, only one minister, Duff Cooper, supported it.

Lord Mountbatten, of course, could not bear to be on the sidelines of such significant events. Earlier in the year he had returned from the Mediterranean to take up, in Ziegler's words, a 'phenomenally early promotion'[54] to the Admiralty. His friendship with Edward continued, although with his new role as King and his relationship with Wallis, there was little time for the two to socialise. At this time it was the Duke of Kent who was Mountbatten's 'closest ally'[55] in the royal family.

The Duke and Duchess of Windsor's biographer Michael Bloch comments that Mountbatten 'suffered from extraordinary inaccuracies of memory'[56] in later accounts of his role in the abdication, claiming to have been present during the fateful discussions at Fort Belvedere in the final weekend of Edward's reign. He wasn't. (He also said that the Windsors failed to invite him to their wedding: the correspondence proves that they did.) Mountbatten adopted his usual strategy of backing both sides until he was sure what the outcome would be. In the beginning of the crisis he and Edwina were Edward and Wallis's closest supporters within the royal family.[57] Mountbatten's inside source of information in the Palace was the King's ADC, Charles Lambe.[58]

Mountbatten thought that he could swing the matter in Edward's favour. On 25 November – the day the King put the morganatic marriage proposal to Baldwin – via the unlikely intermediary of the extreme left-wing MP John Strachey, he approached Claud Cockburn, editor of *The Week*, a left-wing publication with a small but influential circulation. Mountbatten offered Cockburn, in the latter's words, 'certain "inside information" of a particularly sensational character,' emanating from the King himself, that would turn events in his favour.[59] Cockburn agreed to hold *The Week*'s presses until the ultimate scoop arrived. Throughout the night of 25–6 November they waited and waited. Finally, in the early hours of the morning, a messenger arrived with an envelope that contained a single sheet of paper bearing the message, 'The situation has developed too fast.'[60]

Perhaps Mountbatten had heard that Edward had now made the matter official, and so decided to hedge his bets. But, whatever the nature of his 'sensational' scoop, even by implication, the very hint that it existed put Mountbatten in a strong position. Maybe the threat of revealing it was enough – after all, it paved the way for a deal with one or other of the warring factions. Certainly, after this episode Mountbatten adopted a more neutral position, finally coming out in support of the Duke of York when it was clear that he would become King.

THE KING'S PARTY

If powerful figures were lined up against Edward, he too had devoted supporters, chiefly in the form of Lord Beaverbrook and Winston Churchill. As the crisis came to a head, Edward called Beaverbrook back from a visit to New York. The shrewd newspaperman advised Edward to force Baldwin to take the initiative in 'advising' him to abdicate, then refuse to accept that advice – which would compel Baldwin and his Cabinet to resign. Edward could then call on somebody more loyal to him – the ideal candidate being Winston Churchill – to form a new Government.[61] (Beaverbrook, considering it a tactical error, attempted to persuade Edward to withdraw his request for advice on the morganatic proposal, but it was too late.)

In the last days of November Beaverbrook was frantically engaged in trying to keep Edward on the throne. Beaverbrook met with Monckton, Harmsworth, the King's solicitor George Allen and his Lord-in-waiting Peregrine Brownlow, to try to persuade the King to encourage Wallis to leave the country until the situation was resolved. The next day she left for Cannes – and a traumatic dash from hotel to hotel, lying on the floor of her car, seeking refuge from popping flashbulbs. Although many sentimental French folk hailed her as a wronged woman in love, there were also death threats. Wallis's Wonderland was rapidly becoming a nightmare.

Beaverbrook wanted to involve Lloyd George, but he was in the West Indies convalescing from an illness. This was good news for the King's enemies who realised that had the old Welshman been there to rally support for the King, events might have taken an unwelcome turn, as Dawson of *The Times* admitted.[62] It was rumoured that Churchill had said that 'they would not have been able to depose Edward VIII had Lloyd George not been abroad. I alone was too weak.'[63]

Realising the danger, Baldwin had specifically forbidden maverick Churchill from seeking an audience with the King. (Any audience with a Member of Parliament needs the Prime Minister's approval.) On 27 November, after a Cabinet meeting to discuss the issue, the Secretary of

State for India and member of the Cabinet, the Marquess of Zetland, wrote:

> It seems that the King has been encouraged to believe that Winston Churchill would in these circumstances [i.e. if Baldwin and his Cabinet resigned] be prepared to form an alternative Government. If this were true there would be a grave risk of the country being divided into two camps – for and against the King.[64]

(Parliament and the public were told that all the emergency Cabinet meetings were called to discuss the civil war in Spain. The King was not shown the minutes, even though it was a constitutional requirement.)[65] The King's corner was also being fought by another influential lobby, the Imperial Policy Group, whose objectives – especially from today's perspective – seem oddly paradoxical. As they considered the Soviet Union as the greater threat, they wanted Britain to force Germany and Russia into mutual destruction: in Kenneth de Courcy's words, 'bleed each other to death'[66] while Britain watched from the wings. The Group therefore supported Edward VIII for his pro-German stance *and* opposed Baldwin for his soft line on Germany and Italy and his opposition to rearming, reasoning that a militarily strong Britain would deter Hitler, driving him to attack Russia first. Strange, too, was their idea of pairing Edward VIII as King with Churchill as Prime Minister, as they believed that the combination of Edward's pro-German views and Churchill's willingness to stand up to Hitler would be the perfect means to their end. The abdication crisis was therefore ideal, if it resulted in the King staying and the Government resigning. But Baldwin outmanoeuvred them.

One way of defusing the crisis and at least deferring it until after the coronation – if not permanently – was to challenge Wallis's divorce on the grounds that it was the result of collusion between the husband and wife and their respective lovers. Undoubtedly, the Simpson divorce was irregular – in fact, illegal – so it could easily have been stopped simply by bringing this to the court's attention. It would be impossible for Edward to marry and the crisis would be over. The fact that none of the factions opposed to Wallis becoming Queen – i.e. Baldwin's Government and the Palace 'Old Guard' led by Queen Mary – even tried to use this option shows that their overriding concern was *not that Wallis should not be Queen but that Edward should not remain King.*

However, challenging the legality of the divorce was raised elsewhere – only to be mysteriously dropped. Baldwin's Parliamentary Private Secretary met with Kenneth de Courcy, the Earl of Mansfield and the MP A.R. Wise and told them that the issue was about to resolve itself because Wallis's divorce petition was 'irregular' and steps were being taken to ensure that the decree absolute would not be granted. Indeed, a complaint to this effect was lodged by a solicitor's clerk named Francis Stephenson, but then withdrawn: what lay behind this is one of the minor mysteries about the abdication.[67]

After the trio from the Imperial Policy Group reported this to the group of MPs and Lords on the King's side, they relaxed their efforts in support of the King. De Courcy wrote many years later:

> No sooner was the abdication signed than Baldwin's representative wrote to us to deny that any such representation had been made. But I was there when it was made. It was a successful lie.[68]

At some point in the proceedings a trump card was produced – the 'China Dossier' on Wallis Simpson that had been prepared by MI5 for George V two years earlier. This was given to Baldwin, whether by MI5 or the Palace is unclear. As we have noted, many historians dismiss the existence of the Dossier as nothing more than unfounded rumour, on the grounds that there is no evidence for it in any official archive. However, in July 1950, Kenneth de Courcy (whose relationship was so close to the Duke and Duchess of Windsor that their wedding present to him that year was a pair of Georgian silver waiters inscribed with their insignia and the bride and groom's names) wrote:

> I think I should add for the record that in 1936 I heard from Mr Baldwin's supporters almost exactly the same allegations about the Duchess of Windsor's dossier as I have repeated to me by Jack Coke recently.[69]

Although de Courcy never saw the Dossier, the fact that Baldwin's supporters in 1936 and Major Sir John Coke – Queen Mary's equerry, no less – spoke about the allegations it contained is surely evidence of its existence. Indeed, after the Duke of Windsor's death, de Courcy went into more detail in a letter to the Duke's legal representative, Suzanne Blum:

> A secret dossier was prepared by (it was asserted) the Secret Service. That was shown to Queen Mary and was quoted to all important politicians except (in 1936) I think Churchill. I do not know for certain but I do not think it was used on him. It was used on me. It suggested habitual sexual deviations by the Duchess when in China and (also) political deviations and unreliability and particularly in relation to von Ribbentrop.

During later attempts to resolve the Duchess's status there was a meeting between de Courcy, representing Edward, and the royal family's representative Sir John Coke at which, according to de Courcy:

Coke told Churchill [then Prime Minister] and me that we should first consider the 1936 dossier *which Queen Mary had seen* [our italics]. He quoted it to me rather fully and stated that it was the dossier rather than the divorce that deterred Queen Mary.

I believe there was, in fact, a dossier and one which was altogether false put together by very powerful persons to persuade Baldwin and Queen Mary and to influence the Duchess of York (Queen Elizabeth the Queen Mother).[70]

This radically changes the accepted view of the abdication. When the China Dossier was first discussed in the late 1980s, official apologists suggested that de Courcy had simply invented a conspiracy, on the grounds that nobody had heard about the Dossier before. In fact he never mentioned the Dossier publicly until after the Duchess of Windsor's death, out of respect for her. His personal notes, written in 1950, tell the story.

With everything stacked against Edward and Wallis they could no longer swim against the tide. Finally the story broke in the press, although in a clever and roundabout way, using a speech by the outspoken Bishop of Bradford, A.W.F. Blunt, which criticised the King for his lack of support for the Church of England and, without giving any detail, for failing to show a good example to his subjects. This allowed the *Yorkshire Post* on the following day to tie up the loose ends by explicitly linking the Bishop's comments with the Simpson headlines in the American press. The taboo had gone: on 3 December all the national newspapers ran with the story. The British public was stunned, not least because they were the last to know.

Now that the story was out, Edward wanted to put his side to the British people in a radio broadcast, for which he had to have the Government's consent. The Cabinet decided against it, probably because he was still far too popular and might easily mobilise opinion on his side. By now the response from the Dominions had come in. They were unanimously against the morganatic marriage – but not the marriage itself because they were never asked about it. Now the crunch had finally arrived: millions waited with bated breath as Edward VIII decided whether to give up Wallis or the throne.

It was a stark choice. If Edward refused to renounce Mrs Simpson, then either the King or the Government had to go. And Baldwin had already obtained promises from the two opposition leaders, Labour leader Clement Attlee and the Liberals' Sir Archibald Sinclair, that they would not agree to form an alternative government if Edward sent for them. The fact that he sought these promises is revealing: as Baldwin had adamantly refused to give advice on the issue of the marriage, there was no danger of his Government having to resign when that advice was declined. So why did he need the reassurance of the leaders of the opposition? It could only be to neutralise the King's option of dismissing his government – a power the sovereign retains, although it had not been used for 102 years.

The only way out of this unprecedented impasse was if a new party was formed to fight specifically on the issue of the King's abdication. A King's Party . . .

The day after the story broke nationally for the first time Baldwin laid the matter before the House of Commons, and in doing so, also before the people. However, he largely misled them about the real issue, concentrating on the Government's and Dominions' rejection of the morganatic marriage proposal. This gave the impression that the only issue at stake was whether Wallis should be Queen – Baldwin never mentioned that the alternative was abdication. Neither had he made this clear to his Cabinet.[71] The first time that the word 'abdication' was voiced publicly was in *The Times*' editorial the following day.

Churchill made a plea that no 'irrevocable decision' should be made without a Parliamentary debate on the matter and asked for more time for all sides to think. Neither was to happen; Parliament was never allowed to voice its will on the subject until Edward had announced his decision to go. Baldwin refused the reasonable request for time to reflect, preferring to keep the pressure on the King – once again suggesting that his own agenda was to force the crisis to a head.

Edward then formally asked Baldwin that he be allowed to summon Churchill, and the Prime Minister agreed. That evening Churchill dined at the Fort with the King, Monckton, George Allen and the Keeper of the Privy Purse, Sir Ulick Alexander. Characteristically, Churchill was full of fiery fighting talk, urging Edward to stick to his guns and let the Government resign. He would then be appointed Prime Minister, ask for a dissolution of Parliament and fight a general election as the leader of a King's Party. Edward agreed to this.[72] Churchill left well after midnight, his parting words being, 'Sir, it is a time for reflection. You must allow time for the battalions to march.'[73] He returned to London to write a public statement appealing for more time to resolve the crisis and pleading with the Government not to pressurise the King into making a hasty decision – or what he called a 'hastily extorted' abdication. Churchill wrote, 'If the King refuses the advice of his Ministers, they are free to resign. They have no right to put pressure on him by soliciting beforehand assurances from the Leader of the Opposition that he will not form any alternative government.'[74]

However, after Churchill travelled back to London to organise the King's campaign, Edward had a change of heart and decided not to confront Baldwin – but his reasons remain unknown. Perhaps he just got cold feet, his confidence suddenly deserting him (as it did throughout his life). This was characteristic – bursts of energetic and decisive action followed by an attack of self-doubt. That night he decided, in Inglis's words, that 'the risks of calling a King's Party into being were too great'.[75] The next morning, Saturday, 5 December, he told Monckton that he had decided to abdicate. Baldwin was summoned to the Fort. He called a Cabinet meeting for the next day.

Despite Churchill's fighting talk, Edward seemed to doubt that the people were really behind him. Ironically, his retreat to the country to escape the pressures had proved a major psychological mistake, making him feel more isolated than he really was. In fact, public support for Edward was high that weekend.[76] It is a measure of the strange regard in which Edward was held (and a testimony to his own qualities and the success of Stamfordham's policies after the First World War) that during that weekend both the British Union of Fascists and the Communist Party organised marches and rallies in his support.[77] The fact that the Communist Party was marching to *keep* a King on the throne is, in itself, more than a little surreal. But they saw the crisis as an attempt by a Tory-controlled Government and the Establishment to get rid of someone who dared to ask too many awkward questions about the plight of the workers.

The only account of what went on in the King's mind that night – 'a night of soul-searching', as he called it[78] – is Edward's own, published in his memoirs in 1951. Of course, allowances must be made for his desire to justify himself after the event, but at least it reveals what was important to him at the time:

> Even though I might have been able to recruit a commanding majority, I could not have persuaded the entire nation and all the Dominions . . . By making a stand for myself, I should have left the scars of a civil war. A civil war is the worst of all wars. Its passions soar highest, its hatreds last longest. And a civil war is not less a war when it is fought in words and not in blood. The price of my marriage under such circumstances would have been the infliction of a grievous wound on the social unity of my native land and on that wider unity of the Empire.[79]

Although he acknowledged that he would emerge from the crisis still as King, he would have been the ruler of a 'riven and divided' nation.[80] In his memoirs, Edward declared that he was not prepared to overturn the Government and the social order. However, the evidence of his reign, and indeed his time as Prince of Wales in the 1930s, shows that this was exactly what he *was* prepared to do, although he tried to take the credit for *stopping* this happening in his later writings. In the end, it appears that his nerve failed him, perhaps conscious of the enormity of what he was about to do and the uncertainty of the consequences as he moved into uncharted waters in the relationship between the Sovereign, the Government and the people.

Edward spoke of a 'civil war', although one of words and not blood. But was this a real possibility? Just over a week later – three days after he departed from Britain – the newly created Duke of Windsor received a letter from a friend, Colin Davidson, an official in the House of Lords, which included the words:

WAR OF THE WINDSORS

> I must humbly express my intense admiration for your obvious and
> inflexible determination not to encourage a 'King's Party'. It was
> within your power to create Civil War and chaos. You had only to lift
> a finger or even to come to London and show yourself, to arouse
> millions of your subjects to your support.[81]

The fact that Edward chose to quote this letter in his memoirs suggests that
he *had* thought in terms of a more literally bloody civil war. (There is also an
underlying hint of pique that he wished somebody had told him about this
upswelling of public support *before* he abdicated.) But was civil war a real
possibility? From today's viewpoint it hardly seems credible, but it must be
remembered that at that time, in such an unprecedented situation, nobody
could be sure what the consequences would be, and violent civil strife had to
be considered as a very real possibility. To many the core issue would not have
been Mrs Simpson or the King's right to choose his own bride: for a good
many Britons it would have been who rules Britain.

As it was, crowds of demonstrators gathered outside Buckingham Palace
(presumably because they assumed that the King was inside) carrying placards
reading 'God Save the King – from Baldwin', 'Down with the Government'
and – most alarming of all – 'Abdication means Revolution'. Whatever might
have happened if Edward had chosen to challenge the Government and bring
about its fall, the weekend of 4–5 December 1936 was one of the rare
occasions when the ceremonial guards outside the Palace were issued with live
ammunition.[82]

Fear of civil disturbance was very much in the air. After the Cabinet
meeting on 27 November, some of the junior ministers including Alfred Duff
Cooper, Leslie Hore-Belisha and others – many of whom went on to higher
office – held their own meeting. This group, according to Duff Cooper,
considered that 'a *coup d'état* was not impossible. The Government might be
forced to resign; Churchill might take over and go to the country on a
populist platform which would cause great divisions; parliamentary
Government might disappear altogether.'[83] To add to the inflammatory
situation, the head of the British Legion, General Sir Ian Hamilton, told
Baldwin that there would be an 'ex-servicemen's revolution' if Edward
abdicated.[84] It was also recorded at the time that some army officers had
declared that they were willing to 'take up arms against the Government and
for the King'.[85]

ALTERNATIVE SCENARIOS

What would have happened if Churchill *had* formed a King's Party and
fought an election on the abdication issue? What if the King's Party had won?
Churchill would have had the power he had always felt was his destiny – and
as it would have fundamentally changed the nature of the constitutional

monarchy, giving it more overt political power, Edward also would have got what he wanted. No longer just a figurehead, he would be an active participant in the running of the country.

The titanic struggle for the balance of executive power between monarch and Parliament, which had begun in the seventeenth century, had taken place without the people being consulted. The future of the monarchy, or the extent of its powers in Government, had never been part of any political party's manifesto. But if a King's Party came to power, Edward could rightly claim that the people *had* spoken, and that it was their will that he should have some executive power and influence over Government policy. And ironically, if the King's Party had won the day, Britain would have seen a Mussolini-style Government installed with Winston Churchill at its head. But the whole strategy relied on Edward's popularity and the assumption – or hope – that the people would be sympathetic to him (as, indeed, they largely were). That is what needed to be gauged.

Public opinion is enormously difficult to assess with hindsight: there is a tendency for people to adjust their memories in the light of the outcome. (How many survivors of the war were comfortable to admit that they had supported Neville Chamberlain's stance on Nazi Germany in 1938? Although at that time the majority were firmly pro-peace, very few chose to admit as much after war broke out, and even fewer after 1945.) It is very hard to be certain today whether the King's Party could have been successful. The general view now is that before the fateful weekend, people were by and large sympathetic to the King, but that by the Monday morning public opinion had swung away from him, though what might have caused such a sudden change is unknown. (That Christmas a new carol was going the rounds of inner-city playgrounds: 'Hark the herald angels sing/Mrs Simpson's pinched our King'.)

As far as can be judged from the reports of the time – for which we are largely reliant on the press, and the newspapers of the 1930s were blatantly biased towards their owners' political views – it appears that public opinion was split. On the one hand, there was a genuine liking for Edward VIII and the belief that he would make a good king, as well as sympathy for his romantic dilemma. (Most people had no idea about his other affairs or lifestyle.) On the other, people were unsure about having Wallis as their Queen, partly because she was an American and partly because she signally failed to match the traditional, old-fashioned and starchy image of a British Queen. The one compromise that might have resolved this conflict – a morganatic marriage, to which both Edward and Wallis had agreed – had already been ruled out by Baldwin's Government before the public even got to know about the crisis.

This is presumably why Churchill made repeated appeals, both in the Commons and in print, for the King to be allowed more time to put his side of the story to the people, and for himself to organise support for the King's Party. That all-important pause did not materialise.

Many people believed that Churchill's political career had been completely destroyed by his support for Edward. But while history demonstrates conclusively that this was by no means the case, his support for Edward certainly made George VI and his Queen absolutely detest him.

Over the four days following Edward's decision to give up the throne, Fort Belvedere buzzed with frantic activity as all the legal and constitutional details were decided – including the identity of his successor. Although it is usually assumed that the crown passed automatically to Edward's oldest brother, the Duke of York, it was not a foregone conclusion. Although the British succession is set out in law, this only establishes who will succeed on the *death* of a monarch, not on voluntary abdication. In such a situation, Parliament has to pass a new Act to establish who would take the throne: in 1936 the new King could have been any member of the royal family. Indeed, when Edward told Baldwin that he was going to abdicate, the Prime Minister specifically asked him to allow the Government a few days to consider the question of his successor.[86]

The problem was the Duke of York. There was considerable uncertainty about whether he was capable of being King, given his rather too obvious nervous characteristics and lack of training for the role (when he realised he was the new King he exclaimed that he had never even seen a state paper). Although Edward's two other brothers were present throughout the deliberations at Fort Belvedere, York was conspicuously kept away.[87] Even the royal family had doubts about Bertie's suitability. In any case, he himself had made it abundantly clear that the job was not for him. In fact, when his mother told him that he was going to be King, he sobbed uncontrollably for two hours on her silver lamé shoulder.[88]

Other options were considered in those fraught four days at the Fort. One suggestion was that the Crown should pass directly to Princess Elizabeth, who if York succeeded, would be the Heir Presumptive. With Queen Mary as regent until she came of age – although Baldwin thought this inappropriate because Elizabeth was inconveniently female.

Although this rarely features in later accounts of the abdication, the most serious option considered was the Duke of Kent. He seemed to hold all the cards, with his sharp intelligence, good looks and glamorous image (after all, the people were blissfully ignorant about his private excesses) besides his very regal wife and his popularity with the people as the 'Democratic Duke'. Moreover, he also had a male heir.

Although this is another episode that has since been obscured – because of Kent's subsequent activities – there is no doubt that both the royal family and the Government seriously considered giving him the Crown. It was first revealed in two palace-approved books written by Dermot Morrah in 1947 and 1958 respectively.[89] As history demonstrates, Kent did not get the job – but why? He was Queen Mary's favourite and also the logical successor, especially given that York had been distanced from the whole scenario. It can only be because he was unacceptable to the Government, being too much like Edward – sharing the same rebellious streak and political views – for comfort. After getting rid of one troublesome King, they were loath to invite in another. This is supported by the fact that it was ultimately the Government's decision that York should get the throne.[90]

However, there was another player in this drama whom the men would ignore at their peril. Officially, the Duchess of York was out of action, suffering from a severe bout of influenza (or, as the press characteristically described it, a 'slight chill') during the critical Fort Belvedere weekend, and took no part in the deliberations – indeed, as a woman, her views would not have been sought. However, based on information given him by friends of the Queen Mother, royal author Graham Turner suggests that her illness during the crisis may have been 'tactical', and quotes one of her friend's opinions that she was thinking, 'I'll leave it to them and then take over'.

Turner writes, 'None of the people I have spoken to doubts that, during those years, the Queen Mother heartily detested Mrs Simpson and "helped put the bullets in the gun", as one of her ladies-in-waiting put it.'[91] However, it is impossible to assess the scenario with any accuracy because there is a continuing embargo on papers relating to the Duchess of York's part in the abdication crisis – which is somewhat intriguing. If she played no significant role, why are the papers still withheld?

Following her death as Queen Mother in 2002, the Government began to review her previously withheld files to decide which ones might be released, although this only applied to files over 30 years old. Of some that related to the abdication crisis, it was stated that they had been closed because their release would have caused the Queen Mother 'substantial distress'.[92] As she was supposed to be *hors de combat* at the time, this is particularly intriguing. But the content of the files, while clearly significant, must remain the subject of speculation because they are still withheld.

Then there is the mystery of Walter Monckton's papers, which he instructed should be made public in the year 2000. In the event, however, one box was held back because it contained material relating to the Duchess of York. Clearly, when Monckton made his will, he did not anticipate that she would still be alive in 2000. Given Monckton's key role throughout the crisis and his inside knowledge of all the intrigue, it is not outside the bounds of probability that those papers, too, revealed something about the Queen Mother's role that clashed with the received version. (Although, as we shall see, there may be other factors to take into consideration.)

Several royal commentators suspect Elizabeth of having exerted a much more unequivocal influence, not only over the choice of her husband as Edward's successor, but also on the critical chain of events leading to the abdication. Although evidence is hard to come by, there may be a clue in the fact that Geoffrey Dawson of *The Times* was such a key figure in swinging opinion against Edward – indeed, some, such as Beaverbrook, openly accused Dawson of conspiring with Baldwin to oust the King. Therefore it may well be significant that one of the directors of *The Times*, and a friend of Dawson's, was Elizabeth's favourite brother, David Bowes-Lyon, himself no stranger to intrigue.

THE FINAL ACT

On 10 December, Edward signed an Instrument of Abdication, which was then taken to the Commons. The legislation freeing the King of his constitutional duties and responsibilities – His Majesty's Declaration of Abdication Act – was rushed through by a packed and awe-struck House with the full weight of history on its shoulders. By two o'clock in the afternoon the Act had become law, and was taken for the Royal Assent – Edward's final act as King.

That evening Edward made his historic broadcast to the nation, speaking heartfelt words (partly written by Winston Churchill), most memorably: 'You must believe me when I tell you that I have found it impossible to carry the heavy burden of responsibility and discharge my duties as King as I would wish to do without the help and support of the woman I love.' Many a tear was wept throughout the kingdom, but equally there were others who were outraged by the apparent dereliction of duty and abandonment of the greatest sacred trust. And many echoed Queen Mary's disbelieving words: 'To give up all this – *for that* . . .'

That night, Kenneth de Courcy noted his reactions:

> I am shocked and appalled: the King has abdicated. All our efforts have been in vain.
>
> They were determined to force him out. He was very difficult on his part.
>
> But I greatly liked him and more importantly his Foreign, Strategic and Defence Policy was correct. That is what they did not at all like.
>
> Baldwin is lazy: Eden a bad and vain man.
>
> Disaster will follow.
>
> I did my best. I spoke to Churchill and John Buchan [Lord Tweedsmuir, the Canadian Governor-General] in Canada. I saw Salisbury and the Bishop of London. I mobilised everyone I could in both the House of Lords and the House of Commons.
>
> I expect a disaster will follow. First Germany and then of course Russia. I fear for the British Empire.[93]

There are three main views of what really lay behind the abdication. The opinion of the majority was that it was purely and simply about Edward marrying a woman whom the Government regarded as unsuitable. A less popular explanation was that Baldwin (and others), who never wanted Edward as King, used the Wallis issue to get rid of him, turning an awkward but not irresolvable situation into a crisis that could only end with his

Queen Mary visiting her German relatives shortly before the First World War

A young Prince of Wales during the First World War

A young Mountbatten before
he changed his name

Louis F. Battenberg.
1916.

BY THE KING.

A PROCLAMATION

Declaring that the Name of Windsor is to be borne by His Royal House and Family and relinquishing the use of all German Titles and Dignities.

GEORGE R.I.

WHEREAS WE, having taken into consideration the Name and Title of Our Royal House and Family, have determined that henceforth Our House and Family shall be styled and known as the House and Family of Windsor:

AND WHEREAS We have further determined for Ourselves and for and on behalf of Our descendants and all other the descendants of Our Grandmother Queen Victoria of blessed and glorious memory to relinquish and discontinue the use of all German Titles and Dignities:

AND WHEREAS We have declared these Our determinations in Our Privy Council:

NOW, THEREFORE, We, out of Our Royal Will and Authority, do hereby declare and announce that as from the date of this Our Royal Proclamation Our House and Family shall be styled and known as the House and Family of Windsor, and that all the descendants in the male line of Our said Grandmother Queen Victoria who are subjects of these Realms, other than female descendants who may marry or may have married, shall bear the said Name of Windsor:

And do hereby further declare and announce that We for Ourselves and for and on behalf of Our descendants and all other the descendants of Our said Grandmother Queen Victoria who are subjects of these Realms, relinquish and enjoin the discontinuance of the use of the Degrees, Styles, Dignities, Titles and Honours of Dukes and Duchesses of Saxony and Princes and Princesses of Saxe-Coburg and Gotha, and all other German Degrees, Styles, Dignities, Titles, Honours and Appellations to Us or to them heretofore belonging or appertaining.

Given at Our Court at Buckingham Palace, this Seventeenth day of July, in the year of our Lord One thousand nine hundred and seventeen, and in the Eighth year of Our Reign.

GOD SAVE THE KING.

LONDON: Printed by EYRE AND SPOTTISWOODE, LIMITED, Printers to the King's most Excellent Majesty.

Self photographing John.

The Prince of Wales with his youngest brother John

The Prince of Wales with Elizabeth Bowes-Lyon – rumours
of their engagement were leaked by the press

Edward VIII visiting working-class areas to see conditions for himself

A Cecil Beaton portrait
of Wallis Simpson

The Archbishop of Canterbury after leaving Downing Street during the abdication crisis

The Duke of York furtively returning from a clandestine meeting with Prime Minister Stanley Baldwin

Support for the King demonstrating public belief that Baldwin was behind the plot

INSTRUMENT OF ABDICATION

I, Edward the Eighth, of Great
Britain, Ireland, and the British Dominions
beyond the Seas, King, Emperor of India, do
hereby declare My irrevocable determination
to renounce the Throne for Myself and for
My descendants, and My desire that effect
should be given to this Instrument of
Abdication immediately.

In token whereof I have hereunto set
My hand this tenth day of December, nineteen
hundred and thirty six, in the presence of
the witnesses whose signatures are subscribed.

SIGNED AT
FORT BELVEDERE
IN THE PRESENCE
OF

The document by which Edward VIII informed
the Government that he would abdicate

The young Princess Elizabeth with Lord Mountbatten

Lord Mountbatten with his
nephew in 1948

renouncing the throne. As we have noted, much of what Baldwin did at that time, such as totally ignoring possible compromises and resisting pressure for more time to think, bears this out. In particular, de Courcy's evidence that Baldwin lied about stopping the Simpsons' divorce in order to lull the King's supporters into a false sense of security can only be explained by the Prime Minister's desire to see the back of the troublesome monarch. Forty years later, shortly after the Duke of Windsor's death, de Courcy wrote to the Duke's legal representative, Suzanne Blum:

> The main case against King Edward VIII was never really matrimonial. That was only a convenient excuse. Very powerful factions wished to get rid of him for political reasons too complicated here to recite.
> In using the matrimonial excuse the very highest circle did *not* secretly argue the divorce *as such*.[94]

However, this is not the whole story. While there seems little doubt that Baldwin *did* want to get rid of Edward, this fails to explain why the King himself was ridiculously keen to provide an easy target for the Prime Minister – by unnecessarily asking for his formal and binding advice and allowing him, rather than the Palace, to seek the advice of the Dominion Governments. This could be explained by the third view: Edward himself had no desire to be King and used the Wallis issue as a way out – which is why he handed Baldwin the means to turn the issue into a constitutional crisis. After all, Edward repeatedly stated during his years as Prince of Wales that he never wanted the job (although sometimes this may have been his depression speaking, for at other times he wanted to be a new kind of king). This idea is also supported by Monckton, who later said that Edward had decided to give up the throne even before his father died – although, significantly, the lawyer also said that he was unaware of this until the very end of the crisis.[95]

However, there is a quite different interpretation, one that has very far-reaching implications for any in-depth analysis of the abdication. We believe that the real answer is not that Baldwin exploited the Wallis issue to force Edward out: but that Edward was attempting to exploit it to force the *Government* out, so that he could replace it with one that was more to his liking, one that would fundamentally change the constitutional system of Government. This would have effectively given the King more power: as things stood, he had virtually none, being prevented from publicly challenging the Government on issues of domestic or foreign policy. To try to do so under the existing system would have lost him sympathy in the country.

This explains some otherwise curious aspects to the whole affair. Throughout the crisis Baldwin and the Cabinet, although making their objection to his marriage to Mrs Simpson known, never formally advised him not to marry her. If they had done so, and Edward refused to accept their advice – as he had made absolutely clear he would – Baldwin and his Government would have no choice but to resign immediately. Edward was trying to goad Baldwin into formally opposing the marriage and the Prime Minister was doing his utmost to avoid actually doing so. The whole object of the exercise from Edward's point of view was to get rid of the Government. The Wallis issue was a convenient battleground, making it seem as if Baldwin and the Government had precipitated the crisis, so they would be blamed by the public. But it seems that Edward lost heart at the last moment – did Baldwin or the Duchess of York threaten to give the China Dossier to the press?

It appears that the plan to change the constitutional landscape of the country had been jointly worked out by Edward and the Duke of Kent: even before the issue had reached the stage of a political crisis in mid-November, Kent seems to have been anticipating a momentous event. Chips Channon recorded a remark that Kent made in relation to the King at a dinner party, that 'in a month or six weeks' time something terrific will happen. I wish I could tell you now.'[96] It also seems that it had been recognised from the beginning that this game of brinkmanship with Baldwin and his Government could fail, with the result that Edward would be forced to abdicate – but there appears to have been a back-up plan for Edward to abdicate in favour of Kent, who held the same political views and objectives.

However, there is certain evidence to suggest that Baldwin recognised that this would happen – and had already taken steps to prevent it. The day before the story broke publicly, on 2 December, R.A. ('Rab') Butler, Under Secretary of State at the India Office, wrote to Lord Brabourne, Governor of Bombay:

> He [Edward VIII] will abdicate and will be succeeded by a dull dog, who will hold the declining influence of the Church and whose fortune will be linked with that of the middle class.'

By no stretch of the imagination could the Duke of Kent be described as a 'dull dog'! But more tellingly, the next day (3 December) Harold Nicolson, the MP who was to become George VI's official biographer, recorded in his diary:

> The Cabinet met all day. I gather that Attlee and Sinclair have both refused to form alternative governments and that the king will be forced to abdicate. The Duke of York will call himself 'King George VI' . . .'[97]

This is highly significant – and not merely because Nicolson notes that Edward VIII would be *forced* to abdicate. The very day that the crisis became public knowledge, and the two days before the King decided to go, Nicolson was only too aware that he would be succeeded by York but also what name he would take, when the new King is not supposed to have decided until after the following weekend. (The reason for taking the name George was that Albert was considered too German.[98])

During the fateful weekend of 4–5 December, while the King, his advisers and the Dukes of Kent and Gloucester were locked away at Fort Belvedere thrashing out the details of the succession, the Duke of York was deliberately kept at a distance. However, in 1940, the then George VI told Lord Halifax that he had had four secret meetings with Baldwin during that period, being taken in an anonymous car to the garden entrance of No. 10 Downing Street.[99]

All this suggests that Baldwin was manoeuvring to ensure that the malleable Bertie would succeed his troublesome elder brother – and even that his name as sovereign (an adroit link to his respected father) had been decided in advance. And of course, as early as 15 October, Hardinge had taken it upon himself to inform York that he may be called upon to assume the throne. All this demonstrates that the forcing of Edward VIII from the throne and his replacement by Bertie seemed to have been worked out by Baldwin and Hardinge – and presumably others – well in advance of the crisis being made public.

So it was that the Duke of York became King George VI, and his deceptively fluffy little wife finally achieved her great ambition to be the Queen Empress, although the nightmare of the Duke and Duchess of Windsor remained to haunt her for many years yet.

Although Edward VIII is generally written off as an ineffective hysteric who made little real mark on history, the truth is rather different. In fact, his presence on the British throne was an important part of the Nazi game plan for territorial expansion: indeed, it may be significant that Hitler took his first step in confronting the major powers of Europe by reoccupying the Rhineland soon after Edward came to the throne. It would have been a test not only of how the other nations would react, but also how useful Edward VIII would be. His early threat to abdicate if the Government responded militarily showed that he was a valuable ally. What would have happened if he had still been on the throne when the Nazis invaded Poland in 1939? Would he have threatened to abdicate – or refusal to give his assent to the declaration of war? Windsor consistently declared, as in 1940, 'Of course, if I'd been King there'd have been no war,'[100]

There was no reason for the Nazis to believe that Edward, who was only in his early 40s, would not continue to reign for many years – certainly long enough for the immediate unfolding of their agenda. Therefore his abdication came as a considerable shock to Hitler. His importance to the Nazi plan can be detected in their reactions to the crisis and its outcome. At von Ribbentrop's request, Hitler ordered the German press not to make too much of the crisis and to avoid all comment on the subject (if the Nazis took Edward's side it could be used by the King's opponents in Britain).[101] Mussolini adopted the same tactic.

Von Ribbentrop recorded his view of the abdication crisis in his diary: 'I was very depressed and wracked my brains for a possible way in which to influence the course of events . . . King Edward VIII had shown himself a potential advocate of Anglo-German understanding, therefore it lay in our interests that he should remain King'.[102]

In fact, von Ribbentrop had requested an audience with the King during the crisis, but was blocked by Hardinge. During those turbulent days, Hitler personally instructed von Ribbentrop to do everything in his power to prevent the King abdicating.[103] Afterwards, Ribbentrop reported back, advising the Führer that he now doubted any 'understanding' could be reached with Britain, adding with enormous significance, 'Baldwin has already apprehended this, and Edward had to abdicate since it was not certain whether he could co-operate with an anti-German policy.'[104] This summary of the situation is remarkable for the fact that Mrs Simpson is not even mentioned.

Hitler himself had no doubts about who was responsible. This was why, two years later, while watching a newsreel on the visit of George VI and his Queen to Paris, he declared Elizabeth to be 'the most dangerous woman in Europe'.[105]

IMPLICATIONS FOR BRITAIN

The abdication crisis may be seen as the final triumph of politicians over the monarch, the end of a 300-year-old power struggle. Although virtually all executive power had been removed from the monarchy, the Windsor Kings of the early twentieth century still could and did exercise political influence in a behind-the-scenes way – as we have seen, exploiting constitutional loopholes and acquiescent prime ministers – in ways that would be unthinkable in the reign of the present queen and her father, George VI.

Faced with a King who wanted to go even further than his father and claw back some *overt* influence over the running of the country, the politicians reacted sharply. By getting rid of Edward, refusing to make the equally troublesome Duke of Kent his successor and giving the throne to the introverted and easily controllable (or so they thought) Duke of York, the Government had effectively rendered the monarchy politically impotent: from now on the spirit of the constitution would be enforced as well as the letter.

Edward sailed away across the English Channel on HMS *Fury*. Only two British kings have ever abdicated: Edward voluntarily and the Catholic James II when he was deposed – and they both left the country on 11 December, exactly 148 years apart.

FIVE

'THE MOST UNCONSTITUTIONAL ACT'

John Grigg on George VI's reaction to the Munich Agreement

When Edward sailed off into voluntary exile it was not the end of his political ambition in Britain – rather the reverse. Most of what he had wanted to achieve as King had been blocked by the Government or the Palace, always with the same excuse: the constitution would not allow it. But now, although other members of the immediate royal family were still constrained within constitutional limits, Edward found himself with more freedom to take an active political and social role. Far from running away from his grand plans, the new Duke of Windsor fully intended to pursue the work he had started as King. Indeed, this may have been a factor in his decision to abdicate: while ridding himself of the inconveniences of being a constitutional monarch he could still exploit his royal status and popularity to achieve his long-term goals. The fact that his replacement was the weak-willed and easily influenced Bertie only reinforced his belief that he could still play a leading role in guiding Britain into the future.

Having agreed to a two-year voluntary exile, Windsor fully believed he would be allowed to return to Britain – presumably to his beloved Fort Belvedere – and be handed some crucial role within the royal family. But soon he was to discover, to his great disbelief and distress, that this was a radically wrong interpretation of the situation, not to mention of the people involved.

Significantly, in late 1937, just a year after his abdication, he gave an interview to the *Daily Herald* – which the authorities ensured never saw the light of day – in which he said that in the event of a Labour Government coming to power he would be willing to become Britain's first President.[1] This is a remarkably clear statement of intent, which is usually overlooked by most accounts of his life. Obviously, his ambitions had taken a new turn. (It is also interesting in that he seems to have assumed that it was only a matter of time before Britain became a republic, which fits his statement of a couple of years later that he believed the age of constitutional monarchies had passed.)

However, this was not a revelation that was exclusive to him alone: it had also occurred to the Government and the new guiding forces of the royal family: the two queens, Mary and Elizabeth.[2] Much of the stand that they took against the Windsors, which is usually described as 'punishment' for having let his country and family down, is more easily explained by their desire to ensure that the Duke's days were numbered as a *political* force. While Windsor remained convinced that he still had an important role to play, he was oblivious to the fact that the powers that be would move heaven and earth to ensure that he and his wife would be virtual exiles for the rest of their lives.

The first of the Government's moves against him was to get him to agree to stay out of the country for a two-year period. During this absence, under pressure from the Palace and the Government, the British newspapers and newsreels treated the Duke and Duchess of Windsor virtually as 'non-persons'. Clearly, the hope was that those sections of the public who had fond memories of Edward – ex-servicemen and Welsh miners, for example – would forget all about him. The big guns were out: the Government then restricted his ability to re-enter Britain even after the two-year 'exile' had elapsed by using money almost as blackmail.

SKULDUGGERY AND SHARP PRACTICE

Following Edward's decision to abdicate the royal family hotly debated their favourite subject – money. How should a despised ex-King with a hated wife be provided for? As might be expected, the negotiations were bitter, one side intending on granting as little as possible and the other on taking as much as it could grab. In the cold light of history, the ensuing negotiations are remarkable for the fact that both Bertie and Edward were flagrantly dishonest, although predictably attention is usually only drawn to Windsor's duplicity: certainly, he lied to his brother and family. But the new King lied, or tried to lie, to the Government.

At the outset, Edward declared to his brother that he was 'very badly off' and tried, unsuccessfully, to have George V's will changed so that he could get his hands on some of the royal legacy.[3] (As he would inherit the Duchy of Lancaster as King, as well as the private estates of Sandringham and Balmoral, his father had left him no money.) Before Edward left England, George VI had agreed to pay him £25,000 a year in exchange for the properties. This agreement was put in writing and signed by both brothers. That, it seemed, was that.

Within a few weeks it became apparent that Edward had lied about his relative poverty and that the immense fortune he had accrued from the Duchy of Cornwall would be more than adequate – in fact, he had no real need for the annuity at all. (Perhaps curiously, Edward seems not to have been a particularly big spender before he met Wallis.) This revelation, and the mendacity of the ex-King, also angered Churchill.

In the early part of 1937 the House of Commons set about working out the new Civil List, as is customary at the start of a reign. A Select Committee was appointed to assess how much George VI's Civil List income should be, which entailed finding out what he received from other sources. The Duke of Windsor wrote at this time (setting out royal attitudes to their finances – a principle followed by every monarch from Victoria to the present Queen) that it would be a 'grave mistake if the private means of any member of the Royal Family were to be disclosed to the Select Committee'.[4] In other words, if Parliament found out what they were really worth, then their customary pleas of needing more cash would fall on deaf ears.

At this stage, George VI proposed that he and Edward tear up their December 1936 agreement so he could inform the Select Committee that he had never agreed to pay the Duke of Windsor anything – in the hope that Parliament would pay up instead. With some justification, Phillip Hall calls this 'a form of sharp practice'.[5] If Parliament refused to pay, George promised that he would honour the December agreement, though by this time Edward was not inclined to trust his brother's word and refused to agree. (In the event, the Government was adamant that Windsor should get nothing from the Civil List.)

The Government and the King attempted to make any annuity conditional on Windsor not returning to Britain without George's permission, which would only be granted on the advice of his ministers. In other words, the Government would decide if and when the ex-King could set foot on English soil. Not surprisingly, Windsor was incandescent with rage, realising that this was a thinly disguised ploy to prevent him picking up his political agenda.

Yet in some ways he still had the upper hand, being the legal owner of the private estates, so eventually a compromise was reached. George VI paid Windsor £300,000 (around £7 million today) for Sandringham and Balmoral, which was put in trust, from which £10,000 a year (around a quarter of a million pounds today) would be paid to the Duke. The King would pay him an additional £11,000 annually from his own pocket – this part being conditional on asking permission to enter the country.[6]

Under cover of the discussions over Windsor's financial settlement and the re-negotiation of the Civil List, George managed to slip in a deal that finally and completely absolved him of paying income tax. As we have seen, his father ensured that the monarch no longer paid tax on any private income other than those dividends that were taxed at source. George VI had his advisers approach the Inland Revenue directly. They, generously and for no apparent reason, agreed that the King no longer need pay tax on this income (i.e. the Revenue would refund the tax deducted at source to him), provided ministerial approval was given.

The Chancellor of the Exchequer, Neville Chamberlain, agreed to this arrangement – but on what principle is, as usual, shrouded in secrecy. The Treasury's file covering this period was not released to the Public Record Office in the normal way and when in 1991 Phillip Hall persuaded an MP to ask a Question in the House of Commons on the subject, he was told that as the result of a 'clerical error', the file had been accidentally destroyed in the 1970s.[7] This is blatant evasion – after all, presumably there were copies of the missing documents held by the Inland Revenue and the royal family. So all we know is that the King stopped paying tax entirely, but we remain ignorant of the constitutional or legal justification for this convenient arrangement.

George VI also continued the other hallowed royal tradition of transferring money from the Civil List to the Privy Purse – in other words siphoning off funds that were meant to be used in the public's interest into his own pocket.[8]

In 1937 and 1938 George asked his brother-in-law, David Bowes-Lyon, whose career is shrouded in secrecy, to help establish trusts for his daughters in a way that would avoid them paying tax (the exemption he had arranged only applied to him, not to other members of the family). The trusts, to be given to the princesses when they reached 21, were, it is thought, set up using money from a surplus in his Civil List allowance. Princess Elizabeth's trust was started off with £7,000 (over £150,000 today), with £1,000 (over £20,000 today) added each quarter, the money being deposited in a private account at Baring's Bank in the King's name. This account was used so that, following his secret deal with the Inland Revenue, the interest would no longer be subject to tax. He wrote to Bowes-Lyon: 'This will save all taxes as the money is really mine.' Princess Elizabeth's Civil List allowance of £6,000 a year (approaching £140,000 today), in place of the Duchy of Cornwall income that would have been hers had she been male, was also invested in the trust, although this was largely tax-exempt anyway.[9]

George VI's financial manoeuvrings over the trusts were quite unlike his previous modus operandi – and his father's – in their efforts to avoid paying tax on their private income. Their earlier moves were certainly ethically questionable, involving a bending of the law and constitution that was never likely to be put to the test in a court of law. In other words, they used their position to improve their personal finances while remaining on the right side of the law, if only just. More obviously, the method by which the princesses' trusts claimed their income as the King's is flagrant tax evasion, which in the United Kingdom, then as now, was a criminal offence that for others carried stiff penalties, including custodial sentences.

As his letter makes clear, George VI put the princesses' trust money into an account in his own name because otherwise it would be liable for income tax – that is tax evasion, analogous to giving money paid to oneself to a foreign national living in London to bank because they are exempt from UK tax. George's plaintive statement that 'the money is really mine' is nonsense: as soon as he handed it over to the trust legally it belonged to that trust. This is a flagrant breach of British law and if an ordinary individual were to do this he would be prosecuted.

This scheme would have been impossible to expose because of the strict secrecy surrounding royal finances – although undoubtedly Crown immunity would have been invoked if it had been discovered. (However, David Bowes-Lyon was also party to the conspiracy and he would not have been covered by Crown immunity.) How much tax this deprived the Inland Revenue of in the ten years before Princess Elizabeth came of age is impossible to calculate given the scant information available – but a major question remains: since this affair came to light, what has been done to recover the tax?

A GRAVE FALLING OUT

Initially, relations between the two brothers were amicable, but they soon deteriorated as George fell yet further under the influence of the two great Windsor matriarchs, his mother and his wife. Another important influence over the new King was the Palace 'Old Guard' – Hardinge, Lord Wigram (whom he had quickly recalled) and Lascelles, who moved hastily to reassert the old order. Chips Channon wrote that George VI and Queen Elizabeth were the 'puppets of a royal clique',[10] although she, at least, was soon to redress the balance.

Crowned on the day scheduled for his brother's coronation, 12 May 1937, the hesitant George VI found all eyes upon him. After the traumas of Edward VIII's brief reign, the monarchy returned to the much more structured and stuffy style of George V. Temperamentally, Bertie was ideally suited to step into his father's shoes (which is probably why Kent failed to be offered the throne). In fact, the new King's style was almost an imitation of his father's: he was staid, dull, irascible and fixated on routine and formality. (In Brendon and Whitehead's words, in character he was a 'virtual replica' of George V.[11]) It was a very unexciting court, but at least the state papers remained innocent of cocktail stains.

Having basked briefly in the golden glow of Edward's charisma, at first most of George's subjects considered him a distinct let-down. They were slow to take to him. As one commentator put it succinctly, if brutally, 'It was as if people had expected Clark Gable and they'd ended up with George Formby.'[12] Ironically, it would take a war to establish Bertie's reputation – and destroy Edward's.

Now her weaker son was King, Queen Mary could emerge as the matriarch of the royal family, although she was by no means alone in fulfilling this influential role. Lord Halifax, the Foreign Secretary – and Churchill's rival for the office of Prime Minister in 1940 – described the new Queen Elizabeth as 'a steel hand within a velvet glove'.[13] Although she had schemed for Edward's hand in marriage and failed, those who knew her well had no doubt that her ambitions remained undimmed: many observers were unequivocal about the character they detected under the gracious waving and radiant smiles. Historian John Grigg called her 'tough and ruthless', while she herself said later, 'I'm not really a nice person.'[14] During the war, Foreign Secretary Anthony Eden's Private Secretary wrote to him, 'The King is fundamentally a weak character and certainly a rather stupid one. The Queen is a strong one out of a rather reactionary stable.'[15] Another of her detractors, surprisingly, was Mary, then the Princess Royal, who referred scathingly to Elizabeth's 'cheap public smile'.[16] Of all the insights, however, perhaps the most telling comes from George VI's official biographer, John Wheeler-Bennett, who confided to his diary that there was 'a small drop of arsenic in the centre of that marshmallow'.[17]

THE WINDSORS' MARRIAGE

As it was thought advisable that Edward and Wallis should remain apart until her divorce was made absolute, she languished in the south of France while he fretted at Baron de Rothschild's Schloss near Vienna, later moving into an Austrian hotel. He was accompanied by Fruity Metcalfe, who recorded within a month of the Duke's departure from Britain that he had 'become very foreign, talking German all the time'.[18]

Not fully comprehending his change of status, he bombarded George VI with daily telephone calls giving him advice – unknown to either party, tapped by the Germans – and was shocked when he was eventually told that it had to stop. It is now known that it was Queen Elizabeth who urged her husband to take this stand against the ex-King.[19]

In his gloomy Austrian exile, Edward was buoyed up by the prospect of finally marrying 'the most wonderful woman in the world', and by occasional visits from home, including his sister the Princess Royal and the ubiquitous Mountbatten, who offered to be his best man (in return for Edward being his 15 years previously), although Windsor declined. At that time he had no reason to doubt that his brothers would attend the wedding.

(Although Mountbatten showed his customary skill for keeping in with all factions, he had switched sides during the crisis when it became apparent that Edward was on his way out. And his withholding of that 'sensational information' from *The Week* appears to have influenced the outcome. Presumably as a reward, Mountbatten was invested with the honour of a GCVO – Knight Grand Cross of the Royal Victorian Order – in the New Year's honours list. Signalling his approval further, George VI made Mountbatten his personal Naval ADC in January 1937.)

However, on the King's last-minute instructions, no members of the royal family were allowed to attend the wedding: understandably, the bridegroom was devastated and furiously angry. Mountbatten wrote to Windsor that 'others have intervened'[20] and he was not allowed to go either. (As we have seen, Mountbatten later claimed that he failed to turn up because he did not receive an invitation.) In the event, Metcalfe was best man.

Wallis having changed her name back to Warfield by deed poll beforehand, the wedding took place on 3 June 1937 (George V's birthday) at the Château de Candé, near Tours, which was owned by the notoriously pro-Nazi industrialist Charles Bedaux. French-born, he was a naturalised American. Today Windsor is routinely lambasted for choosing to accept the dubious Bedaux's hospitality, but in fact the venue was George VI's suggestion.[21] Although choosing the château was not evidence of Bedaux's influence over Windsor, it did pave the way for such influence in the future.

In the end the wedding of the century was a somewhat subdued affair, although both bride and groom smiled bravely for the cameras. She, ultra-chic as ever in a pale blue suit, was no doubt wondering what she had let herself in for, while he was battered by a maelstrom of conflicting emotions. It was the day he had longed for over months, if not years, but in the event it was, like everything in their fairy-tale story, distinctly bitter-sweet. Without his family, he felt bereft, but much worse had emanated from the Palace, as we shall see shortly.

They spent a three-month honeymoon in Carinthia in southern Austria, Vienna and Venice. The Windsors considered living in Austria and even went castle-hunting there, but eventually settled in Paris. In view of Austria's unification with Nazi Germany a year later, this must have been a relief to both the royal family and the Government.

The Duke of Kent was the first of the family to visit Edward in Austria in the summer of 1937. (The Kents were holidaying in Yugoslavia at the time.) On Queen Mary's orders, however, Marina was forbidden to accompany him – on the somewhat weird grounds that, as Marina was a foreigner, it would be inappropriate for her to be the first royal wife to visit the Duchess of Windsor. Edward was outraged, stating that he would refuse to accept a visit from Kent alone, as it would be an obvious slight to his wife. Although George VI relented, his mother put pressure on him to return to his original decision. In the end, the Duke of Kent went alone.[22]

But even the longed-for honeymoon failed to calm down the new Duke of Windsor, for something had happened just before his wedding day to cause a most serious rift with his family, one that was to last to his dying day. The Letters Patent that bestowed his title, completed just before the wedding, came as a complete shock to Edward. Contained in their formal language was a body blow to Wallis: while she would become Duchess of Windsor, she would not be granted the status of Her Royal Highness. Edward was not only beside himself with rage at this personal spite, but also of the mind that this was illegal. He was not far off the mark: certainly, it was calculated to offend and did indeed flout common law. It is clear that Queen Mary and Queen Elizabeth were behind the move, for weak-willed Bertie had promised Edward the day before he officially abdicated that Wallis would be an HRH.[23]

Edward was of royal status by birth. Although his titles, duties and privileges could be removed from him, nobody could remove that status, represented by the title His Royal Highness (any more than lesser mortals can be prevented from being addressed as 'Mr'). According to common law his wife should have automatically acquired his status upon marriage.

This was precisely the Government's objection to the morganatic marriage solution: without passing a special law she would have taken his status and become Queen. Yet somehow this – the very issue that led directly to the abdication – was suddenly forgotten. Ironically, this principle had been acknowledged by the Palace when Elizabeth had married Bertie: the official announcement stated that she would now be known as Her Royal Highness 'in accordance with the general settled rule that a wife takes the status of her husband'.[24]

When George VI drew up the Letters Patent to make Edward Duke of Windsor, they stated that he would be known as 'His Royal Highness the Duke of Windsor'. This gave the impression that he was bestowing both the Dukedom and the HRH, whereas the latter was not his to bestow or withhold. Clearly, the Duchess's attenuated title actually infringed the law, with the sole purpose of spiting her. The Duke realised this immediately, which is why it rankled so much with him for the rest of his life and why he made strenuous efforts over the years to have the decision reversed. Incredibly, George – presumably voicing a comment of his wife – was later to tell Edward that he should be grateful that he had even 'made' Wallis Duchess of Windsor,[25] which, in Donald Spoto's words, 'would be amusing were it not pathetic'.[26] (In the light of the Windsor title scandal, it is interesting that Spoto makes the point that today's Princess of Michael of Kent is an HRH, even though she is divorced and a Roman Catholic.)

Moreover, the Palace lied by declaring that the Letters Patent were an initiative of the Government. In fact, the Government had only drawn them up on the King's insistence (obviously to cover him against a charge that he and the Queen were being vindictive). George had initiated the terms of the Letters Patent himself.[27]

THE BITTEREST FEUD

The Windsors had little doubt that it was Queen Elizabeth who was behind the many humiliations heaped upon them, including the withholding of the HRH. Although this interpretation of the situation is usually ascribed to Wallis's own spite, given the evidence it is hard not to agree. George VI himself seemed to have preferred a more conciliatory line.

A long-time friend of Edward and Freda Dudley Ward, Angela Fox (whose son Edward was to play Edward VIII in the award-winning 1970s TV series *Edward and Mrs Simpson*) said that, where Wallis was concerned, the Queen was a 'very clever and devious woman'.[28] Undoubtedly, as Queen and Queen Mother – and perhaps also earlier as Duchess of York – Elizabeth had always hated Wallis, taking every opportunity to heap humiliation on her. The antipathy is usually explained as a reaction to Bertie being plunged into kingship by Edward's defection in order to marry the dreadful Mrs Simpson, but there may well have been more to it than that. Not only did Wallis repeatedly hit the headlines as 'the best-dressed woman in the world' while the Windsor women struggled for a mention in the 'worst dressed' lists, and was enviably slim, while Elizabeth was by that time over-amply cushioned – no insignificant considerations for a woman in the public eye with more than her fair share of ego – but of course Wallis had walked off with her man. Edward also had the nerve to be utterly besotted, so much so that he gave up his kingdom for this woman. That was certainly part of the secret that lay behind Elizabeth's cold spite towards the Duchess, which continued to eat away at her as the years passed and the Windsors stayed together, apparently happily enough.

The 40-year vendetta was chronicled by Palace-approved biographer Michael Thornton in his 1985 book *Royal Feud*. It caused an uproar in certain predictable circles: Thornton was even condemned by other members of the royal family, such as Prince Charles, for his indiscretion, and was frozen out of the royal circle for some time. It was only after the Queen Mother's death in 2002 that Thornton was able to reveal that she herself had co-operated with the book, although he had been compelled to bite his tongue on the subject. Thornton had cleared the project with her, through her Private Secretary, and she had authorised people in her trusted circle of friends to give information (some of which undoubtedly came from her) to the author.[29] (Interestingly, this was the same method used by Diana, Princess of Wales, with Andrew Morton, for which she was roundly condemned.)

In the summer of 1938, with the end of the ex-King's exile looming, Walter Monckton, by then the intermediary between the King and the Duke, took part in discussions with George VI and Prime Minister Neville Chamberlain about Windsor's future role. As Chamberlain seems to have taken the view that the two-year 'cooling off period' had lessened Windsor's potential for political interference, and would perhaps restore some much-needed glamour to the royal family, he was in favour of Windsor returning and taking up the same duties as any other brother of the King. In Monckton's words he should be treated as if he were 'a younger brother of the King who could take some of the royal functions off his brother's hands'.[30] George VI agreed, only to have his formidable wife oppose the very idea of Windsor being allowed to return to Britain, specifically on the grounds that his popularity (and ability) might pose a threat to the new King. Walter Monckton wrote in his diary:

> I think the Queen felt quite plainly that it was undesirable to give the Duke any effective sphere of work. I felt then, as always, that she naturally thought that she must be on her guard because the Duke of Windsor, to whom the other brothers had always looked up, was an attractive, vital creature who might be the rallying point for any who might be critical of the new King, who was less superficially endowed with the arts and graces that please.[31]

KENT'S GLITTERING PRIZE

The Duke of Kent was badly shaken by the abdication, not only because of the divisions it caused within his family but also the implications for his own political agenda, which was basically the same as Edward's. Just a fortnight after the abdication, the King's Christmas Day broadcast was cancelled but there was a close substitute: on 28 December the Duke of Kent made a broadcast to the Empire to commemorate the arrival of the first British colonists in Australia. Although not issuing from the lips of the King Emperor, Kent's speech nevertheless went down very well.

The Duke of Kent remained close to his eldest brother, but was also on good terms with George VI who, like his father and brother, availed himself of Kent's intelligence and political acumen. However, Kent's main focus at this time was the situation in Europe rather than domestic problems, and in particular one of the potential trouble spots of the imminent future.

As we have seen, Kent had been considered as Edward VIII's successor, only to be rejected in favour of Bertie. Although whether he wanted the throne is unknown – the deliberations have never been made available – very soon he was to be offered another. This was an integral part of another important agenda: a fight-back by the dispossessed royal families of Europe, who if they could not restore themselves to their old thrones at least were determined to find themselves new kingdoms. This idea appealed to those like Marina who considered such families to be more royal than the House of Windsor, though successively robbed of anywhere to reign over.

One of the obvious countries for the restoration of the monarchy was Poland, which had been created – more accurately recreated, after centuries of being absorbed into the Russian Empire – after the First World War. So it was in 1937 that there were moves to make the Duke and Duchess of Kent the first King and Queen of a new Polish royal line (in much the same way that the Greek monarchy was re-established with an imported royal family in the nineteenth century). Having lost out on the British Crown, Kent now had a second chance of becoming a king and ultra-regal Marina could restore some of the lost family prestige that she believed was her birthright.[32]

In August 1937 the Kents paid a visit to Poland: Marina was a close friend of Zoia Poklewska (whose father was Baron Alexander de Stoeckl, a Russian diplomat who escaped the Revolution), the wife of Polish industrialist Alik Poklewski. It was the Poklewskis who arranged their Polish tour, which, although not an official state visit, in every way resembled one, with George and Marina being greeted by cheering crowds. They visited several towns where Kent gave speeches praising the Polish people for having triumphed in the creation of their new nation. It was very reminiscent of Windsor's visit to Germany two months later: indeed, it seems significant that the two brothers were being fêted in Germany and Poland at more or less the same time.

Clearly, the tour was intended to introduce the Kents to the Polish people in the first move towards making them King and Queen. As Baroness Agnes de Stoeckl, Zoia Poklewska's mother, wrote in her memoirs (*All Not Vanity*, 1950): 'The Polish nation took the Duke and Duchess to their hearts, and from that moment the Duke became for many of them the future King.'[33] From then on Kent studied everything about Poland and Polish affairs, eagerly educating himself for his future role.[34] Of course this was to have a marked effect on his attitude to the war, not only as the European situation deteriorated the year after his Polish tour but also after hostilities had finally broken out.

According to British intelligence writer Richard Deacon, the idea of making Kent the King of Poland originated with Mountbatten[35] – which would make a great deal of sense, given his own dynastic ambitions. At the same time, Mountbatten himself had his heart set on becoming King of Rhineland-Westfalen, an idea he took from Peter Murphy.[36] Clearly, this never materialised because of the war.

A TOUR TOO FAR?

Charles Bedaux arranged for Windsor to make his infamous visit to Nazi Germany in October 1937, in order to study housing and working conditions in the country. The first of a two-nation visit – it was planned that he would then go to the USA for the same purpose – it was clearly, as Walter Monckton later asserted, a fact-finding exercise. But the US tour was abandoned when American unions protested about his favourable attitude to Nazi Germany.

In Germany the Windsors were entertained by the Duke of Saxe-Coburg-Gotha, Herman Göring and Rudolf Hess (Wallis and Hess's wife Ilse got on famously). Repeating his earlier modus operandi in Wales, Edward went down a German coal mine, but his most headline-grabbing meeting was undoubtedly with Hitler in the 'Eagle's Nest' at Berchtesgaden in Austria. Precisely what they discussed is unknown. The only information is a single quote by the Duchess that the main subject of their conversation was how to stop the spread of communism[37] – which perhaps fits with Edward's known views. Although the Germans took minutes of the meeting, the records were removed by the Allies at the end of the war, and – like so many key documents relating to the royals at that time – these have never been made public. It is believed they ended up at the Royal Archives at Windsor, from which they have yet to emerge.[38]

Perhaps strangely to modern eyes, there was virtually no criticism of Windsor in Britain for his German tour, and where there was criticism it was because of his return to a public role. The event even caused something of an upsurge in his popularity due to newsreel coverage – although his Nazi salutes were censored. In fact, Winston Churchill wrote to the Duke afterwards congratulating him on his success.[39]

The Nazis, always keen to promote themselves as the party of the ordinary German people, were also careful to establish cordial relations with the dispossessed, but still important, German royals, particularly because it aided their relations with other European nations – for example, they appointed Prince Philip of Hesse-Cassel governor of Hesse and Hitler's liaison with Mussolini. They also looked favourably on the other line descended from the medieval Hesses, the Hesse-Darmstadts – Mountbatten's family. The marriage of Prince Ludwig of Hesse-Darmstadt, brother of the titular Grand Duke, to Margaret Campbell-Geddes in London in November 1937 (Prince Ludwig was attached to the German Embassy) was seen as important for cementing Anglo-German relations between the ruling classes.

Grand Duke George Donatus of Hesse-Darmstadt, his wife Cecile (Prince Philip's sister and Marina's cousin) and all but their youngest child were provided with a Junkers aircraft by the Nazi Government for the flight to London. The happy couple, together with Louis and Edwina Mountbatten and Prince Philip, were among those waiting to greet them at Croydon aerodrome, when news came through that their plane had collided with a factory chimney in fog as it attempted to land in Belgium. All on board had been killed. (Tragically, the baby daughter who had been left behind also died two years later.) The wedding went ahead – in fact it was brought forward to the day following the crash so there was no time for the grief to set in. Mountbatten was Prince Ludwig's best man and von Ribbentrop one of the witnesses.[40]

Another change in circumstances seriously affected the Mountbattens: in April 1938, George Milford Haven died of cancer and Louis took over as Philip's guardian. Although genuinely grief-stricken for the loss of his brother, the situation had played right into his hands. Now he was not only a major influence on the current royal family, but beginning to influence the next generation . . .

Mountbatten's role as 17-year-old Philip's guardian enabled him to conceive of a new plan to restore the status of his family – after all, the heir to the throne was female and would one day need a husband.

Plotting busily, Mountbatten carefully engineered Philip's first meeting with 13-year-old Princess Elizabeth. Having been persuaded by his uncle to abandon his ambition to join the RAF, and enter the Royal Navy instead, by that time Philip was a cadet at Dartmouth Naval College, which the royal family visited on the royal yacht *Victoria and Albert* on 22 July 1939. Mountbatten arranged for Philip to be entrusted with the task of entertaining the two princesses while their parents went about their official business: in a curious twist, fate seemed to be on their side, for a convenient outbreak of mumps among the cadets (which Philip somehow avoided) meant that he was the *only* cadet to whom the princesses were introduced.[41] Mountbatten also arranged for him to be invited to dinner on the royal yacht. At the end of the two-day visit, according to the custom, the cadets 'escorted' the yacht out of the harbour in a flotilla of rowing boats. Philip was the last to turn back.

The plan worked beyond even Mountbatten's wildest dreams – the blond

Viking prince utterly captivated the young princess's heart. Despite her elevated status, Elizabeth had led a sheltered and confined life; and, it seems, she developed a ferocious crush on the first handsome prince to show an interest in her. In one of her rare admissions on such a personal matter, Elizabeth II has acknowledged that she fell in love with her future husband on that first meeting.[42]

COUNTDOWN TO CONFLICT

In the second year of George VI's reign the tensions caused by Hitler's territorial ambitions significantly increased the possibility of war between Britain and Germany. The reoccupation of the Rhineland in 1936 was the first move, but from May 1938 Hitler began to work towards achieving his ambitions for Germany in earnest, precipitating a series of crises as the other nations of Europe, and particularly Britain and France, had to decide how to respond. First there was the union – Anschluss – with Austria. Then came the Czechoslovakian crisis that peaked in September 1938. Finally came the German invasion of western Poland that was to push Europe over the brink into war a year later.

Throughout this period – right up to the last minute – the royal family remained resolutely opposed to Britain's entry into a war with Germany, for all the reasons discussed in earlier chapters: their fear of the consequences for the monarchy because of the effects of war. Any German loss would be Russia's gain and it was almost inevitable that Britain would have to make an alliance with Stalin. Although this has been neatly airbrushed out of history, the King and his family would go to any lengths, short of jeopardising the support of the British people, to avoid such a war.

This needs to be set against the context of the time. There was far greater opposition to war with Germany than history now admits, and it increased in direct proportion to the social scale: at the top end there was a very substantial and influential lobby in favour of peace, although today the usual impression is that there was only a handful of cowardly 'appeasers'. However, on the whole that lobby was not pro-Nazi or in favour of surrendering Britain's sovereignty to Hitler: in fact, there was a wide spectrum of motives for being opposed to the war. Some felt strongly because of their political convictions – from those, like Oswald Mosley, who actively admired Hitler and embraced the same ideology as the Nazis, to others who, while detesting Nazism, believed that a war would only benefit what they considered to be the greater evil of communism. Yet others based their opposition on what they believed best for the long-term national interest: this too covered a wide range of views, from those who believed that, however just a war with Germany might be, Britain was doomed to lose, to those who thought that even if Britain triumphed, it would ruin the nation's economy, leading in turn to the disintegration of the Empire and a greater dependence on the USA. Other cabals sought to avoid war out of self-interest: City banks and financiers who had invested heavily in German industry, or those, like the royals and aristocrats, who dreaded the social effects of another war. But very few of these people – even the fascist Mosley – wanted to see their country beaten and invaded, and when war did finally break out, except for the small minority of actual Nazi sympathisers, most obeyed the call to arms, fought bravely and many gave their lives; indeed, their sacrifice might even be considered greater because of their views. Put simply: they had no desire for war, but if that horror was inevitable they naturally wanted Britain to win.[43]

As we know, George V strongly opposed war with Germany because, win or lose, of what he believed it would mean for the monarchy. His fears were shared by his son George VI. In the event, of course, their worst fears did not come to pass – George VI and Queen Elizabeth's role as caring national figureheads appealed greatly to a relieved nation, who took the royal family to its hearts in the latter stages of the war and especially after the victory of 1945. (But it is very telling that the code-word that would trigger the evacuation of the royal family in the event of an invasion was 'Cromwell'.)

Alexander Hardinge, who was very anti-appeasement, expressed his disgust that support for Chamberlain's stance among Palace staff ran from 'the highest to the lowest'.[44] The Private Secretary also noted that London society was '99 per cent pro-appeasement'.[45]

For her part, Queen Mary, unsurprisingly, was adamant that there should be no war with Germany. In her case, it seems less of a reasoned political position or concern about the consequences, than because of her German genes. Famously she gave her opinion (presumably based on the contrast between the two countries' standards of living in the late 1930s) that Britain had 'backed the wrong horse' in the First World War.[46] The royal matriarch became the focus for royal and aristocratic opposition to the war – and in this, as in much else, the influence she wielded over her son was all-important.

After the coronation, Neville Chamberlain took over from Stanley Baldwin (who had been persuaded to stay on after Edward's accession, on the understanding that he would only continue until he was crowned; little did he realise how traumatic this extension to his career would be). George VI got on with well with him and, like all the royal family, was firmly behind Chamberlain's 'appeasement' policy towards Germany and Italy.

In April 1939, the King sent Hitler congratulations on his 50th birthday, and on the eve of war twice offered to write to Hitler 'as one ex-serviceman to another' in an attempt to avert hostilities.[47] Not surprisingly, Chamberlain declined this somewhat naïve suggestion, although it shows that the King was desperately considering how he could prevent the war. In personal letters he expressed his view, which he maintained until the last minute, that the war with Germany could be avoided, and it is clear that was his heart's desire.

In fact, George VI's only critical comment about Hitler before the declaration of war came during the Polish crisis in August 1939, when he said that it was 'utterly damnable that that villain Hitler had upset everything'. He was referring not to the climate of fear and apprehension in Europe, or the treatment of Jews in Germany, but to the interruption to his grouse-shooting holiday.[48]

The Queen Consort's attitude to the impending war has never been publicly expressed, but then neither have her views on any other subject. However, it has been suggested that, although less pro-German than the other royals (not sharing their Teutonic background), she was opposed to war with Germany for the same reasons, fearing that conflict would bring the end of the monarchy.

Not unnaturally, there is a great deal of speculation about the notorious 'Box 24' of Walter Monckton's papers that was withheld when the rest were released in 2000. Although it is widely assumed that they dealt with Elizabeth's role in Edward VIII's abdication, the *Independent on Sunday*, based on information from 'senior Government sources', reported that they contained details of her views on war with Germany in the years leading up to the conflict. In particular they were said to include correspondence between the Queen and Lord Halifax, the Foreign Secretary and a close friend of both Bertie and Elizabeth, and a prime mover in the attempts to avoid the war, but who was also involved in secret attempts to negotiate an end to it after it began.[49] The King and Queen wanted Halifax to be Prime Minister, rather than the hated Churchill, when Neville Chamberlain stood down eight months into the war, and it is to this that the letters in Box 24 are thought to refer. Not only are the letters alleged to reveal her dislike for Churchill, but according to *The Independent on Sunday*. 'The letters suggest that preserving the monarchy was a concern which weighed above all others. As leader, Halifax was likely to have sued for peace with Hitler on the understanding that he allowed the monarchy to continue under a Nazi occupation.'[50] The last part is questionable: it was by no means certain that a peace deal would have meant a Nazi occupation. But if the description of the letters is true – and it seems to come from people who have seen them – it does show that the continuation of the monarchy, under any circumstances, was Queen Elizabeth's most heartfelt desire. Indeed, according to the US Ambassador to France, William C. Bullitt, a few months after the King and Queen's state visit to France in July 1938 (the first of their reign), the French Prime Minister Edouard Daladier described Elizabeth as 'an excessively ambitious woman who would be ready to sacrifice every other country in the world in order that she might remain Queen Elizabeth of England'.[51]

The Duke of Kent shared the same views as the rest of his family, although he was more concerned about the effects of the war on Europe, particularly on the few remaining European royal houses. This was partly because he could maintain close connections with surviving and dispossessed continental royalty through Marina. And of course as the prospective King of Poland he had to keep his finger on the pulse of international affairs.

As the situation became increasingly tense, Kent made several fact-finding visits to Europe, some with Marina and some alone. Although these are usually interpreted as social visits to relatives, such as Prince Paul in Yugoslavia, Count zu Törring-Jettenbach in Munich and Marina's cousin Prince Philip of Hesse-Cassel, the very frequency of such trips in 1938 and 1939 suggests that there was more to it than that. In any case, surely it is inconceivable that he would have avoided the subject of the European crisis when talking to his relatives. Marina's family connections and his light public duties in Britain gave him more freedom to act as the royal family's envoy to other countries. Significantly, every time he returned from Europe his first port of call was Buckingham Palace, where he would brief the King.

Kent appears to have assumed the role of the King's unofficial ambassador to the other royal families and politicians of Europe, for which he was ideally suited, being astute and with the advantage of the ready-made cover of his frequent visits to Marina's relatives. In this way, completely unofficial 'back-door' channels could be maintained by heads of state and senior politicians. For example, if Kent had a private word with Philip of Hesse-Cassel, who was in regular contact with Hitler and Mussolini, then all kinds of information and ideas could easily be shared by the network of European movers and shakers. In the absence of official records, Kent's role is a matter for informed speculation, but he must have discussed the European situation with those he met. Indeed, his contacts, via Baron de Ropp and Alfred Rosenberg, reveal that he had fulfilled the same role for his father in 1935. And, as we shall see in the next chapter, he undertook this role for George VI during the war.

Because of the Kents' aspirations to re-establish a royal dynasty in Poland, it was both in the Duke's interests and, in a sense, his duty to act as a peacemaker, particularly in the final months before war when Poland saw escalating tension. He was in an almost unique position, being politically neutral towards Nazi Germany and a respected figure in Poland. But if the Nazis occupied Poland he could see his chances of becoming King slipping away.

As Kent has become virtually a non-person as far as history is concerned, it is the Duke of Windsor's pro-peace dealings that have – predictably – received considerably more attention. In his case, however, they are unequivocally labelled 'pro-Nazi'. He made a speech from Verdun on 7 May 1939, appealing for peace and conciliation, which was arranged with NBC and aimed primarily at an American audience. The BBC refused to broadcast it (although, because the Beaverbrook newspapers informed their readers how to pick it up on shortwave, an estimated one million people heard it in Britain). But equally significantly, German radio was ordered not to broadcast it either, because Hitler realised that the British press would use it as yet further evidence of Windsor's pro-Nazi position.

THE MUNICH AGREEMENT

The lengths to which the King and royal family were prepared to go to avoid war is revealed by their role in the events surrounding the now-infamous Munich Conference between Chamberlain and Hitler. In the summer of 1938 Hitler declared his intention of taking back – either by negotiation or through force – the German-speaking area of the Sudetenland that had been incorporated into Czechoslovakia after the First World War. Britain had the choice of refusing to countenance this move, which could easily have led to war, or finding a compromise. Eventually such a solution was found in the form of the Munich Agreement, in which it was agreed that Czechoslovakia would cede the Sudetenland to Germany. The groundwork was undertaken by a delegation led by former Liberal Cabinet minister Lord Runciman that went to Czechoslovakia in July 1938 to determine how far the Czech Government would make concessions to Hitler. Initially, Runciman refused the mission, but was commanded to go by the King.[52]

As the crisis deepened, there seemed no alternative to war other than a humiliating climbdown by Britain. Despite Chamberlain offering to travel to Germany for direct talks with Hitler, negotiations between the British and German governments stalled. The crisis reached a dramatic head in the House of Commons on 28 September, with just days to go before the deadline after which Hitler would send in the troops. Chamberlain was in the middle of reporting his lack of success to the House when he was handed a message that had just come through from Hitler. The Führer had agreed to meet Chamberlain, Mussolini and French Prime Minister Daladier in Munich the next day. The House went wild with delight and a wave of relief swept across the country.

Hitler's offer was the result of Mussolini's intercession, which in turn came about through requests from both Chamberlain and the royal family, specifically the Duke of Kent, whose contact was Marina's cousin, Prince Philip of Hesse-Cassel, Hitler's liaison with the Italian leader. It is significant that the Duke and Duchess of Kent, together with Queen Mary and the Italian ambassador, were in the gallery of the Commons watching Chamberlain's speech.[53] Especially given such an august audience, the arrival of the note seems suspiciously stage-managed for maximum dramatic impact.

Chamberlain duly flew off for the talks the next day and an agreement was reached whereby Germany's territorial demands would be satisfied in return for a guarantee that it would not use military force. Chamberlain arrived back at Heston aerodrome infamously waving a copy of the agreement that he declared meant 'peace in our time'. Although this was music to the ears of the public, the agreement still needed the endorsement of Parliament – otherwise it would be meaningless.

George VI then committed an astonishingly unconstitutional act, not only to ensure that Parliament and the public knew that the agreement had his support, but also actively to prevent Parliament from being able to block it.

Indeed, it had certainly not met with unanimous political approval – both the Labour and Liberal Parties opposed it, as did a section of the Conservative Party led by Winston Churchill.[54]

Initially, the King wanted to go to Heston aerodrome to greet the triumphant Chamberlain, but Hardinge pointed out that this would compromise him constitutionally. So instead George invited the Prime Minister to Buckingham Palace, where he and Elizabeth proudly took him out on to the balcony to wave his famous piece of paper and receive the rapturous applause of the huge crowd – the first time a Prime Minister had ever been accorded such an honour. The crowds loved it, the King and Queen loved it, and Chamberlain loved it, but there was only one problem. By demonstrating in such a highly visible – not to say slightly hysterical – manner that he supported the deal, George VI revealed an unequivocal political bias. And by publicly endorsing Chamberlain's part in the agreement, he was effectively exerting pressure on the Cabinet and the other parties to accept it. (No politician should be put in the position where he is known to oppose the monarch's wishes.) After the wild scenes of jubilation and the blanket press coverage of the balcony scene, what politician would dare raise his voice against the agreement? Yet the cold fact is that no matter what the situation, George had absolutely no right to display his personal political views so openly. The historian John Grigg calls the balcony scene 'the most unconstitutional act by a British Sovereign in the [twentieth] century', continuing: 'Whatever the rights and wrongs of the Munich Agreement, the relevant point is that it was denounced by the official Opposition and was to be the subject of a vote in Parliament.'[55]

This was undoubtedly the most unconstitutional act carried out in public in the history of the House of Windsor; under no other circumstances would the monarch have been allowed to get away with it. It was only because the majority of the people were behind the agreement (although most of them seemed to have forgotten this by 1945) that it was impossible for anybody to censure the King. It was a move that Edward VIII would have been proud of.

Four months later the King made a less public – but infinitely more shameful – political intervention. At that time the Nazis' strategy for ridding Germany and Austria of their Jewish population was 'voluntary' emigration – making life as uncomfortable for them as possible so that they left the country, some of them without exit visas. (For obvious reasons, the Nazis were not too concerned about Jews illegally leaving the country.) However this unchecked wave of emigration was causing Britain problems: many of the German Jews were going to Palestine, then under a British mandate, and adding to the tensions between the Jewish and Arab communities.

In February 1939, on hearing about the problems in Palestine, George VI asked his Private Secretary to write to Foreign Secretary Lord Halifax expressing his wish that 'steps are being taken to prevent these people leaving their country of origin'.[56] Two days later the Foreign Office asked the British

Embassy in Berlin to take up the matter of 'unauthorised emigration' with the German Government, with the result that it no longer turned a blind eye to irregularities and began to apply the laws more rigorously. Of course – although the King could not have foreseen the consequences – this meant that many Jews who would otherwise have left the country were not allowed to do so. The bleak toll of history shows their fate.

Why George VI felt it necessary to put pressure on the Government over this matter is unclear, but he would have been fully aware of the country of origin of most of the illegal immigrants entering Palestine. And, as historian Andrew Roberts points out, the King's move took place just four months after the outrages of Kristallnacht in Germany, when Nazi mobs took to the streets, attacking synagogues and Jewish homes and looting their businesses.[57] Was he really too foolish to put two and two together? Did he not realise that as a *direct result* of his intervention, thousands more German Jews were immediately condemned – at the very least – to rapidly dwindling civil rights and increasing persecution? Or was it simply that George VI – and his Queen – were not really concerned about what happened to the Jews?

WAR LOOMS

After Hitler reneged on the Munich Agreement and overran the rest of Czechoslovakia six months later there was less chance that a similar deal could be forged over his new territorial demands about the German-speaking parts of Poland. After all, who would trust Hitler now? This crisis began to loom in the summer of 1939 – but this time war looked increasingly certain.

At the end of March, the die was cast when the British and French Governments agreed to give a guarantee to Poland that they would come to its aid if Germany attacked. This made the Polish Government – which was also notably belligerent – less inclined to negotiate with Hitler. In fact, once the treaty was in place there was a widespread feeling in Poland that now they had the backing of Britain and France they should take on Germany in the expectation that they would win. This sentiment was recorded by Baroness de Stoeckl in a diary entry that also shows how Kent was regarded in Poland (as well as revealing some of the less savoury attitudes of the Polish ruling classes):

> Now that Britain is behind them [the Polish people], what need they fear. On every side one hears: 'We fear nothing.' This spirit pervades the very air. Only the Jews are trembling and agitating like mice afraid of a cat. Many shopkeepers beg Zoia to appeal to the Duke of Kent to get them away to England. It is pathetic.[58]

In June 1939 the King and Queen visited Canada and the USA, spending some time with President Roosevelt. The main purpose of this visit was to whip up American support for Britain in the event of war, managing to elicit encouragement that the Neutrality Acts (which prevented the USA selling supplies to any country engaged in a war) might be relaxed. No doubt heaving a massive sigh of relief, the King recorded in his diary the promise – as it turned out, a hollow one – that 'If London was bombed the USA would come in'.[59] On his return he said of US support in the event of war, 'It's in the bag!',[60] another prime example of Providence being only too happy to be tempted. George VI hoped, not so much that much-needed American aid would be forthcoming if war were to break out, but that the promise of American support might effectively deter Hitler.

MOVES TO AVERT WAR

In the summer of 1939 there were several unofficial attempts, by politicians, businessmen and others, to broker an understanding between Britain and Germany that would prevent a war. (In fact, many of these apparently unofficial moves were backed by Chamberlain and Foreign Secretary Lord Halifax.) One of the most important efforts was the delegation of powerful British industrialists and financiers, led by Lord Aberconway, who met with Hermann Göring in August 1939. Although this episode has been known about for some time, it was thought to be a purely private attempt by City figures to avert the war, but in 1999 it was revealed that the delegation had had the full backing of Chamberlain and Halifax. Like several of the peace attempts, it was brokered by Swedish industrialists, particularly those connected with the Electrolux Company. Deeply involved on the British side was Electrolux's British chairman, friend of the King and Queen, Sir Harold Wernher, whose wife Zia was a particularly close friend of the Duchess of Kent.[61] (As we have seen, Zia was the sister of Nada Milford Haven, widow of Mountbatten's brother.)

With his powerful and complex connections on the continent, the Duke of Kent was actively trying to reach an agreement – but clearly not solely on his own initiative: his highly sensitive negotiations would have required his brother's blessing. Although the official biographies acknowledge his role in general, the current restrictions on his papers make it impossible to discover any precise details. It is known that in the early months of the Polish crisis he went to Germany for talks with Prince Philip of Hesse-Cassel, and in July he came up with a plan to talk directly to Hitler – which was approved by the King, Chamberlain and Lord Halifax, but which, for reasons that sadly remain unclear, never materialised.[62] In the five weeks before war broke out both the Duke and Duchess of Kent were particularly active, visiting Paris, Switzerland and Italy, then Marina went on to Yugoslavia while the Duke returned to London.

Baroness de Stoeckl, a frequent visitor to the Kents' country house, the Coppins – indeed she moved in after the outbreak of war – records that on 25 August, just a week before the German invasion of Poland, Kent returned 'from abroad', as she discreetly puts it, and the following day he dined with the King, undoubtedly to brief him.[63] (As the crisis loomed, George VI met with Kent every day.[64]) The day after that the Duchess returned from Yugoslavia.

To underline his escalating importance, Kent had been installed as the Grand Master of the United Grand Lodge of England, the top position in English Freemasonry. The previous incumbent, the elderly Duke of Connaught, had stood aside for him. The installation, at Olympia, was carried out by George VI himself, the first time that a reigning monarch had taken such an active part in Freemasonry. (As Duke of York he had become Grand Master of Scottish Freemasonry in 1936.) Kent now had much wider influence over the Establishment and his rank automatically made him, in the Masonic world of oaths and loyalties, the superior of politicians, generals and admirals – a very convenient situation for such a powerful individual to find himself in with war looming.

Tragically, of course, all the frantic last-ditch peace efforts were in vain, and on 3 September 1939, following Hitler's invasion of Poland two days before, Britain and France declared war on Germany – in Britain's case George VI had to sign the declaration, a source of huge resentment on his part.

Louis Mountbatten, now captain of the new, state-of-the-art destroyer HMS *Kelly*, saw action within 24 hours of war being declared – that is, if his letters and diary, and not the historical record, are to be believed. He wrote to Edwina that the *Kelly* had been attacked by two U-boats, but had narrowly escaped the torpedoes of one and had sunk the other. As captain he was covered in glory. His diary for 4 September records the same. However, as Philip Ziegler notes, there was no enemy submarine within 50 miles.[65]

The first eight months of the war became known as the 'phoney war' (or, as the Duchess of Windsor called it, the 'Bore War', and the Germans the 'Sitzkrieg'): war may have been declared but no hostilities to speak of took place. It is clear that the original intention of Chamberlain's Government, which had been forced to declare a war that it had no stomach for, was to try to negotiate a way out of it as soon as possible.[66]

DID WINDSOR BETRAY BRITAIN?

Just over a week after the declaration of war, hoping for an important and active role in London, the Duke of Windsor returned to the capital for the first time in nearly three years (having been picked up from Cherbourg by Mountbatten's new toy, HMS *Kelly*). In the event, however, Windsor was deemed too dangerous a loose cannon to have in London and, after the King had considered posting him to Wales, he was forced to accept a post with the British Military Mission in Paris with a temporary demotion from the rank of Honorary Field Marshal to Major-General. Even though smarting under this humiliation, he still showed abundant evidence of that dangerous common touch, being immensely popular with the British troops in France in a way that his brother could never hope to emulate. (The Duke of Gloucester was also seconded to the military staff in France, where one of his fellow officers described him as 'very lazy and very, very stupid'.[67])

One of Windsor's main tasks was to inspect and report on the Maginot Line, the famous strip of defences on the French/Belgian border intended to keep the Germans out should they become uppity again. He compiled four intelligent and shrewd reports analysing the strengths and weaknesses of the line, particularly drawing attention to areas that were indeed breached by the Germans when the Blitzkrieg was finally unleashed. Unfortunately these reports were mostly ignored by the British commanders in France and in London, largely because the Duke had become something of a joke in their eyes.[68]

However, since the war evidence has emerged that the Duke's observations were indeed considered attentively – not by the Allies, *but in Berlin*. German files captured after 1945 show that information on the French defences was being transmitted to Berlin by the German Ambassador in Holland, and that the information had been given to the Ambassador by Charles Bedaux (who was to become an economic adviser to the Nazis when France was occupied), who identified his source as the Duke of Windsor. The Duke and Duchess were in regular – sometimes weekly – contact with Bedaux and his wife in Paris, dining and dancing together. Bedaux's information not only included the weaknesses in the Maginot Line but also precise details of how the British and French commanders intended to respond to a German offensive. *Bedaux received all this directly from Windsor.*[69]

Further information from official British files suggests that the War Office may have been aware of the possibility. They had a spy in the Embassy who informed them that Bedaux was a German informer, although this agent had no idea of the identity of Bedaux's source other than that he was codenamed 'Willi' – the name used by Nazi intelligence for Windsor. As a result the British commanders tried to end the Duke's near-treacherous association with Bedaux – although, astonishingly, they accepted his refusal to do so.[70]

On the basis of these reports, in the late 1980s intelligence writer John Costello suggested that the Duke, who was not known for his discretion, had been far too free in his table talk, and that Bedaux was using him to obtain information on the French defences. However, in his 2000 book *Hidden Agenda*, Martin Allen goes the final distance, suggesting that Windsor was knowingly supplying the Nazis with this – and perhaps other – information. Allen bases this on a letter, written in German from Paris on 4 November 1939 (shortly after the first of Windsor's tours of inspection) to 'Lieber Herr Hitler' and signed 'E.P.'. The writer talks in guarded terms about a recent 'trip to the north' and that he had described what he had seen there in detail to 'your acquaintance, Mr. B', and gives his agreement to Hitler's 'suggestions for the future'.[71] The letter was given to Allen's father Peter, a historian and author of an earlier book on Windsor's dealings with the Nazis (*The Crown and the*

Swastika, 1983), by Albert Speer many years before, but Martin Allen did not realise its full significance until he had researched the subject himself. He argues that 'E.P.' stands for 'Edward, Prince', and that 'Mr. B' is Bedaux.

Although the handwriting has been confirmed as Windsor's,[72] the letter's authenticity has been questioned – indeed, in his book Allen does not discount the possibility that it is a forgery. In the final analysis, this disputed 'E.P.' letter is the only evidence that Windsor was knowingly supplying Bedaux vital information as a Nazi agent, rather than just being amazingly indiscreet over the quadruple brandies. But either way, Windsor may have contributed to the success of the German Blitzkrieg that smashed the British and French forces in May 1940, leading to the fall of France and Dunkirk, and the deaths of thousands of Allied troops – the very men who had trusted and adored him. It is a matter of historical record that the Germans concentrated their forces on the areas singled out by the Windsor reports, particularly the Ardennes, and that this was a change of plan ordered by Hitler personally at the time of the Bedaux communications.[73]

Whether by accident or design, on this evidence Windsor had a major effect on the course of the Second World War – to the grave detriment of Britain and France. Certainly, Martin Allen believes that it was quite deliberate on Windsor's part: to him the quickest way to end the war would be an overwhelming German strike that would force Britain to sue for peace. He may have been reassured from the German side that Hitler would offer acceptable terms (as, indeed, he may well have done, as his major concern at that time was the plan to attack the Soviet Union).

During this period, in January 1940, Windsor met with Lord Beaverbrook and Walter Monckton in London – significantly, without asking the King for permission to return to the UK.[74] Another staunch opponent of the war, Beaverbrook discussed with Windsor the necessity of negotiating an early peace and how the Duke might exploit his popularity to get the people on their side.[75]

During this period George VI continued to behave unconstitutionally, interfering in the Government of the country. In January 1940 he was involved in behind-the-scenes intrigue that forced from office the War Minister Leslie Hore-Belisha, one of the 'hawks' in Chamberlain's Cabinet – leader of the 'revolt' that made Chamberlain declare war when, even after the deadline for Hitler's response to Britain's ultimatum over the attack on Poland had passed, he still wanted to give the Führer more time.[76] Apart from being a threat to the 'doves' such as Lord Halifax, Hore-Belisha was deeply unpopular with the army leadership. (He also happened to be the only Jewish member of the Cabinet.) He claimed at the time that the King had been behind the 'conspiracy' that forced his resignation, a view still maintained by some, such as Andrew Roberts,[77] although others[78] think that this overstates the case. But whether or not he instigated the manoeuvres against Hore-Belisha, the King quite unconstitutionally encouraged and supported them.

Significantly, his part in the War Minister's downfall was an open secret even at the time: Chips Channon wrote that it 'would do the Monarchy harm, as they should not interfere or dabble in politics', adding that 'George VI is not George V, and Alec Hardinge is certainly not Lord Stamfordham'.[79]

GEORGE VI AND CHURCHILL

One of the most commonly believed myths about the royal family in the Second World War was that they were almost slavish admirers of Winston Churchill. Certainly at the beginning of the conflict, nothing could be further from the truth. Because of his desire for war with Germany – he was always known in society circles as a warmonger – and his support for Edward VIII during the abdication crisis, they detested the man.

In the summer of 1939, Neville Chamberlain was seated between Queen Elizabeth and the Duchess of Kent at a formal dinner at the Palace. At the time, the Prime Minister was reconstructing his Cabinet and there was political and public pressure to give Churchill a post (in the end he became First Lord of the Admiralty). Chamberlain recorded that 'neither left me in any doubt as to their opposition to the idea of Churchill's inclusion'.[80]

At the beginning of May 1940 Chamberlain had to concede that he was losing the confidence of the House of Commons and that the only option was to form a coalition government for the duration. When the Labour Party refused to serve under his leadership, he was compelled to stand down as Prime Minister. But whom should the King call to succeed him? There were only two candidates, Lord Halifax and Winston Churchill.

Of the two, Halifax was the undoubted front runner. He was the preferred choice of Chamberlain, the Conservative Party and Labour Leader Clement Attlee. He was also a friend of the King and Queen – his wife was one of Queen Elizabeth's ladies-in-waiting and they frequently dined, just the four of them, at the Palace. George VI had even given Halifax a key to the Buckingham Palace gardens: a rare honour indeed.

They were not only close personally, but also politically. Sir Robert Rhodes James writes that 'it would be right to describe Halifax as the King's principal political adviser in 1939'.[81] The politician, like the King, was a firm supporter of Chamberlain's pre-war and wartime policies, and an advocate of negotiating with Germany before the war took a turn for the worse (although he had no way of knowing, this happened within 24 hours of the leadership contest). During the Munich crisis, Halifax had told Hitler's negotiator Fritz Wiedemann that his ultimate aim was to see 'the Führer entering London at the side of the English King amid the acclamation of the English people'.[82]

On the other hand, George VI was 'bitterly opposed' to Churchill becoming prime minister.[83] His official biographer John Wheeler-Bennett stated privately (as recorded in the diary of Robert Bruce Lockhart, wartime head of the Political Warfare Executive) that:

> . . . George VI did not like W.S.C [Churchill]. He was an admirer of
> Chamberlain and was one hundred per cent pro-Munich . . . it is on
> record that he told Roosevelt that only in very exceptional
> circumstances would he consent to W.S.C.'s being made P.M.[84]

Although one of the few occasions when the sovereign is not bound to accept
the advice of the prime minister is the question of his successor, Chamberlain
wanted to make a firm recommendation to George VI by persuading the two
rivals to agree with him on his replacement. The three men, and the
Conservative Chief Whip, met behind closed doors on 9 May 1940 to thrash
it out. The outcome – to everyone's enormous surprise – was that
Chamberlain recommended Churchill to the King.

Clearly, Churchill only came out on top because Halifax had refused the
job, but the reason for this remains uncertain. However, the reason put
forward at the time was that Halifax sat in the House of Lords and believed
he could not be an effective prime minister from that lofty position. This does
have all the hollow ring of a hastily cobbled-together excuse. Lords had been
prime ministers before, and there was no reason why one could not step into
the role then.[85] John Wheeler-Bennett wrote: '. . . none of those who had
previously expressed a preference for Lord Halifax as Prime Minister,
including Mr Chamberlain, saw any constitutional objection to a Prime
Minister in the House of Lords and . . . Lord Halifax's own doubts on
accepting the premiership did not include this'.[86]

Despite repeated efforts to persuade Halifax to change his mind, he
steadfastly refused. Many believe that he simply doubted his ability to lead a
country at war and used his status as a peer as an excuse. Chamberlain's Private
Secretary, John Colville, who was 'inherited' by Churchill, refers intriguingly
in his diary entry for 10 May 1940 to the decision being due to Churchill's
'powers of [presumably political] blackmail'.[87] Having settled the matter, on
10 May Chamberlain went to the Palace to tender his resignation and
informally discuss his replacement. The King's diary on his audience with
Chamberlain records the following:

> We had an informal talk over his successor. I, of course, suggested
> Halifax, but he told me that H. was not enthusiastic, as being in the
> Lords he could only act as a shadow or ghost in the Commons, where
> all the work took place. I was disappointed over this statement, as I
> thought H. was the obvious man, & that his peerage could be placed
> in abeyance for the time being. Then I knew that there was only one
> person whom I could send for to form a Government who had the
> confidence of the country, & that was Winston.[88]

George VI was bitterly disappointed that he had no option but to call
Churchill to meet his 'destiny', as the old British bulldog was to describe it.

(In a calculated break with tradition, the King failed to send Chamberlain a message of regret at his resignation.)[89] Queen Mary was so furious that she attempted to prevent John Colville from transferring his services to the new Prime Minister.[90]

Undoubtedly, despite the retrospective adjustments of history, Churchill did not enjoy the confidence of the King.[91] Nor, it seems, did the new Prime Minister have much confidence in George VI. But at least up to a point, Churchill was right: there was an element of destiny in his appointment. On 10 May 1940, as the final discussions were taking place in Downing Street, news was coming in that the Germans had launched their attack on the Low Countries. In the course of a single day, the war had begun in earnest and Winston Churchill had become the British nation's leader. Both developments represented the worst news that the King and Queen could possibly imagine.

SIX

'THE END OF MANY HOPES'

Baroness de Stoeckl on the death of the Duke of Kent, 1942

Just as the accepted version of history presents a wholly inaccurate picture of the relationship between Winston Churchill and George VI, so most of the famous image of the wartime royal family is equally economical with the truth. The royal family of sober, Hitler-hating Dunkirk spirits who knitted socks for seamen and shared all the people's deprivations is in fact no more than propaganda for posterity, intended to show that Britain was firmly united behind the perfect example of self-sacrifice and valour.

According to historian John Charmley, Churchill's job was made all the harder at the beginning of his time in office because he enjoyed neither the King's confidence nor his trust. It is usually agreed that the situation had improved by 1942, because charismatic and inspirational Churchill had won the King round – but there may be quite another reason for this. After the war, Churchill wrote: 'I made certain that he [George VI] was kept informed of every secret matter.'[1] Like much of what Churchill committed to paper for posterity, the very fact that he felt it a necessity to spell this out inevitably raises suspicions.

The King saw it rather differently. A telling episode involved Sir Louis Greig (who was knighted in the 1930s) – George VI's adviser and 'minder' when he was Duke of York, and also the Duke of Kent's confidant since the 1920s. At the outbreak of war Greig was recalled to serve with the Air Ministry, being assigned to work in the Cabinet War Rooms, the command centre for the whole of Britain's war effort. He was one of the privileged few with access to the Map Room, where information from every theatre of war and all operations was received and collated. Soon after Greig took up this post, George VI wrote a personal letter to him, marked 'secret', in which he asked, 'If you hear of anything which may not come my way please let me know.'[2] This suggests strongly that the King suspected he was being deliberately kept in the dark about some matters.

Greig's great operational advantage – even in the Cabinet War Rooms – was his wide and complex network of contacts: as his grandson Geordie Greig puts it, he was an 'unofficial fixer', adding, 'The advantage of using him was the absence of a paper trail.'[3]

The reason for the mutual mistrust between King and Prime Minister was that Britain was fighting a war in which George VI and the royal family did not wish to be involved, and Churchill was very much aware of this area of tension between them. Queen Mary was furious at both the war in general and Churchill in particular. Still very much a force to be reckoned with, the matriarch continued her career of relentless intriguing at the centre of royal and aristocratic opposition to the war: indeed, for this very reason Churchill attempted to stop like-minded people from seeing her.[4] It may not be totally coincidental that she was packed off for the duration to a country house at Badminton, although it was hardly a privation as she was accompanied by over 60 servants. She spent much of her time driving around the countryside in a horse-drawn buggy requisitioning farm implements to be melted down for the war effort – although her servants discreetly returned them to their owners without her knowledge. She also spent a good deal of time watching movies in the private cinema.

Churchill was also cavalier in his dealings with the King, often turning up late for audiences, and ignoring letters, even, on occasions, royal summonses to the Palace. Although almost certainly he was playing a somewhat obvious power game, perhaps he had seen the new King at close quarters far too often to be impressed by him. In any case, Bertie must have seemed like a callow youth compared not only to Churchill's own age and experience, but also to Edward VIII's easy glamour.

BEHIND THE PROPAGANDA POSES

As the newsreels of the time – and more recent documentaries – never pass up an opportunity to drum into their viewers, the King and Queen played a vital role in keeping British morale up in the Second World War, by visiting the shell-shocked and bombed out, besides workers in munitions factories, Red Cross volunteers and so on. The fact that they had opposed the war made no difference to their role as 'focus of national unity': it was the monarch's role to show solidarity with the nation under all circumstances, but above all the royal family had to be *seen* to be sympathetic, if only for the monarchy's continued survival. However, much of this famous solidarity with the people was never any more than an invention of the Palace's propaganda machine.

When the Blitz on London began, the story was circulated that the King and Queen would remain in Buckingham Palace, at the very heart of the capital. There was even a popular song that boasted the immortal lines 'The King is still in London town / With Mr Jones and Mr Brown'. But while it is true that George and Elizabeth were present in the Palace each day, they left

Lord Mountbatten at
his desk at the Admiralty

Anthony Blunt, Soviet agent at
Buckingham Palace

The Duke of Windsor during
his exile in France

Mountbatten with a young Prince Charles

Princess Margaret sightseeing in South Africa
with group Captain Peter Townsend

A young Prince Charles with
his mother and grandmother

Prince Charles and Princess Anne with Prince
Philip's mother, Princess Alice of Greece

Mountbatten in his finery on achieving
'The House of Mountbatten'

The Princess of Wales a few weeks before her tragic death
© PA

The Fiat Uno whose owner
subsequently died in mysterious
circumstances

The wrecked Mercedes after the
occupants had been cut free
© PA

Flowers at the scene of the car accident that resulted in
the deaths of Princess Diana and Dodi Fayed
© PA

The Heirs: will they break the chains and guide the House of Windsor into the twenty-first century? © PA

every evening by armoured car for the relative safety of Windsor Castle, which was guarded by a contingent of Grenadier Guards.[5]

After Buckingham Palace was bombed in September 1940, Queen Elizabeth famously declared, 'I'm glad we've been bombed. It makes me feel I can look the East End in the face',[6] which was said to have had a great impact on Londoners, especially the stereotypical cheeky chappies and stalwart cockney women who were only too regularly bombed in their East End slums. But what was not reported at the time – and barely known even now – is that the King and Queen's tours of the bombed areas of the East End were by no means always enthusiastically received.[7] Sometimes they were even booed.[8] What was there to cheer about in a pink-and-white woman in her furs delicately picking her way over what was left of your front room and smiling into the cameras, especially when you knew she was going to be swept off to safety and off-ration drinks and fine food? Who did she think she was?

Despite claims to the contrary, at the time and ever since, the royal family did not share their subjects' frustrating dependence on the ration book. Although it is often claimed that food and clothes rationing was enforced in the Palace, of course the wartime privations only applied to the servants. As Piers Brendon and Phillip Whitehead write:

> At a Buckingham Palace luncheon Joseph Kennedy, the American ambassador, was offered the choice of hare or pheasant. Lord Reith [Director General of the BBC] was served a dinner of soup, ham mousse and chicken, strawberry ice and strawberries and cream. Margarine was widely used in the household but only butter, the pats monogrammed with crowns, appeared on the monarch's table. Enormous supplies of tinned food had been accumulated at Buckingham Palace but these were 'reasonable precautions', as the Comptroller of Supply ingenuously recorded, and there was 'no question of hoarding'. In the national interest Churchill exempted himself from rationing, and it is clear that food coupons played equally little part in the life of the royal family.[9]

Food from the royal farms or estates was not subject to rationing: as Frederick Corbitt, the official responsible for procuring food, revealed in 1956, the family continued to indulge in farm produce, salmon and grouse from Balmoral.[10] (Ironically, however, while the leaner population enjoyed the best health it had ever had because of less calorie intake, less fat and less sugar, the Queen herself became noticeably plumper.) And while the people were encouraged to 'make do and mend' – even wedding dresses were usually hand-me-downs – and deny the temptations of the evil 'squander bug', George VI continued to lavish vastly expensive gifts of jewellery on his wife and elder daughter.[11]

WINDSOR'S WAR

As the Germans were overrunning the Maginot Line and sweeping into France, the Duke of Windsor decamped to the south, where he joined his beloved Duchess. Often portrayed as a selfish flight to safety, while his fellow officers remained to face the Nazi invaders, in fact he went to report upon the state of French defences on the Italian border (as it was feared – correctly, as it turned out – that Italy would take advantage of the situation to seize territory in the south). Although this was Windsor's own idea (undoubtedly to give him an excuse to rejoin the Duchess), his journey was agreed by the British Ambassador and the head of the British Military Mission, and he was officially attached to the French Command at Nice. (His sudden departure from Paris caused a rift – later healed – with Fruity Metcalfe, who wrote that the Duke had 'run like two rabbits' and had 'deserted his country', adding scathingly, 'After 20 years I am through – utterly I despise him.'[12] However, Fruity's bitterness seems to have been due to the fact that Windsor left without saying goodbye, or, indeed, offering to take him along too.)

When France surrendered, the Windsors – most unlikely refugees – together with officials from the British Embassy, crossed over the border into Spain, before going on to Madrid. Obviously there was anxiety about a member of the royal family being taken prisoner by the Nazis, especially one as unpredictable, indiscreet and liable to hysteria as Windsor. Just their presence in Spain was dangerous enough: although neutral, it was pro-Hitler and – as indeed events were to prove – the Duke was vulnerable to Nazi agents. Nervous at the turn of events, the British Government wanted him in safer neutral Portugal but at the request of the Portuguese leader, Salazar, Churchill delayed this move. The Duke of Kent was due to visit Lisbon as the King's representative at national celebrations on 24 June (commemorating the 300th anniversary of Portugal's independence and 800 years since its birth as a nation): it was the new policy to prevent the two royal brothers from meeting.

Predictably enough, in Madrid and Lisbon the Duke and Duchess again became the focus for Nazi intrigue, as revealed by telegrams sent between the German Embassy in Madrid and Foreign Minister von Ribbentrop in Berlin, which were captured by the Allies at the end of the war. The 'Madrid telegrams' reveal that from the moment they arrived in Spain the Nazis were keen to contact the Duke and prevent him from going on to Portugal. (For example, they explored the possibility of pressing the Spanish authorities to delay the process of granting them exit visas.)[13] There is no doubt that the Spanish Foreign Ministry was only too happy to inform the Germans about all its dealings with the Duke.

The German Ambassador, Eberhard von Stohrer, reported that, according to the Spanish Foreign Minister, Colonel Juan Beigbeder y Atenzia, Windsor did go to Lisbon for a meeting with Kent (and 'in order to replenish his supply of money').[14] Whether this was simply a misunderstanding, or a reference to a secret meeting between the two brothers, is unclear.

In Portugal, the Windsors stayed with Kent's friend, the banker Ricardo Espírito Santa Silva, just outside Lisbon. Once there, Churchill informed the Duke that he wanted him back in London, but he refused unless they would guarantee him an official post and acknowledge his wife's right to the title of Her Royal Highness. However, he did agree to being sent anywhere else in the Empire, which was clearly music to the Government's ears, for he was promptly assigned, together with his troublesome Duchess, to a very distant outpost indeed. The ex-King became the Governor of the Bahamas. At the time, it was difficult to imagine a more humiliating appointment.

Originating with the Palace, the idea was enthusiastically endorsed by Churchill as an admirable solution. It got the Duke well out of harm's way while maintaining the semblance of granting him the 'important' colonial post he sought. The fact that appointing a member of the royal family to the post of chief political executive of a colony was indisputably unconstitutional was blithely ignored.

All this was duly reported to the German Embassy in Lisbon by certain Spaniards within the Duke's circle. The information was then passed on to the Embassy in Madrid, before ending up in Berlin. A telegram of 11 July reports that the Duke told his Spanish friends that his appointment to the Bahamas 'is intended to keep him far away from England, since his return would bring with it very strong encouragement to English friends of peace', and that he actually feared arrest if he went back to Britain. As a result he intended to delay his departure for the Bahamas for as long as possible 'in the hope of a turn of events favourable to him'.[15]

From Lisbon, Windsor asked the Spanish Foreign Minister to send a 'confidential agent' to Lisbon,[16] and they despatched Javier 'Tiger' Bermejillo, an old friend of the Duke and Duchess. Today it is believed that Windsor merely wanted to discuss the recovery of some of their possessions from their homes in Paris and Antibes. (In the end, one of the Duchess's maids was allowed to travel into occupied and Vichy France to collect their belongings – in itself no small measure of the Nazis' keenness to keep Windsor on side.) But was there another reason for Windsor wanting the services of a 'confidential agent'? Perhaps he was as eager to open a channel with the Germans as they were with him. At this distance in time, it is difficult to be certain, but even if the standard explanation is correct it still means that Windsor was happy to make contact with the Vichy Government and the German overlords of occupied France.

Windsor told Bermejillo that Churchill had threatened him with court martial for desertion if he did not take up the post of Governor of the Bahamas – which was duly relayed to the Germans.[17] Although Churchill couched his threat in somewhat more diplomatic terms, there was no doubt that he meant it.[18] The Duke was in a very serious position.

More incriminatingly, the German telegrams report that Windsor told his friends in Lisbon that: 'He is convinced that if he had remained on the throne war would have been avoided, and he characterises himself as a firm supporter of a peaceful arrangement with Germany. The Duke definitely believes that continued severe bombings would make England ready for peace.'[19] The last comment is particularly significant because it was only the previous day that the Luftwaffe had begun concerted air raids on specific targets in Britain, marking the first day of the Battle of Britain. (At that time, the bombing concentrated on military and other strategic targets – it was not until September that the indiscriminate Blitz on London and other cities began. Although the Duke's approval of the strategy was not, as it is often portrayed, the treasonable encouragement to the Nazis to bomb civilians, it was still a remarkably stupid thing to say.)

As the exchange of telegrams reveals, the German plot was to lure Windsor back into Spain, preferably with his co-operation but 'if necessary by force'.[20] There the Spanish Government would intern him (in order to preserve their neutrality, they routinely did this with members of the British armed forces who made their way to Spain), although probably under elegant house arrest, in order that German agents could talk to him directly. Their objective was that:

> . . . the Duke must be informed that Germany wants peace with the English people, that the Churchill clique stands in the way of it, and that it would be a good thing if the Duke would hold himself in readiness for further developments. Germany is determined to force England to peace by every means of power and upon this happening would be prepared to accommodate any desire expressed by the Duke, especially with a view to the assumption of the English throne by the Duke and Duchess.[21]

Von Stohrer added that if Windsor rejected this plan, then the Germans would provide him with the resources 'to lead a life suitable for a king'. (Whether he would enjoy this glittering existence in Spain, France or Germany is unclear.) It is surely no coincidence that the statement about Germany's opposition to Churchill and his Government (rather than the British people) was echoed precisely by Hitler in his last offer to Britain of peace talks just eight days later.

In order to activate the plan, von Stohrer made contact with General Franco via his (Franco's) brother-in-law Serano Suñer, the Minister of the Interior. In order to put pressure on Windsor the Spanish also ensured that he was fed the line that they had intelligence that the British were planning to assassinate him (a persistent fear of the Duke's).

On 21 June Windsor cabled the King to propose that he appoint Lloyd George as Prime Minister (which of course would entail dismissing

Churchill).[22] Lloyd George was the centre of the pro-peace lobby and leader of the opposition to Churchill in the Commons.[23]

A second Nazi 'confidential emissary', this time from the Spanish Minister of the Interior but another pre-war friend, Don Miguel Primo de Rivera, then entered into regular contact with the Windsors. (Both Don Miguel's and 'Tiger' Bermejillo's names were kept out of the German communications, being referred to only as the first and second 'confidential emissary' respectively.) Apparently not only were the Windsors ignorant of the fact that Don Miguel was representing Germany, but even he was not aware that reports of their conversations were being relayed to Berlin.[24] At these meetings – with the Duchess also present on occasions – Windsor announced that he was considering going public with his opposition to the continuation of the war.[25]

Don Miguel was instructed to tell Windsor that it might be possible to return him to the British throne (of course with the clear implication that this time he could reign with the woman he loved by his side). Both Windsors were reportedly astonished at the possibility, especially when the Duke pointed out that the constitution would not permit such a revolt against the current regime. 'When the confidential emissary then expressed his expectation that the course of the war might bring about changes even in the English constitution, the Duchess especially became very pensive.'[26]

Towards the end of July, with time fast running out before the Windsors' departure for the Bahamas, the Nazis sent one of their top covert agents, Walter Schellenberg, to supervise the operation. (Four years later he became chief of all German intelligence services.) His orders were to organise the Windsors' crossing of the Portuguese/Spanish border and then act as their chief of security. Schellenberg was also authorised to offer the Duke 50 million Swiss francs, with a promise of more to come. Meanwhile, a team of 18 Nazi agents was assigned to the Windsor mission.

Under pressure from all sides, the Duke dithered. Eventually he told Don Miguel that the best long-term strategy would be not to jeopardise his standing by being seen to enjoy unauthorised contact with the Germans, which would destroy his reputation in Britain. Instead he determined to go to the Bahamas while holding himself in readiness to act as an intermediary when the situation was right. Although he firmly believed that there was still a strong enough peace lobby in Britain to make it a real possibility,[27] this ran counter to the Nazi plan – they wanted him in Spain.

Schellenberg refers to a last-minute visit to the Duke to persuade him not to leave for the Bahamas by an individual whom he identified only by the code-name 'Viktor'.[28] It has been speculated that this might have been none other than Deputy Führer Rudolf Hess.[29] However, a more likely candidate was surely Prince Philip of Hesse-Cassel. According to Miranda Carter, in her recent biography of Anthony Blunt, Philip visited the Duke of Windsor in Lisbon.[30] As we have seen, Prince Philip of Hesse-Cassel was an important member of the Nazi Party: Hitler's liaison officer with Mussolini and in close contact with the Duke of Kent before the war – not to mention the royal family's 'back-door' contact with Hitler. While he was the obvious person to despatch to Lisbon to try and talk Windsor round to the German plan, there is no possibility that the Duke was ignorant of Philip's status as a Nazi emissary when the two met in Lisbon. This visit makes nonsense of the idea – maintained since the war – that the Duke was unaware of being the focus of a Nazi plot.

However, despite all the desperate and ingenious attempts to keep them in Europe, the Windsors eventually departed for the Bahamas on 1 August on the SS *Excalibur* (to the great excitement of the other passengers who saw them as the last word in romance and chic). But on the morning of their departure Don Miguel made a final attempt to persuade the Duke not to sail. Tellingly, his reply – as reported in Schellenberg's final report – shows that he knew full well that his words would be relayed back to Germany:

> . . . the Duke paid tribute to the Führer's desire for peace, which was in complete agreement with his own point of view. He was firmly convinced that if he had been King it would never have come to war.[31]

He made it clear that although for the time being he would obey the Government's orders, he firmly believed that the British would soon come round to the idea of a negotiated peace. When they did admit the inevitable he expected either to be called back to participate in the negotiations, or failing that the Germans could seek his services as a major negotiator. The German Embassy reported to Berlin the day after Windsor's departure:

> He would remain in continuing communication with his previous host [Espírito Santo Silva] and had agreed with him a code-word, upon receiving which he would immediately come back over . . . The statements of the Duke were, as the confidant [Don Miguel] stressed, supported by firmness of will and the deepest sincerity, and had included an expression of admiration and sympathy for the Führer.[32]

The *Excalibur* took the Duke and Duchess to Bermuda, where they spent a few days acclimatising before moving on to take up their post. On the day they left Bermuda, the German Ambassador in Lisbon, Baron Oswald von Huynigen-Heune reported to von Ribbentrop that 'the confidant' in Lisbon had received a telegram from the Duke, asking that he be given sufficient notice of being required to 'act'.[33] Clearly, the Windsors were holding themselves in readiness for a glorious *coup*.

The telegrams were in the German Foreign Ministry archives that were captured by the Americans in 1945. Churchill wanted them destroyed and it is clear that, had the Americans not seen them, they would have been.[34] They were included in an official publication of captured German documents in the 1950s, although Churchill (who had by then been returned to office) wrote to Eisenhower to try to prevent their being published, and indeed the President agreed they should be suppressed.[35] It was the French Government that insisted that they should be made public.

The usual line adopted by war historians and official biographers about the telegrams is that, while there was undoubtedly a German plot to seize control of the Duke of Windsor for propaganda purposes, they provide no especially significant insights into the Duke's attitudes to the war at that time. This is largely based on the fact that when the telegrams were made public in the 1950s, Windsor bluntly denied making many of the comments attributed to him – especially the 'treasonable' remark about the bombing of Britain – declaring he had no idea that the Spaniards such as Don Miguel and 'Tiger' Bermejillo were German agents. However, as we have seen, as Bermejillo was sent in response to his request for a conduit to the Nazis in order to retrieve belongings from France, it is hard to believe that the Duke was unaware that what he said would be reported back. And, of course, he was contacted by Prince Philip of Hesse-Cassel.

While it is admitted that there was Nazi intrigue surrounding the Duke, the accepted line is that he was unaware of it. According to the usual story, the information transmitted to Berlin was based on the Duke and Duchess's typically unguarded and indiscreet comments. Those that apparently revealed that the Duke was aware of what was going on – such as his willingness to act as peace negotiator, and the invention of the code that would recall him from the Bahamas – are put down to the Spanish agents' desire to inflate their own importance, and wishful thinking on the part of the German officials in Madrid. But why bother with such contrived explanations when the more obvious interpretation is that they accurately report the Duke's words at the time? It is obvious he was aware that he was speaking to agents of the German Government. Not only do his sentiments match his pre-war beliefs, it is hard to see how sending his good wishes to the Führer can be ascribed to exaggeration. Moreover, the accuracy of the telegrams is supported by evidence from other, non-Nazi, sources.

The American Ambassador in Madrid reported that Windsor was well known for expressing his view that negotiations to end the war should begin immediately.[36] More importantly, he had a conversation with Count Nava de Tajo that became the subject of a note by a secretary at the British Embassy – not released to the public until 1996. The Duke had forecast that Churchill's Government would soon fall, to be replaced by a Labour Government that would enter into negotiations with Germany. He also anticipated George VI would abdicate because the people would lose confidence in him and the ruling classes – and his own return to the throne as a result. Windsor stated that this would leave Germany free to attack Russia while the other nations of

Europe stood on the sidelines, exactly the position he had advocated while Prince of Wales and King.[37]

There is also the very telling note by Alexander Hardinge, dated 7 July 1940. After being shown intelligence reports to report to the King, he wrote:

> Germans expect assistance from Duke and Duchess of Windsor, latter desiring at any price to become Queen. Germans have been negotiating with her since June 27th. Status quo in England except for undertaking to form anti-Russian alliance. German purpose to form Opposition Government under Duke of Windsor, having first changed public opinion by propaganda. Germans think King George will abdicate during attack on London.[38]

When the Government posted Windsor to the Bahamas, the task of drafting the announcement to the Prime Ministers of the Dominions fell to Lord Caldecote, Secretary of State for the Dominions. It read:

> The activities of the Duke of Windsor on the Continent in recent months have been causing His Majesty and myself grave uneasiness as his inclinations are well known to be pro-Nazi and he may become a centre of intrigue.[39]

Churchill personally amended this to read:

> The position of the Duke of Windsor in recent months has been causing His Majesty and His Majesty's Government embarrassment, as though his loyalties are unimpeachable, there is always a backwash of Nazi intrigue which seeks to make trouble about him.[40]

As usual, it was Churchill's view of events that was adopted by history.

Yet despite this evidence official historians and biographers remain unconvinced. Ziegler, for example, concludes that Windsor would never have been party to such treasonable plans and that 'Ribbentrop deluded himself'.[41] On the other hand, others who reject the official line, such as John Parker, believe that Windsor was in active collusion with the Nazis in order to be restored to the throne – but neither is this borne out by the German telegrams, which state that although the idea was put to him, at best he appeared lukewarm at the prospect. (Remember, it was the Duchess who became particularly 'pensive' at the suggestion.) Instead, Windsor made arrangements to assume the role of negotiator or go-between in the event of peace talks. As we have seen, it was Windsor's ambition to have a position of power in Britain, so that he could guide the country in his chosen direction; he did not necessarily want to return to the throne – even though the Nazis assumed his most heartfelt desire was to be King again.

Wallis was another matter. Kenneth de Courcy's comment on this subject, in a note that he made after reading Michael Bloch's *Operation Willi* (1984), reads: 'The Duke would never on his own have accepted restoration from the Germans. But the Duchess would have . . .'[42] Presumably she considered this the ultimate revenge for the HRH humiliation.

At the same time as the flurry of Madrid and Lisbon communications, Hardinge was informed that British intelligence had information about the Germans' plan to restore Windsor to the throne, as they expected George VI to 'abdicate during [the] attack on London'. Why they thought the King would take such a radical step is unclear – after all George would realise that a second abdication in quick succession would spell the end of the monarchy in Britain, not to mention personal ignominy on an unimaginable scale. Surely it made more sense to expect the King and the rest of the royal family to be evacuated, presumably to Canada. But the idea that the Germans would reinstall Edward on the throne – should George VI leave the country – does appear to have played a part in Hitler's strategic thinking.

Despite Churchill's rousing promise to 'fight them on the beaches' in the event of a German invasion, in reality of course this would not have applied to himself, the Government, the military commanders or the royal family. At the first sign of an enemy landing they would have been whisked out of the country and continued to run the war from the safety of Canada.[43] If the King left the country, then the German plan to restore Windsor would become a serious possibility. John Parker argues that such a plan had more chance of success than might be thought today. He points out that Edward's return in George VI's absence would have had a fair chance of being accepted by the British people at that time; Bertie and Elizabeth had made little headway in the popularity stakes and Windsor was still remembered affectionately by many as a promising golden boy.[44]

Elsewhere we have argued that Hitler never seriously intended to invade Britain, and that the alleged invasion plan, Operation Sea Lion, was a cover for preparations for the German offensive against Russia.[45] Not only did he consider the campaign against the USSR to be considerably more important than engaging in hand-to-hand fights on the beaches of Skegness and Margate, but the more logical, efficient – and cost-effective – option where Britain was concerned was surely to starve the island into surrender through a U-boat blockade. However, the Nazis may have anticipated that the royal family would be taken out of the country for their safety during the bombing of London.

This may explain George VI's apparently paranoid idea, when the Palace was bombed in September 1940, that it was a deliberate plot by the Nazis to kill him and put the Duke of Windsor on the throne.[46] His anxiety makes little sense otherwise, and we know that he was briefed by Hardinge on the skulduggery centring on Windsor in Lisbon. The first bomb dropped on Buckingham Palace just a few days into the Blitz, in daylight on 9 September, when the King was at the Palace, but it failed to explode until the early hours of the next morning. On Friday, 13 September 1940, during an (unusual) daytime air raid, one of the Luftwaffe bombers broke off from its formation, flew up the Mall and dropped six bombs on the Palace while the King and Queen were inside.[47] The Palace seems to have been specifically targeted – the King wrote in his diary that 'There is no doubt that it was a direct attack on the Palace.'[48]

Certainly, Hitler may have considered it worthwhile to divert one bomber to attack the Palace, in the hope of either killing the King or driving him out of the country, providing a golden opportunity of restoring Windsor to the throne. Another telling sign of Hitler's attitude to the ex-King is the fact that the Windsors' homes in Paris and Antibes remained completely unscathed throughout the war, whereas many thousands of others were wrecked or looted by their temporary Nazi residents.[49] As late as October 1941, Hitler declared that the Duke of Windsor was 'no enemy of Germany' and that 'when the proper moment arrives, he will be the only person capable of directing the destiny of Britain'.[50]

Even in the out-of-the-way Bahamas, Windsor continued to cause headaches in Britain and the USA, chief among them being his contact with the immensely wealthy Swedish industrialist Axel Wenner-Gren, lord of the Bahamian Hog Island. The founder of Electrolux, he is often unquestioningly labelled as pro-Nazi because of his continued business interests in Germany during the continuation of hostilities. But in fact there is no evidence that he was ever an active supporter of Nazi ideology. Moreover, Wenner-Gren was one of the group of Swedish businessmen that attempted to avert the war – holding personal discussions with Göring in May 1939. Indeed, we have seen that individuals connected with Electrolux were at the forefront of the peace movement. Most significantly, its British chairman, Sir Harold Wernher, helped to arrange Lord Aberconway's delegation to Göring in August 1939. Married to Lady Zia, Mountbatten's sister-in-law, he was also a close friend of the Duchess of Kent.[51] The Wernhers' country house, Luton Hoo in Bedfordshire, was a hotbed of intrigue intended to bring about a compromise peace, which included the dramatic but failed Rudolf Hess mission.[52]

While it is inaccurate to label Wenner-Gren a Nazi sympathiser, the very fact that the Duke and Duchess of Windsor were in regular contact socially with a prime mover in the cause of a compromise peace was more than enough to worry Churchill. And Windsor amply demonstrated that he was still capable of profoundly embarrassing the British Government. In December 1940 he gave an interview to American journalist and novelist Fulton Oursler – published in the magazine *Liberty* three months later – in which he made what were widely seen as distinctly defeatist statements: he doubted that there would be any one victor in this war and intimated that it would be wrong to depose Hitler as he had the support of the German people.[53]

One of the most telling responses to the interview was something that failed to materialise, like the Sherlock Holmes dog that didn't bark in the night. On Goebbels' personal instruction, the Nazi propaganda machine made nothing of Windsor's amazing indiscretion, even though it was a gift from the gods.[54] It would have been easy enough to present it as evidence of the serious division among the British ruling classes. Goebbels still considered it more important not to compromise the Duke's popularity in Britain – presumably because the Nazis thought he would still have his uses there.

COURTS IN EXILE

The opening stages of the Second World War seemed to confirm the royal family's worst fears about the fate of the other European monarchies. As legions of Nazi jackboots stamped their way through the continent, the dispossessed sovereigns of the occupied countries – one by one – ended up in Britain. Theo Aronson writes that by the end of 1940, 'All the other Sovereigns [of Europe] were either in exile, in disgrace or virtual prisoners of the Nazi regime.'[55] The royal family played host to a number of their European counterparts: King Haakon VII of Norway; Queen Wilhelmina of the Netherlands; King George II of the Hellenes; King Peter II of Yugoslavia; and King Zog of Albania, together with most of their families.

The focus for the behind-the-scenes diplomacy surrounding the exiled royals was Kent's country house, the Coppins, becoming almost an unofficial Court of St James. The Duke was George VI's personal liaison officer – even perhaps his ambassador – not only with exiled royals but also the Governments-in-exile, such as General Sikorski's Free Poles.

At the outbreak of hostilities, Kent had been given a job at the Admiralty, but soon moved on, for a brief spell with the Ministry of Labour and then the RAF, where he became Chief Welfare Officer – using his royal glamour in morale-boosting visits to RAF bases. Whether by accident or design, this proved very useful for his considerably less public role, allowing him greater freedom to travel and the necessary cover for meeting with representatives of foreign governments, the governments-in-exile and the dispossessed royals.

The King himself was accustomed to using relatives to establish 'unofficial' contacts with foreign heads of state: for example, David Bowes-Lyon was appointed to British intelligence's Political Warfare Mission in Washington, under the famous spymaster Sir William Stephenson in 1942. As David Duff writes, Bowes-Lyon was 'used unofficially to carry messages between the King and President Roosevelt'.[56]

George and Marina invited their Polish friends, Alik and Zoia Poklewski, with Zoia's mother Baroness de Stoeckl, to move into a cottage in the grounds of the Coppins. Writing in her memoirs of the closing months of 1940, Baroness de Stoeckl said:

So many important people were coming down to visit the Duke, and many would end the day in our small house. General Sikorski rented a mansion quite close . . .

The King and Queen, Queen Mary, the King of Greece, in fact all the Royal Families of any country would come to Coppins – the Ministers, etc – it was a constant stream of visitors.[57]

Hitler's merciless Blitzkreig throughout the Low Countries had brought calamity to the royal houses of Belgium and Holland. In Belgium, Leopold III ordered his forces to lay down their arms on 28 May 1940 (as in Britain, the Belgian armed forces swear loyalty to the monarch rather than government). This has always been interpreted either as an act of pragmatism, to avoid further loss of Belgian lives faced with inevitable defeat, or straightforward cowardice. However, although presumably he would have preferred the Nazis not to invade his country, Leopold had no real problems with them – certainly Hitler 'considered Leopold to be Nazi-friendly'[58] – and his own position in Belgium was barely affected by the occupation. Although a 'self-proclaimed prisoner'[59] in his palace just outside Brussels, Leopold was allowed out on excursions to Paris and various resorts, even being supplied by the German occupiers with call girls, some of whom he even took with him when he went to Berchtesgaden in November 1940 to negotiate a political settlement with Hitler about his country's future.[60] To clarify his position yet further, Leopold denounced the Belgium Government-in-exile in London as traitors.[61]

Leopold's order for Belgium to surrender was denounced by Britain and France as a stab in the back because it allegedly came as a bolt from the blue. In fact, he had given those governments several days' warning of his intentions, even setting them out in a personal letter to George VI, who was disturbed by the virulence with which the Belgian King was widely scapegoated.[62]

Queen Wilhelmina of the Netherlands, who was 60 at the time of the German invasion of her country has – along with her son-in-law Prince Bernhard – gone down in history as the symbol of her people's defiance against the Nazi occupation, particularly because of her plucky and upbeat radio broadcasts from London to her conquered nation. However, as with the British royal family, there was a wide gulf between Wilhelmina's true convictions and those she chose to display publicly as national figurehead. There are still many taboos in the Netherlands about probing too deeply into Wilhelmina and Bernhard's real war, although a small band of researchers are willing to challenge the cosy myths: one such is Charles Destrée, who as a teenager worked with his father in the Dutch Resistance and has since spent decades researching occupied Holland and the Dutch Government-in-exile, and whose insights will be discussed shortly.[63]

Queen Wilhelmina had more direct political influence over her kingdom than Leopold or even George VI over their respective countries, chiefly because of her unique financial position: from the 1880s the Dutch royal family had owned a substantial share of the oil company Royal Dutch Shell (as it was then called), founded on oil reserves in the Dutch East Indies. Because of this investment, Wilhelmina herself was said to be the 'richest woman in the world'. (Ironically, Royal Dutch Shell was a major supplier of oil to Germany. As Charles Destrée points out, when the Luftwaffe began bombing Rotterdam on 14 May 1940, they were using Dutch fuel.)

Wilhelmina did not have any particular ideological quarrel with Nazism when it first rose to prominence in Germany, and made efforts to promote good relations with the new regime. In return, Hitler gave her a guarantee, which of course proved worthless, of Dutch independence within the New Europe. (To the Nazis, the Dutch, like the British, were part of the Aryan 'master race', so deserving of some respect.) Like her royal counterparts throughout Europe, Wilhelmina was opposed to the conflict, urging Britain, France and Germany not to go to war over Poland.

Moreover, Destrée argues that Wilhelmina displayed distinctly pro-German – if not actually pro-Nazi – sympathies. She was happy to accept the pledge of allegiance from the Dutch Fascist League (the ANFB) when it was formed in 1932, and in an astonishing move, decreed that the Dutch national anthem should change, from one whose opening line was 'Netherlands' blood . . . free from alien taint' to one that began: 'Wilhelm of Nassau am I, of German blood.'[64]

Her daughter and heir, Princess (later Queen) Juliana, had been a close friend of the Duchess of Kent since they were teenagers.[65] In 1932 it was Juliana who introduced Göring to the elderly Kaiser Wilhelm II (exiled in Holland since the First World War). More significantly, five years later she married the German Prince Bernhard von Lippe-Biesterfeld (better known as Prince Bernhard of the Netherlands), who had been a member of both the Nazi Party and the SS.[66]

Queen Wilhelmina found herself in Britain largely without her consent. Three days into the assault on Holland, the British sent a destroyer to take her from danger in the Hague to Zeeland in the south. However, as the German advance continued, it was deemed safer for her to go to Britain, so the ship changed course – much to Wilhelmina's annoyance. That, at least, is the official explanation: it is possible that this was a deliberate move by Churchill, who thought it best to remove her from occupied Holland, as she might have proved too willing to compromise with the Germans, or might even have echoed Prince Leopold's surrender. Her first request on landing at Harwich was to be allowed to return to the Netherlands, a request she was to repeat several times, but to no avail.[67] Queen Wilhelmina had been virtually kidnapped by the Royal Navy.

Also on board were Juliana and her husband Prince Bernhard: as the only child and direct heir to the throne, she was sent to Canada for safety, while

Bernhard remained in Britain, becoming active in the Dutch Government-in-exile. Scandalously, the fact that he was not only German, but a former member of the Nazi Party and of the SS, does not appear even to have marked him out as a security risk – and unlike all other Germans living in the UK he was not interned.

During the German occupation of the Netherlands, through her radio broadcasts Wilhelmina established herself as the symbol of the Dutch resistance and freedom fighters, although researchers such as Destrée regard this as a sham. All the indications are that she would have preferred to stay in Holland so that, once the initial fighting was over, she would be able to work for her nation's independence by co-operation with Germany. Relations between the Dutch royal family and the Nazi leaders had always been good, and having a Nazi son-in-law would have helped. Her true objective is revealed by her letter to Princess Juliana in Canada in August 1940 in which she spoke of reaching 'an agreement with the Germans . . . by which the Netherlands in a German Europe nevertheless would keep a certain independence'.[68]

Queen Wilhelmina easily imposed her will on the Dutch Government-in-exile that controlled the Free Dutch forces in Britain, having much more constitutional power to appoint and dismiss ministers than the British Sovereign. In August 1940, she dismissed the Prime Minister in exile with her, De Geer, officially on the grounds of ill health – but, according to post-war historians, in reality because of his desire to make a compromise peace with Germany. De Geer left Britain, ostensibly for the Dutch East Indies, but after playing for time in Portugal, made his way back to occupied Holland. Although widely condemned and even prosecuted for this after the war, he received only a nominal sentence. However, there is evidence that this was all a charade and that De Geer's return to Holland was engineered so that a back-door channel could be opened between Wilhelmina and the Nazis to pursue secret negotiations to restore Holland's independence.

Although it lies outside the scope of this book, Charles Destrée's research has uncovered considerable evidence that Wilhelmina's control of the Free Dutch provides the key to one of the Second World War's most notorious intelligence deceptions: the Nazi operation known as the Englandspiel ('England Game'). Dutch agents parachuted into Holland by the Special Operations Executive (SOE) were all betrayed, being picked up one by one by German squads that were lying in wait, then compelled to contact London.[69]

Wilhelmina was not alone in relentlessly pursuing her own agenda while based in Britain. Many of the other royal houses continued to exploit their own network of contacts, in which the Duke of Kent almost always played a pivotal role. Perhaps it is no coincidence that Marina was close to the Dutch royal family and Kent worked closely with Prince Bernhard of the Netherlands.

Clearly, because the various exiled royals and heads of state always put their country's best interests first, they did not necessarily concur absolutely with the Allies' overall war aims. This became more and more obvious as the war progressed. Although initially Britain had famously gone to war to curb the Nazis' territorial ambitions, all that soon changed. Particularly after the 'Triple Alliance' with the USA and USSR was in place at the beginning of 1942, that objective evolved into the Churchillian vision of the annihilation of the Nazi regime and the total destruction of Germany. The interests of the smaller nations became less and less important in the grand scheme, and sometimes the two actually came into conflict.

The example of Poland is particularly instructive: the aims of Sikorski's exiled Free Poles were straightforward enough – to regain their nation's independence. Although the issue over which Britain and France declared war was the Nazi invasion of Poland, it is usually forgotten today that it was a joint invasion by Germany and the Soviet Union, Hitler and Stalin having made a secret deal to divide the country between them. (The question of why Britain only declared war on one of the aggressors, but became an ally of the other, has never been satisfactorily answered.) When, in 1942, the USSR became Britain's ally, the Free Poles were faced with a choice of the lesser of two evils – literally. If the Allies triumphed, the whole of Poland would be under Soviet domination: the Poles laboured under no illusion that Stalin would return their autonomy. In fact, there was more of a chance of compromise with the Germans, especially if Kent – who had the respect of both sides – was involved in the negotiations. In this way, the interests of one of the smaller nations in the alliance became diametrically opposed to those of the major powers – and the overall policy of the Grand Alliance.

Because of his pre-war relationship with Poland, Kent was close to Sikorski and the Polish Government-in-exile, as well as the troops stationed in Britain, mainly in Scotland. Because of the way events had turned out, Kent would have been even keener to negotiate an end to the war. His overriding concern was that the war should not end in a victory for Russia, which would leave Poland under communist occupation.

His championship of the Polish cause resulted in Sikorski's formal offer of the Polish Crown, giving the Duke an added incentive to find an end to the war that left Poland free. Baroness de Stoeckl writes: 'It was their [the Polish exiles'] wish that he should become King of Poland when once their country was free – but death came, and with it the end of many hopes!'[70] Published in 1950, the Baroness's memoirs contain the only public reference to this plan for Kent, but Sikorski's offer was revealed in official papers released in 1972, which also disclose the Government's disquiet about Kent's close relationship with the Free Poles.[71]

The exiles' attitudes, plans and decisions depended on how they saw the result of the war: at that time, at least from the summer of 1940 to the end of 1941, it seemed obvious that either the Germans would win outright or that a compromise peace would have to be reached eventually.

THE HESS PLAN

In our book *Double Standards: The Rudolf Hess Cover-Up* (2001) we unravelled the complex mystery of Rudolf Hess's flight to Scotland in May 1941, but the most relevant arguments are summarised here.

On 10 May 1941, Hitler's Deputy flew alone in a Messerschmidt fighter-bomber from Augsburg, near his hometown of Munich, to Scotland. He parachuted out close to the village of Eaglesham, to the south of Glasgow, where he ended up – somewhat farcically – in the custody of the Home Guard. Giving the name of 'Alfred Horn', he claimed to be attempting to make contact with the Duke of Hamilton, the Premier Peer of Scotland and the King's representative north of the border. (At the Scottish coronation of the monarch, it is the Duke of Hamilton who presents the crown of Scotland.) Indeed, it became apparent that Hess planned to land on the private airfield at the Duke's estate at Dungavel, but had lost his bearings and baled out some eight miles away. The morning after his capture Hess revealed his true identity to Hamilton and was subsequently transferred to England, where he spent the rest of the war as a top-security prisoner.

In *Double Standards* we argued that, far from being the inconsequential sideshow dismissed by most post-war historians, Hess's flight was one of the pivotal events of the Second World War. Officially both the British Government and Hitler (the only thing on which they agreed) ascribed the incident to Hess's delusion that there was still a substantial peace movement in Britain and that, if only he could make contact with its members, he could persuade them to oust Churchill and create a government that would negotiate an end to the conflict. The accepted story goes that in reality there was no peace movement and such terms that Hess brought with him were no more than a madman's bluster.

However, our evidence reveals that this is far from the true picture, and that the conventional view of the Hess affair is the result of one of the most successful cover-ups of the twentieth century. Briefly, we concluded that there *was* a substantial peace lobby in Britain – the same influential individuals and groups that had always opposed war with Germany – which knew that Hess was coming, and indeed had been planning the event for months through intermediaries in Portugal, Sweden and Switzerland. Those involved on the British side included leading aristocrats, senior politicians and even MI6 – its chief, Sir Stewart Menzies, being an important figure in the anti-war lobby. Another major group involved in the plan was the Free Polish Government.

Our investigation revealed that Hess's mission represented a real chance to end the war, and the proposals that he brought were not the babblings of a madman or a mess of vague ideas, but detailed terms for a compromise peace. In fact, they comprised a substantial document – seen by several people – which went into great detail about the fate of different territories. Whether the terms would have been acceptable to the majority of politicians and the public at that stage of the war is difficult to judge, as only their broad principles are known: if Britain allowed Germany a free hand in Europe, Germany would not interfere with the British Empire. However, with astounding deviousness and arrogance, Churchill unilaterally rejected the proposals, not even putting them to the Cabinet, let alone Parliament; indeed, their non-appearance in governmental circles led to the widely accepted belief that they were pointless ramblings.

However, the most important aspect of the Hess affair as far as this book is concerned is that the Duke of Kent was intimately involved in the plan. We have testimony that Kent was actually among the group that clandestinely waited to greet the Deputy Führer at Hamilton's home, Dungavel House. It appears that as usual Kent was acting on behalf of George VI, *and that the King had sanctioned the Hess plan* – one of the major reasons for the carefully maintained post-war cover-up.

The King's part in the Hess cover-up also involved the bizarre and disturbing fate of one Lieutenant-Colonel William S. Pilcher of the Grenadier Guards. After a distinguished Army career, suddenly he became a 'non-person' in 1942, completely disappearing from society, his name even being removed from *Who's Who*. Several researchers have linked Pilcher with the Hess affair.

An informant told us that, on the orders of the King, Pilcher was kept isolated in a cottage on the Balmoral estate, where he lived – virtually incommunicado – until his death in 1970, nearly 30 years later. Apparently the reason for this strange, almost man-in-the-iron-mask scenario, was that he knew too much about George VI's support of the Hess peace plan: it is said that Pilcher had even signed a letter of safe conduct for the Deputy Führer in the King's name, although in the absence of solid evidence this must remain hearsay.

Kenneth de Courcy was a close friend of Pilcher, who had been the commanding officer of his school cadets and who later introduced him to Sir Stewart Menzies of MI6, and made strenuous efforts to keep Pilcher's name alive. He tried to persuade his influential friends to find out what they could about his fate. In the letters he wrote to Pilcher's son Jeremy in 1989 – now in our possession – he says: 'I conclude that your father was disgracefully treated.'[72]

Other researchers have suggested that if any member of the royal family was involved in the Hess mission, it must have been the Duke of Windsor – and even that an integral part was to depose George VI and put him back on the throne.

George VI and the Duke of Windsor's aims were essentially the same as far as the war was concerned. Neither thought that Britain should be at war with Germany. There was no conflict between the brothers on that point, nor about who should be King. We have seen that Windsor's ambition was for a political role in Britain, not necessarily restoration to the throne (although no doubt he could have been persuaded by the Nazis – and Wallis). In his secret dealings with the Nazis, he had simply offered himself as a negotiator between the two countries – a position for which he was well suited, being (at that time) popular in both.

Therefore it is possible that Windsor did feature in the Hess plan to some extent, and may even have been aware of it, if only because of his possible role as negotiator. Kent always maintained good relations with his eldest brother, presumably including the period in which the Hess plan was being organised. During the Windsors' turbulent time in Lisbon, they stayed with Kent's friend, so probably they communicated in some way at that time, and it was Kent's German contact, Philip of Hesse-Cassel, who visited the Duke there. It is also significant that Churchill went to great lengths to prevent Windsor and Kent meeting during the war. Although – officially – it was the Portuguese Government that requested they should be kept apart when Kent attended the anniversary celebrations in Lisbon in June 1940, in September 1941 when they were due to visit America at the same time, Churchill ordered Windsor to delay his planned trip until Kent had left.[73] Why should Churchill have been so anxious to prevent two members of the royal family from meeting? Under the circumstances, as Windsor had been effectively isolated in the Bahamas, it can only have been because of what actions *Kent* might take as a result of such a meeting.

However, it is unlikely that Windsor instigated the Hess plan. The British end of the operation required quite complex organisation – even moving army officers supportive of the cause into the area, as well as transferring German internees who were to act as Hess's aides in the peace talks. The plan was supported by various politicians, officials and army officers, and a number of peers, most of whom would have been opposed to the restoration of Edward VIII. There was also the substantial involvement of the Free Poles, whose participation was crucial (as the war had started over Poland, they would have had to have been an integral part of any attempt to end it). But although Kent was undoubtedly the major royal figure behind the plan, he was acting on behalf of the King, not Windsor. (The Duchess of Windsor wrote somewhat cryptically of the Hess affair to her aunt in the US, 'This mystery is something. If only it meant the end of this war.'[74])

THE COUP THAT NEVER WAS

If Hess had successfully landed at Dungavel for negotiations with the Kent group what would have happened next? We believe that Churchill would have been presented with the fait accompli of an acceptable resolution to the conflict. If, as seems likely, he had rejected it, the King would have used his prerogative to remove him from office and appoint someone in his place who would accept it. (This would have been relatively easy for the King at that time: as Britain was being governed by a War Cabinet, neither Parliament nor a general election would have been required to make the change.) The most likely candidate was Lloyd George, although other leading members of the pro-peace movement such as Lord Halifax or Sir Samuel Hoare – both of whom Churchill had cunningly sent abroad – might have been recalled. (Halifax had been removed as Foreign Secretary in 1940 and appointed Ambassador to the United States, while Hoare was Ambassador to Spain.)

However, the plan failed, and Hess ended up under Churchill's control, with two important consequences. The wily old Prime Minister now possessed the means to blackmail those in the House of Commons and House of Lords who opposed his furtherance of the war. In fact, the degree of opposition to Churchill was far greater than post-war history will admit and until the middle of 1941 he was in a very insecure position, but the advent of Hess and his peace proposal – and the threat of Regulation 18b, the wartime law which gave Churchill the power to arrest without trial anyone who engaged in, or even advocated, unauthorised dealings with the Nazi Government – provided him with the leverage he needed. Indeed, when faced with a vote of confidence in the Commons in January 1942, he quite blatantly used the Hess affair to quell any rebellious MPs.[75]

Because of Kent's involvement in the failed Hess mission, this also gave Churchill the same power of blackmail over the King. Not only did George VI oppose Churchill's appointment as Prime Minister in the first place, but relations between the two were not good during the early part of Churchill's tenure: he did not enjoy the King's confidence, to put it mildly. However, it was noticeable that their relationship had improved by 1942, when the King appeared to be much happier to co-operate with his Prime Minister. This is usually thought to be because George VI had come to realise that Churchill was truly a great man and the right leader for the country in such a crisis. We would, however, suggest another motive: after the Hess debacle, Churchill had the King precisely where he wanted him.

The wartime Prime Minister is usually held up as the staunchest champion of the monarchy: it was said of him that he was the last remaining person to believe in the literal divine right of Kings. Maybe this is something of an exaggeration, but Churchill had an overriding belief in another divine right – his own. Besides, believing in the monarchy as an ideal institution is quite different from agreeing with an individual monarch, who might from time to time need to be prodded in the right direction. Churchill's great hero was his most famous ancestor, the first Duke of Marlborough (of whom he wrote a lengthy biography), Queen Anne's eminence grise. Churchill seemed to have relished the idea of fulfilling the same role for George VI.[76]

The truth about the Hess mission reveals how far reality departs from the usual bluff certainties of mainstream history. Churchill exploited the Hess affair to his own advantage in another highly significant way. By pretending to negotiate with the captive Hess, Churchill reached a de facto armistice with Hitler that lasted until the summer of 1942. Unthinkable though this may seem, the evidence is there: remarkably little happened in terms of direct confrontation between Britain and Germany during this period – the Blitz, for example, ended on the very night Hess arrived in Scotland. His main impetus was his and Hitler's eagerness to pursue what they regarded as the 'real' war: the offensive against Stalin's Russia, code-named Operation Barbarossa. This was due to begin six weeks after Hess's flight and, although Britain was effectively contained at that time, Hitler and his deputy considered it vital that resources should not be tied up in watching Germany's back: it would be an ideal time for Britain to go on the offensive. (Indeed, this was Churchill's plan all along – to wait for Hitler to turn east and then attack – although, for reasons not easily explained other than by the 'secret truce' theory, when Barbarossa actually began he abruptly dropped the idea.) By persuading Hitler that a deal was still possible through Hess, effectively Churchill had adopted the strategy advocated by the Imperial Policy Group and endorsed by Edward VIII before the war – to let Germany and the Soviet Union fight it out. This was the 'carrot' to the King and those members of the peace group who opposed the war on the grounds that Russia was the greater enemy. It may not have been exactly what they wanted, but it was close.

The truth about the Hess affair was suppressed by an unprecedented – and highly effective – cover-up. First, the relevant official documents were closed under an unusual, though not unique, 75-year rule, rather than the usual 50 years for secrets relating to national security, thereby keeping them from public scrutiny until 2017. This allowed ample time for the carefully cultivated official version to be established: Hess was mentally unstable and brought nothing of importance with him to Britain.

However, following Hess's death in Spandau prison in Berlin in 1987 and the end of the Cold War, pressure was put on the Government for the early release of the Foreign Office files, which was agreed in 1992. Researchers were sceptical that this would finally answer the many questions that remained – quite rightly, as it turned out. There was no way of checking that the files had not been 'weeded' before release – in fact, some of the most significant reports from the period after Hess's arrival were missing. (We know that they once existed because of memoranda that remain in the files – a bad mistake.) In any case, the then Foreign Minister Douglas Hurd told the Commons that one file would still be withheld because it contained 'certain records which pose a risk to national security'.[77]

However, a contact in the Foreign Office who has seen the 'file' (and must therefore remain anonymous) told us what it contains. In fact, it consists of a set of individual files, each of which contains a single sheet of paper – which states that the contents have been transferred to the Royal Archives at Windsor. This did not come as a major surprise.

TO THE GLORY OF HIS NAME

The Hess plan reeks of Establishment intrigue and desperate cover-ups. Richard Deacon[78] suggests that Mountbatten was behind the plan, but although he would have loved the power games involved – and the sense of forging history in one's own image – he lacked the opportunity. For most of the planning phase he was at sea, captaining his destroyer, without the means of maintaining regular contact with fellow plotters back in Britain.

Mountbatten had a slightly different angle on the war from the royal family because under Peter Murphy's influence he took the pro-Soviet rather than the pro-Nazi line (during the Spanish Civil War he had favoured a communist victory).[79] For this reason, he took an anti-appeasement stance before the war, although he did rather exaggerate its extent afterwards.[80]

Mountbatten and his family, the Milford Havens – particularly Nada, now the dowager Marchioness – also had their back-door channels to the German ruling houses, which they maintained through neutral Sweden. Conveniently, Mountbatten's sister was married to the Swedish Crown Prince so it was an easy matter to arrange for their letters to be conveyed in the diplomatic bag through the Swedish Embassy. At least in the early stages of the war, this channel appears to have been used purely to allow the Mountbattens to keep in touch with their German relatives. According to Charles Higham and Roy Moseley, authors of *Elizabeth and Philip: The Untold Story* (1991), although documents relating to the Mountbattens' secret channel have disappeared from official files, enough remains to show that it existed.[81] Of course, clandestine communication with the nation's enemies is for others a treasonable offence.

In any case, Mountbatten had considerably less interest than the royal family in seeking an end to the war: as far as he was concerned, he was having the time of his life making his name through some real, but mostly imagined, heroics.

As we have seen, as captain of the HMS *Kelly* Mountbatten celebrated the first day of the phoney war with an imaginary battle with not one, but two, U-boats. But providence decreed that he was to mark the last day of the phoney war with an all-too-real, if rather one-sided, encounter with a German submarine.

On 9 May 1940 HMS *Kelly* was torpedoed 100 miles off the Danish coast, killing 27 of the crew, whose deaths can be laid squarely at Mountbatten's feet. Although the destroyer was supposed to be on escort duty, he had disregarded orders to chase a U-boat, which promptly turned on him. Insisting that his ship could not possibly sink, the *Kelly* took four days to limp home. Typically, Mountbatten managed to turn this near-disaster – caused by his own almost psychotic recklessness – to good advantage, the return of the *Kelly* against all the odds being rapidly 'spun' into the stuff of legend. The adventure was even turned into the classic film *In Which We Serve*, with Noël Coward as the noble Mountbatten character (the dialogue included the latter's verbatim address to the crew on taking command). Later, this unsavoury episode was also fêted in *This Is Your Life*, when Mountbatten regally accepted the plaudits of the *Kelly's* survivors in a televisual extravaganza for which the subject himself had essentially provided the script. It was an interesting version of what was in real terms a complete debacle and, for many families, a tragedy for which no fine words or retrospective fantasy would ever compensate.

Adding insult to injury, Mountbatten firmly believed he should be rewarded with a DSO for his feat and elicited the help of the Duke of Kent to canvas the Admiralty on his behalf. He also asked Edwina to exploit her most influential friendships – while cannily demanding that she pretend to do so at the request of his officers, not himself.[82] The Admiralty declined, on the grounds that although he had claimed to have sunk two U-boats, there was no evidence for it – and because the *Kelly* fiasco was his own fault.

Despite his incompetence, Mountbatten was given the command of a flotilla of seven ships led by his own HMS *Javelin*, which was also torpedoed in November 1940, this time while in night-time combat with three German destroyers – five according to the incorrigibly innumerate Mountbatten – which escaped unscathed. Not only did his tactic for approaching the ships give the Germans advance warning of the attack – full speed, making as much noise as possible – but during the engagement he ordered his ships to turn broadside to the enemy, making them unmissable targets. He wrote that they were 'lucky to escape with 50 killed'.[83] Unbelievably, he finally received his DSO for this carnage, but only because the King himself shamelessly lobbied Churchill for it.

In December, the *Kelly* was repaired and Mountbatten resumed command, only to run into another British vessel on its first day out and return to the dock. As Andrew Roberts observes, 'The comedy of Mountbatten's errors would be funny had not sailors died as a result of them.'[84] There is no doubt that despite his astonishingly cavalier attitude to orders, his recklessness and downright incompetence, he saw his career flourish simply because of his royal connections. Anyone else would have been court-martialled for the *Kelly* and *Javelin* fiascos. Dickie was untouchable.

However, for some reason, the usually shrewd Churchill seemed to have fallen for Mountbatten's self-publicity – possibly because they shared the same arrogant belief in their supreme destiny and a love of romantic *Boys' Own* derring-do. Indeed, it was partly due to the Prime Minister's favour – not forgetting the King's support – that Mountbatten never looked back. At the end of 1941 Churchill appointed him to Combined Operations in London, initially as an adviser, then as Director. (Combined Operations co-ordinated the activities of the three services, previously somewhat slapdash but now that war required proper co-ordination of the army, navy and RAF, it was organised on more formal lines by Churchill.) The appointment astonished Mountbatten's superiors in the Admiralty for two reasons: it was unheard of for the captain of a destroyer to leap-frog over his seniors and betters into such a powerful position – the equal of admirals and generals – and because the man was crassly, jaw-droppingly, incompetent.

The best known – and certainly most controversial – of the combined operations carried out under Mountbatten's command was the Dieppe Raid on 19 August 1942. Officially code-named Operation Jubilee, this was a cross-channel attack in which Canadian troops were landed on the French coast. In one of the greatest Allied military disasters of the war, nearly 5,000 soldiers were landed, of which over 3,300 – two-thirds – were killed, wounded or taken prisoner. Much about the Dieppe Raid remains a mystery to this day – particularly what it was designed to achieve. Was it a cynical deception, in which the Canadian troops were sacrificed towards some other end? Was it intended to deceive Stalin,who was bearing the brunt of the war at that stage, into believing that the British and Americans were prepared to open a second front (even though Churchill realised they were nowhere near ready for it)? Or, conversely, was it to prove to the Americans that their intended invasion of northern France was impossible by deliberately botching the operation? Or was it part of a longer-term deception aimed at the Germans? The standard line is that Jubilee was an ill-conceived and badly planned operation that should never have been allowed to go ahead, and that, as the Director of Combined Operations, the fiasco was Mountbatten's fault. Lord Beaverbrook – a Canadian himself – pulled no punches: he loudly condemned him as a murderer.

Although the complexities of the Dieppe Raid lie outside the scope of this book, suffice it to say that, despite Mountbatten's incompetence and often criminal disregard of the lives of his men, on this occasion he was possibly the 'fall guy' for an operation approved by Churchill that was never meant to succeed. However, there is evidence that Churchill did not know of the raid, at least officially, which would mean that Mountbatten bears even greater responsibility.[85] Only when all the records concerning this debacle are revealed will the truth be known. But whatever lay behind the Dieppe Raid, the fact that it happened at all added to the royal family's mounting list of reasons for wanting the war to end.

THE STRANGE DEATH OF THE DUKE OF KENT

The Hess mission was – almost – the last throw of the dice by the peace group. Fifteen months later there was to be an even more desperate gamble, resulting in the death of the 40-year-old Duke of Kent. As far as the royal family was concerned, between May 1941 and August 1942 the situation had seriously worsened. Following the launch of Operation Barbarossa in June 1941 and the Japanese attack on Pearl Harbor the following December, the USA and the USSR were now Britain's allies. At the end of May 1942 the British Government made a treaty with Stalin's Russia, committing the two nations to a 20-year alliance – and also to closer co-operation after the end of the war. To the royal family, to whom the Soviets were the ultimate bogeymen, this was a nightmare indeed. As Sovereign, George VI not only had to sign the treaty, but – to rub salt in an already suppurating wound – was also compelled to make a speech celebrating the alliance with the brave and resolute Soviet Union.[86]

This alliance posed a real threat to the royals at home and those exiled in Britain, but also carried serious implications for the smaller nations, especially the Free Poles who realised they were about to be betrayed by the very nation that had promised them their freedom. If the Allies were victorious Poland would come under Soviet domination – for them an even worse prospect than Nazi occupation. Although the Triple Alliance made it more likely that the Allies would be victorious – though this was by no means certain even in the summer of 1942 – the triumph would come at the cost of increased Soviet influence in post-war Europe. In Britain such an alliance would surely result in the wider popularity of left-wing – and very likely *republican* – ideas.

With the Americans in the war, the de facto truce that had kept Britain largely out of the war since May 1941 and encouraged Germany in its war with Russia was coming to an end. The Dieppe Raid was a tangible sign of that. American aid was now pouring into the Soviet Union, increasing the likelihood that the Russians would defeat Germany – precisely the wrong outcome as far as the royals were concerned. Meanwhile the American commanders in London were pressing for the opening of a second front. Another sign of the ending of the 'truce' was the intensive air raids on Germany by the American 8th Army Air Force under the command of General Carl A. 'Tooey' Spaatz, which began in August 1942. The situation looked bad for the royal agenda, and if it was going to be resolved in a way favourable to them it had to be now. There were certainly signs that the King's usual man for the job, the Duke of Kent, was up to something in the summer of 1942 – but, as it turned out, that plot was to lead to his untimely death.

Now an Air Commodore, since May 1941 Kent had continued both his official work with the RAF's Welfare Branch and his unofficial job as liaison with foreign heads of state, both based in Britain and abroad. George VI had also appointed Group Captain Sir Louis Greig as Kent's personal assistant – in Geordie Greig's words, 'a sort of minder'.[87] In 1941, Greig had left the Cabinet War Room (where he was the King's unofficial 'eyes and ears') to take up a new post as Personal Secretary to the Air Minister (and Liberal Party leader) Sir Archibald Sinclair, with specific responsibility as Sinclair's liaison with foreign heads of state – in his grandson's words, a 'political fixer on a grander international scale'.[88] It was shortly after this appointment that George VI gave him the job with Kent. This was an ideal pairing, not only because of the close friendship between the two and Greig's skill in getting things done through unofficial channels, but also because they were both secretly working as top liaison officers with foreign heads of state.

In August 1941, Greig accompanied Kent on his six-week visit to Canada and the USA, where the Duke had meetings with President Roosevelt. (The two got on well: the Kents' third child, Prince Michael, who was born on 4 July 1942, became President Franklin D. Roosevelt's godson, taking the unusual middle name for a royal prince of Franklin.)

In late August 1942, Kent undertook the trip that ended in his death, which is officially described as a hastily arranged, morale-boosting visit to British forces in Iceland. However, as we shall see, there is compelling evidence it was nothing of the sort, the 'Iceland' story being a cover for a much more dangerous and sensitive mission. In the weeks leading up to the tragedy, Kent had been busy with several secret meetings. Shortly before the flight (the exact date is unclear) he met General Spaatz, commander of the Eighth US Army Air Force, in a Mayfair restaurant.[89] This was arranged through the American movie star Douglas Fairbanks, Jr, then serving with the US Navy in London – the two had become friends when he had been assigned to Kent as an aide on his Canadian and US tour in 1941. (Fairbanks was due to spend the weekend before Kent's fatal flight at the Coppins, but he received an apologetic note from the Duke postponing it because he had to leave on a 'special assignment'.[90])

Kent also met with Mountbatten a few days before the flight, possibly for a briefing on the Dieppe fiasco and also – like the meeting with Spaatz – to garner information about the Allies' plans for the next stages of the war. He was also visited by Crown Prince Bertil of Sweden at his Buckinghamshire home. The Duke of Kent left the Coppins for what was to be the last time on the morning of 24 August. Baroness de Stoeckl recorded his departure in her diary – noting that there seemed to be something special about this leave-taking. Certainly the Duke himself seemed to have had intimations of the coming tragedy:

> He stoops and strokes 'Muff' his chow, turns to the butler Bysworth: 'What will you do with him when I am gone?' Strange question, as he was so often leaving![91]

The Baroness's diary also reveals that he was to meet Alik and Zoia Poklewski in Scotland on 8 September, where he would visit the Polish troops stationed there. (In Sikorski's tribute following the Duke's death, he said that this visit was to have been for Kent to 'declare his sympathy to the Polish cause'.[92])

His exact movements from the time he left the Coppins to boarding his flight at RAF Invergordon in Scotland shortly after midday the following day remain unclear. According to official accounts he took the overnight train directly to Invergordon, but there is evidence that he broke his journey at Balmoral, where the King and Queen, along with the Duke and Duchess of Gloucester, were in residence. Significantly, Prince Bernhard of the Netherlands has stated that he dined with Kent at Balmoral the night before his death.[93]

A MYSTERIOUS DEATH

Although the mystery of the Duke of Kent's death is discussed in much greater detail in *Double Standards*, because of its relevance to this book, it will be summarized here. He died on 25 August 1942 when his Sunderland flying boat, flight number W4026, crashed into the side of a hill known as Eagle's Rock in Caithness in the far north of Scotland. Of all the crew and Kent's entourage, only one man survived, Flight Sergeant Andrew Jack. The crash that killed Kent is an acknowledged mystery of the Second World War, not least because of the obvious official cover-up: records have been withheld or gone missing, and Andy Jack was ordered to keep silent about what had happened – a silence he maintained to his death in 1978.

Although the flying boat was supposed to have been taking Kent to Iceland for a straightforward morale-boosting visit to the British forces stationed there, many clues suggest that the real purpose of the flight – and its true destination – was very different.[94]

There are too many anomalies, including the fact that the aircraft left from the wrong coast of Scotland for a journey to Iceland. The normal point of departure was Oban on the west coast, whereas this flight left from Invergordon on the east coast – an oddity compounded by the fact that W4026 was stationed at Oban and had to be specially moved to Invergordon for this flight. Secondly, why did the Sunderland crash in that particular area? Why was it flying over land in the first place? After all, for obvious reasons, a flying boat should stay over water where possible. And why did the pilot descend so low? As mechanical failure was ruled out, the crash was officially blamed on pilot error. Finally, why – if this was just a tragic accident – was there such an obvious cover-up?

Our research uncovered two additional – and potentially exciting – facts. The crash had occurred between half an hour and one hour later than it should have done, given the distance and flying time to Eagle's Rock. More astoundingly, *there was an extra person on board*: one body too many was recovered from the wreckage. The inescapable conclusion is that flight W4026 had diverted somewhere to pick up an extra passenger, which would also explain what the flying boat was doing in that particular area. An obvious candidate for the pick-up point was the remote Loch More, on the Caithness estate of Air Minister Sir Archibald Sinclair – whose assistant, Sir Louis Greig, was also aide to the Duke of Kent. (Although Greig usually accompanied Kent on his overseas trips, he was inexplicably absent from this one.)

As to the identity of the mystery extra passenger, we have suggested that this was none other than Rudolf Hess. Although of course he is believed to have lived out his long life as the lone inmate of Spandau Prison, it has been persuasively argued over the years that the prisoner who emerged from Britain and was imprisoned for life at the Nuremberg trials was not the real Rudolf Hess, but a double. This is supported by evidence given to us by Sir Archibald Sinclair's son, that in the summer of 1942 Hess was held in a house on the Duke of Portland's Caithness estate (in fact, just two miles from the crash site) and also, briefly, on a cottage on the shores of Loch More itself.

Although it is impossible to prove now – without a body to test forensically

– whether the extra passenger really was Hess, given all the facts it is at least clear that the 'special mission' on which Kent died was not a simple flag-waving tour of Iceland but one with a much more secret purpose. We believe that his destination was actually neutral Sweden, which is why the flying boat left from Invergordon. In *Double Standards* we also link the timing of the flight to a plot to oust Churchill from power, involving many of the same figures as those involved in the Hess plan.[95]

As to what caused the crash, again in the absence of precise information it is impossible to be certain. Unusually, every last scrap of wreckage was cleared from the crash site, and the official report – which would have included the technical analysis of the aircraft – has never been released. According to some researchers it was swallowed up by the Royal Archives at Windsor. However, the convenient timing, besides the presence in the area that day of unidentified military personnel, at least raises the possibility of sabotage. The exact objective of Kent's special mission will probably never be known, but it does seem to have been a desperate last-ditch attempt by the royals to end the war because of the alliance with the detested Bolsheviks. The German Ambassador to Portugal, Baron von Hoyningen-Huene, reported to von Ribbentrop that according to the British community in Lisbon, the flying boat was sabotaged in order to kill Kent because he was in favour of peace with Germany.[96] Once again, it is significant that the Nazis made no propaganda advantage out of this high-profile tragedy.

Reactions to Kent's death were peculiar, to say the least – and they remain so to this day. Although it did provide a few headlines, the reports were curiously muted (this was put down to the royal family's desire not to detract attention from the wartime bereavements of ordinary people). He was buried at Windsor on 29 August, in a private funeral attended by family and friends, including Noël Coward and Douglas Fairbanks, Jr. Winston Churchill was conspicuous by his absence: he was not invited. General Sikorski ordered that a special tribute to the Duke should be read to all Polish servicemen, wherever they might be in the world.

The Duke of Windsor organised a memorial service for his beloved youngest brother in the Bahamas, on 29 August 1942, the day of his funeral at Windsor. According to one of Windsor's aides, the Duke 'broke down and wept like a child all the way through'.[97]

It is very curious that although Kent was the only member of the royal family to die on active service for 500 years, his life and (presumed) valour remain unsung. How many people have heard of him today? Even during the national celebrations to mark the end of the war, and the annual Cenotaph ceremony he is rarely mentioned, and then only in passing as a hasty acknowledgement of the Kent family's loss. There is no sense of heroism or national grief – and no obvious desire to dwell on his death. It is no exaggeration to say that it is almost as if the royal family wish to pretend he never existed in case too many questions are asked. There are only two memorials to him – the cross raised by Marina at the remote crash site and a stained-glass window in the Savoy Chapel in London.[98] Significantly, Marion Crawford, governess to Princesses Elizabeth and Margaret Rose, likened the royal family's avoidance of the Kent tragedy to their reaction to the Duke of Windsor – but why, when one was presumably a hero and the other painted as a villain? She says: 'The Royal Conspiracy of silence had closed about him as it did with so many other uncomfortable things.'[99]

Kent's death marked the final chapter of the royal campaign to end the war. It was now out of their control. They could only wait to see what would happen when the dust had settled. And of course when the war did end, the Palace spin doctors went into overdrive to cover up their less acceptable activities. The myth with which we are only too familiar today was already in place: the King and Queen always hated Hitler and Nazism, always loved Mr Churchill and were adored by every last one of their subjects, especially the humble cockney folk. They voluntarily stuck to the meagre wartime rations. Every member of the royal family was quietly heroic in their hatred of the Germans and unstinting devotion to all our Allies, from Americans to Poles and Russians. Not a single member of the family was involved in anything that might be construed as treacherous or underhand throughout the whole period of the war.

Perhaps because it was what the nation wanted to hear, that is what it has heard unremittingly since 1945. Cynics may suspect other agendas, but rarely do they uncover the full story.

– SEVEN –

'THE HOUSE OF MOUNTBATTEN NOW REIGNS!'

Earl Mountbatten of Burma on the death of George VI, 1952

The Duke of Kent's death effectively marked the end of the royal family's behind-the-scenes intrigues during the war: after August 1942 there was little option but to toe the line, provide the impeccable 'focus for national unity' and nervously wait to see how things would turn out.

Kent's death also assisted the further rise of Mountbatten, who seems to have taken over some of his unofficial – and highly sensitive – liaison work with the family's German contacts. Tellingly, three years after the end of the war George VI supported legislation that would improve Mountbatten's financial standing on the grounds that he needed the extra income because he had taken over 'many of the representational duties of the Duke of Kent'.[1] Yet a glance at Mountbatten's naval career and public life between 1942 and 1948 reveals nothing that matches such a description. What was he up to during that time that deserved such recognition? Mountbatten also took on some of the responsibility for providing for Kent's children.[2]

As we have seen, Mountbatten and his family had back-door channels to Germany, which initially seem to have been used simply to keep in touch with his relatives. However, after Kent's death those channels were probably used to communicate with his former contacts such as Prince Philip of Hesse-Cassel.

HIDING THE EVIDENCE

As thousands surged up the Mall to celebrate an end to the war in Europe on VE Day, 8 May 1945, they flocked to cheer the focus of national pride – the royal family, who took several 'curtain calls' on the Buckingham Palace's war-battered balcony, together with Winston Churchill. This picture of patriotic unity can still bring a lump to the throat, an upsurge of emotion that the

Palace has carefully fostered ever since, particularly on the commemoration of VE Day, the Queen Mother's many milestone birthdays and, of course, on the occasion of her death.

While basking in the glow of popular support, the royal family knew it had to execute some fancy footwork very swiftly if it was to keep ahead of the game. In the immediate aftermath of the German surrender, their worst fears seemed to be confirmed. They emerged from the Second World War – just as they had from the First – anxious that Britain stood on the brink of becoming a republic. It seemed everything they stood for was disappearing rapidly in the bleak realities of the second half of the twentieth century. Emerging from their bombed-out cities and ravaged countryside – not to mention the many thousands of members of the armed forces gradually returning from nightmare experiences all over the globe – the British people were desperate for a brave new world. And it seemed that their wish would be granted.

According to the long-standing agreement, Churchill asked for a general election to be called as soon as Germany was defeated. (In the event, he tried to postpone it until the war with Japan was over, but Clement Attlee held him to his promise.) Like any monarch, George VI was unhappy to see the end of the coalition and the return to party politics, but had no option but to accept the situation.[3] The election in July 1945 saw Churchill swept out of office as Clement Attlee surged to power at the head of the first majority Labour Government.[4]

However, George VI was still able to exert some influence over the Government, by persuading Attlee – though according to a note by Lascelles the King 'begged' the new Prime Minister[5] – to appoint the moderate Ernest Bevin as Foreign Secretary in his first Cabinet, instead of his preferred choice of Hugh Dalton. Apart from being of the extreme left, Dalton, as wartime Minister of Economic Warfare, had made the bad mistake of falling foul of his subordinate, the Queen's brother, David Bowes-Lyon.[6] (Another who fell foul of a Bowes-Lyon was Sir Alexander Hardinge, who had been compelled to resign in mid-1943 because the King had made it apparent that he had lost confidence in him. It has been claimed that the Queen was behind this because of her personal dislike for Hardinge.[7] This was why Lascelles was promoted as his replacement.)

The jewel in the crown of the new Labour Government was the – then sensational – creation of the National Health Service, which involved taking independent, charity-based hospitals under state control. This was another blow for the royal family, who preferred welfare to be provided on a voluntary basis – after all, their patronage of hospitals and charities was a potent signal that they cared for the poor and needy. They were particularly concerned to ensure that the nationalised hospitals continued to bear the title 'Royal' where it had been granted.[8]

There was much worse on their horizon. The British Empire was visibly crumbling, for a number of reasons. It was impossible for economically devastated post-war Britain to maintain the administration and defence of its sprawling overseas possessions. The ousting of the British by the Japanese in the battered possessions in Asia, such as Burma and Malaya, had – after the Japanese surrender in August 1945 – created a power vacuum that militant nationalist groups were only too willing to fill. It was simply no longer possible, after a long and bloody war fought in the name of democracy, to deny the colonies the right of self-determination. Worst of all for the pride of the once imperial royal family, Indian independence was inevitable. Small wonder then, that in 1948, when the novelist Vita Sackville-West lamented that her childhood home had been given to the National Trust, George VI replied, 'Everything is going nowadays. Before long, I shall have to go.'⁹ A Labour Government, the welfare state and the disintegration of the Empire – how could the royal family possibly survive this time?

The same strategies that worked before were brought into play again – shows of empathy with ordinary people and an emphasis on the royal family's Britishness (easier now than after the First World War). Moreover, the war itself had given the royal family a role and direction that could continue in peacetime. Largely due to the ubiquitous images of the newsreels, never before had the King and Queen played quite such an important part as a 'focus for national unity', whereas George V and Queen Mary had remained regal and relatively remote during the Great War. Few Britons would forget VE Day, and the sight of their King and Queen, and the princesses, together with 'Old Winnie', on the balcony of Buckingham Palace. (Conveniently, it helped to obliterate the memory of the last time George VI had accorded a Prime Minister such an honour, and the reasons why.)

The King had emerged from the war riding on a huge wave of respect from the British people, who had come to regard him as their national figurehead. Between them, Churchill and the King covered the two instantly recognisable national archetypes – Churchill as the squatly defiant John Bull who would win or die in the attempt, and the King as the decent chap who, if perhaps not very bright or glamorous, still managed to muddle through somehow, even in the end quite heroically. These were typified by their wartime broadcasts – Churchill belligerent and rousing, George empathetic and quietly confident, if somewhat hesitant. His nervousness and stammer – which despite all efforts to conceal was widely known – worked in his favour: the English in particular like nothing better than cheering on the disadvantaged and triumph over adversity.

The King had never really succeeded in controlling his extreme nerves and stammer. Lionel Logue, the speech therapist who had done much to tackle the problem since the mid-1920s, was on hand to school him before each wartime broadcast and – with the aid of some BBC wizardry – George managed to produce a competent performance, if somewhat slow and tired-sounding. But his temper tantrums, or 'gnashes', became much more frequent as the war progressed. Not only was this nervous wreck on display almost every day as he visited the new bombsites, he also had the extra burden of inside knowledge of the progress of the war, including some grim facts and prognostications.

He was still petrified of appearing in public. In June 1943 – travelling incognito as 'General Lyon' – he had made his first and last visit of the war to British forces overseas, in North Africa. Before one review, he sat in his tent saying, 'I can't, I can't . . . I'm not going to do it.' When his equerry, Sir Piers Legh, told him he had no choice in the matter, the King said, 'No, I'm going home . . .' When Legh eventually persuaded him to leave his tent, he made a competent enough job of the inspection.[10]

Given all George VI's personal demons, it was a remarkable achievement to come through all the pressures of reigning over a country at war (a conflict he had never wanted) without cracking up completely – although he had come to rely rather too heavily on the bottle to give him extra courage. But he had one great advantage: by this time Queen Elizabeth had honed her famous people skills, always exuding an effortless charisma as she picked her way delicately across the rubble in her high heels, always the epitome of empathy as she murmured, 'I *do* understand . . .' over and over again. But could they keep up the same level of success in peacetime? Or would they become the focus for discontent in the Britain of post-war austerity?

In response to the disintegration of the Empire, the royal family moved to create the British Commonwealth. (In fact, the dominions, colonies and dependencies had properly been known as the British Commonwealth of Nations since 1931, but the old term 'British Empire' died hard.) In many ways the Commonwealth may seem an illogical concept – an association of independent nations across the world whose only common characteristic is that they were once conquered, leased or otherwise acquired by Britain. Moreover, it is a curious mix of nations, some of which acknowledge the British monarch as head of state, others (for example, Brunei) have their own Sovereign, while yet others are republics. But despite its very British eccentricities, the Commonwealth has proved strangely enduring. (Today it consists of 54 nations with a total population of 1.7 billion, or 30 per cent of the world's population.) There is no doubt that it was inspired, for the Commonwealth allowed the Sovereign to retain the status as the head of an Empire that in reality had already imploded.

At home, there was some totting up to do. After the war, George VI gave back to the Treasury the sum of £100,000 (over £1.5 million today) saved from the Civil List during the conflict (less had been spent on wages, overseas visits, entertaining state visitors and so on). However, he only did this as a sweetener when asking Parliament in 1948 for an increased annuity for Princess Elizabeth following her marriage.[11] Princess Elizabeth was granted £40,000 a year (approaching £700,000 today) which was 90 per cent tax free. Princess Margaret received £10,000 (around £175,000).

More potentially embarrassing was income from the No Kin Investment

Fund, which derived from a fourteenth-century law by which the property and land of anyone who died intestate in the county of Lancashire went to the Duchy of Lancaster – in other words, into the King's coffers. In the words of the Duchy's historian Sir Robert Somerville, writing in 1953, the Duchy did 'surprisingly well' during the war, with payments of £85,000 (in the order of £1.5–£2 million today) being made annually to the Privy Purse. Part of this was the income from those who died without having made a will, listed in the Duchy's accounts together with 'forfeitures' (fines imposed by Lancashire Quarter Session Courts, another archaic right that was ended in the late 1960s). During the 1930s, this forfeiture income averaged £7,000 a year (about £175,000 today), but shot up during the war years, reaching a peak of £41,500 (about £850,000 today) in 1945, after which it slumped once more. This made up a substantial part of the Duchy's 'surprising' profits during the war.[12]

Of course it was not surprising at all. The war ensured that many more people from Lancashire (as elsewhere in Britain) were dying – intestate or otherwise. Every time one of his Lancastrian subjects was killed without making a will, the King pocketed their money and property. It is hard to be sure exactly how much he made from Lancashire's war dead – the No Kin income is aggregated with the fines in the Duchy's accounts. But, because there is no reason for the fines to have shot up in the war (quite the reverse), it is reasonable to conclude that the extra money came from the intestates. If so, then George VI made somewhere between £1 million and £1.5 million in modern terms from the war dead of Lancashire. Similar figures are not available for the First World War, so George V's profit from the fund is unknown.[13]

COMPROMISING DOCUMENTS

In the immediate aftermath of the war, the royal family's urgent priority was to prevent their secret communications with the Nazis, including Kent's dealings with Prince Philip of Hesse-Cassel and his involvement in the Rudolf Hess mission, from leaking out. All the most compromising documents were hastily tidied away in the untouchable Royal Archives at Windsor Castle, most urgently those concerning the Duke of Windsor. He was to serve a very useful purpose in diverting attention from the royal 'goodies' while he, as the black sheep, provided a convenient focus for accusations of treachery, a strategy that only really came into its own after his death, when he was in no position to defend himself. With Windsor the focus for all blame, it was hoped no one would notice what Kent – or, much worse, George VI and Queen Elizabeth – got up to. Under no circumstances must their involvement with secret negotiations with the Nazis come out, including the potentially explosive Hess affair.

One of the cache of compromising documents that ended up in the Royal

Archives is believed to be the German record of the meeting between Windsor and Hitler in 1937.[14] Certainly the eminent war historian Professor Donald Cameron Watt, who was one of the British officers responsible for analysing the captured German documents, states that they kept all material relating to the Duke of Windsor separate, but he was surprised that the record of the Hitler meeting was not included, and he believes that it was 'quite possible' that it had been extracted before it even reached the army historians. Watt says: 'The royal archivists have proper historians to advise them these days but at that time they were very secretive.'[15] It will come as no surprise to discover that the Duke of Kent's personal papers and diaries have never been made available to historians and biographers.[16] And, according to our own information, the detailed peace proposals brought by Rudolf Hess in 1941, although originally kept in Foreign Office files, were also transferred to the Royal Archives.

Based on her interviews with several individuals in a position to know the true circumstances, controversial author Kitty Kelley identifies the driving force behind this wholesale removal of these documents from the public domain as Queen Elizabeth, claiming she was even able to put pressure on the Government not to release certain documents relating to the Windsors when she was in her 90s.[17] However, our research identifies another self-appointed custodian of the royal image as the culprit – Lord Mountbatten. Of course his – and his family's – correspondence with relatives in Germany during the years of war gave him an excellent incentive to instigate the cover-up. But whoever was responsible, the use of the Royal Archives as a dumping ground for unacceptable material is a major scandal, akin to concealing evidence in a top-level case of treason.

The Royal Library and Archive falls into that usefully grey area of ownership between the Sovereign and the state. Like the Royal Collection (the art and antiques acquired by the royal family over the centuries), it is officially held by the monarch 'in trust' for the nation: while in theory it belongs to the nation, in practice the monarch owns it. The monarch may control it, but by and large the state pays for it.

The release of official documents to the Public Record Office is governed by law, although the Government has some discretion about the length of time such records are withheld. The usual period is 30 years, 50 in the case of national defence and matters of security. In certain circumstances a 75-year rule can be invoked (most often for records of court martials, although those relating to Hess's 1941 mission were also originally closed for this period). Lastly, there is the 100-year rule for matters concerning Northern Ireland – and the royal family. However, as the Public Records legislation only covers government and military records, it does not apply to the Royal Archives, access to which is – ultimately – controlled by the monarch.

While the royal family may legitimately claim that it is their decision whether purely personal papers – private correspondence and diaries, for example – should be made public, where they relate to affairs of state and matters of public interest there is no doubt that they should be accessible to scholars and researchers. And where the documents have been taken from Government departments they should certainly be in the public domain in accordance with the Public Records legislation. Because it is not even certain what the archive contains (unlike the Public Record Office, where the files are generally catalogued, even if access is forbidden), the contents are a matter for speculation, but documents that fall into this category are thought to include the record of the Hitler–Windsor meeting, the official inquiry into the Duke of Kent's crash, and – the most important historically – the peace plan brought by Rudolf Hess. But perhaps the greatest mystery surrounds papers recovered from Germany soon after the end of the war by the notorious Anthony Blunt, later unmasked as a Soviet spy.

A 'VERY HUSH-HUSH' MISSION

During the Second World War, Blunt – then a respected art historian at London University – achieved two positions of importance. Like many scholars and intellectuals, he was recruited into MI5, where he specialised in deception operations. Then in 1943, during the course of his research for his book about the drawings of Nicholas Poussin, he visited the Royal Library at Windsor, whose archivist, Owen Morshead, he already knew through his old tutor at Cambridge. This led to the offer of a job cataloguing the Library's Old Masters, as the whole collection was somewhat chaotic. (It may appear incongruous that the royal family would devote valuable resources to such a task in the middle of a war, but perhaps they needed an inventory in order to carry them off if they fled the country.)

What was not known then was that Anthony Blunt was also a Soviet spy, having been recruited into the Communist Party, and subsequently the NKVD, in the mid-1930s by another notorious traitor, Guy Burgess. Blunt later explained at the press conference in 1979 following the public revelations of his double life that he felt at that time that 'the Communist Party and Russia constituted the only firm bulwark against fascism, since the Western democracies were taking an uncertain and compromising attitude towards Germany'.[18]

Blunt was unmasked as a spy in 1964 (although there is evidence that MI5 knew of his treachery ten years previously, and were forced to take action against him only because of pressure from the United States). By this time he was not only the Surveyor of the Queen's Pictures, but also had been knighted by Elizabeth II as a member of the Victorian Order, so his royal connections meant that his case had to be handled with kid gloves. The outcome of the MI5 investigation – as a scandalised public was to learn 15 years later – was that although Blunt confessed, he was given immunity from prosecution and allowed to continue as before. He retained both his knighthood and his job in the Royal Household.

Three years later, MI5 officer Peter Wright, whose task was to seek out Russian 'moles', wanted to question Blunt further, particularly to try to elicit the identity of his fellow agents. (Even this process was immensely civilised: Wright conducted his 'interrogations' over drinks on a regular basis covering a period of some years.) However, before beginning his investigation, Wright was first called in by the Palace to be given an extraordinary – and highly significant – injunction. He writes in *Spycatcher*:

> Before I began meeting Blunt I had to attend a briefing by Michael Adeane, the Queen's Private Secretary. We met at his office in the Palace. He was punctilious and correct, and assured me that the Palace was willing to cooperate in any inquiries the Service thought fit. He spoke in the detached manner of someone who wishes not to know very much more about the matter.
>
> 'The Queen,' he said, 'has been fully informed about Sir Anthony, and is quite content for him to be dealt with in any way which gets at the truth.'
>
> There was only one caveat.
>
> 'From time to time,' said Adeane, 'you may find Blunt referring to an assignment he undertook on behalf of the Palace – a visit to Germany at the end of the war. Please do not pursue this matter. Strictly speaking, it is not relevant to considerations of national security.'[19]

This is breathtaking. Who were the Palace officials to judge that 'strictly speaking' Blunt's German trip had no connection with national security? They knew he was a Soviet agent, so anything he did, anyone he met – and especially any information he gleaned during that assignment in occupied Germany – most certainly *was* relevant to national security. In any case, surely Adeane's judicious phrase 'strictly speaking' is civil service-speak for an admission that there *were* such security implications. According to the official version, Blunt was only sent to Germany to collect some letters and other papers of purely family interest (besides some works of art). So why was the Palace so keen to prevent Wright from inquiring about the assignment? At the very least, Adeane's injunction reveals that the Queen and the Palace regard their own affairs to be more important than the defence of the realm.

Wright comments: 'Although I spent hundreds of hours with Blunt, I never did learn the secret of his mission to Germany. But then, the Palace had had several centuries to learn the difficult art of scandal burying. MI5 have only been in the business since 1909!'[20]

Clearly, the Palace has no intention of permitting the public to know something in particular about the affair – but what was it? Nothing about the 'assignment' – even the fact it had taken place – emerged into the public arena until the 1980s, when a reference to it was found in a Foreign Office file relating to captured German documents.[21] It appears that Blunt had been sent to recover letters from Prince Philip of Hesse-Cassel's twin brother, Wolfgang, at the Schloss Friedrichshof, the Hesse-Cassels' family seat at Kronberg in the Taunus Mountains, just north of Frankfurt-am-Main.[22] This provides a clue about the sensitivity of the mission: Friedrichshof was the home of Philip of Hesse-Cassel – the Duke of Kent's contact with the Nazi (and Italian) leadership who visited Windsor in Lisbon during the time of the 'Willi plot'. Moreover, in 1979, Prince Wolfgang of Hesse-Cassel revealed in an interview for the *Sunday Times* that Philip had conducted '"unofficial" mediation' between the Duke of Windsor and Hitler – 'discussions conducted with King Edward VIII through his youngest brother, George, Duke of Kent'.[23]

By the end of the war, Prince Philip of Hesse-Cassel had been arrested on Hitler's orders for intrigues (whether real or imagined is unknown) connected with Mussolini's deposition in July 1943, and thrown into a concentration camp. His wife, the King of Italy's daughter, was killed during an Allied air raid while an inmate of Buchenwald. Philip was freed by the US Army at the end of April 1945 – only to be promptly arrested by the Americans because he was number 53 on their wanted list, as the governor of Hesse.[24] Although they were keen to proceed with his prosecution, for reasons unknown he escaped the fate of fellow Nazis and lived on in comfort until 1980 (having inherited the title of Landgrave of Hesse from his uncle in 1945).

Since the story of the Blunt mission leaked out, the Royal Archive has allowed historians and biographers to see some of the documents relating to the affair that – they claim – reveal it to be all quite innocent. However, the very fact of the Palace's over-eagerness to set the record straight is in itself suspicious. Brendon and Whitehead suggest that their willingness to allow Philip Ziegler access to the Royal Archives for his authorised biography of Edward VIII was a direct response to speculation about Blunt and the 'Hesse letters'[25] – did this reflect a desire to sweep the episode under the carpet once and for all?

The story that emerges from the official records is that the then Archivist, Owen Morshead, and Blunt, sometimes together and sometimes singly, made several trips to Europe to recover property belonging to the British royal family, in case it should disappear in the confusion of the Allied occupation of Germany. The first trip took place in August 1945, when both men travelled to Friedrichshof, then a US Army rest and recuperation centre, with the aim of retrieving some 4,000 letters written by Queen Victoria to her eldest daughter (Victoria, the Princess Royal), Emperor Frederick III's wife and the mother of Kaiser Wilhelm II. (These are known as the 'Vicky letters' as both sender and recipient were called Victoria.) Morshead returned with the letters the following day, while Blunt remained on what Morshead described as 'military business'.[26]

Morshead subsequently made a 'similar trip' to Holland, about which there are no details, and over the next two years Blunt undertook three more assignments on the King's behalf after he had left MI5 in October 1945. In December 1945 and March 1946, two trips – both using George VI's private plane – took him to Westphalia to meet with the Duke of Brunswick (the heir to the Kingdom of Hanover) and bring back what are described as 'historic Royal Family possessions'.[27] Blunt returned with a sealed package that was not opened by Customs. According to Windsor documents, the 'possessions' included a twelfth-century manuscript and a diadem that had belonged to George III's Queen Charlotte. There is a rumour that they also included Queen Mary's letters to the Duke of Brunswick.[28] Leo Long, Blunt's former colleague in MI5 (the source of information he passed to Moscow), who was selected to be his driver on the first Westphalia trip, described Blunt's mission as 'very hush hush'.[29]

His last secret mission, in August 1947, took him to the Kaiser's former home, Haus Doorn in the Netherlands, to examine 'some objects that had once belonged to Queen Victoria' together with (as Morshead tellingly puts it in a letter to Alan Lascelles) anything relevant to 'relations between the Courts of England and Germany during the past hundred years'.[30] Blunt also returned from this excursion with some portraits.

These letters and memoranda from the Royal Archives have been used by historians and biographers to debunk reports that the purpose of the assignment was to recover compromising letters to Philip of Hesse-Cassel from the Dukes of Windsor and Kent, or to the Duke of Brunswick from Queen Mary. However, this fails to explain why these trips were never mentioned until after they became known through other channels in the mid-1980s – and why the Palace ordered Peter Wright not to pursue them in 1967, or even to pay attention to whatever Blunt might have volunteered on the subject. While the royal family in the immediate aftermath of the war might not wish to remind the British people of their close ties with Germany, surely the matter of their German blood would hardly matter so much 22 years later.

It is also significant that Adeane referred to 'a visit' by Blunt to Germany at the end of the war – not three to Germany (and one to Holland). It appears that only the first visit to the Hesse-Cassel castle at Kronberg was particularly sensitive. With their usual flair, the Palace mafia only succeeded in drawing attention to an episode they wanted to be ignored.

Given the secrecy and the nature of Hesse-Cassel's role, besides some of the more unlikely elements of the story (why should Queen Victoria's letters to her daughter end up in the possession of the Hesse-Cassel family, rather than that of Kaiser Wilhelm II?), few researchers believe that Morshead and Blunt were sent to recover letters of purely family interest. But given the shroud of secrecy and the fact that these mysterious documents – whatever they contain – disappeared into the Royal Archive, their contents have had to remain a matter of speculation. After all, nobody outside that tight royal circle has even seen them – or so it was believed.

PHOENIX'S STORY

Shortly after the publication of *Double Standards* in April 2001, we were contacted by an individual who claimed to have accompanied Blunt on one of his German trips – and to have read some of the letters he collected. Naturally, we were initially cautious, not to say sceptical. (Any controversial book attracts readers with all manner of outrageous claims.) Because at first he preferred to use a pseudonym – requesting us not to reveal his identity because of his involvement in this and other sensitive matters – we will refer to him by the somewhat melodramatic code-name he adopted of 'Phoenix'.

Phoenix claimed to be a former MI5 agent who worked in Peter Wright's teams of 'spycatchers' in the 1960s and early '70s – and as fate would have it, was one of the officers involved in Blunt's interrogation in 1964. He came to us because during his career he became seriously disillusioned by the behaviour of the royal family and the way the security services are used to protect their interests – not to mention the manner in which 'spycatcher' Peter Wright was treated by the Establishment. Now elderly and in ill health, he has no desire to court unwelcome publicity.

Over the course of several months, we were able to learn Phoenix's real identity and, besides receiving his written testimony about Blunt's mysterious German trip, we eventually arranged several face-to-face interviews. These were recorded on both audio and video tapes (some of which have been seen by our publishers).

Obviously, our first priority was to confirm his identity. Through our own contacts in the British security and intelligence community we found evidence that he had indeed worked for MI5 on Wright's team. However, there was a surprising twist: apparently Phoenix is *persona non grata* with today's MI5 – although he had described his stormy relations with the Service and the reasons he left (which are unrelated to the Blunt affair).

The story Phoenix tells is as follows. During the Second World War, he served with the RAF, including as a glider pilot in the disastrous Arnhem offensive in September 1944. By the time of the victory over Germany, he was serving with the RAF's Special Investigations Branch (SIB) in Berlin, where, under the name 'Lieutenant Graham', he also worked in intelligence. After the war, following a brief return to civilian life, he was recruited by MI5. While serving in Berlin, he was called in for a special assignment – to accompany someone named Colonel Blunt on a trip to the south 'to recover properties of the Crown'. His superior made it clear that, although officially he was simply Blunt's escort, he was to stay close to him and report back on his every move.

Dressed in the uniform of a staff officer, Blunt left the next morning with Phoenix and a driver on the long journey to the Frankfurt area. After stopping overnight at Worms, they proceeded to Kronberg and Schloss Friederichschof. Phoenix writes:

Except for a few American officers on R&R, the place seemed somewhat deserted. Blunt, showing his written authority to the custodian of the private apartments, was allowed in, with myself in tow.

I quickly realised that he either knew the place or had good directions. He went directly to the exact room, to the exact writing bureau and began emptying the bureau drawers and cubbyholes into a box he brought with him, superficially examining the papers as he did so. After this, he retrieved other knicknacks from the room, which I could not see, and placed them into a cloth bag and put that into his pocket. The whole enterprise took less than an hour from arrival to departure.

On the return journey to Berlin, they stopped overnight at a hotel where, to Phoenix's surprise, Blunt – whom he describes as being in an irritable mood throughout – handed him the box with the order to keep it safe until the next morning. (Blunt wanted to go out for the evening.) Phoenix was even more astounded to find that the box – a simple cardboard affair – was unsealed. Bearing his secret orders in mind, he then spent the night examining the letters. Astounded by their revelations, he wrote down the details on the only material that was to hand – one of his pillowcases, which he handed to his superior on his return to Berlin.

Nearly 20 years later, Phoenix – now with MI5 – was one of the officers present when Blunt was brought in for interrogation. Initially, Blunt failed to recognise him, but eventually when Phoenix reminded him about their mission, his jaw dropped. And when asked why he had left the box unsealed, he replied simply: 'I was tired from the trip. I just forgot.'

Given their sensational content, perhaps it is not surprising that Phoenix can still recall the letters in detail. Dating from both the immediate pre-war period and the early stages of the war, there was correspondence between the Duke of Windsor and Franz von Papen, Hitler's original Vice Chancellor and, until the Anschluss, Ambassador to Austria, discussing possible peaceful solutions to the impending conflict. There was also correspondence between Windsor and Rudolf Hess relating to the possibility that – in the event of George VI and the royal family fleeing to Canada – the Duke would return as King. There were other letters, covering the same subjects, from the Duke of Kent and Göring. One surprising name among the letter writers was Duff Cooper, Edward VIII's only supporter in the Cabinet during the abdication crisis and wartime Minister of Information. The documents even included a letter on Reichs Chancellery notepaper from Hitler to Windsor offering season's greetings for Christmas 1938.

If Phoenix's testimony is reliable, clearly the papers retrieved from Friedrichshof comprised either both sides of the correspondence, or just Windsor's. This makes sense: presumably he had left these letters in Paris when he hurriedly went south in 1940. If so, he would have been keen to recover them before they fell into either Allied or, because of their propaganda potential, Nazi hands. This would explain why he asked for an emissary through whom he could communicate with the Germans about recovering certain possessions from his homes in France, and why Philip of Hesse-Cassel turned up later, being trusted to keep the letters safe. But the big question remains: *is* Phoenix's testimony reliable?

Frankly, at first we had serious doubts. Although little is known about Blunt's royal missions to Germany and Holland, we realised that Phoenix's information was suspect on several points. He claimed the trip took place in September 1945, whereas it happened in August – an understandable slip given that he was remembering an event that took place over half a century earlier. Phoenix had always referred to his charge as 'Colonel Blunt', yet Blunt, who had been briefly in the army between 1939 and 1940, had only reached the rank of captain. However, those on certain assignments were often made up to higher acting ranks, so it is possible that it happened on this occasion. But the major discrepancy is that, according to Phoenix, the Kronberg group consisted solely of himself, Blunt and a driver, whereas it is known that Owen Morshead accompanied them. Could Phoenix have confused this trip with one of Blunt's later solo missions to Brunswick? Phoenix was adamant that this took place in 1945 (Blunt's next assignment happened in March the following year). Tracing the career of Phoenix's superior – who assigned him the duty – we were able to establish that he was no longer in that post by the end of 1945, so it had to have been the Friedrichshof trip.

However, two important facts in particular about the Kronberg trip emerged in Miranda Carter's biography of Anthony Blunt, published in 2001. Although Morshead and Blunt had visited the Hesse-Cassel castle together, Morshead had returned alone the next day, leaving Blunt behind – according to Morshead, on 'military business'. This additional information – while not confirming Phoenix's story – at least helps resolve some of the discrepancies, suggesting the following scenario: both Morshead and Blunt made an initial visit to Friedrichshof, to win the confidence of the elderly Margaret, Hesse-Cassel's mother, who was still living in the castle's private apartments. Presumably Morshead did take some of the family letters into safe-keeping: according to the Windsor Archive, certain documents collected on this occasion were returned to the Hesse-Cassel family in the 1950s. Then Blunt, who had remained in Berlin, returned a few days later to collect the more compromising letters, presumably deemed too sensitive even for Morshead's eyes. Blunt's official reason for staying behind – 'military business' – may account for the fact that, according to Phoenix, Blunt was in uniform on the second visit.

It must be admitted that Phoenix's testimony adds little to what is already suspected or deduced about the content of the Hesse letters: that they compromised the Dukes of Windsor and Kent. The surprise is that other unexpected individuals, such as Duff Cooper, were also implicated. Phoenix also told us that Blunt remained in Berlin for a day or two after their excursion, and obviously the letters would have remained in his possession during this time. Presumably he seized the opportunity to pass their details on to his Russian masters, who probably photographed them. This would clarify certain aspects of subsequent events, such as why, even after confessing to being a Russian spy, Blunt was protected and continued to be treated with favour by the royal family. Because of the letters, he had the power to blackmail the Palace and the royal family. But then so did the Soviet Union.

Michael Adeane's injunction to Peter Wright in 1967 has several implications. The Palace should have reacted very differently. If the person entrusted with a secret mission on behalf of the royal family was later revealed to be a Soviet agent, surely they would have encouraged MI5 to investigate *everything* about that trip. Where else did he go? To whom did he speak? Did he have the opportunity to show the letters to the Russians? Under normal circumstances the Palace would have been close to boiling point at the very thought. But these were not normal circumstances – as well they knew.

Instead, the episode was dismissed as being of no interest either to MI5 or the Palace, which suggests that the Palace already knew whether Blunt had passed on the secret of the letters to Moscow. They were fully aware that the NKVD, or its successor the KGB, had the power to blackmail them – because they had already used the letters to do so. If nothing else, the Palace's ban on Wright effectively impeded an investigation involving national security in a way that was not only unconstitutional but would in any other circumstances be criminal. Even if the official story about Blunt's German assignments is correct (although highly unlikely for the reasons given above), the Palace seemed to assume that whatever else he did there bore no relevance to the investigation. Yet the Palace already knew that he stayed on in Germany on 'military business' which, by implication, had no connection with his royal assignment. Inevitably the question is raised: did he take the opportunity to make contact with other Soviet agents in Germany? Wright was forbidden to ask – indeed, he was instructed to ignore anything Blunt may have even volunteered about those trips – and so the possibility of identifying other agents was compromised by royal request. Again the question must be asked: why jeopardise a highly significant security investigation unless the Palace had something to hide?[31]

Whatever they involved, these mysterious tasks on behalf of the royal family proved very advantageous for Blunt. George VI appointed him Surveyor of the King's Pictures (an honour continued by the Queen on her accession in 1952) and in 1947 he was invested as a member of the Royal Victorian Order, a mark of special favour, becoming Sir Anthony on his elevation to the title of Knight Commander of the Order in 1956. Undoubtedly, his sensitive role in the Hesse-Cassel assignment contributed to the reason he was protected when his treachery was exposed in 1964. But is that the whole story? After all, he had other potentially embarrassing connections with the royal family – most damagingly, his then illegal sexual liaison with the Duke of Kent in the late 1920s.

Phoenix also handed us this potential bombshell: when Blunt was brought in to MI5 in 1964, he repeatedly asked to be allowed to telephone *Lord Mountbatten*, who was obviously heavily implicated in the whole murky business, presumably as Blunt's secret royal protector. But why should he of all people undertake this role? As Mountbatten became the self-appointed protector of the royal family and its image after the war, it appears that he, rather than the King, masterminded the post-war 'clean up' operation to recover all compromising documents. (Although Supreme Commander of the Allied forces in South East Asia during that period, he was in London at the specific time of the first of Blunt's assignments.)[32] But if Mountbatten specially selected Blunt for the Hesse-Cassel mission, did the Russians threaten *him* with blackmail over the letters? This is all the more disturbing because he was about to enter a phase of considerable influence – not to say control – over the royal family.

LOVE, MARRIAGE – AND MOUNTBATTEN

The King and Queen's policy of accepting only royal spouses from British families was almost immediately thwarted by the heir to the throne, Princess Elizabeth, who had other ideas. As did Lord Mountbatten. Although dismissed for many years, the idea is now accepted that he engineered the marriage of Prince Philip of Greece to the future Queen to fulfil his own blatantly dynastic ambitions.[33] However, he was aided and abetted by other members of the Greek royal family, including King George II and Marina, Duchess of Kent.

As early as 1940, Philip confided to the captain of his first posting, HMS *Ramillies* (an old friend of Mountbatten), 'My uncle has ideas for me; he thinks I could marry Princess Elizabeth,'[34] and said the same thing to a cousin in 1939 and 1941.[35] In July 1941, Chips Channon noted in his diary a party conversation with Philip, then on leave in London: 'He is to be our Prince Consort, and that is why he is serving in our Navy.'[36] (Like many in his circle, Channon was surprised that a Greek national should be serving in the British Navy: at the outbreak of war, as Greece was neutral, Philip should not have been fighting at all – but when his country did join the conflict, he should have been transferred to the Greek Navy.[37]) That same summer in Cape Town, Philip's cousin Princess Alexandra of Greece saw him writing to 'Lilibet' (Elizabeth's pet name). Indeed, after that first meeting at Dartmouth in the summer of 1939, Philip assiduously kept up his correspondence with Princess Elizabeth throughout his war service. This suggests collusion: without Uncle Dickie's intervention would a worldly wise naval officer be so smitten by just one day in the company of a particularly immature 13-year-old girl?

Philip may have been playing his own game, but for Elizabeth it was the real thing: by September 1942 she was already speaking of him as 'the one'.[38] He began to crop up in her immediate circle: together with David, Marquess of Milford Haven, he was a guest of the royal family at Sandringham for Christmas 1943, much to Elizabeth's delight. (And also Margaret's, judging by her letters of the time.) He may have been 'the [only] one' for Elizabeth, but there is no evidence that he returned the compliment. As might be expected with a handsome 'man's man' like Philip (especially with the Milford Havens and Mountbattens as role models), by all accounts he took full advantage of his shore leave – particularly with his long-term drinking partner, Lieutenant-Commander Michael Parker, whom he met when they served on the destroyer HMS *Wallace* in 1942. Philip was known for enjoying his share of affairs, both casual and serious. It is said that he wanted to marry a Canadian debutante named Osla Benning, but – seeing his grand plan about to go up in flames – Mountbatten hastily stepped in.[39] It is also reported that Philip proposed to American socialite Cobina Wright, but she turned him down.[40]

In 1944, when Elizabeth became 18, the King of Greece put the idea of the engagement to George VI, but was rebuffed with the reply that both he and the Queen considered her too young to think of marriage. Another matchmaker was the Duchess of Kent, who was always very close to Philip. In fact, according to Chips Channon, she arranged most of the meetings between Philip and Elizabeth – and they took place at the Coppins.[41]

Philip finally proposed to the Princess at Balmoral in September 1946, and – in an unusually independent move – the besotted Elizabeth accepted, even without asking her parents. Although without the King's approval it was very much an unofficial engagement, somehow the story leaked out and within days the wrong-footed Palace issued a formal denial that there were any plans for Princess Elizabeth to marry Philip. Although deliriously happy, she faced an uphill struggle. Both parents were against the match: her mother opposed the marriage in principle – she wanted her daughter to marry either a British Duke or an heir to a Dukedom[42] – but also because she thought Philip personally unsuitable largely because of his German relations. (Although his brash and breezy style may also have been a factor.)

When the rumours of their engagement surfaced a newspaper poll found that 40 per cent of its readers opposed the marriage. To add to Elizabeth's problems, the Beaverbrook press ran a campaign against the marriage, on the grounds that Philip was German. Indeed, being 7/8 German, 1/8 Danish and 0/8 Greek, his family connections were certainly enough to cause serious ripples among the post-war xenophobes. Not only did they clash with the King and Queen's policy of finding British husbands for their daughters (especially the future Queen), but they threatened to reverse all the good work of the post-Stamfordham era to 'de-Germanise' the royal family.

As we have seen, all three of Philip's surviving sisters were married to Germans who were active in the Nazi Party, SS or German armed forces during the war. The most potentially embarrassing was Sophie, whose husband was Prince Philip of Hesse-Cassel's brother Christopher, an SS officer who was killed in 1943 in circumstances that are still shrouded in mystery. He died on a plane over the Apennine Mountains in Italy on what is described as a 'secret mission' – accounts differ on whether the plane accidentally crashed or was shot down by the Allies. (The Palace has claimed he was killed on Hitler's orders for denouncing Nazism, but there is not a shred of evidence for this.[43]) Philip's family connections make an interesting comparison with the public outcry that greeted revelations in the 1980s that the father of Princess Michael of Kent (the former Marie-Christine von Riebnitz) was an ex-SS officer. At that time the Palace countered that he had not been a particularly high-ranking or active member, who had been expelled from both the Party and the SS in 1944 – which appears to be true.[44] While the same cannot be said of Philip's brothers-in-law, their uncomfortable history was carefully concealed at the time of his marriage and for many years afterwards.

On the other hand, a strong faction actively supported the union, obviously headed by Mountbatten, but also including King George II of Greece, Queen Mary (largely because it would *keep* German blood in the family) and the Duchess of Kent.

Faced with the prospect of losing her beloved Philip, Princess Elizabeth was uncharacteristically obstinate. The US Ambassador to London, Lewis Douglas, who was close to the royal family, reported back to the State Department that she had even threatened to abdicate if her parents refused her permission to marry Philip. (When Kitty Kelley put this to one of George VI's former aides in the 1990s, he told her that Elizabeth had not 'exactly' made that threat, but merely said that she could understand what had made her uncle, Edward VIII, abdicate for love.[45] Surely, this was threat enough. Given Elizabeth's near-mystical belief in the sanctity of the monarchy and her total agreement with her parents about Edward VIII's calumny, this shows just how desperate she was.)

In February 1947 the King, Queen and the two princesses went on a three-month goodwill tour of South Africa, the true purpose of which was to counter the growth of republicanism. In fact, it was quite blatant electioneering on behalf of the South African Prime Minister Jan Smuts (a general election was due in the Dominion and the republicans looked set to do well). During this trip, one of the press entourage, James Cameron, noted that for much of the tour George VI was the worse for drink due to the stress of being constantly on show[46] – and perhaps, too, sadness that he was about to lose his elder daughter.

On her 21st birthday, Princess Elizabeth broadcast a speech to the Commonwealth that encapsulated perfectly her attitude not only to her future reign but also to her far-flung subjects. In her characteristic high, clear voice she said: 'I declare before you all that my whole life, whether it be long or short, shall be devoted to your service and the service of our great imperial family to which we all belong.' Note that she refers pointedly to 'the great *imperial* family' – and in the present tense. It was ironic that this appeal for harmony came from the infamously divisive South Africa: when presenting medals to those who served in the war her father had been asked not to shake hands with the black soldiers. To give him his due, it is said that it annoyed him greatly, but nonetheless he complied.

On their return, faced with the immoveable rock that was their elder daughter, the King and Queen finally surrendered and gave their permission for her to marry Philip. This marked the beginning of a series of hasty changes for the bridegroom-to-be: to become an acceptable husband for the future Queen, he converted from the Greek Orthodox Church to the Church of England and confronted the problem of his surname – Schleswig-Holstein-Sonderburg-Glücksburg – guaranteed to raise a few eyebrows among listeners to the marriage service, especially just two years after the end of the war. It was decided that he should take the Anglicised form of his mother's maiden name, and so conveniently – even suspiciously – became Philip Mountbatten. When he changed his name he also renounced the title 'Prince of Greece', but in time for the wedding George VI made him the Duke of Edinburgh (as well as Earl of Merioneth and Baron Greenwich). Curiously, although bestowing the status of His Royal Highness, the King did not also confer the title of Prince. (In 1957 Elizabeth herself made him a Prince of the Realm, although he had been customarily – but incorrectly – referred to as 'Prince Philip' since their wedding. He is still waiting to become Prince Consort.)

There was also an unnecessary commotion over rushing through his British nationality in time for the official wedding announcement: it had been forgotten that all descendants of the Electress Sophia of Hanover – which included Philip – are automatically British subjects by law. All this done, and the very German Philip of Greece consigned to the hidden alleys of history to re-emerge as the perfect British prince, the Palace made the official announcement on 10 July 1947. But while Elizabeth herself floated through the days on clouds of Oscar and Hammerstein, her parents and courtiers still worried about Philip. Something told them he was going to be trouble.

Philip's love of nightclubbing in red-blooded male company presented all kinds of ripe opportunities for scandal. Shortly before the wedding, rumours began to circulate about his particularly close relationship with Parisian Hélène Cordet, then a nightclub owner and singer in London. She and Philip had been close friends since childhood – her parents had supported Philip's family financially in Paris – and he had given Hélène away when she married in 1938, becoming godfather to her two children. It has also been frequently rumoured that Hélène's son Max Boisot was his, but this has been denied by everyone concerned.

Whether there was any truth in this and similar stories, the very fact his lifestyle guaranteed such damaging rumours was enough to alarm the King and Queen, and the Palace. Philip enjoyed going out to the West End and Soho clubs with a circle of aristocratic and celebrity friends, including the harmonica player Larry Adler – who quipped shortly before his wedding, 'Be glad your zipper can't talk.'[47]

In 1946, David, Marquess of Milford Haven (heir to the infamous pornography collection), had introduced Philip to the Thursday Club, an all-male gathering that met weekly in the upstairs room of a Soho restaurant for eating, drinking and laddish ribaldry. The Thursday Club was the innovation of Italian-born society photographer Baron Nahum (just 'Baron' professionally – it was his name, not a title). He owed his success to the patronage of Lord Mountbatten – he and his family had been Baron's first major commission, which opened doors for him into the exclusive world of royalty and celebrities. A close friend of Milford Haven, Baron soon became one of Philip's gilded circle.

The Thursday Club's members included Larry Adler, the actors James Robertson Justice and Peter Ustinov, *Daily Express* editor Arthur Christiansen, *Tatler* editor Pip Youngman Carter, MP Iain McLeod (later Leader of the House of Commons), artist Vasco Lazzolo and, occasionally, Lord Mountbatten. Among the guests was Harold 'Kim' Philby, the Soviet spy.[48] Another frequent guest, who later achieved notoriety in the Profumo scandal, was the Harley Street osteopath Stephen Ward, a close friend of Baron who first met Philip at a New Year's Party in 1946.[49]

Philip had his 'unofficial' stag night with the Thursday Club crowd the night before the wedding, at Baron's flat, and although that passed off without a hitch, there were other embarrassing problems: Philip's best man, Milford Haven, promptly sold the story of the stag night to a newspaper for £1,500 (£25,000 today), for which astonishing indiscretion he was unsurprisingly frozen out of the royal circle.

As if to rub his nose in the fact that the King and Queen were not too keen on their prospective son-in-law, Philip was only allotted two invitations to the wedding – which he gave to Mike Parker and Hélène Cordet's mother (Hélène herself could not attend because she was by then a divorcee). Perhaps this was part of a move to prevent his Nazi-sympathizer sisters from attending, especially Sophie, widow of the SS's Prince Christopher of Hesse-Cassel (already remarried, to a Prince of Hanover). The Duke and Duchess of Windsor were not invited, which so appalled the Princess Royal that she stayed away in protest.

After all the politicking and behind-the-scenes adjustments and intrigue, the marriage finally took place in Westminster Abbey on 20 November 1947 – to Elizabeth's great joy and Mountbatten's enormous satisfaction. What the groom thought of it is harder to judge, but there is no doubt that he was – and still is – genuinely very fond of his wife. Although questions were raised about the cost of the pageantry, on the whole the great occasion was greeted enthusiastically by the public, who enjoyed the unaccustomed colour and spectacle after the shabby war years and the tight rein of continued austerity.

Fittingly, the newly-weds spent their honeymoon at Mountbatten's estate at Broadlands, a holiday abroad being out of the question in those economically bleak days.

Hailed as the perfect love match, more properly the marriage represented the culmination of many years' work on Mountbatten's behalf. Not only had he successfully merged his own family with the ruling British house – thus ensuring that future generations of the reigning dynasty would carry Mountbatten blood, and therefore Hesse-Darmstadt genes – but he was also now guaranteed influence over the future Queen, a position that he spent the next years consolidating in preparation for her accession to the throne. (George VI's declining state of health more or less guaranteed that Elizabeth would accede sooner rather than later.)

There was another twist: by the device of bestowing his own family name on his nephew, it was also now the future Queen's – an exquisite irony, as the heir to the British throne bore a name that had been foisted upon Mountbatten's father by her grandfather. After the wedding, and until Elizabeth's succession five years later, nobody seemed to have questioned that in common law she had taken her husband's family name and was now Elizabeth Mountbatten. It was acknowledged by the King's Assistant Private Secretary who, shortly before the birth of Prince Charles in November 1948, wrote in relation to the granting of Letters Patent to smooth out certain irregularities in the rules governing royal status, 'Princess Elizabeth having married no longer has the name of Windsor, but is in fact Mountbatten.'[50] Nobody queried this at the time.

CONTINUING CAREER OF A KINGMAKER

Mountbatten had ended the war on a high note – in 1943 Churchill had appointed him Supreme Commander of Allied Forces in South-East Asia Command (SEAC), promoting him to acting Admiral. As with his previous position as Chief of Combined Operations, the appointment baffled the other commanders. Field Marshal Montgomery wrote, 'Dickie Mountbatten is, of course, quite unfit to be a Supreme Commander . . . his knowledge of how to make war is really NIL.'[51] While acknowledging these somewhat basic flaws, Churchill continued to like Mountbatten's style – his skill at public relations and lifting morale – and considered that his shortcomings where strategy and planning were concerned would be offset by the more experienced commanders around him.

Mountbatten's specific brief had been to turn the tide against the invading Japanese in the former British colonies of Burma, Malaya, Ceylon and Sumatra, although military historians generally acknowledge that his contribution to Allied triumph in South East Asia was negligible. In August 1945, just before the Japanese surrender, Field Marshal Alan Brooke wrote in his diary that: 'Seldom had a Supreme Commander been more deficient of the main attributes of a Supreme Commander than Dickie Mountbatten.'[52] In his immature and arrogant manner, he continued the policy he had adopted at Combined Operations – blaming others for ideas that failed and taking the credit for those that succeeded. One of his staff officers at Combined Operations composed a poem on this theme, which runs in part:

> Of each new plan which came his way
> He'd always claim in accents pat
> 'Why, I myself invented that!'
> Adding when he remembered it,
> For any scoffers benefit,
> Roughly the point in his career
> When he'd conceived the bright idea,
> As 'August 1944'
> Or 'Some time in the Boer War'.[53]

Mountbatten was working at the Admiralty, planning attacks on Malaya and Sumatra – which, had they gone ahead, in Andrew Roberts's words 'would have made the Dieppe Raid look like a textbook example of military planning'[54] – when news of the Japanese surrender came through. Mountbatten claimed later that he had been the first to hear the momentous news and had rushed to break it to Prime Minister Clement Attlee. However, John Colville records that it was he who brought the news to the Cabinet rooms 'where Attlee was closeted with Lord Louis Mountbatten, who was professing Labour sympathies'.[55] But he did get the share of the action he craved, returning to Singapore to receive the formal surrender of the Japanese on 12 September 1945. Not only did this give him the satisfaction of seeing the enemy humiliated – especially after their treatment of Allied POWs, which had genuinely appalled him – but it also put him centre stage at a moment when history was made.

Following the victory over Japan, Mountbatten was given overall charge of the newly liberated territories in South East Asia. SEAC's role was extended to cover other former European colonies, such as the Dutch East Indies and French Indo-China. As Supreme Commander, this effectively made Mountbatten governor of nearly 130 million people – a terrifying thought.

His task was to administer and maintain law and order in these territories and manage the transfer of power to new governments for the future – a complex problem, for the end of the war had created a power vacuum in which independence movements, often of conflicting political ideologies, were flourishing. It would be difficult, if not impossible, to restore them to colonial rule – particularly as the Americans were now so powerful in the Pacific and South East Asia, giving them the opportunity for economic and political influence in those territories they never had when the region was almost entirely dominated by Europe. The future of each country had to be decided by resolving the interests of the former colonial masters – Britain, France and the Netherlands – the indigenous political groups and the USA. Into this sensitive scenario strode the Supreme Commander of SEAC, Lord Mountbatten, intent on taking over. In this transition period, it was noted that he consistently favoured handing the power to nationalist movements, particularly communist groups.

Since 1937, Burma had been a semi-independent British colony with its own elected House of Representatives under a British governor. Immediately after the war, Britain re-established its imperial control and the displaced governor, Sir Reginald Dorman-Smith, was brought back. However, Mountbatten opposed his proposal for free elections to decide on Burma's new government, instead backing – successfully – communist leader U Aung San's appointment as head of the first post-war Government. (And Mountbatten successfully lobbied Attlee for Dorman-Smith's removal.) Aung San promptly set about negotiating Burma's independence, which took effect in January 1948 (although he was assassinated just before this). Later, Mountbatten was to claim that had he been in overall charge Burma would still be in the Commonwealth, but the others had 'mucked it up'. In 1955, Dorman-Smith successfully sued a newspaper that printed these allegations, although it did nothing to stop Mountbatten from repeating them ten years later.[56] A very similar thing happened in Malaya, where he backed the extreme left-wing Malayan Peoples' Anti-Japanese Union, which was hardly in favour of the restoration of colonial rule.[57]

Before the war French Indo-China (comprising modern Vietnam, Cambodia and Laos) had been ruled, for the most part, by the indigenous royal families under a French governor. But after the Japanese surrender the communist Viet Minh League (the forerunners of the Viet Cong), led by Ho Chi Minh, took control of Vietnam. The Allies then stepped in, giving the south to SEAC's jurisdiction and the north to China. The French wanted to regain their former control of the region, but Mountbatten favoured the Viet Minh and persuaded the French to negotiate with them. Again, in the Dutch East Indies (modern Indonesia), he sided with the independence movement, in the form of the left-wing party led by Dr Ahmed Soekarno (whom the Dutch regarded as a Japanese collaborator).

By May 1946 SEAC was disbanded, its job done. Mountbatten lost his rank as acting Admiral and returned to service with the Royal Navy. But back in London, it soon became apparent that his lust for glory remained undiminished as he discussed the possibility of taking up a political career with the aim of becoming Prime Minister – indeed, some noted that he was watching the progress of the Labour Party in 1946 with the aim of becoming the first President of the British republic.[58]

When offered a baronetcy in the 1946 New Year's Honours list he refused it on the grounds it was too lowly for him. The hint was taken: although he was created Viscount Mountbatten of Burma, in October 1947, in time for his nephew's wedding, George VI elevated him to the title of Earl.

Although describing it euphemistically as the 'fulfilment of Britain's mission in India', Attlee's government realised that it had no option but to fulfil the promise that Churchill had made to Roosevelt in 1943 and grant India its independence. If there was one person who could make a humiliating retreat look like a victory it was Mountbatten, so in February 1947 he was appointed the last Viceroy, with a brief to organise the end of British rule by June 1948. The Viceroy of India represented, and was answerable to, the Sovereign, controlling the Indian civil service, army and police – governing directly about two-thirds of the country (then made up of today's India, Pakistan and Bangladesh). The other third was ruled by Indian princes.

Disengaging Britain from India was an extremely complex and delicate task. The British officials and the army would have to be withdrawn without leaving a power vacuum that would be fought over by the various factions. Then there was the problem of handing over administrative and legislative power to a native Indian Government. All this was set against a background of the threat of explosive violence between the bitterly divided Hindu and Moslem populations.

In short, Mountbatten faced a thankless task, and whether anyone else could have achieved a more peaceful transition is, of course, impossible to answer. Perhaps, for once, his overweening arrogance came in useful, for surely lesser mortals would have wilted at the enormity of the job. However, the situation was hardly helped by his fired-up impatience. Instead of adhering to the June 1948 deadline, he insisted that the handover of power would be achieved within just six months – by 15 August 1947 (the second anniversary of the Japanese surrender).[59]

The newly created Earl Mountbatten of Burma took Edwina and their daughter Pamela to India – along with the ubiquitous Peter Murphy, which caused another potentially ruinous situation: within a week Edwina was embroiled in a passionate love affair with Jawaharlal Nehru, who was to become independent India's first Prime Minister. Although the affair became the stuff of common gossip among the aristocracy, once again the Mountbattens managed to escape the disaster of overt scandal.[60]

The transfer of power was duly carried out at the stroke of midnight on 14 August 1947 (Indian astrologers having pronounced Mountbatten's preferred date of 15 August inauspicious). Of course the most immediate and hugely significant change was the partition of the former Indian states into Hindu India and Muslim Pakistan – and it was Mountbatten's task, now as Governor-General, to use the remainder of the transition period to keep the peace between the two religious factions. In this, he conspicuously failed, as riots, massacres and acts of atrocity became daily occurrences in the Punjab, the region most affected by the partition – although, given the tensions and passions aroused, it is doubtful whether any other Governor could have prevented it.

However, Mountbatten managed to cause enormous offence by leaving India at the height of the trouble to attend the wedding of Elizabeth and Philip. Rubbing salt into wounds being his speciality, and swept away with the overwhelming sense of triumph as London celebrated the union of the Mountbattens and the Windsors, he appalled some of the guests by his speech at India House when he proclaimed that 'only' 100,000 people had died in the riots.[61] In fact, although the true figures will never be known, it is estimated to be at least double, and perhaps as much as a million.

Mountbatten left an India in turmoil, taking with him the last vestige of British rule, on 21 June 1948 (a date he chose in order to be back in England for his birthday four days later).[62] He returned to find a frosty atmosphere at Court: the loss of the sub-continent, while a relief for the British Government, was a bitter blow to the King and the royal family. George VI (who had wanted to imprison Gandhi and other independence leaders) was particularly upset at losing the title King Emperor.[63] Queen Elizabeth never forgave Mountbatten for his part in giving away the 'jewel in the crown' of the British Empire. While not blaming him for the upheaval, she could not understand how a member of the royal family could willingly have taken such a prominent role in the end of Empire.

No doubt with a sense of anti-climax, Mountbatten returned to the Royal Navy with the Mediterranean fleet based on Malta. He was promoted to Vice-Admiral the following year.

Back home, it was time to face reality. The Mountbattens were not doing well financially. The post-war economy was bad, and income tax for the wealthy was exorbitantly high – over 95 per cent (although, to his great relief, the King was exempt). Edwina's capital was tied up in a complex trust, and although it yielded her £45,000 (the equivalent of something approaching £1 million today) annually, the increase in income tax during and after the war reduced their net income to about a tenth of that. As a result, Mountbatten introduced a Private Bill in the House of Lords to change the law specifically so that Edwina could break the trust. The Bill was passed by the Lords but, because of understandable opposition in the Commons, it was amended, becoming a bill that would apply to all women in Edwina's situation.[64]

Mountbatten had accepted the Labour Government with equanimity, having an understanding of socialism because the left-wing Peter Murphy had been his closest associate for the last 20 years. Indeed, Mountbatten undertook to become the royal family's liaison with the Labour Party.[65] Bizarrely, it seemed almost a marriage made in heaven, for the Labour Government also approved of Mountbatten. In February 1949 they even asked him to become Minister of Defence, but he declined because a minister's office is always temporary and taking the post would damage his long-term plans for his naval career.[66]

THE POST-WAR EDWARD AND WALLIS

The Duke of Windsor returned to Britain in October 1945 – regretfully leaving Wallis at home – keen to discover what job his brother had earmarked for him in the post-war world. Perhaps a governorship of one of the Dominions, or an ambassadorial post? He could scarcely believe it, but George VI refused to give him any public or diplomatic role of any sort. Neither would he allow Windsor to live in Britain. (In 1946, the Duke heard that his beloved Fort Belvedere – which had only been his on 'grace and favour' terms – was to be sold, but when he offered to buy it as his English home it was abruptly taken off the market.)

It was at this time that the deeply embarrassing papers about the Duke of Windsor's wartime activities began to emerge from the captured German archives. As we have seen, Churchill made strenuous efforts to destroy them or suppress their publication to preserve both Windsor's and the royal family's image. No doubt Churchill realised that no matter how murky Edward's wartime activities occasionally became, the record of his brother the King was by no means lily-white. Presumably that is why, on his return to office as Prime Minister as 1951, he also made vigorous attempts to rehabilitate the Duke – and especially the Duchess – by trying to resolve their grievances. This led to the meetings to discuss the vexed HRH issue at which Kenneth de Courcy represented the Duke, although Queen Mary, through her equerry Sir John Coke, simply refused to budge.[67]

Clearly the war had done nothing to bridge the gulf between the warring royals – if anything, their positions were more entrenched. The Duke had his first meeting with his mother in nine years, but Queen Mary refused to receive the Duchess. When Windsor visited the King, Queen Elizabeth even refused to meet *him*. He was also ideologically light-years away from Mountbatten, having greeted the advent of the Labour Government with dismay, voicing his opinion that it was the beginning of the slippery slope that would lead to communism, writing of 'these crazy and dangerous Socialists'.[68]

Although the Duke – and sometimes his wife – paid several visits to England in the late 1940s, they decided to make their permanent home in France. The lease on their Paris home about to expire, they lived in their Antibes villa, La Cröe (although spending several months of each year abroad, mainly in the USA, in the 1940s and '50s). In 1952 they bought a country house, Moulin de la Tuilerie, an hour's drive from Paris, and the City of Paris gave them a bargain-price lease on a mansion in the Bois de Boulogne. All of their homes became a byword for elegance and comfort, due to the Duchess's exceptional gift for interior design and hospitality.

Settled in France they attempted to establish their own 'alternative Court' that would outshine that of the stuffy and uninspired Buckingham Palace. In some respects they were successful, their table usually humming with witty conversation. But although they were perceived as the epitome of style and romance, their lives became increasingly empty and aimless. The Duke in particular became a pathetic figure, endlessly whining about his diminished circumstances and indulging in unattractive ploys to secure the proverbial free lunch (toying with a restaurant bill for several hours until someone snapped and paid it for him being one of his tricks). Despite his obsession with money, in fact he was extremely wealthy – besides his annuity, he made a fortune on the stock market (something for which he had a genuine acumen), as well as lucrative illegal currency deals.[69] But while complaining of poverty he continued to lavish gifts of jewellery on his beloved Wallis. Reports differ about their relationship: certainly they were close, but the Duchess's noticeable brusqueness with her husband may be understandable. His obsessive dog-like devotion – undiminished with the passing years – no doubt proved extremely wearing.

MR AND MRS MOUNTBATTEN

After their honeymoon Elizabeth and Philip began what was to be a short but idyllic life on the island of Malta, where he served with the Mediterranean fleet. Staying at the Mountbattens' house, they could live an almost normal life as an aristocratic naval couple. Elizabeth enjoyed doing things most young wives took for granted, such as having her hair done at a salon and taking tea with other British families on the island. She was intensely happy, although the idyll was not to last for long. Meanwhile, at home, the plotting continued . . .

The marriage of Mountbatten's nephew to Princess Elizabeth had caused disquiet among the Palace mafia, which worried about the degree of influence he might wield over the couple, especially as Elizabeth would one day be Queen.[70] But despite Palace reservations, Mountbatten still managed to get his daughter Pamela appointed as Elizabeth's lady-in-waiting.

The marriage also saw the beginning of a new power struggle within the family for influence over the next generation, between Mountbatten and Queen Elizabeth, representing the old royal Europe and the British aristocracy respectively. The Queen treated Mountbatten with reserve and caution because of his undisguised ambition and desire for influence over the royal couple. But very soon another opportunity presented itself to the kingmaker-in-waiting, for Prince Charles Philip Arthur George was born on 14 November 1948, providing the requisite male heir – and another target for Mountbatten's long-term plan.

Shortly before Charles's birth, it was realised that there was a problem. When George V had changed the rules to restrict royal status, he had failed to envisage that one day there might be a female on the throne. Under the 1917 rules, even though she was the heir, none of Elizabeth's children would enjoy royal status.[71] In order to circumvent this, the Queen had to change the rules. Then on 15 August 1950 Princess Anne Elizabeth Alice Louise was born. Blonde like her father, she was also possessed of many of his more idiosyncratic traits. Already the two royal children were like chalk and cheese. Pained, vulnerable and timid, the heir was often in awe of his tomboyish sister, who was afraid of nothing.

Mountbatten's position was further enhanced when he was called in by the King to sort out Philip's errant ways. After his marriage the Duke of Edinburgh had appointed his old navy confederate Mike Parker as his Private Secretary, continuing his West End nightclubbing and association with the Thursday Club. Not unnaturally, royal eyebrows were raised. His obvious enjoyment of London nightlife while his wife stayed at home with supper on a tray presented golden opportunities for straying and – even if he failed to take advantage of them – provided fertile ground for rumours.

Over the years, the press has become increasingly fascinated by Philip's close relationships with beautiful women, mostly from the world of show business and the ranks of randy 'polo wives'. Always strenuously denying any impropriety, still less infidelity, in the early 1990s he turned the tables on an inquisitive reporter, asking, 'Have you ever stopped to think that for the last 40 years I have never moved anywhere without a policeman accompanying me? So how the hell could I ever get away with anything like that?'[72] This is more than a little disingenuous. After all, others such as Prince Charles and Princess Diana 'got away' with their affairs for some years.

Whatever the facts about the prince and the showgirls, the King and Palace were alarmed at Philip's behaviour, which was not only hurtful to his adoring wife, but also a threat to the newly burnished image of the royal family as a whole. When Princess Elizabeth was pregnant with Charles, Philip was seen dining and dancing with singer Pat Kirkwood (to whom he had been introduced by Baron), which naturally caused ripples. Although Kirkwood has always maintained they were just good friends, even the heir's husband being seen out with another woman was bad enough at such a time.

As a result of the Pat Kirkwood incident a furious George VI called in Mountbatten to bring his nephew to heel.[73] This earned Mountbatten more royal gratitude and, because he held the key to a possible royal scandal, he was no doubt delighted to gain some extra power over the family.

Undoubtedly, Mountbatten's ambitions extended far beyond persuading the royal family to adopt his name. Prince Nicholas of Greece warned John Gordon, the editor of the *Sunday Express,* that the Mountbattens were intent on becoming 'the power behind the throne when Elizabeth succeeds'.[74] Gordon reported to the *Express*'s owner, Lord Beaverbrook – who had kept a careful eye on Mountbatten ever since the Dieppe Raid – that his ambition was for Philip to be elevated, not simply to the status of Prince Consort, but to King Consort and co-ruler. Then he would wield power through his nephew, effectively becoming the King. However, *Daily Express* editor Arthur Christiansen – Philip's close friend and fellow member of the Thursday Club – told Beaverbrook that the heir's husband had seen through his uncle's ambitions.[75]

MOUNTBATTEN AND THE RUSSIANS

During the handover of power in South East Asia, Mountbatten's preferment of communist nationalist groups had not gone unnoticed – and nor had the warmth with which he greeted the advent of the first majority Labour Government. Although this may seem paradoxical in someone so obsessed with royalty and status – in Brian Hoey's words, the self-appointed 'patriarch of European royalty'[76] – this tendency was so marked that some Conservative MPs were beginning to mutter about his left-wing sympathies. Even Churchill, who was returned to power as Prime Minister in the general election of 1951, chided Mountbatten over his expression of 'left-wing views'.[77] Some reactionary Americans went further, unhesitatingly denouncing him as a Marxist, citing the influence of his close companion Peter Murphy.

They had a point. Peter Murphy had been part of the Mountbattens' household since the mid-1920s and was certainly his closest relationship. Although without any formal position on Mountbatten's staff, he had always been around, with the exception of the periods when Mountbatten was at sea. As John Brabourne, husband of Mountbatten's daughter Patricia, said:

> Few people actually knew what Murphy's role was in Dickie's life, but his real position was a sounding board. He was brilliant at spotting mistakes in something that Dickie was planning, and he wasn't afraid to speak up. Dickie would show him a letter he had drafted and Peter would read it and say what he thought the reaction of the recipient would be.[78]

Unofficial it may have been, but Murphy's was a very significant role when Mountbatten's own power and influence is taken into consideration. During the war Murphy had worked for the Political Intelligence Department but, after the Japanese surrender – he was with Mountbatten at the ceremony – Mountbatten had managed to sweep him off to South East Asia as his unofficial adviser. During the handover of power in the region, Mountbatten consistently took Murphy's advice – indeed, it was he who actually drafted Mountbatten's report on his period as SEAC's Supreme Commander. (Ziegler says of this, 'Mountbatten never doubted that his reputation would survive any calumny and emerge unblemished in the eyes of posterity, but he was not above giving the eyes of posterity a little help.'[79])

As Peter Murphy had been openly and unashamedly a Marxist when he first met Mountbatten at Cambridge more than 20 years earlier, and had never wavered in his allegiance since, it is not difficult to understand the Americans' suspicions about Mountbatten's motives in favouring left-wing groups. Not only was Murphy a communist and pro-Soviet (not too much of a problem during that part of the war when Stalin was on the same side), but he was also known to be promiscuously homosexual – which would normally have made him a security risk because of the possibility of blackmail. It is incredible that Mountbatten was allowed to associate with him, still less to take him to South East Asia where he would be involved in sensitive negotiations with important long-term consequences for the region. It seems to be another example of the security services being unwilling to challenge a member of the royal family (just as they had been unable to stop Windsor's association with Charles Bedaux in France in the early months of the war).

It was not until 1952 that MI5 investigated Murphy – and even then at Mountbatten's own instigation, because of the increasing clamour of the Americans' allegations.[80] The MI5 investigation is said to have cleared Murphy, but it would be fairer to say that it reached a 'not proven' verdict. Although he was not a member of the Communist Party, and there was no hard evidence that he was either working for the Party or for the Soviet Union, it did note his Marxist sympathies and sexual proclivities. At the very least, MI5 and Mountbatten – who saw the report on Murphy – were condoning a criminal offence. (While in these more enlightened days one might be tempted to cheer on those that got away with acting according to their sexual nature, the fact remains that this was another example of one law for the royals and one for the common folk. In the year of their investigation, in England and Wales alone, there were nearly 700 prosecutions for sodomy, over 3,000 for attempted sodomy and 1,700 for gross indecency between males.[81])

MI5 seemed to have taken the line that because nothing specific could be proven against Murphy, he was in the clear, a view they would be unlikely to take with anybody else of his political persuasion and sexual orientation. Yet Murphy remained close to Mountbatten as he continued his inexorable climb to positions of yet greater power, which were increasingly concerned with national security.

Even if Murphy was not technically a member of the Communist Party, he was certainly close to people who were – for example, Harry Pollitt, a friend since the 1920s and later wartime head of the Party in Britain.[82] Mountbatten's relationship with Murphy should also have made him a security risk – perhaps not as an active agent, but an unwitting source of confidential information. The gravest danger was that Mountbatten was what is known in espionage jargon as an 'agent of influence' – an influential individual who, while not knowingly a foreign agent, is clandestinely guided by those who *are*.

Edwina Mountbatten had also had become steadily more left-wing over the years – probably partly the result of Murphy's influence, but in her case there also seems to be a strong element of disgust at the hypocrisy she had witnessed among the rich and powerful. Yet once again, Edwina's politics should also have alerted the security services well before she became Vicereine of India and a force to be reckoned with in widespread Asian charities.

An additional factor was undoubtedly Mountbatten's bisexuality, which in itself should have made MI5 cautious. As a CIA source put it, 'What we could never understand was how Mountbatten, a known homosexual and therefore a security risk, managed to achieve the kind of promotion and jobs he got.'[83] There is no doubt that the security services' reluctance to challenge a member of the royal family – presumably for fear of upsetting George VI and later Elizabeth II – was seriously jeopardising national security. This situation is all the more incredible because there is evidence that Mountbatten was not simply an agent of influence, *but actively in league with the Soviet Union.*

With or without Murphy's influence, virtually everything Mountbatten did after the war played perfectly into the hands of the Soviet Union, working against British and – in particular – American interests. After the end of the war, the Anglo-Soviet pact for a 20-year alliance having quickly proved worthless, the former Allies were now realigning for what was becoming the Cold War, with East and West vying for influence over different parts of the world. Mountbatten's actions in South East Asia seem designed to move the whole region into the Soviet sphere of influence – indeed, this was only prevented by the communist takeover of China in 1948, after which the South East Asian communist groups allied themselves to that country instead. Many saw his handling of the British withdrawal from India as a blatant move to steer that vast country towards Russia. He opposed Britain's post-war 'special relationship' with the USA, particularly in defence matters – which brought him into head-on conflict with Churchill.[84] From supporting the communists in the Spanish Civil War in 1936 through the handover of power in South-East Asia, to opposing Britain's involvement in the Suez crisis in 1956 and advocating nuclear disarmament in the 1960s, *everything that Mountbatten did worked in the favour of the USSR.*

Some argue that his actions were not so much pro-Soviet as anti-American – particularly in South East Asia. Although he had always loved the United States and its people, he was opposed to increased American influence on the world stage. Perhaps he favoured communist regimes in South East Asia because even if the old European countries were no longer main players, he would be damned if the Yanks would take over.

Convinced that it was only a question of time before socialism triumphed both at home and abroad, and as ever angling for a powerful position when it did, at his own request Mountbatten had established contacts in the Soviet Union during the war, through the physicist – and committed Marxist – Professor John Desmond Bernal, one of the scientific advisers to Combined Operations, who became a close friend.[85] In the early 1930s Bernal was also part of the Cambridge circle that included Blunt and Guy Burgess, and after the war he received the Stalin Prize and became a member of the Soviet Academy of Sciences.[86] No doubt under the influence of the likes of Murphy and Bernal, Mountbatten departed from the usual royal line on Britain's alliance with the USSR and on the preferred outcome for the German–Russian conflict. Perhaps significantly, by August 1942 this would have put him in the opposite camp politically to the Duke of Kent.

While the British security services were reluctant to investigate Mountbatten, those of other countries were increasingly suspicious. Intelligence writer Richard Deacon (the pen-name of Commander Donald McCormick, who served in the Royal Navy under Mountbatten during the war and in naval intelligence) writes:

> . . . when first in America and then in England in the 1940s the name of Lord Mountbatten of Burma was first raised as a possible security risk, backing for detailed investigation seems to have been badly lacking. Yet American, French and other security services have on various occasions produced evidence which pointed to his having pro-German sympathies in the early days and pro-Soviet sympathies latterly. The response over here [i.e. in the UK] was that he was a World War II hero whose integrity should not be questioned.[87]

Countering those who dismiss Mountbatten's pro-Soviet activities as unthinkable, Deacon writes:

> What those who took this view failed to appreciate was the obsession of Mountbatten with his royal connections in Germany and Russia just as much as in Britain and his almost grotesque vanity which sometimes led him to believe that he could achieve far more in international politics than anyone else. Vanity and treachery go together.[88]

CIA sources have complained that Mountbatten personally blocked investigations into the activities of a senior Royal Navy officer whom they had reason to suspect was passing information to the Russians.[89] Most incredible of all, in the mid-1950s Mountbatten was in secret contact with the Soviet Ministry of Defence. This was revealed by Captain Geoffrey Bennett, the Naval Attaché in Moscow, who handled the correspondence. According to Bennett, Mountbatten not only disclosed his hostility to US foreign policy to the Russians, but in one letter even stated bluntly that in the event of a war between Russia and the USA, 'I should be on the side of the USSR'.[90] This is an unbelievable and treasonable statement, especially coming from a high-ranking NATO officer.

Deacon ascribes Mountbatten's underlying reason for establishing contact with the Soviet Union to his overweening vanity and sense of self-importance. His supreme skill at self-preservation was another – Mountbatten had always presented himself as everybody's ally until it was clear which way the wind was blowing, but here he had excelled himself, trying to convince Britain's Cold War enemy that in principle he was on their side. However, there is a strong possibility that there was another reason: blackmail. The evidence suggests that Anthony Blunt had told his masters in Moscow about the contents of the

Hesse-Cassel letters, so the Soviet Union now had the power of blackmail over the royal family itself. And if – as seems to be the case – Blunt had been selected for the task by Mountbatten, then he had even more of an incentive to be amenable to the Russians. (Given Peter Murphy's influence over Mountbatten, it is of course possible that he had chosen Blunt on Murphy's advice, which would explain a great deal.)

But how could even the staggeringly egotistical and unprincipled Mountbatten square this with his ambitions to set his own family on the British throne and direct the future of the monarchy? A major clue lies in the other thread that runs through Mountbatten's career from the earliest days, a mostly unconscious but deadly motivation: the seething hatred of Britain, originating in the humiliating treatment meted out to his father, his family and himself during the First World War – when his father was stripped of his princely status and forced to change his name. Seen in this light, Mountbatten's whole career had been about restoring his personal and family pride: indeed, he often spoke of his ambition to become First Sea Lord in order to redress the wrong done to his father (an ambition he was soon to achieve). Ultimately, his revenge would be fulfilled by controlling the British Crown. But inevitably, the other side of this desire to teach the British a lesson must at least have manifested itself in a secret pleasure whenever Britain suffered. Is that why he was so uncharacteristically competent in dismantling its Empire?

Whatever else was going on inside his over-heated mind, his personal ambitions for becoming the power behind the throne were just a step away from fulfilment. Only the King stood in the way – and soon he would be gone.

MOUNTBATTEN'S TRIUMPH

The stress of being plunged into kingship had exacerbated the heavy smoking and the drinking that is such a dangerous Windsor trait, ruining George VI's health by the end of the 1940s. He suffered from arteriosclerosis and in 1951 had a lung removed because of cancer. (At the State Opening of Parliament in November, after the return of Churchill as Prime Minister, the King's Speech had to be read out for him.) It was realised then that he probably had no more than a year to live, although this was kept from the public, so his death of a thrombosis in his sleep at Sandringham in the early hours of 6 February 1952 took the nation by surprise. Alan Lascelles telephoned his assistant, Edward Ford, at the Palace with the code-phrase – 'Hyde Park Corner' – setting the official wheels in motion. Churchill and Queen Mary were the first to be informed. (On hearing the news the distraught Princess Royal ran into her mother's room, only to be greeted by the rebuff from Queen Mary, 'Please do your hair properly when you come before the Queen.'[91])

Princess Elizabeth famously heard the news on holiday in Kenya, with

Philip, Mike Parker and Lady Pamela Mountbatten. This slight 25-year-old mother of two was now Queen Elizabeth II, but if she was pole-axed by personal grief and a sudden consciousness of her heavy fate, her husband was also devastated, though for quite different reasons. Literally overnight his freedom to enjoy simultaneously a naval career and royal perks was gone: instead lay a bleak future of cutting ribbons, laying foundation stones – and, much worse, walking a few paces behind his wife. Not even Prince Consort, Philip had no official role, no job, no prospects except to support the new Queen. It was not a future that appealed greatly to him.

A third of a million people filed past the King's coffin as it lay in state in Westminster Hall. The Duke of Windsor came back to London for the funeral – without his Duchess, who was not invited – but to his astonishment the Queen Mother (as she had become) was present when he was received by Elizabeth and Philip at Buckingham Palace.

At George VI's funeral procession, Mountbatten tried to insist that it was his right to walk immediately behind the coffin and was put out to find that this was the position of the new Queen.[92] Less than a week after the funeral, raising his champagne glass, the new Queen's Uncle Dickie announced triumphantly to guests at Broadlands that: 'The House of Mountbatten now reigns!'[93] Rarely has such naked ambition been so swiftly and comprehensively rewarded.

EIGHT

'THAT GERMAN PRINCELING'

Sir Alan Lascelles on Prince Philip, 1952

Mountbatten's triumphant – but exceptionally tactless – declaration was a bombshell for the royal family. It was immediately reported to Queen Mary, who, after a sleepless night, branded him an 'ambitious upstart'[1] – perhaps somewhat belatedly. The day after his announcement, Churchill and his Cabinet expressed their 'strong opinion' – but, significantly, not their advice – that the name of the royal house should remain 'Windsor'. (After all, 'Mountbatten' was almost a German reversion, which was the reason for all the trouble in the first place.) They objected that if the House of Windsor became the House of Mountbatten, inevitably it would confer extra status on the man himself in the eyes of the public. Kitty Kelley writes, 'Churchill and his ministers felt that anything less would cause political insurrection, so suspicious were they of Mountbatten's dynastic ambitions and liberal policies.'[2] But by not giving their formal advice, the politicians left the decision up to the Queen.

Part of the reason for the royal family's nervousness was that Mountbatten was right, or, perhaps more accurately, nobody was quite sure that he was wrong. (The customs concerning the naming of the royal house – whether it changes automatically or has to be decreed – seem to be a bit of a mystery even to the custodians of the constitution.) However, there was a precedent – Queen Victoria's marriage to Prince Albert had changed the name of Britain's royal house to Saxe-Coburg-Gotha with effect from the next generation. Therefore the House of Mountbatten *would* reign, at least when Prince Charles succeeded. But, in Victoria's case, the name had only changed with her successor because she had ascended the throne as a Hanover – Elizabeth came to the throne already married to Philip Mountbatten, so was she actually the first monarch of a new royal house? That this was the case is demonstrated by the fact that Elizabeth II had to issue a decree specifically changing it *back* to Windsor. After some discussion, at the beginning of April 1952 she issued a declaration, on similar lines to that of George V in 1917, that 'I and My children shall be styled and known as the House and Family of Windsor, and that my descendants who marry and their descendants, shall bear the name of Windsor.'[3]

The Queen had decided that both the name of the royal house and her family name should be Windsor. The family name of the House of Hanover was Guelph and that of Saxe-Coburg-Gotha was Wettin, so the Mountbatten family could as easily have reigned as the House of Windsor. However, it was deemed that even that was too much. This was not only a snub to Lord Mountbatten but also, of course, to her husband – after all, since their marriage her surname had been taken to be Mountbatten. And her declaration meant that although Philip's name remained the same as his uncle's, his wife no longer bore it, thus setting him apart from every other man in the kingdom. Philip took this very hard, famously exploding, 'I'm nothing but a bloody amoeba!' although it has been reported that his actual word was 'sperm', which makes considerably more sense, especially in the context as provider of the requisite 'heir and a spare'.

The Palace claimed that the Queen resisted the change of name because George V had intended that the royal house would always be Windsor. However, Elizabeth II had just as much power to change it as George V – if she had wanted to.

Mountbatten refused to abandon the fight, although it did not become a pressing matter again until the Queen became pregnant for the third time in 1959. By then Queen Mary was no longer around to oppose the change, and so Elizabeth gave in, or at least reached a compromise. In February 1960, shortly before giving birth to Prince Andrew, she asked the Cabinet to advise her to make the change, and then decreed that her descendants other than those of royal status (i.e. those without the titles of HRH or Prince/Princess) would have the surname Mountbatten-Windsor.[4]

This meant that Andrew and Edward's grandchildren would use the new double-barrelled form (Anne's children would take their father's surname). However, both Princess Anne – the closest of the royal brood to her father – and Prince Andrew adopted it themselves, both signing their respective marriage registers as Mountbatten-Windsor. Of course Mountbatten was delighted with the new name, describing it as his 'greatest happiness',[5] but others were appalled.

There was great concern about the influence Mountbatten might exert over the new Queen through her husband. A few days after George VI's death Mountbatten wrote to Edwina:

> Four different people have come to me in the last two or three days to say that London is buzzing with rumours and talk in the clubs, etc. that I was being offered an immediate post abroad so as to remove us from being able to influence Lilibet through Philip. My own influence

was viewed with apprehension, and there was also the view that I would be passing on extreme left-wing views from you![6]

DOUBLY QUEEN

Papers released under the 30-year rule in 1982 revealed that the formal declaration of Elizabeth II's accession to the throne to the Privy Council had been delayed for 24 hours because of a sudden fear that her mother might be pregnant. She had missed two periods, and although this was almost certainly the onset of the menopause – she was 51 – even the remote chance that she might be with child could not be ignored: if a boy was on his way he would automatically pre-empt Elizabeth's claim to the throne. In the event, this exciting eventuality did not materialise.[7]

The accession of her daughter brought the former Queen Elizabeth not only a new role, as matriarch and power behind the throne, but also a new title. On 17 February 1952, two days after her husband's funeral, she issued a statement declaring: 'My only wish now is that I may be allowed to continue the work we sought to do together.'[8] The question has often been asked – what exactly was this 'work'? The widow of a monarch has no constitutional or public role. However, the statement reveals that she had understood perfectly well why she and Bertie had been such a success, not so much because of their constitutional duties but because of their potent role in fostering the magic and myth of royalty. That 'work' had been vital to the survival of the monarchy, and it was to this that she was to devote the last half-century of her life, with emphatic success.

In her statement she also asked for the people's 'loyalty and devotion' for her daughter – 'in the great and lonely station to which she has been called she will need your protection and love'. This seems remarkably condescending towards her daughter, but it was entirely consistent with her character. Elizabeth II's biographer Sarah Bradford writes, ' . . . the Queen Mother could not help feeling jealous of her daughter, who had suddenly become the focus of all the attention and the possessor of the power that had recently been hers.'[9] (It was noticed that she had made no reference to Prince Philip or their two children, so a 'corrected' version was issued by the Palace for the newspapers.[10])

The statement also announced her new title: Queen Elizabeth the Queen Mother. The formal title normally adopted by the widow of a King is usually Queen Dowager, although in practice just 'Queen' – as in the case of Queen Mary. However, at this particular time there were two problems: first, as both mother and daughter had the same name, it would be confusing to have two Queen Elizabeths; secondly, there was already a Queen Dowager in the form of Queen Mary, hence the adoption of the new title of Queen Mother, which the media soon turned into the incongruously cuddly 'Queen Mum'. However, as biographer Penelope Mortimer points out, the full title had the advantage of mentioning the word 'Queen' twice[11] – a final victory for the woman who had schemed to be Queen since the early 1920s, and a cruel slap in the face for the HRH-less Duchess of Windsor. It also allowed her to retain another little piece of her former status: only a female monarch or the consort of a King is called '*the* Queen', but now Elizabeth was '*the* Queen Mother'.

DEATH BY ROYAL APPOINTMENT

Too ill to attend George VI's funeral, the 85-year-old Queen Mary watched the procession from Marlborough House, after which her health went into a steep decline and it became increasingly obvious that it was touch and go whether she would make it to the coronation, which was set for 2 June 1953. In fact, it appears that there was no danger that her death would spoil the celebrations: once again it seems that the Palace machinery went into deadly action. She died on 24 March, conveniently allowing ample time for Court mourning to be observed.

Two days previously, reporter Gordon Winter was told by a member of the Duke of Winsor's staff in London (whom he does not name), not merely the day on which the matriarch would die, *but also the hour*, and that this was decided specifically in order that the period of mourning would be over by the time of the coronation.[12] As we have seen, in 1936 her husband King George V had been despatched simply to fit the newspaper deadlines, so doing the same to prevent a complete reorganisation of the coronation would hardly pose much of a problem.

When at the beginning of March the physicians realised that this was her final illness, the Duke of Windsor as her eldest son was summoned from New York. After consulting his tax advisers (to ensure he would not exceed the number of days he could be in the country before being liable for UK tax) he took his time and sailed home, arriving on 11 March.[13] The fact that he hardly came speeding back tends to support Winter's information, as does Windsor's relaxed visit to France and golfing weekend while his mother was dying. Moreover, the contradictory and evasive way Queen Mary's death is dealt with in official biographies also suggests that something is being covered up and it is hard to think what else it would be.[14] The evidence strongly implies that Queen Mary's life was unaturally terminated. Unlike the case of George V, it seems likely that Queen Mary's death was assisted at her own request. Royal watchers know that she had always made it clear that her death should not interfere with the coronation, which is usually taken to mean that *if* she were to die at that time, her funeral should be suitably low-key so as not to create problems for the organisers of the Queen's big day. But her words are open to quite another interpretation. Although her sense of duty essentially precluded her from wrecking the Queen's coronation with her own obsequies, perhaps she went yet further, and had given her permission to be eased out of this world at a more convenient time. But laudable though this may seem on the surface, the fact remains of course that even today voluntary euthanasia remains firmly illegal.

Interestingly, the morning after Winter was told about this plan, he tried to place a bet with a leading bookmaker on the hour of Queen Mary's death – and although they quoted odds of 2000–1, they refused the bet on the grounds that if he won the attendant publicity would do them no good at all. In the event, he would have pocketed £10,000.[15]

However, are these the only two instances of royal euthanasia? Knowing that it was acceptable to both the family and the Palace inevitably raises questions about other expedient demises. There was the convenient death of the debauched Prince Albert Victor, source of multitudinous scandals – and Queen Mary's original intended – allegedly from typhoid fever in 1892, and little Prince John who was shut away because of his 'shameful' epilepsy and who died just at the moment that the royal family were keen to reinvent their image in January 1919. And more recently, following the death of the Queen Mother on Easter Day, 2002, Ephraim Hardcastle of the *Daily Mail* wrote, pointing up the curious phenomenon:

> The circumstances of the Queen Mother's death are similar to those of the last Queen Consort to die in Britain – her mother-in-law, Queen Mary, widow of George V. She died on 24 March 1953, at the age of 85, stipulating that her death should not interfere with the coronation of her granddaughter, Elizabeth II, on 2 June 1953. The Queen Mother's last ambition was to see her daughter's Golden Jubilee in June. Historians may wonder if the effort became too much for her and she willed herself to go now rather than risk wrecking the jubilee by dying in June.[16]

Whatever the arguments for and against euthanasia, the fact is that ordinary people who assist their loved ones to die are still subject to criminal proceedings – some are even sentenced to months in jail.

After lying in state in Westminster Hall, Queen Mary's coffin was taken to Windsor to be interred beside her husband in St George's Chapel. The Duke of Windsor came for the funeral, but was not invited to join the other guests for dinner at Windsor Castle afterwards. After the obsequies, Windsor wrote to Wallis, 'My sadness was mixed with incredulity that any mother could have been so hard and cruel towards her eldest son for so many years and yet so demanding at the end without relenting a scrap. I'm afraid the fluids in her veins have always been as icy cold as they now are in death.'[17] This was kind compared to his comments about his other female relatives: 'What a smug, stinking lot my relations are and you've never seen such a seedy worn-out bunch of old hags most of them have become.'[18] Certainly, he had a point when comparing the plump Queen Mother in her unflattering crinoline frocks and the plain and well-upholstered Princess Royal to his svelte fashion plate of a wife.

THE NEW ELIZABETHAN ERA

The first royal event to be televised, the glorious pageant of the coronation of Queen Elizabeth II was the envy of millions across the world, adding unimaginably to the mystique of the British monarchy. However, the broadcast was very nearly a non-event: when the idea was first mooted the Cabinet advised the Queen against it, but she rejected their advice (obviously the Cabinet did not feel strongly enough about the issue to resign en masse). The royal family had entered the television age: there was no going back now. Daylight had been let in on the magic.

The Duke of Windsor was not invited, on Elizabeth II's express instructions. (She also stopped paying the £11,000 annuity her father had granted him.) The official reason – invented by him as a face-saving measure and approved by Churchill – was that it was against precedent for a former sovereign to attend a coronation (which was true, but only because it was a long-established custom for former sovereigns to be dead). But the Duke ensured he was part of the historic occasion by writing an article for the *Sunday Express* to coincide with the coronation, which was published later in the year in book form as *The Crown and the People.*

Thanks to her father, Elizabeth II was the first monarch to ascend the throne without being liable for income tax. During the usual beginning-of-reign debate over the Civil List, Rab Butler, the Chancellor of the Exchequer, stated that the Queen 'naturally' does not pay tax[19] – but as we have seen, there is nothing natural about it. It is unlikely that Butler was deliberately misleading the House, but as so often happens, simply passing on the information he had been given by the Treasury.

Constitutionally, from the outset Elizabeth II was very different from her father and grandfather. As far as we know, she has shown little inclination to try to influence the political direction of a government. (The caveat 'as far as we know' is important because her predecessors' political acts took decades to surface publicly.) In part this was probably due to her relative inexperience when she came to the throne (she relied heavily on Winston Churchill for advice in her first years). But in any case Britain's post-war political landscape was very different from its pre-war counterpart: there was little inclination for coalitions and Labour could no longer be ignored or contained, both factors leaving little room for the Sovereign to meddle in political affairs. And, as we have seen, the reigns of Edward VIII and George VI largely saw the 'taming' of the monarchy by the politicians. A final factor was the Queen Mother's influence: she had seen that the key to the monarchy's survival was not political influence, but winning the hearts of the people.

Another major difference was Elizabeth's role as Head of the Commonwealth, which had always been dear to her heart, and to which she has enthusiastically devoted much of her 50-year reign. Five months after her coronation, the Queen and the Duke of Edinburgh set off on a six-month tour of the Commonwealth, leaving Charles and Anne behind. However, they were reunited at Tobruk when the children – who seemed doubtful about the identity of their parents – sailed over on the newly commissioned royal yacht *Britannia*. Mountbatten had been the prime mover in getting approval for the cost of the new yacht to replace the 50-year-old *Victoria & Albert*, which was finally granted in 1951.[20] The *Britannia* cost £2 million (over £30 million today) and was paid for and maintained by the state. It became a much-beloved floating home for the Queen and her family.

Just after the coronation a major change in the Palace was the departure of Sir Alan Lascelles, the Private Secretary Elizabeth had inherited from her father. The indications suggest that the parting was not amicable, although the reasons for this are unclear. (While the more innocuous parts of Lascelle's diaries have been published, the full volumes are embargoed indefinitely.[21]) It is likely that antagonism between him and Philip (whom Lascelles reportedly called 'that German princeling')[22] was at the root of it. Lascelles refused the customary peerage on leaving his post as Private Secretary.

Lascelles's successor had been Assistant Private Secretary since 1937 (apart from his war service) and was to remain in this important office until 1972. This was the formidable Sir Michael Adeane – who, by a happy coincidence, was Lord Stamfordham's grandson.

MARGARET CAUSES MAYHEM

The first constitutional crisis of Elizabeth II's reign – which threatened to re-open some of the issues of Edward VIII's abdication – was not long in breaking. With a symbolic flourish, the first clue happened in full view of the press immediately after the coronation: when the family gathered outside the Abbey awaiting their carriages, Princess Margaret was seen to casually brush some fluff from the uniform of one of the equerries, Group Captain Peter Townsend. The unmistakeably intimate gesture was reported, with fevered speculation, by the American and European media – although of course it was not mentioned in British newspapers.

By then, Margaret had already told her family that she and Townsend were in love and wanted to marry. A Battle of Britain pilot, Townsend had become one of the King's equerries during the Second World War, when he rapidly became the focus for the teenaged Margaret's infatuation. It is unclear exactly when the affair 'blossomed', although rumours about them were already current in 1948, when she was 18 and he 34, though Townsend himself dates it to two years later. By the time of the coronation, Margaret already had a reputation as a girl-about-town – including a brief affair with Danny Kaye, to whom she was introduced by David, Marquess of Milford Haven, when she was 18.[23] (The American entertainer was also the great love of Marina's long widowhood.[24])

George VI and Queen Elizabeth had decided long before that Margaret should marry a British husband in order to redress the imbalance caused by

Elizabeth's marriage to a German-Dane. The leading contender was the young Earl of Dalkeith, son of the Duke of Buccleuch (who had been stripped of royal duties during the war because of his only too public opposition to the conflict, and had played an important part in organising the Hess mission).[25] It has been said that, had George VI lived, he would have insisted on Margaret marrying Dalkeith.[26]

As a royal husband, Townsend was out of the question. First, although a war hero he was essentially a *servant* (by then Comptroller of the Queen Mother's Household at Clarence House, where Margaret also lived at that time). Secondly, he was 16 years older than the Princess. And finally, he was divorced, having severed all ties with his wife on the grounds of her adultery in late 1952. The Townsend affair had become more serious after – probably because of – the King's death, when Margaret needed an older man in her life.

Elizabeth II herself seemed sympathetic – when Margaret broke the news she invited the couple to dine with her and Philip that evening – but she was faced by the implacable opposition of Lascelles and Churchill, both of whom refused even to consider a royal marriage to a divorcee: after all, that was the official reason for Edward VIII's abdication. Another factor was that it was very early in the new reign – nothing must rock the royal boat before Elizabeth had established herself. Both men advised the Queen not to grant permission for the marriage, which was required by law as Margaret was under 25. The Queen Mother was also set against it, because she wanted Margaret to marry someone much grander.

(Curiously, David Milford Haven had married an American divorcee – and a Mrs Simpson – without asking permission, even though, as a descendant of George II, the Royal Marriages Act should have applied to him. Nobody seems to have noticed and there was no fuss.)

The story of the affair broke in *The People* on 14 June 1953, instantly becoming a national sensation. A poll by the *Daily Mirror* found that almost 97 per cent of its readers were in favour: as far as the people were concerned there was no problem with the marriage, which was largely seen as the epitome of romance – the dashing pilot winning the heart of the beautiful princess, almost Cinderella in reverse.

Characteristically uncomfortable with emotional crises, Elizabeth ducked the question by turning it over to the Cabinet, saying she would not give her consent to the marriage unless that is what they advised. They chose not to do so. At the beginning of July Townsend was duly transferred to Brussels as Air Attaché to the British Embassy.

Margaret was comforted by the fact that, if she waited until she was 25 – August 1955 – she would no longer need her sister's permission to marry. However, when Lascelles explained this to her, astoundingly he neglected to add that she would still have to put the matter to the Privy Council, and if they or the Government objected there was no way she could marry without forfeiting her royal status and Civil List income.[27] (She was also prevented from marrying in Church, since according to the eighteenth-century Royal Marriages Act any clergyman who officiated would be imprisoned and have all his property and money confiscated.) When she turned 25 press speculation was once again rife. In October 1955, Prime Minister Anthony Eden (successor to Churchill, who had retired because of ill health six months previously) told the Queen that the Cabinet would not approve of the marriage. On 31 October Margaret made her famous forlorn but achingly stiff upper-lip public statement:

> I would like it to be known that I have decided not to marry Group Captain Peter Townsend. I have been aware that, subject to my renouncing my rights of succession, it might have been possible for me to contract a civil marriage. But, mindful of the Church's teaching that Christian marriage is indissoluble, and conscious of my duty to the Commonwealth, I have resolved to put these considerations before any others.[28]

Fine words, but complete nonsense. (The part about her duty to the Commonwealth is a dazzling non sequitur.) It is clear that her decision was really the result of pressure from the Queen, the rest of the family and certain courtiers and politicians, never mind the Church. But what finally tipped the balance was the threat of losing her Civil List income and status as a royal princess. So much for the fairy tale.

The Townsend affair marked a watershed for Margaret. She had been publicly humiliated and lost her chance of happiness – or so she saw it at the time – becoming bitter and rebellious, often using her sacrifice over Townsend as emotional blackmail in order to get her own way with her family. Her mother and sister often felt they were walking on eggshells and had no idea how to rein her in, even when the sensational newspaper headlines screamed 'Is Margaret Too Daring?' over close-ups of her teetering cleavage, or shook their heads over her chainsmoking and late hours in louche company. Added to this were growing grumbles about the way she conducted her royal duties: often late, usually haughty or indifferent to those who had waited hours in the rain to catch a glimpse of her, and not infrequently downright rude. But after her Townsend 'sacrifice' she knew she could get away with almost anything.

After Townsend, Margaret – no doubt mischievously – turned her attentions briefly to her cousin Prince Christopher of Hanover, a grandson of Kaiser Wilhelm whose sister had been in the Hitler Youth.[29] Perhaps she just wanted to scare her family. But at the beginning of 1960, immediately on hearing that Townsend was about to marry, she agreed to wed Antony Armstrong-Jones (later Lord Snowdon). (A friend reports her saying later, 'I received a letter from Peter in the morning and that evening I decided to marry Tony. It was not a coincidence.'[30]) They were married in Westminster Abbey on a Friday in May: according to superstition, a doubly inauspicious day. (Armstrong-Jones's first two choices of best man, the second being later controversial Liberal leader Jeremy Thorpe, were dropped under pressure from the Palace because they were gay.[31])

The slight and artistic Armstrong-Jones had begun his photographic career as Baron's assistant, though he set up on his own after his mentor's death in 1956. Margaret met him a few months before this, and had been involved in an affair with him more or less ever since. (This time the Queen Mother much approved: like the Queen, she was very fond of Armstrong-Jones.)

PHILIP'S NEW LIFE

The Duke of Edinburgh had greeted the news of George VI's death with shock: he knew that it meant the end of his independent life. He was to sum it up in the early 1990s in an often-repeated quote, 'It was not my ambition to be President of the Mint Advisory Committee, and I didn't want to be President of the World Wildlife Fund. I'd much rather have stayed in the navy, frankly.'

When, just a few weeks after the old King's death, Philip sat in the Peers' gallery to watch a debate in the Commons, he was criticised by MPs and never did so again. Any hope that he could adopt a similar role to Prince Albert, effectively joint Sovereign with Victoria, was not to last. The Queen refused to allow him to participate in any of her duties connected with the Government – he was not allowed to help 'do the boxes' – and he was never to become Prince Consort. Again, this seems to have been more to pre-empt Lord Mountbatten's influence rather than because of any doubts about his own ability. The Queen Mother's hand can be seen quite clearly in this. But on Elizabeth's initiative, in November 1953 Philip was named as regent for the infant Charles in the event of her death or incapacity. This role had been assigned to Margaret, but because of the Townsend affair it was thought she was not quite right for the job.

Philip – a stickler for naval efficiency – was exasperated at the archaic practices and stifling formality of the Royal Household and took steps to modernise it. In place of the system of sending messages throughout the Palace via a series of footmen ('bloody pages running all over the place'), he instituted an intercom system. He had his rooms in the Palace decorated like a ship's cabin. But mostly he questioned everything – why is it done this way? Could it be done more efficiently? The Palace was abuzz with resentment.

Philip believed that the monarchy must change with the times if it was to survive – a philosophy he expressed in an interview for American TV in the late 1960s: 'Most of the monarchies in Europe were really destroyed by their greatest and most ardent supporters. It was the most reactionary people who tried to hold on to something without letting it develop and change.'[32] This, of course, set him on a head-on collision course with the Queen Mother, who was famous for her reactionary view of the monarchy. His undisguised hostility towards pressmen also worried the Palace, who could see trouble ahead.

The Duke accepted his role as the Queen's consort (with a small 'c'), albeit very reluctantly at first. He had no constitutional duties or responsibilities as such, other than to ensure he did nothing that would compromise *her* constitutional duties or responsibilities (not always easy for someone so forthright and uncompromising). As he put it to Mike Parker when he first employed him in 1948, his job 'first, second and last, was never to let her down'.[33]

By 1956, all his attempts to modernise or innovate being received coldly, essentially he gave up. Frustrated at every turn, he began to spend more time with his old friends from the Thursday Club and other like-minded males. Much of his socialising took place at Mike Parker's flat, at riotous parties with flocks of beautiful women.[34] The photographer Baron was a regular, but an occasional guest was Prince Bernhard of the Netherlands – another guest, Larry Adler, recalled Philip making the telling comment to Bernard about how he envied him: 'You can go anywhere you like, see who you like, and even have affairs, and no one knows. I am known everywhere, and I am constantly being trailed by secret service men.'[35]

There are still stories circulating about Prince Philip's less-than-impeccable morals at this time. Despite his laddish behaviour, on the whole Philip was a miracle of discretion – at least compared to his other pals from the Thursday Club, and it was this constant threat of having them drag his name into their own scandals that really worried the Palace.

Both Baron and Lord Milford Haven (following in his father's footsteps) held wild orgies – for which Stephen Ward provided some of the girls. Milford Haven held parties at his flat in Grosvenor Square, Mayfair, which involved games such as 'Find the Lady' and 'Chase the Bitch', which leave little to the imagination. Society photographer Baron and the artist Vasco Lazzolo were frequent guests and – according to journalist Warwick Charlton – a member of the royal family was also a regular participant, although he refused to identify him.[36] Baron held even more orgiastic parties at his flat in Piccadilly that featured parodies of Masonic rituals, with girls dressed only in Masonic aprons.[37]

Stephen Ward, too, held functions at his Cavendish Square flat, which – at that stage – were non-orgy parties. (Ward appears to have branched out into that area only after Baron's death in 1956.) Before his marriage – but during his engagement – Philip attended at least one of these, possibly more. Ward later acknowledged Philip's attendance at one party with a Canadian model named Mitzi Taylor, and some of Ward's guests recall him being at others.[38]

As a close friend of Milford Haven and Baron, it is unlikely that Philip was unaware of these abandoned revels – and the same applies to Mountbatten. And although news of the parties was kept within a fairly exclusive circle, the Palace spies almost certainly knew about them – their antennae for potential scandal being unusually well honed. The very fact that Philip was well acquainted with people who were part of this circuit – and even friendly with the organisers of the fun and games – threatened to embroil him in scandal if they were exposed. Indeed, this very nearly happened.

Unaware of Palace machinations against him, at the end of 1956 Philip blithely came up with the ultimate plan to return to his bachelor life, away from the security men and reporters who were cramping his style. Invited to open the Olympic Games in Melbourne, Australia, he decided to do it in style, turning it into a four-month, 40,000-mile tour on the *Britannia* that took in the USA, New Zealand, the Seychelles, Malaya and many other places, with the occasional stop for official business – but mostly to have fun. His companion was the recently separated Mike Parker. Baron was supposed to come with them, but died of a heart attack following an operation just a few days before they were due to leave – conveniently for the Palace mafia.

Leaving in October 1956, their trip was nearly called to a premature halt as the Suez crisis blew up – the *Britannia* being earmarked as a hospital ship – but it blew down again before the royal yacht was needed. Rumours have circulated ever since about what Philip and Parker got up to on the cruise – there were plentiful stories of women being brought aboard at each port of call. Other authors have even suggested that he left an illegitimate child behind in Melbourne.[39]

Perhaps inevitably, the protracted trip fuelled press speculation of a rift in the royal marriage. When the Queen granted Philip the title Prince of the United Kingdom in February 1957 it was, at least in part, a symbolic answer to the rumours. But during the cruise Parker's wife divorced him for adultery, which the Palace mafia insisted meant that he had to leave Philip's staff. The Palace, who disapproved of Parker and his influence over the Queen's husband, was delighted. When Parker arrived back at Heathrow airport, alone, he was met by Press Secretary Richard Colville, who simply told him, 'I've just come to let you know that from now on, you're on your own.'[40] While it is almost unimaginable that the Palace should have sent a high-ranking official to greet Parker with this odious one-liner, this distasteful little scene acted as a clear warning to Philip himself: thus far with your fun and games but absolutely no further. In fact, Parker was the third of Philip's boon companions to have disappeared from his intimate circle: Baron had died and Philip had already dropped his cousin, Lord Milford Haven, probably on Mountbatten's advice, on one occasion in Cannes refusing to meet him with the words: 'Not him. I've got enough problems already.'[41]

(Clearly having acquired a renewed taste for the quasi-bachelor life, the Duke of Edinburgh made so many solo overseas trips in the ensuing years that in 1959 one newspaper ran the headline 'The Duke visits Britain'.)

However, the *Britannia* cruise seems to have been Philip's last major fling. After his return he began to carve out his own niche in the royal sphere, supporting, besides the many patronages and presidencies thrust upon him, organisations whose objects particularly interested him. He became President of the British Association for the Advancement of Science and patron of the Industrial Society – being keenly interested in science and technology, especially if useful to the British economy – and, following a suggestion by Kurt Hahn, setting up the now-famous Duke of Edinburgh Award Scheme for young people. (Presumably, it was because Hahn had been the founder of Salem School in Germany – where Philip was exposed to the Hitler Youth – that the Queen Mother always referred to the Duke of Edinburgh Award Scheme as 'the Hitler Youth'.)

A NEW ERA FOR MOUNTBATTEN

By the mid-1950s Mountbatten must have thought he was in paradise. His nephew was married to the Queen – although the name issue was still unresolved – and in 1955 his 40-year-old ambition was fulfilled when he became First Sea Lord, the post from which his father had been forced to resign at the beginning of the First World War. (Curiously, Winston Churchill opposed the promotion and only gave in after sustained pressure from the Admiralty – clearly he now had second thoughts about Mountbatten's abilities.) Surely this was as good as it gets.

(Finally he had been promoted to Admiral in February 1953. The same rank was given to Prince Philip when he left the navy on the Queen's accession. Soon after uncle and nephew met, each wearing their admiral's uniform, and someone queried who salutes whom in such a situation. Philip replied, 'We both salute, but only one of us means it.'[42])

First Sea Lord is the top job of the Royal Navy, the operational head and Chief of Staff, directly answerable to the First Lord of the Admiralty, the Government minister responsible for the navy. But given the evidence that Mountbatten was either an agent or an agent of influence of the Soviet Union, his elevation to this position was extremely dangerous. It put him at the forefront of Britain's defence policy and gave him access to even the most sensitive of national secrets.

One of the enduring mysteries of Cold War espionage revolves around the disappearance of Commander Lionel 'Buster' Crabbe in 1956. By then officially retired, he was the navy's top diver, having taken part in many underwater operations in the Second World War. In April 1956 the Soviet Prime Minister Nikita Khrushchev paid a state visit to Britain (during which he was entertained to tea by the Queen at Windsor Castle), arriving on a Russian cruiser, escorted by two destroyers, which anchored in Portsmouth Harbour.

Crabbe was sent on some kind of underwater mission beneath Khrushchev's ship, the *Ordzhonikidze*, from which he never returned – a complaint was received from the Russians that a diver had been spotted near their ships. A year later a headless body in a wetsuit was washed ashore at

Chichester and subsequently identified as his, although doubts remain about the identification. Whether he was killed by the Russians or died accidentally is unknown. (There is even a theory that Crabbe was a Soviet agent and had defected, or was kidnapped.) The episode caused a diplomatic incident: Eden stated in the Commons that the operation had been arranged without the Government's knowledge, and it led to the departure of MI6 chief Major-General Sir John Sinclair.

What Crabbe was up to has never been fully explained. The accepted version is that it was a botched operation by MI6, which had asked the Admiralty's assistance in carrying out an underwater survey of the *Ordzhonikidze* in the belief that important information could be gathered from an examination of the ship's hull.[43] Such an operation would normally have required the sanction of the First Sea Lord but Mountbatten was on a tour of India and Burma at the time. But just how much did he know about the operation? How much was he involved? Certainly, on his return to London a few days after the incident, some MPs called for him to go because it seemed impossible for him not to have given his approval. And if he was unaware of it, he was unbelievably useless at his job.

An objective analysis of the situation is made more difficult by the fact that, as usual, Mountbatten's later account of events bears little resemblance to what was recorded at the time. He claimed that before he left on the tour he gave specific instructions that no such operation should be carried out (which implies that he knew something like it was at least being considered). However, his second-in-command, Admiral William Davis, maintained that Mountbatten gave no such instruction. Mountbatten also said that as soon as he heard about it on his return, he ordered the reluctant Admiral Davis to inform the First Lord of the Admiralty immediately. Davis says that Mountbatten did not want the First Lord informed until it became clear that the story was going to break in the press. (Even Mountbatten's official biographer Philip Ziegler gave more credence to Davis's version.[44])

However, there is a bizarre twist to the story, in the shape of a letter apparently written by Mountbatten that purportedly tells the real story of the Crabbe affair, which was circulated, strictly confidentially, among various interested individuals – including Crabbe's fiancée, Patricia Rose. The letter was marked 'Most Secret' (then the highest security classification, equivalent of the American 'Top Secret'), with the strict condition that its contents should not be revealed until permission was given to do so. (Patricia Rose did reveal its contents to Richard Deacon, on condition that he said nothing about it until after her death.) Another person who saw the letter – or a slightly but significantly different version – in the 1980s was Derek Jameson, then editor of the *News of the World*. According to this letter, Crabbe had been *protecting* the ship against an attack by the Americans, whom MI6 had learned were going to attach limpet mines to its hull. In the version seen by Jameson, it was the KGB which, as part of an internal power struggle, was attempting to assassinate Khrushchev. But tellingly, in both versions, Mountbatten was responsible for covering up the truth.[45]

Clearly both versions are complete nonsense – how could anyone be sure of killing the Soviet Prime Minister by sinking his ship, especially while in harbour? But the fact that it appears to have emanated from Mountbatten, who insisted on secrecy, suggests that for some reason he was covering his back. But if he had nothing to hide about the affair, why bother?

Later in 1956, as First Sea Lord, Mountbatten was at the forefront of planning the military intervention in the Suez crisis. As the Suez Canal was originally constructed by Britain and France it remained under their auspices until 1956, when President Nasser took it under Egyptian control. Worried about Nasser's move towards co-operation with the Soviet Union, which threatened to hand control of this vitally important sea route to the Russians, Britain and France came up with a desperate plan to get it back. They made a secret deal with the Israelis, whereby they would invade the Sinai desert – and in response Britain and France would send in troops ostensibly as a peace-keeping force, while actually reoccupying the canal zone. The result was a debacle that seriously damaged Britain's international standing, as well as its economy, through an American attack on the pound. It was one of the most cataclysmic political misjudgements of modern history and it led to the resignation of Anthony Eden as Prime Minister.

Mountbatten, whose job it was to organise the Royal Navy's role in what was known as Operation Musketeer, strongly opposed British intervention from the beginning because of the political consequences, even – uncharacteristically – threatening to resign. He wrote a letter of resignation to Eden, though before sending it he discussed it with the First Lord of the Admiralty (Lord Cilcennin) and the Minister of Defence (Walter Monckton). They told him it was not his job to worry about anything other than carrying out the Government's orders. In the end he reluctantly continued with the planning and never sent his letter of resignation.[46]

Mountbatten also asked the Queen to persuade Eden to abandon the operation,[47] but, short of threatening to abdicate, there was nothing she could do apart from warn the Prime Minister of the possible consequences. (It is not known whether she did this, but she wrote a letter to Mountbatten, which although never published has been seen by historians, stating her opposition to the operation.[48])

Even as late as 2 November, two days after the RAF began bombing strategic targets in Egypt and with 72 hours to go before the first British parachute drops, Mountbatten took the unheard-of step of writing direct to Eden appealing to him to call off the operation. (Military commanders should *never* become involved in the political side of hostilities. It is surprising that Mountbatten survived with his job intact.)

Inevitably, the question is asked: if Mountbatten felt so strongly that the Suez operation was wrong, why didn't he resign? That was hardly his style –

in any case, such a resignation implies that he possessed strong principles, whereas his main motivation had always been self-interest. His career was not likely to suffer if the Suez operation went wrong – it would be the politicians, not the commanders, who were left to face the music. All of which makes his opposition to Operation Musketeer very uncharacteristic, so why was he so set against it?

He later claimed that he was opposed to the intervention because he knew it was doomed and would land Britain in a political mess. Predictably, 20 years later he said that he had proposed another plan that would have worked, but the Government had refused to listen to him.[49] In fact, contemporary documents show that he had vigorously opposed all military action from the outset.[50]

The Suez affair succeeded magnificently in uniting the world – but only against Britain and France. It was seen for what it was: a blatant conspiracy to invade territory belonging to another sovereign nation. The action was condemned by the United Nations and virtually unanimously by the Commonwealth, as well as by both of the world's superpowers, the USA and USSR – the latter even threatening to use nuclear weapons to right the wrong.

Seen in this light, Mountbatten was correct: Britain should never have gone into Egypt. But was this really why he opposed any intervention from the outset? Or was it because, if it had been successful, the nation that would have lost the most would have been the Soviet Union? Significantly, the Russians did know about the highly secret Anglo-French plan: it was even published through the Moscow news agency Tass on 15 September, several days before it was sanctioned by the British Cabinet.[51] Who gave the information to them is still unknown, but it is suspected that it came via Blunt from Buckingham Palace.

Faced with disaster, Eden suffered a breakdown and resigned in January 1957. After Sir Michael Adeane had taking soundings from senior Conservatives and the Queen had consulted Winston Churchill, she called Harold Macmillan to form a new Government. (This was a controversial move: the other candidate, Rab Butler, had strong support within the party.)

In July 1959 Mountbatten climbed even higher towards the apotheosis of his career when he was appointed Chief of the Defence Staff, a post he held for six years. This was an extremely powerful and new office (he was only the second holder), giving him overall responsibility for all three services, and directly responsible to the Minister of Defence. His task was to head the complete review, overhaul and restructuring of Britain's defences, both in terms of the relationship between the armed forces and their relationship to the Ministry of Defence, an exercise that was completed in 1963. This was an extraordinary appointment for the presumptive head of the royal household.

After this, Mountbatten was again approached about the office of Minister of Defence, this time by the Macmillan Government – and again declined the honour. To have been head-hunted as Minister of Defence by both a Labour and Conservative Government is a rare achievement.

Again, inevitably questions are raised: why was someone known to associate with communists and left-wing sympathisers – including his own wife – and who was already under suspicion in the United States allowed to hold such an important post? It is also likely that the security services knew about his bisexuality (after all, he had virtually lived with a known homosexual for 30 years). Even if somehow this had been overlooked, Mountbatten was the most outspoken advocate of friendly relations with the Soviet Union on the defence staff (and, less overtly, a strident critic of Britain's post-war alliance with the United States). In 1956, as First Sea Lord, he famously declared, 'If I were Prime Minister I'd go to Moscow tomorrow to meet Khrushchev . . . I know they killed all my family but that mustn't stand in the way of getting on with them now.'[52] And all this at the coldest period of the Cold War!

He was hardly the only man for the job. In the end, the only explanation for his preferment was his closeness to the Queen: because of his niece he was deemed so untouchable that no one dared argue against his appointment.

But although members of the royal family are not allowed to hold such offices, Mountbatten's blood relationship to the Queen was sufficiently distant to allow him to play it whichever way suited him: in matters of status and ceremony, he was a member of the royal family, but when it came to high command and political matters, he was too far removed to be considered royal. However, his blood relationship was not the only issue. He was the uncle and, to all intents and purposes, the father figure to the Queen's husband, and consequently had influence over her both through Prince Philip and on his own account. This unofficial, personal influence circumvented official protocols and lines of authority. For example, as Chief of the Defence staff, Mountbatten was subordinate to the Minister of Defence, who was subordinate to the Prime Minister, who (constitutionally) was subordinate to the Queen – who was influenced by Mountbatten. Was this the secret of his success?

Through Elizabeth, Mountbatten could also influence Government policies that, as First Sea Lord and Chief of the Defence Staff, he would then have to carry out – a serious breach of the usual protocol. He attempted to persuade the Queen to intervene during the Suez crisis – an avenue that should never have been available to a military commander. If for no other reason, his very closeness to the Crown, let alone his own view that he headed the household, should have debarred him from holding these important posts.

At around the time of Mountbatten's great promotion Colonel Oleg Penkovsky of the Soviet Army's intelligence department, the GRU, offered himself to the West as an agent. Twice in 1961 Penkovsky visited the UK with trade delegations, and on both occasions spent time being debriefed by a team of MI6 and CIA officers. He passed over some 10,000 photographs of Soviet military documents, including details of their latest missiles, as well as detailed information on his fellow GRU agents at home and abroad. Between the two sessions in London, he also passed information to his MI6 contact in Moscow, the businessman Greville Wynne, and a husband and wife team, Roderick and Janet Chisholm, stationed at the British Embassy.[53]

However, at the beginning of 1962 Penkovsky, in Moscow, realised that the KGB were on to him, and plans were made for him to defect. Before they could be put into effect, in October 1962 Penkovsky was arrested, as was Greville Wynne shortly afterwards. At the very public trial in Moscow in May of the following year Penkovsky was sentenced to death and Wynne to eight years' imprisonment, though less than a year later he was exchanged for the Russian spy Gordon Lonsdale. However, some commentators believe that Penkovsky had been a plant all along – the whole thing had been a sham, and he was not really executed. They point to the KGB's marked delay in taking action against Penkovsky, who believed that he had been compromised by a meeting with Janet Chisholm in January 1962, as this was when he first noticed that he was under surveillance – so why did the KGB wait until October to arrest him? A possible answer is that Penkovsky was not identified by KGB surveillance, but by a Soviet mole – for example, within MI6 – during his London debriefings, and if action was taken too soon the British and Americans might realise they had a spy in their midst.

In this light it is perhaps significant that, during Penkovsky's second visit to London in July 1961, he met Mountbatten. Penkovsky was staying with the Soviet delegation at a Kensington hotel while meeting his MI6 and CIA debriefers in a nearby safe house – a flat in Coleherne Court. The GRU man, who was nervous and suspected that he might be being lured into some kind of trap by MI6 and the CIA, had asked to see the Queen as a token of good faith. Of course, this was out of the question – but MI6 did arrange for the next best thing, Lord Mountbatten, to be brought to Coleherne Court to reassure him.[54]

None of these affairs – Crabbe, Suez and Penkovsky – can be laid directly at Mountbatten's door. The most that can be said is that he was involved in them and, like everything he touched from at least 1945 onwards, they turned out in Russia's favour, but whether he was an agent or an agent of influence is impossible to tell. (Did he tell Peter Murphy about Penkovsky? Or about Crabbe? Did he ask him for advice over the Suez plan? Did he tell Blunt?) But the affair of Anthony Blunt and the Hesse-Cassel letters would have given the USSR leverage over Mountbatten and the royal family. His vanity – his belief that he could turn any situation to his advantage – would have done the rest.

'TRAGEDY'

Not everything went Mountbatten's way. In February 1960 Edwina died while on a tour of Borneo on behalf of the St John's Ambulance Brigade. Mountbatten's diary entry for the day he heard the news was the single word, in capitals, 'TRAGEDY'.[55] It was her wish to be buried at sea, which was carried out from a Royal Navy ship escorted by a small flotilla, including an Indian Navy frigate sent by Nehru. Her death and burial at sea received international news coverage. When the Queen Mother watched it on the TV news, she remarked, 'Well, Edwina always did like making a splash.'[56] Although by all accounts Mountbatten laughed at this, there is no doubt that her death affected him deeply – his colleagues report him being distracted and unusually indecisive at that time. Edwina's death was also a financial blow: after death duties and bequests to their two daughters, his income from her fortune was reduced by 80 per cent. (The Queen Mother was to suffer her own great loss in 1961, when her beloved brother David died.)

Not long afterwards Peter Murphy began suffering from multiple sclerosis and although Mountbatten paid for his medical treatment and gave him £600 a year (about £6,000 today), eventually his closest friend and ally died in September 1966. It was the bleak end of a golden era, but Mountbatten was by no means finished yet.

PROFUMO AND AFTER

One of the GRU agents in London identified by Oleg Penkovsky in 1961 was the Assistant Naval Attaché at the Soviet Embassy, Lieutenant-Colonel Yevgeny Ivanov, who was to become a central figure in the biggest spy-and-sex scandal of the post-war era – one that threatened to embroil the royal family directly.

In March 1963 stories began to circulate that the Secretary of State for War, John Profumo, was having an affair with a 21-year-old model named Christine Keeler, who was also Ivanov's lover. Eventually the stories reached the stage where Profumo, after assuring Conservative Party bosses that the rumours were untrue, made a personal statement in the House of Commons denying any illicit relationship with Keeler, although he admitted that she was a friend of himself and his wife, the actress Valerie Hobson. He said that he had been introduced to Keeler by Stephen Ward at a party at Cliveden, the Buckinghamshire estate of Lord Astor, in July 1961, at which Ivanov had also been present. After making the statement, the Profumos went to a race meeting with the Queen Mother. He also started legal actions against two French magazines that had published the story.

However, at the beginning of June, after more press attention, Profumo admitted that he *had* been engaged in a sexual relationship with Keeler, and resigned from the Government in disgrace amid enormous furore. That was not the end of it. After Profumo's resignation, a solicitor named Michael Eddowes – a former member of the Thursday Club – revealed that he was aware that Keeler had tried to find out state secrets from Profumo on Ivanov's behalf, specifically when the United States was due to deliver nuclear warheads to West Germany. Keeler – who has always maintained that she only had sex with Ivanov once, although this was on the same weekend that Ward had introduced her to Profumo – admitted that Ward *had* asked her to find this out from the War Minister, but claimed he only made the suggestion half-seriously and that she never asked the question. However, as this was clearly a highly worrying development, Harold Macmillan appointed the eminent judge and Master of the Rolls, Lord Denning, to investigate and report on the role of the security services and police in the business.

As media attention was focused on Stephen Ward, the man who had introduced Keeler to both Profumo and Ivanov, a second, related sensation began to unravel, based on the nature of Ward's relationship with Keeler and various other girls that he had introduced to his rich and influential friends. Clearly their relationship was difficult to define, but were they just good friends or was he a sinister Svengali figure, as some have suggested? Keeler had lived in his flat on and off for four years, but their relationship was never sexual. In fact, although he did occasionally bring prostitutes back home, Ward's own enjoyment of sex seems to have been vicarious.

Undoubtedly, Ward was singled out as the fall guy for the Profumo affair. After extensive police enquiries, he was charged on three counts of living on immoral earnings and two of procuring women for sex. His trial, which took place in July 1963, revealed only too starkly that he had been set up. It was alleged that Christine Keeler and her friend Marilyn ('Mandy') Rice-Davies had taken money for sex, some of which 'immoral earnings' they had given to Ward. Although the charges create the impression that Ward was a pimp running a number of prostitutes that included Keeler and Rice-Davies, the real issue was whether the girls had accepted money for sexual favours and given any of it to him, even just to pay their rent or repay a loan.

The 'procuring' charges were frankly bizarre, alleging that Keeler had arranged or attempted to arrange a liaison between Ward and another woman solely for the purpose of them having sex: in 1963 it was an offence for anyone to arrange a purely sexual encounter with a woman under the age of 21 – a discovery that caused some panic among the press pack.

In the words of Ludovic Kennedy, who covered the trial as a reporter, there was 'a growing suspicion among many of us that the prosecution were hoping that by bringing enough charges, however absurd they might be, some were bound to stick'.[57] These represented the best the police could come up with, despite having interviewed 140 people – Keeler alone was questioned 24 times. It has since emerged that several witnesses lied, and that some had been intimidated by the police into testifying against Ward: prostitute Ronna Ricardo was told that her child would be taken into care if she refused to co-operate.[58] Some of the officers involved later admitted that they had been promised promotion if Ward was successfully prosecuted, although some refused it after his death.[59] Clearly, people in high places were out to get Stephen Ward. As Ludovic Kennedy writes:

To sum up then, two of the prosecution's four main witnesses, Mandy [Rice-Davies] and Ronna Ricardo, admitted that the police had put pressure on them to say what they wanted, while the other two Christine [Keeler] and Vickie Barrett, had been placed in positions where they were very susceptible to pressure (and one of these admitted pressure later). Ronna Ricardo agreed that she had lied at the Magistrate's Court, Mandy Rice-Davies was proved to have lied, Vickie Barrett's evidence was a series of lies and Christine Keeler had lied about going to Scotland Yard to see Inspector Partridge. The evidence of one of the police officers involved had been very much less than frank. Indeed, the more one looked at the prosecution's case, the more dubious a thing it appeared.[60]

As the thinness of both charges and evidence became apparent, most observers expected Ward to be acquitted. However, the prosecutor, Mervyn Griffiths-Jones (who had recently lost the *Lady Chatterley's Lover* obscenity case) managed to confuse the jury by bringing in lurid and salacious testimony about the orgies Ward arranged or attended, which featured various colourful fetishes and sado-masochistic activities. The 'Swinging '60s' being much more sedate than pop culture retrospectively allows, most members of the jury were shocked to hear about such things. Of course none of this had any connection with the charges against Ward, and in any case, these practices were not illegal – they happened behind closed doors between consenting adults. But by establishing him, in Lord Denning's phrase, as a man who catered for the 'perverted tastes' of others, the jury found no difficulty in believing him capable of anything. The case for the prosecution was almost entirely based on innuendo, and also acted as a deterrent to his rich and influential friends testifying on his behalf. The summing up by Judge Sir Archibald Marshall was one of the most biased ever heard in a British court. Begun on 30 July 1963, it was adjourned mid-way through, to be continued the next day, after which the jury would retire to consider the verdict – although it seemed to be a foregone conclusion. That night Ward took an overdose of barbiturates and was in a coma for three days. Although the initial prognosis was that he would survive, he died on the afternoon of 3 August. In the meantime, Marshall ordered that the trial continue to the point of the verdict. Ward was found not guilty on the procuring charges, but guilty on two of the three counts of living off immoral earnings.

The outcome for the Establishment was extremely satisfactory. Ward had been branded a pimp and pervert, but – best of all – he was no longer around to cause further embarrassment by not being able to offer a plea of mitigation, attempting to appeal or telling his story when eventually released. (As the judge never passed sentence, estimates vary between 2 and 14 years imprisonment, although the lower was more likely.) In Lord Goodman's famous phrase: 'Stephen Ward was the historic victim of an historic injustice.'[61]

Ward's death also meant that he could be singled out as the villain in Lord Denning's report, published in September 1963. Christine Keeler also came in for harsh treatment. But as more information has leaked out over the years it has become increasingly clear that Denning's report was a deliberate whitewash – while MI5 and the police were exonerated of any errors of judgement or lapses, Ward was branded a pervert and a pro-Soviet sympathiser.

Even 40 years on, it is still hard to be certain about exactly what lay behind the Profumo affair, although it is now obvious that the episode was considerably more complex than it was portrayed in the Denning report, especially where the intelligence agencies were concerned. There are now two diametrically opposed views. The first – supported by Christine Keeler – is that Ward was an active Soviet agent, and that the purpose of the exercise was to entrap Profumo, possibly with the intention of blackmailing him into giving information to the Russians, or simply to sow seeds of suspicion and mistrust in Britain and between Britain and the USA. The other is that Ward was working for MI5, and that the aim was to entrap Ivanov, by compromising him with Keeler and blackmailing *him*. Other intelligence agencies, including MI6 and the CIA, have also been implicated. The problem – typically for the murky world of Cold War espionage and counter-espionage – is that there is persuasive evidence either way. However, though it is usually assumed that Ward's downfall was connected with the intelligence aspects of the business, we believe that he was persecuted because of his connections – both direct and indirect – with the royal family.

For many years there have been suggestions that Prince Philip was involved in some way. He certainly knew Stephen Ward through the Thursday Club, and had attended at least one of his parties in the late 1940s. On 18 June 1963 an FBI report on the Profumo affair stated that 'There are indications that Prince Philip . . . may be involved.'[62] On the day that Lord Denning began his enquiry on 24 June, the *Daily Mirror* printed this tease:

> The foulest rumour being circulated about the Profumo Scandal, has involved the Royal Family. The name mentioned in the rumour has been Prince Philip's.

The *Mirror* went on to say that the rumour was 'utterly unfounded' – but frustratingly failed to describe what the rumour was. A complaint was made to the Press Council, which decided that the story was in bad taste, but was left in something of a quandary. Although it had drawn attention to Philip's rumoured connection with the Profumo/Ward affair, it had dismissed it as unfounded, and gave no details about what Philip was rumoured to have done.[63]

Many rumours centred on the identity of the mystery character known as the 'man in the mask' who, naked except for his mask, acted as waiter at the colourful sybaritic affair in Knightsbridge in December 1961 called 'the Feast of the Peacocks', which featured in the testimony given at Ward's trial. Was it a famous person – perhaps, as persistent rumours had it, Lord Mountbatten himself or even the Queen's husband? Another popular candidate was Cabinet Minister Ernest Marples. However, the best-accepted identity of the masked waiter was film director Anthony Asquith, son of the former Prime Minister.[64]

On the day that Ward's trial opened, so did an exhibition of his chalk portraits of his rich and famous friends at the Museum Gallery in Holborn, London, among them sketches of several members of the royal family, including Philip, Princess Margaret and the Duchess of Kent. Five days into the exhibition – and the trial – an anonymous man went into the gallery and bought all the portraits of members of the royal family for £5,000 (over £50,000 today). According to Arthur Martin, one of the MI5 officers who interrogated Anthony Blunt the following year, Blunt volunteered that he was the mystery man who snapped up the royal portraits.[65] This makes sense: Blunt, the Queen's art expert, was the obvious person to send, with the purpose of removing the evidence that they had been acquainted with the pariah Ward.

The portraits at the exhibition had originally been commissioned in 1961 by the *Illustrated London News* for a series of royal sketches – his portrait of Philip appeared on the cover of their 24 June edition (a month before Ward introduced Christine Keeler to Profumo and Ivanov at Cliveden). The reason for this commission was because in July 1960 he had held an exhibition of his work at Leggatt's, the Queen's art dealers.[66] This was an unprecedented honour: they had never invited any other portrait artists to exhibit their work there, but he had the advantage of royal patronage.

In order to raise money for his defence, Ward had also put on sale photographs taken at parties he had either organised or attended. One of these, showing Ward with Prince Philip and two girls, was acquired by the newspaper magnate Cecil Harmsworth King, owner of the International Publishing Corporation (IPC) and Chairman of the Daily Mirror Group.[67] King suppressed the photograph, but arranged for the story of the Philip/Profumo rumours to be featured in the *Mirror*. In fact, its purpose was to protect Philip and the royal family – by simultaneously raising and discrediting the rumour of his involvement, it killed the story stone dead, preventing other newspapers from attempting to exploit similar photographs. Even so, there were copies circulating. According to *Today* journalist Warwick Charlton, his newspaper had acquired one from Ward, but it was confiscated by the police.[68] There is no suggestion that there was anything untoward about the photograph, and the indications are that it had been taken many years before – possibly in the late 1940s – but the mere fact that it revealed that Philip knew Stephen Ward at the time of the sensational trial was seen as dangerous.

In his remorseless character assassination of Ward, Lord Denning made a great point of the fact that the osteopath was an inveterate name-dropper, who habitually pretended that high-profile slight acquaintances were great friends. But Ward had no need to fantasise. He had set up as an osteopath after the Second World War, and through some lucky breaks when working in fashionable Park Lane, had established himself in very exclusive circles. His patients included Winston Churchill (who suggested that he take up painting), Elizabeth Taylor, Frank Sinatra, Douglas Fairbanks, Jr, and Danny Kaye, as well as many politicians and diplomats. He was a good friend of Lord Astor. Another of his closest friends in the early 1950s was the photographer Anthony Beauchamp (another Thursday Club member), husband of Winston Churchill's daughter Sarah.[69] Among his first celebrity friends whom he persuaded to sit for portraits were Paul Getty and Sophia Loren. And of course his membership of the Thursday Club brought him in contact with the Queen's husband. Clearly, there was no need for Ward to pretend to know rich and famous people: indeed, he probably knew as many, if not more, than Lord Denning himself.

The image that the prosecution was so careful to establish of a pathetic Establishment wannabee was clearly an attempt to persuade the jury that he had no real acquaintance with members of the royal family. But if that was the case, why did Denning find it necessary to interview Michael Parker, Philip's former Private Secretary?[70] However, although Ward's connections with the Queen's husband have attracted the most attention, he had many other links, either directly or indirectly, with the royal family.

As we have seen, there is evidence that Stephen Ward provided girls for the sex parties hosted by David, Marquess of Milford Haven, and the photographer Baron – both Thursday Club members. After Baron's death in 1956, Ward stepped into his shoes, organising sex parties for the rich and titled, probably in order to maintain his useful connections. He was undoubtedly close to Milford Haven, whose reputation was already causing him grief. By the time of the Ward scandal Philip had cut his cousin out of his life, but was still friendly with other Thursday Club members, such as Vasco Lazzolo and Baron, also orgiastic revellers. The truth is that many of the cast of odd characters who circled around the Ward affair were involved with royalty in one way or another. Vasco Lazzolo was a leading portrait artist who had painted both the Queen and Prince Philip. Baron, who owed his career to Mountbatten's patronage, had photographed several members of the royal family. Antony Armstrong-Jones, now Lord Snowdon and married to Princess Margaret, had begun his career as Baron's assistant. Even John Profumo (who was a friend of the Queen Mother) is said to have had an affair with Marina, Duchess of Kent.[71]

If the Ward scandal had been allowed to unravel completely, many of these connections would have become apparent and the royal family would have become mired in speculation and dirty jokes. In the inevitable process of suppression, Ward was the sacrificial lamb: first his reputation went up in smoke, then his life. If orders had come down, to protect the royal family, that he was to be destroyed, it would explain the almost fanatical zeal of the police and why Lord Denning devoted so much of his report to demolishing Ward's character – which was a completely irrelevant issue, the brief being only to examine the security implications of the affair. Unsurprisingly, the evidence on which Denning based his conclusions has never been released. Indeed, in 1977 he told the House of Lords that the files had been destroyed – but Prime Minister James Callaghan contradicted him, saying that they were still held in the Cabinet Office.[72] Wherever they are, they are officially withheld until 2015. The question must be asked: why did Denning lie to the House?

Certainly something very sensitive was being frantically covered up. Earlier in the evening before he committed suicide, Ward had called over to his flat *Daily Express* journalist Tom Mangold, who had taken photographer Bryan Wharton with him. Ward was writing letters, including one to Home Secretary Henry Brooke, and Wharton took photographs of them, but the next day the negatives had disappeared from the *Express* offices.[73] The cover-up appears to have taken a drastic turn: in the wake of Ward's trial several of the girls involved mysteriously met their deaths. One of his girlfriends, Yvonne Brooks, died of a drugs overdose in the Hilton Hotel a year later. Frances Brown, one of the witnesses, and Hannah Tailford, whom Ward had provided for Lord Milford Haven's orgies, were both murdered in 1964 – at least officially at the hands of a serial killer known as 'Jack the Stripper' who preyed on London prostitutes, and who was never caught.[74] It has been suggested that these murders were carried out by the KGB in order to cover up the espionage side of the Profumo/Ward affair. However, it is more likely that the women died because they knew too much about Ward's connections with those close to the royal family, such as Milford Haven and Baron, and which might have compromised the royals themselves. There are those within the security services who take the motto 'Defend the Realm' very seriously and see it as their role to protect the monarchy at all costs, regardless of the views of the Government.

Ward's connection with Lord Astor provided an entry to another network, through Astor's gay step-brother Bobbie Shaw. Anthony Summers and Stephen Dorril in their book, *Honeytrap* (1987), describe Shaw's milieu as 'the world of upper-class homosexuality and of the generation that produced Britain's most infamous traitors this century: Burgess, Maclean and Anthony Blunt'.[75] Blunt's long-term lover was Peter Montgomery, whose brother Monsignor Hugh Montgomery was Bobbie Shaw's lover.[76]

In her 2001 book *The Truth at Last* Christine Keeler added a new piece to the jigsaw. She claims that Ward had frequent meetings in his Wimpole Mews flat – at some of which she was present – with MI5 Director Roger Hollis and Sir Anthony Blunt.[77] Hollis has long been suspected of being a Soviet agent, although the case against him has never been proven. (As we have seen, he was also a major contributor to the 1936 China Dossier that smeared Wallis

Simpson. But if Hollis *were* a Soviet agent, this would suggest that it was part of a Russian plan to force Edward VIII to abdicate.) Keeler also insists that she gave this information to Lord Denning during his enquiry, but he ignored it.[78]

The Profumo affair seriously damaged Harold Macmillan's government – but how much it contributed to Macmillan's resignation, on health grounds, in October 1963, is uncertain. This marked the last occasion on which a sovereign has had to exercise their prerogative in appointing a Prime Minister. Acting on Macmillan's recommendation, the Queen appointed Sir Alec Douglas-Home as his successor. (A few weeks previously she had given her assent to an Act that permitted peers to renounce their titles, enabling the Earl of Home to become an MP and sit in the Commons.) There was some controversy within the Conservative Party over the appointment, which led to reforms in the Party after which the leader was elected. Since that time the Queen has never been required to exercise her prerogative, as the political parties now effectively make the decision for her: all she has to do is appoint the leader of the party with the majority in the Commons.

A year after Douglas-Home's appointment, a general election brought Labour back to power, this time headed by Harold Wilson. The defeat of the Conservatives probably owed a great deal to the public perception that they were all as corrupt and mendacious as John Profumo.

BLUNT'S GREAT SECRET

According to our contact 'Phoenix', it was a connection between the Profumo/Ward affair and the investigation of Sir Anthony Blunt that led to his confession in early 1964, although details were hard to come by. In fact, Phoenix claimed that the Soviet spy had been under suspicion for at least a decade – some questions were raised as early as 1943 – but mysteriously no action had been taken against him. We can hazard a guess that this was either because of his close connection to the Queen or the direct intervention of Mountbatten. Significantly, other researchers have also concluded that Blunt was under suspicion from the early 1950s.[79]

According to the usual version, there was no connection between the Profumo affair and Blunt's unmasking, and the tip-off came from the United States, when Michael Straight, a Cambridge-educated American who had been recruited by Blunt in 1937, confessed to the FBI. However, the fact that the Blunt exposure happened in June 1963, the same month that the Profumo scandal broke – not to mention both the CIA and FBI's high level of interest in the affair – suggests that there was indeed a link. In fact, it seems that MI5 finally took action against Blunt at that time because they could no longer ignore the increasing American clamour to take drastic steps.

Before questioning Blunt, Roger Hollis and Sir Charles Cunningham of the Home Office briefed the Palace's representative, Sir Michael Adeane, advising that the Queen should take no action at that time because it could forewarn both Blunt himself and other Soviet agents in his network.[80] After this Blunt was brought in for questioning and confessed – but only because he was promised immunity from prosecution.

The immunity from criminal charges – as an inducement to name other Soviet agents – is perhaps understandable. What is bewildering and disturbing is the fact that the Queen – who, it is claimed, was informed of Blunt's confession – took no action against him. This traitor against the Crown and the British people was allowed to remain as Surveyor of the Queen's Pictures until his retirement in 1972, and even then he continued to be a special adviser on the royal art collection. Blunt even kept his knighthood and membership of the Victorian Order (although the customary upgrading to GCVO was withheld). Officially, it is said that the Queen was advised to turn a blind eye by the Home Secretary, Henry Brooke,[81] but why? Why allow an admitted traitor not only to keep his honours and comfortable lifestyle, but also to have such regular proximity to the Head of State? It is incredible that a Soviet agent should be allowed into Buckingham Palace, let alone have access to the Queen.

Although it is argued that any obvious sign of her disapproval might cause unwelcome publicity, including awkward questions about his immunity, courtiers have fallen from royal grace before without so much as a paragraph in the papers. Surely it was not beyond the talents of the Palace to ensure he went quietly. The truth is somewhat different: the Queen did not keep him on to save MI5's face, *it was MI5 that smoothed Blunt's passage to protect the royal family.* The other semi-official explanation was that MI5 wanted to keep Blunt sweet, especially as he was co-operating. This is just as unconvincing: it was not until three years after his confession that Peter Wright began a systematic debriefing, in an attempt to identify former or active Russian agents, and even then he had to seek the Palace's permission first. And, as far as can be ascertained, information about such a highly placed spy was even withheld from both the Prime Minister, Sir Alec Douglas-Home, and his successor Harold Wilson.[82]

Why was knowledge of Blunt's treachery restricted to so few people? When Wright began his debriefing in 1967 the Palace seemed most anxious about Blunt's part in the recovery of the letters from Schloss Friedrichshof in 1945: were they afraid it would leak out? Even that seems hardly sufficient to explain why the Queen and Palace totally ignored the fact that Blunt had betrayed his country. In any case, why did the royal family choose him of all people for that highly sensitive mission? Not only has Blunt's KGB controller Yuri Modin stated that Blunt was a 'friend' of George VI, but he was said to be excused the usual formality of addressing the present queen as 'ma'am'.[83] Even Prince Philip uses that form of address in public.

During our own enquiries into the Blunt affair, we were given an astonishing – and initially unbelievable – piece of information by a contact in the Foreign Office who has seen the intelligence file compiled on Blunt when he was publicly unmasked in 1979, which was made up of the separate MI5 and MI6 files. (As Peter Wright apparently had never heard of this new information, and Phoenix definitely had no inkling of it, it was presumably in the MI6 documents.) The bombshell was as follows: Blunt had enjoyed the Queen's protection because he was, in fact, one of the family. *Anthony Blunt, Soviet spy, was the illegitimate son of George V* and therefore *the Queen's uncle.* Of course if true this would explain a great deal – but is there any evidence?

Curiously, we found that the rumour had surfaced in the press in 1981 – close enough to 1979 when leaks would have begun circulating from those who had seen the consolidated file. Author Andrew Boyle, whose *Climate of Treason* (1979) was the catalyst for the public unmasking of Blunt, also acknowledged that he had heard the story, adding: 'There might be something to it.'[84] But this is still just rumour – probably all stemming from the same source, the consolidated file. While supporting the information from our source, this has no bearing on the accuracy of the file. We are no closer to the origin of MI6's information. But are there any clues in Blunt's personal history about his true parentage?

Anthony Blunt was born in September 1907, the youngest of three sons. His father was the Reverend Stanley Blunt, vicar of the village of Ham, and his mother Hilda Masters, ten years his junior, the daughter of a retired magistrate from the Indian Colonial Service. They married in 1900, and in 1906 – the year before Anthony was born – moved to Bournemouth on the south-west coast of England.

Anthony Blunt's royal favour is sometimes ascribed to the fact that he was a distant cousin of the Queen Mother, although their relationship was extremely remote – on his mother's side they shared a great-great-great-grandfather. On this basis scores of people could have demanded a golden career at the Palace. But there was a much closer connection. Both Blunt's parents were directly connected to royal circles, although in his father's case unimpressively: his father had been a chaplain to Queen Victoria.[85]

However, the Masters family, then living in Petersham, enjoyed a friendship with their neighbours – the Tecks. Hilda Masters and the future Queen Mary used to go blackberry picking together, and Blunt's mother even used to get Mary's cast-off dresses.[86] The two women remained friends for the rest of their lives. According to Robin Bryans (the real name of the writer Robert Harbinson, who knew Blunt, Burgess and their associates from their Cambridge days), when interviewed by journalists Barrie Penrose and Simon Freeman in 1985: 'They were very, very close. They were so close they [the Blunt family] were let into royal secrets.'[87] Perhaps they were even closer: being an intimate friend of Queen Mary inevitably meant contact with her husband, the future George V. But were Hilda and George more than friends? Even this allegedly most uxorious of royal husbands was known to have mistresses – at the seaside resort of Bognor, for example. Like many Victorian ladies, Mary may have welcomed the reprieve from the horror of sexual intimacy, even if it meant her great friend took her place in her husband's bed.

In 1912, Reverend Blunt was appointed chaplain to the British Embassy Church in Paris, reportedly through the direct influence of George V.[88] (Visits to the Louvre during this time inspired Blunt's lifelong interest in art.) Although of relatively humble circumstances, all three Blunt sons attended Marlborough College, eventually rising to prominent enough positions to be listed in *Who's Who*.[89]

Anthony Blunt won a scholarship to Trinity College, where he studied mathematics (being equally gifted in the sciences as in the arts). It was at Cambridge in the early 1930s that he first encountered communist ideology and was recruited to the Communist Party, and subsequently the NKVD, by Guy Burgess.

In 1943, while writing a book on artist Nicholas Poussin, Blunt visited the Royal Library at Windsor, where he met Owen Morshead – a confidant of Queen Mary – which led to the job of cataloguing the Old Master drawings. During his two years at the Royal Archives Queen Mary used to go out of her way to call in on him.[90]

It was during the war that he was recruited by MI5, but Blunt was not the minor spy as he is sometimes portrayed. Indeed, his post-war KGB controller, Yuri Modin, stresses his importance:

> Blunt had done sterling work for us during the war. Without the slightest risk of exaggeration I can affirm that over the years he supplied us with literally thousands of documents. He had helped change the course of the war, and his work unquestionably spared the lives of tens of thousands of Soviet soldiers.[91]

During the early stages of the war, when the USSR was a German ally, Blunt routinely informed the Russians of any MI5 operations directed at them.[92] He even recruited MI5 agents from within the personnel of governments-in-exile, whose names, of course, he duly passed on to the NKVD.[93]

George VI offered Blunt the position of Surveyor of the King's Pictures in 1945, at around the time of the Friedrichshof mission – although ironically Blunt had to ask the permission of his NKVD masters to resign from MI5 in order to accept the post.[94] But he continued to be a 'talent spotter' for new KGB recruits and was the contact man between Guy Burgess, Kim Philby and their masters in Moscow.[95]

Swaddled in the royal comfort blanket despite his horrific crimes against the nation and the Crown itself, Blunt's gilded life was suspicious, to say the least. But was the homosexual Soviet spy really the Queen's uncle – albeit from the wrong side of the blanket? Although it is impossible to know for certain – the royal family not being keen to leave incriminating documents in the public domain – there was a marked family resemblance between the art historian and the royal family, especially the generation that included

Windsor and Kent. (And if this suspicion is correct, what does it mean about Blunt's liaison with the Duke of Kent?) Although facial similarities can be subjective, in this case they are so distinctive as to reinforce the suspicions as to why a traitor was allowed to work in the Queen's own house and bask in continued royal favour.

NINE

'IN SPITE OF EVERYTHING, HE WAS A GREAT MAN'

Philip Ziegler on Earl Mountbatten of Burma, 1985

In the history of any family, some years may be seen retrospectively to have greater significance than others, when the clan begins to move in directions that will forever change its fortunes, for better or worse. One of those watershed years for the Windsors was 1965, when society began to tap its feet to the irreverent rhythms of the prototypical 'cool Britannia' and the royal family suddenly seemed frumpy, starchy and irrelevant to the colourful new era of the Swinging '60s. Symbolic of the dichotomy between the two worlds was the time of the death and funeral of Winston Churchill in January. Elizabeth II granted him, as her first prime minister and guiding light of the early years of her reign – and by then the almost mythical hero of the Second World War – the exceptional honour of a lying in state and a state funeral. But even as the embodiment of bulldog Britain was laid to rest amid great panoply on a freezing winter's day, the wind of change had brought in a Labour government, headed by Harold Wilson, which was to last until 1970.

Among his government's many innovations was the mushrooming of new universities and a new wave of working-class students, few of whom understood or cared about Elizabeth II and her burgeoning family. But they were not alone in their disaffection: during the decade public interest in the royal family had dwindled dramatically. Viewing figures for the Queen's annual Christmas message had plummeted and few theatres or cinemas kept up the time-honoured tradition of ending their entertainment with the National Anthem – and where it was still a feature, only the most reactionary audiences bothered to stand respectfully.[1] Even the tenth anniversary of the coronation in 1963 had gone unnoticed (which the spin doctors would ensure could never happen now): as the outspoken journalist Malcolm Muggeridge said on an American TV chat show, 'The English are getting bored with their monarchy.'[2]

The Swinging '60s, with its irresistible rise of youth culture, had made it cool to be working-class. The new heroes were the Beatles and the Rolling Stones, actors like Michael Caine and sportsmen like Bobby Moore. By the end of the 1960s, it was more likely that young aristocrats would assume 'mockney' accents than that social climbers would feign the cut-glass tones of the upper class. (Princess Anne's Liverpudlian twang in homage to the Beatles was a source of worry to the Palace.) Sexual permissiveness, fuelled by the widespread availability of the contraceptive pill, led to the questioning of traditional institutions and, particularly among the young, it was a time of irreverence in which satire flourished in the hands of the likes of David Frost and Peter Cook. The upper class was now little more than a source of comedy, and royalty always good for a cheap laugh.

Elizabeth II's staid and resolutely tweedy style, which had suited the country up until the early 1960s, was out of step with the times, which saw greater individual freedom, especially where sex and marriage were concerned. The year of 1967 saw a direct threat to one of the most entrenched royal traditions, when George Lascelles, Earl of Harewood, son of the Princess Royal and 18th in line to the throne, was divorced – the first royal divorcee since Henry VIII.[3] When Harewood, who had been living with a divorced woman and their son for three years, was divorced by his wife and wanted to marry his lover, Harold Wilson's Cabinet advised Elizabeth II to give her consent. She did so, but ordered them to marry outside the UK.

Harewood's divorce and remarriage in the USA set a precedent and had an immediate effect on the previously unyielding attitude to the Duke and Duchess of Windsor. In June 1967 for the first time the Duchess of Windsor was invited to accompany her husband to a royal occasion – the unveiling of a memorial plaque to Queen Mary in London. Even the Queen Mother was present, although the Duchess, while dropping a respectful curtsey to the Queen, pointedly omitted even to incline her head to her old enemy. (Elizabeth II had met the Duke and Duchess in March 1965 when the Duke was in London for an eye operation. Although he was glad to see his niece and conscious of the honour after all that time as a royal pariah, the occasion was not remarkable for its warmth and spontaneity. The Queen was her usual remote and cool self.)

A year later, the Duke of Windsor – this time without his Duchess – was back in England for the funeral of George, Duke of Kent's, widow. The ever-elegant dowager, Marina, who had been given a grace and favour apartment in Kensington Palace, had enjoyed an eventful love life during her widowhood. Her name had been linked with many worldly and glamorous men including Douglas Fairbanks, Jr, David Niven, John Profumo – and there is even a suggestion that she was romantically involved with Sir Anthony Eden.[4] However, the great love of her later years was the American entertainer Danny Kaye (whose name has also been associated with other senior royal ladies).[5] But the doomed Duke of Kent was always her grand passion and soul mate, their closeness even being reflected in the date of her death. Diagnosed with an inoperable brain tumour some weeks previously, she collapsed in Kensington Palace in August 1968 on the 24th anniversary of his death, dying without regaining consciousness two days later.

Marina's funeral seems to have turned Windsor's thoughts to his own mortality: while in England he sought Elizabeth's permission for himself and his Duchess to be laid to rest in the royal burial ground at Frogmore. Perhaps surprisingly, this was granted. He was also concerned about providing for his wife if he died first, asking for the £10,000 annual income from the Sandringham and Balmoral estates – which would end at his death – to be paid to the Duchess. This was more difficult to deal with, presumably because it involved money and a troublesome living, rather than conveniently dead, Windsor. Elizabeth took six months to decide and finally agreed to pay her £5,000 a year (a little under £50,000 today).

MOUNTBATTEN IN 'RETIREMENT'

The year 1965 also saw the departure of Mountbatten as Chief of the Defence Staff and his reluctant retirement from public office altogether. (He had managed to extend his tour of duty as Chief of the Defence Staff twice, but it was thought undesirable for any one person to hold the post for too long.) Of course, Mountbatten had no intention of spending his twilight years sniffing roses and walking the dog. He was still an influential figure on the world stage and was determined to keep it that way, being involved in one way or another with nearly 180 organisations. Many of these, such as the British–Burma Society and the Royal Naval Film Corporation reflected his career, while others showed his sometimes surprising interests: while his membership of the Society of Genealogists is entirely in keeping with his obsession with imperial claims, his membership of the Magic Circle was more unexpected, although symbolically perfect for such a master of illusion.

Retirement was also an opportunity for his voluminous papers – numbering some 4,000 files that eventually ended up with Southampton University – to be organised with an eye to posterity. It was also, of course, the perfect time to rewrite history, a hobby of his since his youth. One academic who was involved with the archives found evidence that some of the papers are much more recent than they are supposed to be – presumably Mountbatten's latest version of events that had previously painted him in an unacceptably less-than-perfect light. He branded Mountbatten an 'awful crook'.[6]

Even Mountbatten's admirers admit that he falsified the story of events in which he was involved, always making himself out to be the hero of the hour, being obsessed with self-publicity. Philip Ziegler writes at the end of his official biography of the Earl:

His vanity, though child-like, was monstrous, his ambition unbridled. The truth, in his hands, was swiftly converted from what it was to what it should have been. He sought to rewrite history with a cavalier indifference to the facts to magnify his own achievements. There was a time when I became so enraged by what I began to feel was his determination to hoodwink me that I found it necessary to place on my desk a notice saying: REMEMBER. IN SPITE OF EVERYTHING, HE WAS A GREAT MAN.[7]

Many others were much more brutal. Lord Reith, one-time Director-General of the BBC, who, during the war, became Minister of Information before working with Mountbatten in Combined Operations, bluntly called him a 'fraud and a counterfeit'.[8] Another wartime Minister of Information, Brendan Bracken, described him as 'a miserable creature, power-mad, publicity-mad',[9] while the daughter of Caspar John, Vice Chief of Naval Staff during his time as First Sea Lord, summed up her father's view of him: 'He deplored the flamboyance, the self-promotion, above all the deviousness of the First Sea Lord.'[10] Later history is even blunter in its condemnation: the *Daily Mail* of 24 August 2002 carried an article entitled 'And now... the 100 Worst Britons' in which Simon Heffer cited one of his choices for the unenviable title as Earl Mountbatten of Burma, describing him as: 'Charlatan, poseur, incompetent, disastrous Viceroy of India, mediocre service chief, complete phoney.'

First-hand accounts of dealings with the duplicitous Mountbatten reveal the extraordinary lengths he went to in order to present his own unique angle on the past. When Madeleine Masson – a friend of both Mountbattens and a regular guest at Broadlands even after his wife's death – was writing her 1952 biography, Edwina was happy to give her unrestricted access to her diaries and papers. However, when she had finished the book Mountbatten asked to see the manuscript – and altered it in his own hand, using blue pencil, the traditional tool of the military censor. In Madeleine's words, 'He rewrote history by taking out anything, however petty, that did not show the Mountbattens in a good light, and inserted new information.' Horrified, she summed up his uniquely annotated version as 'lies, pure lies'.[11]

But worse was to come. After the book – or rather Mountbatten's version of it – was published, Masson placed the incriminating manuscript in her bank in London's Portman Square for safekeeping. At a subsequent meeting, when he casually asked her where it was, she made the innocent error of telling him. Then the manuscript vanished from the bank.

A similar episode involved writer Gwen Robyns, who was collaborating with David Hicks, the interior decorator husband of Mountbatten's younger daughter Pamela, on a biography of Hicks. This included candid details about Hick's homosexual relationships, based on taped interviews with several of his former boyfriends. Anxious as ever to protect his family's image, Mountbatten invited Robyns to lunch, during which he asked her to 'Be a good girl and give me those tapes'. When she refused (partly because the interviewees had also regaled her with uncomplimentary words about Mountbatten himself) he threatened to sue her. Robyns said, 'I couldn't fight a man with his money, so we ended up going to his lawyer's office and burning the tapes.'[12]

One of Mountbatten's early retirement projects was the production of a 12-part television series, *The Life and Times of Lord Louis Mountbatten*, broadcast in early 1969, which, needless to say, was very much his own brainchild and over which he scrupulously maintained editorial control. As such, of course, it was almost pure fiction. Andrew Roberts comments, 'It presented a totally distorted view of his career and induced equal mixtures of anger and hilarity amongst those who knew the truth.'[13] His concluding remarks to the series include the priceless remark, 'All I want to know is was I right, were they wrong?'[14] (The alternative questions 'Were they right?' or 'Was I wrong?' obviously never entered his head.)

His absurd egotism rumbled on. In 1953 he had complained to *The Times* when his name appeared on the line below those of other (more senior) members of the royal family.[15] His entry in *Who's Who* (as is the custom, written by himself) was by far the most extensive in the book, dwarfing those of far more eminent people. He loved being lionised as a legendary figure by the rapt audiences of his worldwide lecture tours, but what he still relished most was exerting influence over Britain's royal family. He already had his sights set on the next monarch, Prince Charles, who was caught between the two equally strong – but opposing – figures that stood behind each of his parents.

As with many aspects of the future king's life, there was a struggle between Mountbatten and the Queen Mother over Charles's education. While she wanted him to go to Eton, Mountbatten and Philip agitated for Gordonstoun.[16] Charles became a Gordonstoun boy in May 1962 and hated every minute of it – but while it was one more nail in the coffin of his relationship with his father, once again Mountbatten emerged scot-free. In Charles's eyes, he could do no wrong.

Writing of this period in the Prince's life, Sarah Bradford comments:

> Mountbatten by this time was coming to occupy in the Prince's life the place of both his father and his mother. His had been the influential voice in the plotting of the Prince's education, something in which Elizabeth, unsure of herself because of her own lack of experience in the field, had acted passively, leaving the initiative to her husband and his uncle. After Cambridge, it had been Mountbatten who pressed upon the Prince the importance of joining the Navy rather than any other service.[17]

Mountbatten's bisexuality was another aspect of his character that critics seized on. During the debate over the Mountbatten-Windsor name in 1960, one Cabinet minister referred to him as 'that Battenberg buggerer'.[18] On this subject, writer Nigel Blundell comments tellingly:

> The Royal Family had always turned a blind eye to homosexual practices among its members – but it has often been marvelled at that Prince Charles was allowed to become so close to his adoring Uncle Dickie. Few fathers would have been as trusting and as understanding as Prince Philip when his son spent so long in the company of a surrogate father with such sexual predilections.[19]

His imperial game plan always in mind, Mountbatten had also cultivated influence over the other royal families of Europe. In the words of Brian Hoey, he 'liked to think of himself as the patriarch of European royalty'.[20] Less flatteringly, Harold Wilson described him as the 'shop steward of royalty'.[21] Indeed, King Constantine II of Greece regarded Mountbatten as one of his chief advisers.[22] In the early 1970s Mountbatten tried to persuade his brother-in-law, King Gustav VI of Sweden, who was approaching his 90th birthday, to abdicate in favour of his grandson and heir, over whom the obsessive kingmaker had carefully established his influence. When Gustav died in 1973 and the unmarried Carl Gustav ascended the throne, Mountbatten did his best to find a suitable – British – bride for him. (Carl Gustav eventually married a German commoner.) Mountbatten also wielded powerful influence over Juan Carlos of Spain, set on the throne by General Franco to rule after his death. The Spanish monarchy had been in abeyance since the Civil War, but Franco decided to hand power to the son and heir of the titular King, even though the latter was still alive. Mountbatten urged Juan Carlos's father to agree to this arrangement, and also lobbied President Nixon to press Franco for an early handover of power.[23] Mountbatten's chief interest in this skulduggery was because he had cultivated his own influence over the future King of Spain.

But if Mountbatten had unprecedented influence, actual power had always eluded him. Except for the tentative plan to make him King of Rhineland-Westfalen in the 1930s and his brief periods in post-war South East Asia and India, he had never had real political authority. For a man with virtually psychopathic ambitions, being the power behind the throne fell way short of the mark. Why not be a king in his own right? This burning desire may explain his involvement in a bizarre episode that took place towards the end of the 1960s.

THE COUP THAT NEVER WAS

In 1981 – after Mountbatten's death – details of a remarkable would-be conspiracy of 13 years before emerged into the public arena for the first time. Apparently inspired by the military takeover in Greece the previous year –

ending in the exile of Constantine and the Duke of Edinburgh's family to London – the idea was mooted for a similar military *coup d'état* in the United Kingdom, after which a Government of National Unity would be established. While it is now acknowledged that Mountbatten was approached to be the figurehead leader of the coup, the extent of his involvement and his reaction to the proposition remains unclear.

The conspiracy is usually attributed to the powerful newspaper magnate Cecil Harmsworth King, chairman of the International Publishing Corporation (IPC) and leading light of the great Harmsworth dynasty that had produced Lords Northcliffe and Rothermere. King was alarmed at what he saw as the economic and moral decline of Britain, for which he placed the blame firmly on Harold Wilson. Taxes had increased dramatically, the pound had been devalued and unrest was fomenting among the unions. Also involved was Hugh Cudlipp, managing director of the *Daily Mirror*, a friend of Mountbatten with links to MI5.[24] It was King who had suppressed the photograph of Prince Philip and Stephen Ward that threatened to drag the royal family into the Profumo affair in 1963 – which suggests an established connection between him and Mountbatten; it is a reasonable assumption that King suppressed the photograph at Mountbatten's request, but if not it would at least have earned the newspaper magnate Mountbatten's gratitude.

The centrepiece of the plot lay in persuading the Queen to dismiss the Government, and then, with the backing of the armed forces – always loyal to the Sovereign – to set up the Government of National Unity. Mountbatten would come into his own as a respected national figure, but his influence over Elizabeth II would also endow the conspiracy with the chance of success. Ideologically, he was ready to bite: although initially approving of Harold Wilson, it seems he had become disenchanted with the Labour Government and dismayed about what was happening in the country.

At the beginning of May 1968 Mountbatten attended two meetings about the projected coup, the first with Cudlipp at Broadlands and the second with both King and Cudlipp at his own London flat – which Mountbatten had asked Sir Solly Zuckerman, then Chief Scientific Advisor to the Government and a friend since he served with Combined Operations, to attend. According to Zuckerman, although Mountbatten tried to prevent him, he stormed out of the meeting denouncing it as 'rank treachery' and declaring, 'I am a public servant and will have nothing to do with it. Nor should you, Dickie.'[25] But Mountbatten stayed. Zuckerman was later to write that the ultimate egotist was 'impulsively interested in almost any suggestion that looked as if it might lead him back to the national stage'.[26] In 1975, referring to these events, Zuckerman wrote in his diary, 'Dickie was really intrigued by Cecil King's suggestion that he should become the boss man of a "Government".'[27]

According to Cecil King, however, events were rather different. The meetings were initiated by *Mountbatten* because, he said, of the Queen's concern over Britain's decline.[28] This version is also favoured by intelligence historian Nigel West (the pen-name of the former Conservative MP Rupert Allason), who writes: 'Mountbatten reported that the Queen had become concerned over the very large number of letters she had received protesting about the Wilson Government . . . He asked, in the broadest terms, what action should be taken.'[29] West is unsure whether the 'plot' ever went further than that, but does note that Mountbatten, having been Chief of the Defence Staff, had the right connections in the armed forces.

The full story of this episode has yet to see the light of day, although from the information that has emerged since 1981, it certainly seems to have been much more serious than it is usually portrayed. This putative military coup was certainly more real than just some eccentric idea of King's – and overlapped with another series of events that is only partially in the public domain even now. Since Harold Wilson came to power, groups within MI5 and the CIA had become convinced that he was a Soviet agent. This is explored by David Leigh, associate editor of the *Observer*, in his 1988 book *The Wilson Plot*, in which he argues that it was pressure from MI5 that caused Wilson's surprise resignation from his second term of office in 1976. One of those convinced of Wilson's guilt was Peter Wright, who obsessively devoted much of his energy to proving the case against the Prime Minister. In our view the suspicions against Wilson are unfounded (a view shared, despite his admiration for his former chief, by Phoenix), although it is more than likely that Wilson was an agent of influence: two of his closest advisers, Lords Kagan and Plurenden, both of whom owed their peerages to Wilson, have since been identified as having been under Soviet control.

It appears that a faction within MI5 supported King's idea of a coup because it believed that Wilson was a Russian agent. Wright claimed that Cecil King had agreed to publish leaks from MI5 that would help put the pressure on the Prime Minister.[30] It is also clear that King did more than simply arrange a couple of meetings with Mountbatten to sound him out. David Leigh writes:

> Next [after the Mountbatten meeting], King addressed young officers at Sandhurst, astonishing them by his calls for the Army to rise up . . . There were reportedly other meetings, one at the Defence Ministry itself. One senior Army officer at the Ashford Intelligence services, said privately at the time that planning had reached the stage of designating the Shetland Islands, in the far North of Scotland, as a home for 'internees'.[31]

This alarming episode is particularly difficult to evaluate because, in 1975, Mountbatten, Zuckerman and Cudlipp agreed on an 'official' version they would trot out if and when the coup became public. (Cecil King – who claimed the plan was Mountbatten's – was not party to this arrangement.) Mountbatten showed the correspondence between the three men that established their joint story to Harold Wilson in November 1975.[32] But undoubtedly, the quasi-hero also gave Wilson his own spin on the affair: a few years later the latter was quoted as saying that 'two people high up in the press' had tried to involve Mountbatten in a coup but he had 'sent them packing in the best quarter-deck manner'.[33] As we have seen, this is not exactly what happened.

Mountbatten's diary entry for that day simply states 'Dangerous nonsense!' and there is correspondence to show that, when King attempted to revive the plan in 1970, Mountbatten declined the proffered role on the grounds that his views had not changed.[34] Although this appears to show that Mountbatten had rejected the plot, his unique way of rewriting history makes it impossible to know what to believe even in his own archives.

Was there any more to this conspiracy than bellicose huffing and puffing by a handful of disaffected members of the Establishment? Were any serious attempts made to recruit others to support the military takeover? Another factor that makes these questions difficult to answer is that while the initial 1968 meetings were on somewhat vague lines, there are indications that the plot later became a much more serious proposition. The coup idea was revived in 1970 (when Mountbatten was approached again) and again in 1975.

A key figure in this was George Kennedy Young, an extreme right-wing former Deputy Director of MI6 (he left the post in 1961), who in the early 1970s formed a group called Unison which recruited like-minded retired and serving officers from the armed forces, special forces and security services. (Ironically, Young viewed Edward Heath's Conservative government, which was elected in June 1970, with as much alarm and distaste as he did Labour, blaming Heath's failure to take on the unions for worsening industrial unrest in Britain.) By 1975, after Wilson and Labour had been returned to power, the sketchy plan of seven years before seemed to take on a more definite form: that summer, as reported in *The Sunday Times* in 1987, the famous shipping line Cunard was approached by senior figures in the army and security services in preparation for the liner *QE2* to be requisitioned as a detention centre for the Cabinet.[35]

Set against this background, the fact that Mountbatten, Zuckerman and Cudlipp decided to get their stories straight in 1975 – when the idea of a coup seems to have been a much more serious proposition – is rather significant. Wilson's political secretary Marcia Williams said later that Mountbatten had been a 'prime mover in the plan': apparently he even had maps detailing how key locations in London would be taken over.[36] This is usually dismissed as a flight of fancy on her part, on the grounds that the 1968 plans never got off the ground – but in fact that confuses the first plot with the 1975 conspiracy.

Despite some fancy footwork after the (non-)event, Mountbatten appears to have played a major role in the plan. Certainly, he failed to send King and Cudlipp packing at the first suggestion of a *coup d'état*; he was interested enough by Cudlipp's initial approach to want a second meeting, at which he remained even after Zuckerman had walked out at the 'rank treachery'. Secondly, as far as can be ascertained (and surely Mountbatten would have ensured it was known if it had happened), he did nothing to report this treasonable talk to the authorities.

THE ROYALS FIGHT BACK – AGAIN

Faced with the ominous decline in their popularity, the royals – under guidance from the Palace – adopted their usual strategy: try to become closer to the people, and revive the pageantry and colourful ceremonial. With this game plan in mind, the first major event was the production of a 'fly on the wall' television documentary about the Queen and her family, the idea of Assistant Press Secretary William Heseltine. At first the Queen was reluctant to agree, objecting that she would sound 'silly and trite', but was persuaded it was a good idea by the publicity-mad Mountbatten, then putting the finishing touches to the mammoth 12-part *The Life and Times of Lord Mountbatten*.[37]

For nearly a year – from June 1968 to May 1969 – the Queen and Prince Philip with their children were followed around by a television crew, who filmed them on both state and private occasions (although carefully stage-managed to look natural). The resulting film, *The Royal Family*, was broadcast simultaneously on both major channels (BBC and ITV – there was only a choice of three then in any case) on 30 June 1969, the day before the investiture of Charles as Prince of Wales. Although the Queen's fears appear to have been partly justified to twenty-first-century eyes – if not 'silly' she does sound 'trite' – it was a huge success at the time, being seen by 40 million viewers and repeated five times in the next two years. Although far from a 'warts and all' documentary, it gave the people in Britain and across the world the most intimate view they had ever thought possible of the life of the Queen and her family.

Although a great success in refocusing attention on the royals – the 1960s being characterised less by republicanism than by apathy where the monarchy was concerned – the prying television lens soon proved to be a double-edged sword. While many considered it necessary to show the people that the royals were human, others feared that *The Royal Family* would eventually destroy the mystique and magic on which royalty relies in order to survive. After all, allowing the Queen's subjects to follow her daily life so closely from the comfort of their living-rooms was the ultimate letting in of daylight on magic. And now, of course, it would be much more difficult for the Queen to complain about press intrusion.

Another innovation in moving the Queen closer to the people – literally in this case – was the 'royal walkabout' in 1970. Although both she and Prince Philip soon learned to 'work' the crowds with professionalism and some charm, the real walkabout queen with the star quality was soon to eclipse them in this, and other, royal performances. But in the 1970s, the future Princess of Wales was only a rather mousey schoolgirl, with little to suggest the threat she would come to embody.

As it was axiomatic that the royal fight-back also had to focus on the heir to the throne, image makers were hired to ensure that he was presented in the best possible light to the public. With his big ears, tortured mannerisms and sensitive and insecure nature, Charles was hardly the best material to work with (even his parents nicknamed him 'Windy' – a somewhat cruel reference to his often extreme timidity). Although he became the first royal to be brought up in front of the television cameras, he never made friends with the lens. Charles is not a TV 'natural'. The first time he really found himself in the world's spotlight was his investiture as Prince of Wales on 1 July 1969.

After his private hell at the emotionally bleak Gordonstoun, Charles was sent to the much more congenial Timbertop school in Australia for a few months in 1966, to build up his Commonwealth credentials – he was the first royal to be partly educated outside of the UK. This may also have been intended as preparation for his becoming Governor-General of Australia when he had finished his education and customary period in the services: indeed, the idea was certainly considered seriously when he left the navy ten years later.

In 1967 Charles went to Trinity College, Cambridge, to study archaeology and anthropology, where he was taken under the wing of Rab Butler, then the Master of Trinity. Still socially awkward, and aware of the problems involved in making friends among social climbers and hangers-on, he kept very largely to himself. However, his Cambridge days were distinguished by his achieving a competent lower second honours degree, being the first royal to do so without significant upgrading by obsequious authorities. In 1969 he attended the University College of Wales, Aberystwyth, for a few months to learn Welsh in order to prepare him for becoming Prince of that country. It says much for Charles's innate integrity that despite initial republican demonstrations – and inevitably attendant security nightmares – he soon came to be a popular figure to both the people of Aberystwyth and fellow students. He was much missed when he left.

The investiture took place at Caernarvon Castle on 1 July 1969. Designed by Lord Snowdon (Constable of Caernarvon since 1963), it was a strange mix of ancient and modern: the material with which the great canopy was made giving the ceremony the soundbite description of 'Pomp and Perspex'. Wearing a very modernistic crown, Charles knelt to his mother – with whom he exchanged a very human grin – and in sonorous quasi-Arthurian language swore to be her 'liegeman of life and limb'.

When Charles became Prince of Wales at the age of 21, he inherited the Duchy of Cornwall and its income of £248,000 – approaching £2 million today – of which he voluntarily gave 50 per cent of the profits to the Treasury. (On his marriage in 1981 this was reduced to 25 per cent.) When the voluntary payment was announced, Charles's Private Secretary stated that the Prince was simply following the precedent established by Edward, the last Prince of Wales. What he did not mention, however, was that prior to 1921 the Duchy *had* paid tax. As we saw earlier, Edward had negotiated a secret (and highly questionable) deal with the Inland Revenue in which income from the Duchy would be exempt, in lieu of which he would pay a voluntary contribution from the profits (less than half of the tax he would otherwise have paid) to the Treasury. We also saw that this arrangement was kept secret until it was unearthed by an independent researcher in the early 1990s, and that until 1969 the Palace had routinely lied about the tax status of the Duchy of Cornwall.[38]

'INTO THE RED'

By the end of the 1960s, the royals had another problem: they had serious money worries. Although they were hardly threatened with bankruptcy, the payments they received from the state no longer covered their expenses – the Queen was even compelled to subsidise herself and her family from the Privy Purse. The problem was inflation. According to the practice of setting the monarch's Civil List at the beginning of the reign, the sum agreed in 1952 was £475,000 a year – the equivalent of over £7 million today – but by the end of the 1960s it was worth only roughly half of that. And although it had a built-in allowance for inflation, it was simply not enough to cover the spiralling inflation of the 1960s. In the past, there was usually something left over from the Civil List at the end of each year (which generally disappeared into the royal coffers), but by 1962 the Civil List no longer covered the cost of maintaining the Court, which by the end of the decade was £750,000 – around £5.5 million today. The deficit was paid out of the Privy Purse.

The first time the public heard about the crisis was from the horse's mouth when Prince Philip told an American TV interviewer in 1969 that, unless something happened, by the following year the royal family would 'go into the red', adding, 'we may have to move into smaller premises'.[39] At the time this was widely seen as one of Philip's characteristic flippancies, but the Palace took it seriously enough, even attempting to persuade NBC not to broadcast his remarks – unsuccessfully.[40] For the first time, the debate over funding the royals entered the public arena – and it was all the doing of the Queen's own husband.

Clearly, it was not such an off-the-cuff bit of nonsense. Philip's 'gaffe' was actually a shrewd move to get the issue of the royal money debated publicly (all the more reason to do it abroad) in order to head off a secret plan being drawn up by Harold Wilson's Government. In the words of the *Independent*'s legal affairs correspondent Robert Verkaik, writing in May 2002, Philip had revealed 'the truth about the running antagonism between the Royal Family and the Wilson Government over the funding of the Windsors during the 1960s'. He goes on:

Back in 1969, the prime minister's records of the day show Whitehall had drawn up a secret plan for a Scandinavian-style monarchy to put an end to centuries of arguments over how much money parliament should give to the monarch. The record shows that Prince Philip was right to have been worried. One part of the plan did indeed include proposals for the Queen and her immediate family to move out of Buckingham Palace into a private home, financed entirely from her own private means.

Prince Philip's comments forced Wilson to come clean and, a few weeks later, he admitted to the Commons that the Royal Family had been in the red since 1962 and that the Civil List reserves would be exhausted by the end of 1970.[41]

Even many royalists questioned the need for the royal family to live on quite such a grand scale at the taxpayers' expense, especially when compared to the lifestyles of the other royal houses of Europe. Elsewhere – particularly in the Scandinavian countries – the state had drastically reduced its financial provision for the monarchy. The kings and queens were provided with luxurious residences and given the means to impress visiting heads of state, but this was restricted to the immediate family: others not in the immediate line of succession were expected to make their own way in the world like everyone else (although of course, they started out with the advantage of royal connections). This strategy of 'slimming down' the monarchy prompted the inevitable question: if this system worked in Sweden, Norway, Denmark, the Netherlands and Belgium, why not adopt it in the UK? Does the Queen really need three palaces (Buckingham Palace, Kensington Palace and Windsor Castle) when surely one would suffice? And why do so many of the Queen's relatives receive money from the Civil List, besides grace and favour apartments in the state-maintained Kensington Palace? Even today, the British royal family receives more from the Government (or rather the taxpayer) than the seven other surviving European monarchies put together.

The result of the controversy launched by Philip's comments was that Prime Minister Harold Wilson set up a Select Committee to look into the whole question of royal finance. The ensuing debate – in Parliament, in the press and among the public – was the first time the sacrosanct issue of royal financing had ever been aired. The Sovereign's immunity from tax was suddenly talked about openly: most people, if they had thought about it at all, no doubt assumed that no monarch had ever paid tax. In 1971 the Treasury informed the Select Committee that, 'as part of the Royal Prerogative, the Queen is not liable to pay tax unless Parliament says so explicitly or by inevitable inference', although royal finance expert Phillip Hall declares this statement to be 'false'.[42]

However, although the Queen and Palace remained tight-lipped about her personal wealth, Mountbatten, realising that this struck a discordant note with the public, encouraged her to put a figure on it.[43] In the Parliamentary debate, it emerged that the actual cost of the monarchy to the state far exceeded the Civil List. Since the beginning of the 1950s the responsibility for various expenses previously paid by the monarch out of the Civil List was shifted directly to government departments – the running costs of the *Britannia,* for example, were now paid by the Ministry of Defence (which is why they could call on it during the Suez crisis). Figures produced for Parliament showed that, in addition to the Civil List, the taxpayer was finding just under another £3 million – in excess of £20 million today.[44]

Faced with these alarming figures, the Select Committee began to ask questions about the allowances paid to members of the royal family – allegedly to meet the expenses of their official duties. Princess Margaret, for example, while receiving her apartment in Kensington Palace and £15,000 a year (over £100,000 today), only spent 31 days on official engagements. The ailing and largely unknown Duke of Gloucester, who was on £35,000 a year (£250,000), had not carried out an official engagement for 19 years. And the infant princes Andrew and Edward were each receiving £10,000 (£75,000) – but nobody knew for what. (Prince Edward Antony Richard Louis – the Antony for Snowdon and the Louis for Mountbatten – was born in March 1964. He rapidly became his father's favourite son.) The committee expressed particular puzzlement over the justification for the Queen Mother's allowance of £70,000 (£500,000). It also emerged that the allowances given to the Queen Mother, Princess Margaret and the Duke of Gloucester were entirely tax free and that many of the others were virtually immune – for example, Princess Anne only paid tax on 5 per cent of hers. (This makes her 1989 rant about tax dodgers who 'cost people like you and me money'[45] all the harder to comprehend.)

Predictably, the Select Committee recommended that these allowances be reduced or in some cases abolished altogether. However, by the time the committee reached its conclusions in 1972 the Conservatives were now in power. Parliament rejected all of its recommendations, instead doubling the Queen's Civil List and most of the other allowances.[46] The Civil List Act of 1972 also established that it should be reviewed every ten years, rather than only at the start of each reign – and also forbade Questions about royal finances from being asked in the House outside the review period.[47] (Is there any other subject of national importance that the British people's elected representatives are forbidden to talk about?) The monetary crisis was resolved very much in the Queen's favour, with a 100 per cent Civil List increase (at a time when wage demands were causing great industrial unrest) and the public financing of the royal family being further removed from Parliamentary scrutiny.

THE BANK OF ENGLAND NOMINEES

In early 1973 new legislation governing the ownership of shares was proposed by the Heath Government. This would force stockbroking companies to disclose the names of the individuals on whose behalf they bought shares (to prevent them gaining a controlling interest in a company by buying shares in several different names). The Queen was concerned that this would mean that details of her private investments would be made public, which would allow her personal wealth to be calculated – which the royal family had always strenuously avoided – and asked her Private Secretary, Sir Martin Charteris (who had succeeded Sir Michael Adeane in 1972), to express her anxiety to Edward Heath.

The legislation was delayed, but eventually became law – under Labour – in 1976 as the Companies Act. However, a special clause was included that exempted a new shareholding company, Bank of England Nominees. This was established with the purpose of handling investments solely on behalf of heads of state and their immediate families. This allowed the Queen's investments and those of her family – along with those of other heads of state, such as the Sultan of Brunei, who were quick to take advantage of the exemption – effectively to be concealed. Extraordinarily, not even the Chancellor of the Exchequer is permitted to know about the Queen's personal investments. Andrew Morton writes:

> The result of this legislation has been to cocoon further the royal finances in a web of mystery. Journalists who delve into dusty share registers find the impenetrable phrase 'Bank of England Nominees' staring back at them when they try to find a hint of royal investment in a company.[48]

The justification for the clause was that public knowledge about where the Queen invested her money might influence the market. However, that this was just an excuse is revealed by a memo sent from the Palace to the Government saying that it is 'to be congratulated on a neat and defensible solution'.[49] In other words, the Palace were pleased that the Government had come up with a way of justifying the secrecy.

MATCHMAKING

The major relationship of Mountbatten's later life was with his goddaughter Anastasia ('Sacha'), Marchioness of Hamilton and later (when her husband James inherited the Dukedom) Duchess of Abercorn, who was 50 years his junior. The daughter of Edwina's long-term lover, 'Bunny' Phillips, and the granddaughter of Sir Harold and Lady Zia Wernher, her husband was aware before marrying her of what Hoey describes as their 'special bond'.[50] Both were frank and open about the relationship (although nothing was made public before Mountbatten's death): he even declared that she was the only person apart from Edwina that he would ever consider marrying.[51]

Mountbatten was still seeking to extend his already considerable influence over the royal family – especially Charles. Sarah Bradford writes that he was delighted to have the opportunity to shape the personality and future life of the heir, especially because he could strengthen his hold on the rest of the royal family through the Prince of Wales.[52] Charles was not only heir to the throne, but on his 18th birthday in 1966, he had replaced Philip as the designated regent in the event of the Queen's incapacity.

At the end of 1971, *The Genealogist's Magazine* asked Mountbatten to write an article to mark the forthcoming silver wedding of the Queen and Prince Philip. He declined, suggesting instead the respected genealogist Clare Forbes Turner, whose article used historical precedent to argue that the royal house should not be Windsor, but Mountbatten. Unsurprisingly, the article was actually written by the man himself, Clare Forbes Turner being the daughter of the Broadlands' archivist. As it happened, the editor saw through the trick and removed several glaring errors in the historical argument.[53]

As Charles entered his early 20s, Mountbatten's influence over him increased. This was easy enough, for the young man had no congenial male role model, never having been close to his brusque and intimidating father who, although capable of kindness, was terribly domineering.[54] Athough Prince Philip (no doubt resentful of the way that Mounbatten had run *his* life) cautioned against letting him have too great an influence, in the words of Sarah Bradford, 'By the time Charles was 23, Mountbatten had become his closest confidant and the greatest single influence on his life. The Prince called him "grandpapa" to his face and "honorary grandfather" in his letters; in return Mountbatten referred to him as "honorary grandson".'[55] But their closeness only added to the already critical strain on Charles's relationship with his father and also brought Mountbatten and the Queen Mother into direct opposition.

One way in which Mountbatten sought to influence Charles was in his choice of bride – indeed the old sailor's private secretary John Barratt described him bluntly as a 'royal procurer',[56] arranging weekends at Broadlands for the prince and a string of aristocratic girls. Charles was allowed to take his girlfriends there for – in Sarah Bradford's gentle euphemism – 'relaxing, unsupervised weekends'.[57] Mountbatten wrote to Charles, 'I believe, in a case like yours, the man should sow his wild oats and have as many affairs as he can before settling down, but for a wife he should choose a suitable, attractive and sweet-charactered girl *before* she met anyone else she might fall for.'[58] The relationships encouraged in this way included those with Lady Jane Wellesley (daughter of the Duke of Wellington) and – momentously – Camilla Shand, the future Mrs Parker Bowles. In that, at least, Mountbatten succeeded in making royal history.

Although Charles first met Camilla in 1970, their love affair only really began two years later. Mountbatten considered her more suitable as a mistress than a possible wife.[59] Their relationship was put on hold when Charles joined the navy in 1971 (again, on Mountbatten's urging), and by the time he left she had married Princess Anne's one-time boyfriend Andrew Parker Bowles.

However, Mountbatten's greatest ambition was for Charles to marry his granddaughter, Amanda Knatchbull, just 15 against Charles's 24 years when he first began to match-make in 1972. Mountbatten arranged weekends at Broadlands and holidays, including a romantic tryst in the Bahamas. (Philip's comment when he heard of his uncle's ambitions for Amanda was, 'Good, it beats having strangers come into the family.'[60]) The match was greeted with some warmth by the Queen and Prince Philip, and Charles did apparently propose to her in 1979, but allegedly she declined the honour.[61] However, according to Donald Spoto, the match with Amanda was blocked by the Queen Mother.[62]

DEATH OF THE DUKE OF WINDSOR

When Prince Charles reached his 20s, Mountbatten angled for a reconciliation between the royal family and the Duke of Windsor, in the hope that the Duke would leave Charles his property and money.[63] With this aim in mind, Mountbatten began visiting the Windsors in 1970, although the Duke and Duchess complained that he was continually preoccupied with the fate of their treasures when they died (usually suggesting they bequeath them to Prince Charles). Appalled by his impertinence – and amazed by his thick skin – the Duke once exploded: 'How dare he! He even tells me what *he* wants left to him!'[64]

No doubt for this reason, Charles was persuaded to pay a visit to the Duke and Duchess in October 1971: just a month later the Duke was diagnosed with terminal throat cancer. In May 1972, when the Queen was due to pay a state visit to Paris, the British Ambassador, Sir Christopher Soames, went to see the Duke's doctor, Jean Thin, and stressed that it was important that he did not die while the Queen was in France asking, according to Dr Thin: 'Was there anything I could do to reassure him about the timing of the Duke's end?'[65] Elizabeth and Philip did pay Windsor a visit: although very weak he insisted on getting up and dressing to receive his regal niece. The Duke died nine days later, having considerably unsullied the royal visit with his embarrassing demise.

He died, with Wallis by his bedside, on 28 May 1972, his last word being 'Mother', which was taken by those who knew him not to refer to Queen Mary, but to his wife. His body was flown back to Britain and lay in state in St George's Chapel, Windsor, where some 60,000 people came to pay their last respects. The Duchess was met at the airport by the ubiquitous Mountbatten, who then proceeded to behave astoundingly badly. Michael Thornton describes the scene:

> When she came to the waiting Rolls Royce, Wallis found that Mountbatten, instead of giving her precedence, had unchivalrously climbed into the car ahead of her. Her face, caught in a television close-up, reflected surprise and a certain distaste at this boorish discourtesy to a widow five years his senior.[66]

The distraught and increasingly confused Duchess of Windsor was invited to stay at Buckingham Palace for the funeral, where she was sufficiently alert to be appalled by the coldness of the royals towards her.

The funeral took place on 3 June. At the burial, the Queen Mother was heard to say to the Duchess, 'I know how you feel. I've been through it myself',[67] which although taken to be an example of her kindness, was probably nothing of the sort. As she considered that the abdication had effectively caused her husband's premature death, no doubt she delivered the lines through gritted teeth.

At the BBC's request, Mountbatten broadcast a tribute to the departed ex-king, in which he claimed, with silver-tongued mendacity, that 'He was more than my best man, he was my best friend all my life.'[68] Following the Duke's death, he tried to take control of the disposal of his assets – but met his match in the Duchess's formidable lawyer, Maître Suzanne Blum.[69] Mountbatten also tried to persuade the Duchess to bequeath her money and possessions (including her legendary jewellery collection) to Prince Charles and other members of the royal family – including himself – but to no avail. Cruelly, he piled pressure on the increasingly sick and traumatised Duchess, who told a friend, 'He wanted me to make out a will right there and then, giving everything to David's family and of course some to himself. He had it all worked out, just where everything should go.'[70] He wanted to set up a charitable foundation, to be headed by Charles, which would absorb the income from the Duke's estate, but failed in this too.[71]

Mountbatten also wanted to get his hands on the ex-king's private papers, in which he was more successful – and predictably, they were lodged in the Royal Archives.[72] But once again questions have been raised about Mountbatten's methods in acquiring the documents. According to Maître Blum's letters to Kenneth de Courcy in 1979, they were effectively stolen.[73] The Duchess had given her consent to the return of letters from George VI and Queen Elizabeth, as well as other documents dealing with the abdication that were of historical interest. But this was not all that disappeared: the entire contents of the Duke's boxes and confidential filing cabinets were put in packing cases and collected by a lorry that came at night. All this happened while the Duchess was still in a state of shock after her husband's death, and without her knowledge. Blum wrote, 'Of course, the person behind this operation is Mountbatten.'[74]

During a trip to Paris in 1976, the Queen Mother intended to visit the Duchess but in the event Wallis was too ill and confused to receive her, due to rapidly advancing senility. The Queen Mother gave precise instructions that her old enemy be sent a dozen red and a dozen white roses, bearing the message 'In Friendship, Elizabeth'. But what did the colours symbolise, so specifically chosen? One interpretation is that they stand for 'unity', but to superstitious hospital workers the combination of red and white flowers has long been considered unlucky, the harbingers of imminent death.[75] Indeed, some hospitals refuse to accept them for this reason. Even if her intention was to build bridges at long last, was the sharp-minded Queen Mother really unaware that her gift could so easily be misinterpreted?

The Duchess of Windsor eventually died in April 1986, after years of pitiful mental and physical decline. The woman for whom a king had given up his throne ended her days a wasted, uncomprehending zombie, subsisting on silver mugs of iced vodka, occasionally rousing herself to mutter, 'He really *loved* me' . . . As agreed, she was buried at Frogmore beside her husband. Bizarrely, during her burial service in St George's Chapel (attended by both the Queen and Queen Mother), her name was not mentioned once. The plaque on her grave bears her name, 'Wallis, Duchess of Windsor'. Of course there is no HRH.

NOT HAPPY EVER AFTER

The first royal wedding of the new generation took place in 1973, when the forceful and tomboyish Princess Anne married Captain Mark Phillips. Educated at the progressive girls' boarding school, Benenden, hers was an unremarkable education which she abandoned as soon as possible in favour of a career in riding. With her real equestrian talent, she qualified for the Badminton Horse Trials and won the European individual championship in 1971. The trophy was presented by her mother.

After a few brief relationships – including Andrew Parker Bowles, who later married Camilla – she married fellow equestrian Captain Mark Phillips, a career officer in the Queen's Dragoon Guards. From the royal family's point of view, he was hardly the ideal choice – a commoner, upper middle-class, and not from a titled family. Neither the Queen nor Philip ever really approved of him – and Charles was particularly appalled. But they gave their consent. (During the courtship the Palace displayed its usual economy with the truth, claiming that Anne and Mark had never even met, even after photographs of them kissing had appeared on most front pages.) The engagement was announced at the end of May 1973 and they married at Westminster Abbey on 14 November, Charles's 24th birthday. The Queen's first grandchild, Peter Phillips, was born four years and one day later, feisty Zara arriving in 1981.

As already noted, Anne was married under the name of Mountbatten-Windsor – incorrectly – the direct result of Mountbatten's intercession. He persuaded Charles to write to the Lord Chamberlain to have the marriage certificate made out in this name, and in 1976 he also wrote to Charles asking him to make sure the same happened when Prince Andrew eventually married. Mark Phillips refused a title, which had been offered so that their children, although deprived of royal status by the rules of 1917, would not be commoners. However, he and Anne were content that their two children were simply Mr and Miss Phillips.

Meanwhile, Princess Margaret was locked in an increasingly acrimonious and seemingly endless feud with her husband. The marriage between two such highly strung, artistic and passionate individuals was bound to be difficult, and soon it all began to fall apart. They both strayed, Margaret starting an affair with Robin Douglas-Home (the Prime Minister's nephew) at Christmas 1966, which contributed to his suicide two years later.[76] And in the mid-1970s she enjoyed a highly damaging affair with garden designer Roddy Llewellyn, 18 years her junior, which was made public in 1976 when the *News of the World* published photographs of the couple on holiday on the island of Mustique. This resulting embarrassing furore caused Margaret and Snowdon to separate. They divorced in 1978 – another sign that the times were catching up with the royal family, and a bitter irony for the woman who had given up her beloved Townsend because she respected 'the Church's teaching that marriage is indissoluble'.

At much the same time, a problem arose, not of the ending of a marriage but the beginning of one. In 1976, Prince Michael of Kent, the younger son of George, Duke of Kent, asked permission to marry Marie-Christine Troubridge (née Baroness Marie-Christine von Reibnitz), who could hardly have been less suitable, being foreign, previously married (though technically not a divorcee, as her first marriage had been annulled) and Roman Catholic.

Realising that he was in for a bumpy ride with the senior royals, Prince Michael enlisted Mountbatten to talk to the Queen, the Church and the politicians. Michael said afterwards, 'I am quite sure without his help things would not have gone so smoothly. He was an elder figure in the family and so everyone tended to listen to him and he could say things that no one else could have got away with.'[77] No doubt persuaded by Mountbatten's gilded tongue, the Queen duly gave her consent, although to avoid problems with the Royal Marriages Act the wedding took place in Vienna in June 1978. Sixteenth in line, Prince Michael had to renounce his rights to the throne, but as their children were brought up Protestants, they retain their rights. Tellingly, by common law, the new Princess Michael automatically took her husband's status and the title of Her Royal Highness, reinforcing the contention that the withholding of the Duchess of Windsor's HRH was not just spiteful, but actually illegal.

A further complication that was not publicised at the time (although the Palace were aware of it) was revealed in 1985: Princess Michael's late father was a Nazi, having been a Sturmbannführer (Major) in the SS. This was uncovered by Phillip Hall in documents in the Berlin Document Centre, to satisfy his curiosity about why the Palace always described Baron Günther von

Reibnitz as Austrian whereas German reference books describe him as German.[78] The Baron joined the Nazi Party in 1930 – before it came to power – and the SS in 1933, although he was expelled from both in 1944 and despatched to the Russian front, while his wife, the Czech Countess Marianne Szapáry, was sent to a concentration camp (from which she was released because she was pregnant, as it was against German law for a woman to give birth in prison). Although it is often claimed that he earned this treatment for disowning the Nazi cause, it is more likely to be due to the fact that when he married Countess Marianne in 1941 he returned to the Catholicism he had renounced on joining the SS. (To complicate matters further, there is evidence that his marriage to Marianne was bigamous.[79])

Princess Michael declared that she was 'shocked' to discover her father had been in the SS, although her ignorance seems strange, particularly as the Palace already knew of this from their background checks on her before the marriage.[80] The revelation was also a major embarrassment to the royal family, although they clearly knew about Baron von Reibnitz's past and presumably had also approved of the Palace's cover-up.

PRINCE CHARLES MOVES ON

Charles served for five years with the Royal Navy, which he reportedly hated apart from training as a helicopter pilot. When he left in 1976 he was faced with the usual dilemma of a Prince of Wales – what to do next?

Without much enthusiasm, he faced the paradoxical life of the heir-in-waiting: the role as perpetual understudy, bound by the constitutional rules but without any of the concomitant responsibilities and duties. (The Prince of Wales is not subject to any specific constitutional rules, but as one day he will have to abide by them, at all costs he must avoid compromising them.) And it seemed that his vague and dilettante existence would stretch into the distant future; after all, the Queen was only 50 – and clearly of very hardy stock, certainly on her mother's side – so there was little prospect that he would accede to the throne imminently.

The Queen gave him his own offices and staff – his Private Secretary was Edward Adeane, son of Sir Michael and great-grandson of Lord Stamfordham – at St James's Palace, and left him to get on with it. Not being a dedicated libertine like Edward VII or indeed Edward VIII while Prince of Wales, Charles's natural reaction to almost unlimited time and money was to dither, dabble and flounder – although he did found the Prince's Trust, an organisation dedicated to helping disadvantaged youth into private enterprise, which was to become remarkably successful and highly respected. Back then, however, it seemed like just another worthy cause without any special merit.

The idea was floated that Charles should be made Governor-General of Australia but it was a bad time for such a move. In 1975 the Governor-General of Australia, Sir John Kerr, had used his powers to dismiss Australia's

Labour Prime Minister, which had not gone down well in that country. The official reason for this was that Gough Whitlam was refusing to hold an election that, in Kerr's judgement, was necessary to resolve an impasse that was stopping the country being governed effectively. (The two chambers of the Australian Parliament were controlled by different parties.) But as the Governor-General is the Queen's representative and her constitutional powers are effectively delegated to him, it was impossible to prevent Her Majesty's name being dragged into the row. Kerr always maintained that – deliberately in order that no blame attached to her – he did not inform the Queen of his intentions, but many Australians refused to believe this. Nor did it help that Kerr ended the proclamation that officially dismissed Whitlam with the words, 'God save the Queen'.[81] Whatever the truth about the Queen's involvement, it was not the best time to put a member of the royal family in Kerr's place.

Like other Princes of Wales – most obviously Edward – Charles sought an important role without wanting to be bothered by the detail. ('He wanted to be a dabbler', as one Government minister put it.[82]) Some of his comments sound remarkably like those of the earlier Prince of Wales, for example, 'You can't understand what it is like to have your whole life mapped out for you a year in advance. It's so awful to be programmed. At times I get fed up with the whole idea.'[83]

Charles became increasingly frustrated with Buckingham Palace's power to restrict his activities and prevent his initiatives, creating a division between the two households that lasts to this day. It also marked the deepening rift with his mother. As he floundered in this sea of doubt and ill-feeling, he began to pursue more spiritual and philosophical interests, his 'guru' being the South African mythologist Laurens van der Post, also a friend of the Queen Mother. In an effort to understand himself and find some peace of mind, he kept a dream diary, went on retreats, took up painting and talked to plants – all of which heaped lasting ridicule on his head from the media. And *still* he was a bachelor, despite the endless nagging from his family, who no doubt had sleepless nights over the possibility that another Mrs Simpson might pop up and destroy their lives.

Perhaps, though, there was a way of giving him a meaningful job. Throughout Elizabeth's reign, the idea had periodically resurfaced that she should effectively retire, by abdicating in his favour. (Queen Wilhelmina of the Netherlands had done so in favour of her daughter Juliana.) Whether this has ever been a serious possibility is a matter of speculation: it was not until 1991 that Elizabeth II publicly demolished the idea by insisting that she was Queen for life. However, in the late 1970s it does appear that Mountbatten was persistently encouraging her to abdicate, while simultaneously encouraging Charles to believe that she would do so.[84] (As we have seen, Mountbatten also tried to persuade the King of Sweden to do the same.) Given Mountbatten's powers of persuasion – even with the Queen's almost mystical devotion to her life's work – it is possible that he might have succeeded if she had been older, or if he had lived until she was in her 60s or 70s, nearer to the usual retirement age.

Charles was still closer to his great-uncle than to his parents – in fact, Sarah Bradford describes Mountbatten as a 'vital channel of communication' between Charles and his mother.[85]

The other question uppermost in the thoughts of the public and the media when Charles re-emerged on to the royal stage in 1976 was when he was going to marry – after all, he had stated that he intended to be married by the time he was 30 (i.e. by 1978).[86] Every move he made where girlfriends were concerned was carefully watched and splashed on the pages of the world's newspapers. Indeed, there was plenty to splash. Of his many serial girlfriends, two – Anna Wallace and Davina Sheffield – were deemed unsuitable by the Palace because they had lived with previous boyfriends. In 1977 there was some excitement when the press reported that Charles was about to wed the Catholic Princess Astrid, granddaughter of King Leopold III of the Belgians, and even that the Queen had given her consent. Of course, this was a non-starter. Ironically, such is the Palace's customary economy with the truth, that their – for once – genuine denial was taken as confirmation by the media![87] And at this time Mountbatten revived the plans to marry him to Amanda Knatchbull.

Then in 1977 all eyes were on the person of Her Majesty the Queen, on the occasion of her Silver Jubilee: for 25 often sticky years she was believed, as the favourite saying of royal watchers went, 'never to have put a foot wrong', although there were some who would disagree. For some months at the start of the year there were dire prognostications about the summer's celebrations: nobody except hardened royalists would come to cheer the Queen, and even the monarch herself was dubious about the depth of her welcome. In the event, however, the public demonstrations of loyalty and affection were numerous and heartfelt, and the Queen was genuinely moved by such outpourings of emotion. Yet this was also the time when many – the youth in particular – were either apathetic or actively opposed to the monarchy and all it stood for. (Was the success of the Sex Pistols' Jubilee week hit 'God Save the Queen' a serious political statement or just an example of teenage irreverence? It was hard to be sure.)

NEMESIS

At the end of the decade, another skeleton threatened to emerge from the royal family's closet. In 1979 it became increasingly clear that the wall of silence surrounding Sir Anthony Blunt was about to be breached. Writer Robin Bryans, who had first-hand knowledge of the main players since the 1920s and was appalled by the hypocrisy, had for years been trying to expose Blunt and his connections with Mountbatten. His information about Blunt was used by the satirical magazine *Private Eye*, which delighted in dropping broader and broader hints about the scandal and its cover-up.[88]

In early 1979 Blunt was actually named as a possible Soviet agent by Richard Deacon in *The British Connection*, although the book never reached the shops because of an unrelated legal action. It was intended to publish a revised version, but according to Deacon, pressure was put on his publishers, not only by left-wingers but also by 'banking and big business interests' to prevent this from happening.[89] But in any case, it was clear that it was only a matter of time before Blunt was exposed. The bomb finally exploded with the publication of Andrew Boyle's *The Climate of Treason*, although the identification of the 'fourth man' in the Cambridge spy ring was hidden behind a pseudonym. It was enough, however, to get a question asked in the House of Commons, which led to Margaret Thatcher's statement of 15 November 1979, admitting that Blunt had confessed 15 years earlier. In the immediate furore, questions were asked about why he had continued to enjoy royal favour. As we have seen, the evidence is that it was Mountbatten who was Blunt's main protector.

However, fate overtook events. By the time Blunt was finally exposed in public, Mountbatten was dead, having been killed by a terrorist bomb some ten weeks earlier. Given his connection with Blunt, the timing inevitably raises questions about the real story behind his assassination. Was he killed simply because he was a member of the royal family who was so foolhardy and arrogant as to holiday in the same Irish seaside town every year without taking more than the most elementary and erratic security precautions?

Since Edwina's death, it had been Mountbatten's practice to spend the whole of August on a family holiday at Classiebawn Castle (actually a mansion house) at Mullaghmore, County Sligo, in Eire, which Edwina had inherited from her father in 1938. Mountbatten took pleasure in presiding over the gathering of the ever-growing families of his two daughters, which after 15 years had become a family custom. There had never been any security problems.

On the morning of 27 August 1979, a Bank Holiday Monday (the day after the BBC had broadcast an interview with Mountbatten in which he talked about the plans he had made for his funeral) he and several members of his daughter Patricia's family went from Classiebawn Castle to the harbour at Mullaghmore for a trip in his fishing boat *Shadow V* to collect lobster pots. They were accompanied by a car from the Garda, with two armed officers of the Irish Special Branch, who customarily watched the boat from the clifftops while it was at sea.

Fifteen minutes after leaving the harbour, 200 yards off shore, a huge explosion ripped *Shadow V* apart. A bomb containing 50 pounds of plastic explosives had been hidden on board and set off by remote control. Mountbatten was killed instantly, as was his 14-year-old grandson Nicholas Knatchbull and 15-year-old Paul Maxwell, a Northern Irish boy whom

Mountbatten had invited to Classiebawn for the holiday. The 83-year-old Dowager Lady Brabourne died of her injuries the next day. Mountbatten's daughter Patricia, her husband, Lord Brabourne, and their son Timothy Knatchbull (twin brother of Nicholas) were severely injured.

The Provisional IRA claimed responsibility. (On the same afternoon, 18 soldiers were killed in two explosions at Warren Point on the border between Northern Ireland and the Republic.) The police believed that a team of six were involved, although only one man was ever convicted of the murders. This was Thomas McMahon, who was in police custody at the time of the explosion, having been stopped by a routine police patrol 70 miles from Mullaghmore on suspicion of driving a stolen car. Residue from explosives and paint from the *Shadow V* were found on his clothing, and he was convicted in Dublin in November 1979. (No charges were brought against a second man arrested with McMahon, Francis McGirl, as there was no evidence against him.) Sentenced to life imprisonment in Mountjoy Prison, McMahon was the seventh prisoner to be released under the terms of the Good Friday agreement of 1998.

Although there is little question that the Provisional IRA was responsible for the killings, why did that cell choose to do so at that time and in that place? It was very odd, for two reasons. First, although the IRA had often threatened the royal family, they had always steered clear of doing anything about it for fear of alienating support in America. More importantly, they had avoided carrying out bombings in the Irish Republic to prevent a crackdown by the Irish Government. These unusual factors in the Mountbatten case raise the possibility that the assassination had been sub-contracted to the IRA by someone else. But if so, who? The MP Enoch Powell has suggested that the CIA were behind it because of Mountbatten's outspoken opposition to the United States' policies on nuclear weapons.[90] However, a more likely candidate, given what we now know about Mountbatten's Soviet connections, is the KGB. As Richard Deacon comments, 'It would not be the first time that the KGB has used a foreign terrorist organisation to carry out such a killing.'[91] It is known that Russian intelligence did have contact with the IRA, even supplying them with weapons and money. But there were many organisations who would have been keen for Mountbatten to die a hero's death before the Blunt story began to unravel. The IRA's decision to kill Mountbatten at that particular time is at least suspicious.

According to some Belfast journalists, Mountbatten lived a secret life both in Eire and, more particularly, Northern Ireland. Frank Doherty of the *Sunday News* writes, 'Lord Mountbatten was interested in what homosexuals call "the rough trade" and liked to have contacts with working-class youths. He was particularly attracted to boys in their early teens.'[92] (Robin Bryans has linked Mountbatten with the notorious scandal surrounding the Kincora boy's home in Belfast, where a network of teenage boys were made available to prominent individuals.[93]) Doherty and others allege that the IRA was aware of this, and used his homosexual contacts to monitor his movements, which often involved him slipping away from his bodyguards. If this is true, then from their point of view it would have been easier – and infinitely more embarrassing for the British Establishment – to have assassinated him during such a liaison.

The man who would be king was given a state funeral. Like the Queen Mother, he had been planning his obsequies in detail for years – in his case since the end of the 1960s – even down to stipulating what the Prime Minister would say in the eulogy.[94] Prefiguring her reaction to Princess Diana's death nearly two decades later, the Queen refused to interrupt her holiday at Balmoral. Neither did she write letters of condolence to Mountbatten's children.[95] But whatever his mother may have felt – or not felt – Charles was devastated, completely grief-stricken by the loss of his 'honorary grandfather' and beloved mentor. It has been reported that when Charles finally accedes to the throne, he will decree that the name of the royal house will be changed – to Mountbatten.[96] Then the stylish old fantasist will have fulfilled his dearest ambition.

– TEN –

'AFTER ALL I'VE DONE FOR THIS F——ING FAMILY'

Diana, Princess of Wales, on the royal family, 1989

It is probably no coincidence, given the tussle between his grandmother and his 'honorary grandfather' over the choice of his bride, that it was only after Mountbatten's death that Charles finally married. There is little doubt that his union with Lady Diana Spencer was an arranged marriage, and that it was the Queen Mother who arranged it.[1] It has often been said that Diana's grandmother, Lady Ruth Fermoy, the Queen Mother's principal lady-in-waiting, was a gleeful co-conspirator. However, shortly before her death in 1993, Lady Fermoy reportedly stated that she had never been in favour of the match – although she did acknowledge that Charles had been 'driven' into the relationship.[2] (But by that stage no one would willingly take credit for the most publicly wrecked marriage in the world.) And it is probably not a coincidence that Charles had dated Diana's eldest sister, Lady Sarah Spencer, in 1977. Clearly, the Spencers were uppermost in the Queen Mother's mind as breeding stock, and at the time Diana had the clear advantage. She was utterly infatuated with Prince Charles, whom she had known as an acquaintance for some years: he made her go weak at the knees and his photograph graced her bedside table like a real-life hero from one of her favourite Barbara Cartland romances.

Theoretically, Diana seemed the perfect bride for the Prince of Wales: a young, beautiful, allegedly virginal – and apparently compliant – 19-year-old from a good aristocratic British family. (Although it was widely reported that Diana was a virgin until, if not her wedding night, then at least her courtship with Charles, this may well be a piece of Palace and Spencer family myth-making, as her friends have suggested otherwise.[3]) But, of course, marriages do not remain theoretical: as subsequent events proved, it was a disastrous choice that nearly tore the royal family apart, and in many ways changed it forever through the baptism of fire caused by tragedy and heartbreak.

Ironically, in her haste to propel Charles into the besotted Diana's arms, the Queen Mother came close to destroying everything she had fought to create and preserve since her own marriage into the family nearly 60 years before.

Apart from Lady Fermoy's relationship with the Queen Mother, the Spencer family had long been close to the royal household. Diana was the daughter of the eighth Earl Spencer, formerly an equerry to George VI and subsequently to the Queen Mother, while her paternal grandparents were close friends of Queen Mary. Diana's elder sister Jane was married to the Queen's Assistant Private Secretary, Robert Fellowes (who was to become Private Secretary in 1990, an acutely awkward position as the Wales's marriage unravelled during the first years of that decade). But, in the late twentieth century, blue blood and royal connections were no longer enough to make or sustain a royal marriage. In temperament, taste and interests, Charles and Diana could hardly have been more different: he, the tortured quasi-mystic with intellectual and idealistic aspirations, and a 'young fogey', who wore a suit and tie even to a rock concert, while she was an outgoing giggler who loved gossip and clothes. Fun though she was, dangerous undercurrents swirled in her psyche, driving her to hysteria, eating disorders and a desperate need for constant demonstrations of affection. With the emotionally detached Queen as his mother, Charles stood no chance of ever being able to give Diana what she craved.

The ill-matched pair started their somewhat muted courtship (at least on Charles's side) in the summer of 1980, when Diana was working in a kindergarten in south London and sharing a flat with other 'Sloaney' girls in Kensington (coincidentally in Coleherne Court, where Mountbatten met Oleg Penkovsky in 1961). The Prince of Wales proposed to Lady Diana in February 1981 – and was almost knocked flat by her haste to accept him.

In the first flush of enthusiasm – and relief – all the royals approved of her: Philip commenting, as if on breeding stock, that she could bring some much-needed height into the family. The press and public were immediately captivated, too. As soon as the engagement was announced, the still-teenage 'Lady Di' became the centre of press attention that was never to relax its iron grip. The chubby-faced child-bride with her enormous dancing eyes and giggle in her voice was astonishingly free of affectation and seemed to exude an infectious happiness. Already mass adulation surrounded her like a cloud of incense.

However, all was not well. Tormented by the desire to lose her puppy fat before the wedding, and desperate to exert some kind of control over her life, Diana was in the grip of the bulimia that was to haunt the rest of her days. Charles was also tormented, writing to a friend a matter of days before proposing to Diana, 'I do very much want to do the right thing for this Country and for my family – but I'm terrified of making a promise and then perhaps living to regret it.'[4] (He also spoke of his 'duty' to marry Diana, a remark reminiscent of his grandmother's 60 years before when faced with a lifetime with her second choice, the uncharismatic Bertie.) Most famously, when interviewed on television in the lead-up to their wedding, a squirming Charles replied to the question of whether they were in love with the words, 'Yes. Whatever "in love" means.' (The blushing and champagne-fuelled Diana responded with an enthusiastic 'Of course!') It did not augur well.

According to the book she organised, *Diana: Her True Story* by Andrew Morton (1992), during one of their early arguments Charles told her that Prince Philip had agreed that, if the marriage failed, he could revert to his 'bachelor habits' after five years.[5] *Philip* had agreed? It was small wonder that the new Princess of Wales felt her already tentative autonomy was rapidly flooding away. Charles already knew that Diana was no conservative and staid Lilibet, whose heart may be breaking but who stoically accepted her husband's serial disloyalty and long absences. Diana did not wish to obey the age-old rules of the aristocracy, whereby the husband was expected to have mistresses and the wife never to enquire or complain. But the very modern Diana not only demanded fun, compliments and love – she refused to accept anything less than total commitment and constant presence. Brought up by the old school, Charles simply could not understand and resented having to account for his absences.

Mountbatten's death had another consequence. Now floundering and in desperate need of a confidante, Charles had chosen the ever-sympathetic and amenable Camilla Parker Bowles – which led to the rekindling of their affair.[6] Camilla was to become the spectre haunting the Wales's marriage: John Barratt, Mountbatten's former secretary, said, 'Five days before the royal wedding Charles told myself and [Mountbatten's grandson] Lord Romsey that Camilla was the only woman he had ever loved.'[7] Diana, too, knew about her rival before the wedding and even tearfully told family and friends that she wanted to call it off. But with the world's media camped outside the Palace and her face on millions of posters, mugs and tea towels, what could she do?

The fairy tale burst upon a romance-hungry world on 29 July 1981. St Paul's Cathedral was chosen rather than the 'traditional' Westminster Abbey (that particular tradition dating all the way back to 1922) as a much more fitting backdrop for a drama on such a mammoth scale. The venue was more spacious, allowing for more guests – and television cameras, which beamed the ceremony into over three-quarters of a billion homes around the globe. With a national holiday and a fantastic firework display – not to mention a genuinely blushing bride in her crumpled crinoline, all blonde fringe and sexual promise – it was a stupendous occasion. As the event that was supposed to revive the fortunes of the royal family, it was a massive success: opinion polls in the wake of the wedding recorded the Queen at the peak of her popularity. It seemed not to have dawned on her that she was merely borrowing some of Diana's glory, a strange and worryingly unfamiliar phenomenon.

The newly-weds spent their wedding night at Earl Mountbatten's house,

Broadlands – in the same bed that his parents had spent theirs 34 years together – before sailing off on board the Royal Yacht *Britannia*, where the bikini-clad Diana caused a sensation among the crew, while Charles went off on his own, sketching, reading or telephoning Camilla.

THE UNRAVELLING

In retrospect, the 1980s was the best decade for the royal family where their relationship with the nation was concerned, their popularity reaching an all-time high after the royal wedding, and their image remained largely unsullied by scandal.

The Prince and Princess of Wales dutifully – and quickly – produced the required 'heir and spare': William Arthur Philip Louis ('Wills'), was born on 21 June 1982, and Henry Charles Albert David ('Harry'), on 15 September 1984. Both parents departed from the usual royal custom, being excited and involved in their babies' lives in their own ways, Charles by devouring every book he could find on parenting and Diana with lots of play, kisses and cuddles. But it was outside the nursery that she was causing comment, rapidly reaching the status of the most photographed woman in the world; few, if any, in the Palace noticed that she was beginning to eclipse the royal family itself in the public's estimation. If they did, it seemed harmless enough, merely a passing phase. It was assumed that the public would soon get tired of 'Shy Di'. Charles, on the other hand, was already beginning to know the pangs of jealousy as the crowds made their disappointment clear when he approached them, while those to whom Diana chatted were virtually ecstatic. Nothing in his upbringing had prepared him to be second best – and to a slip of a girl with barely a coherent thought in her head. He fumed, his jealousy contributing to the seemingly endless tears and rows out of the public's sight.

In July 1986, there was a sequel to *the* royal wedding, when Prince Andrew married Sarah Ferguson at Westminster Abbey. For the occasion Andrew was made Duke of York (and Earl of Inverness and Baron Killyleagh), the title last held by the Queen's father. The red-haired jolly Sarah was an unconventional choice for a royal wife, but her explosion into the stuffy corridors of power seemed to signal that the new generation was finally in tune with the modern world.

As it had fallen to Andrew to take up the role – real or imagined – of the royal prince with the common touch, he had enthusiastically projected a laddish image, dating actresses and models, earning him the nickname of 'Randy Andy'. His career as a helicopter pilot in the Royal Navy – particularly during the 1982 Falklands campaign – had added to his carefully cultivated macho image. Some of his girlfriends, such as the actress Koo Stark, who had appeared in a soft-porn movie (albeit one with a good pedigree, being produced by the Earl of Pembroke), occasionally caused his mother and the

Palace some sleepless nights, but as the Queen's favourite son, where she was concerned he could do no wrong.

If it was humanity they wanted, Sarah had it in abundance. A larger-than-life young woman with rumpled clothes and freckles, and given to pulling faces and practical jokes, 'Fergie' had earned her living as a publishing assistant and was very much a girl-about-town. And if her background was by no means virginal, it hardly mattered for the bride of the *second* in line. Like a big, over-friendly puppy, she soon became the Queen's favourite, a new and refreshing link with the real world that the Sovereign in her ivory tower found fascinating.

The only sour note as the decade ended was sounded by the separation of Princess Anne and Mark Phillips in 1989 (ironically, two years after the Queen had bestowed on her the title of Princess Royal in recognition of her sterling work). Even this hardly seemed to matter: of all the Queen's children, Anne has best fitted the traditional royal role, performing her duties and charity work diligently and without fuss. Despite the break-up of her first marriage, she married Commander Tim Laurence in a modest ceremony in Scotland (to avoid controversy over the remarriage of divorcees in church in England) in 1992 and has managed to keep her private life well away from the glare of the media.

The other discordant note was Prince Edward's resignation from the Royal Marines at the beginning of 1987. Why it was believed for a single moment that someone with his artistic temperament could cope with the brutal life in the toughest of the services is deeply puzzling. Perhaps, as Philip's favourite son, it was assumed he had it in him – or maybe he was allowed to join up simply because he had set his heart on it. When he abandoned the Marines, Edward became the first royal offspring to have a career outside the military – and it could hardly have been more different. His position precluding him from fulfilling his ambitions to be an actor, he turned to film and the arts, initially working for Andrew Lloyd Webber's production company, then forming his own, the vexed Ardent Productions.

Edward's first foray into the world of television after his departure from the Marines was the deeply embarrassing gameshow *It's a Royal Knockout!* in 1987, in which he, Andrew and Anne took part. (Charles soon scuppered Diana's desire to join in.) The stunt acted as a dire warning of a new and potentially disastrous direction for the royals: despite their decade of unprecedented success, they were in danger of becoming celebrities rather than the respected representatives of a hallowed and age-old institution. Anne and Andrew appeared on TV chat shows; Andrew and 'Fergie' sold photographs of themselves at home to *Hello!* magazine. The royal family was turning into a soap opera, but the most successful series only keep interest going with unhappy and tragic storylines. As the 1990s quickly revealed, the apparent success of the royal family in the previous decade was just a cosy illusion.

THE THATCHER YEARS

The 1980s also saw a marked absence of problems in the two areas that had always caused controversy throughout the history of the House of Windsor: finances and the monarch's political role. Both their public and private finances were more than healthy enough to weather the recession of the '80s, and the quibbling about the cost of occasions such as royal weddings could always be dismissed as the inevitable carping of the left wing. For the whole of the decade Britain was in the secure grip of a royal-friendly Conservative government, under the indomitable Margaret Thatcher, the provincial grocer's daughter made good. The longevity of her government removed constitutional crises or the need for the Queen to make any decisions about the exercise of her prerogative (as had happened during the 'hung' parliaments of the mid-1970s). But was there really no close royal involvement in politics in the 1980s and '90s – or have we simply not heard about it yet? The Queen's personal papers – which may not tell the full story but could well allow it to be pieced together – will only be made public after her death, and even then perhaps not for many years. It will probably take another half-century after her demise for the full picture of the constitutional side of her reign to be assembled from the scattered pieces of the jigsaw. Even now, however, there are indications that Elizabeth II has not been quite as acquiescent as she may appear.

It is now an open secret that the Queen did not get on with Mrs Thatcher, whose mammoth period in office straddled the decade (from May 1979 until November 1990). The Queen, a traditionalist at heart, disapproved of a female prime minister and found the premier's personal style affected and abrasive, but the gulf between them went much deeper than that. Sarah Bradford comments, 'Both the Palace and loyal Thatcherites protest that the two women got on very well, but the indications are that while Elizabeth was always perfectly professional and correct in her relations with her prime minister, in her heart of hearts she did not like her or approve of all the changes that she was making to the fabric of Britain.'[8] It is reported that in private she referred to Mrs Thatcher as 'that woman'.[9]

On the Prime Minister's part, while her curtseys were almost risibly deep, and her apparently heartfelt royalist words never less than effusive, in practice she treated the Queen and the royal family almost as an irrelevance. (Paradoxically, the strongest prime ministers, such as Mrs Thatcher, Winston Churchill and David Lloyd George, while among the staunchest supporters of the monarch as national figurehead, have always regarded his or her constitutional powers as a political encumbrance.) A.N. Wilson writes, 'With her upstaging of the Royal Family themselves, her use of the royal "we" to describe herself, her immense appeal at election time, her genius in front of television and film cameras, Margaret Thatcher had begun to displace the Queen and to demonstrate that the British could have a plausible national leader who was not a monarch but an elected representative.'[10] Mrs Thatcher also began to abrogate the role of 'national figurehead', taking it upon herself to visit the scenes of national disasters or the casualties in hospital. It is even reported that, on the occasion of the Zeebrugge ferry tragedy in 1987, she gave instructions that any royal visit should not interfere with her own.[11] (In the event, the Duke and Duchess of York fitted in with her plans.)

Often astute and, of course, extremely experienced in political matters, the Queen seems to have been one of the first to recognise that Mrs Thatcher's policies would have a divisive effect on the country – the 'changes to the fabric of Britain' referred to by Sarah Bradford. But Elizabeth also recognised a more personal problem: the Prime Minister's showdown with the trade unions also marked the polarisation of left and right wings that posed a potential threat to the monarchy. Storm clouds were gathering over the political landscape, and they loomed large over the throne.

Labour had never become the republican monster it had been feared at the beginning of the century, and extreme anti-monarchists (such as the Scottish MP Willie Hamilton, the arch-critic of the royal family in the 1970s) had been regarded as mildly eccentric mavericks even by their own party. And, as we have seen, monarchs prefer coalitions to governments in which one party – even the Conservatives – rule the roost. For all these reasons – as well as her personal dislike of the Prime Minister – the Queen would have disapproved of Mrs Thatcher. And there are indications that her disapproval took a more concrete form than has ever been suspected.

In 1981 and 1982 secret discussions took place between senior Palace officials and leading politicians about the need for a National Government to deal with the country's escalating economic and industrial problems. These clandestine meetings took place in a basement restaurant in Horseferry Road in London, after the founding of the Social Democrat Party (SDP) by breakaway senior Labour politicians in January 1981. The plan was to form a coalition made up of the SDP, the Liberal Party, centre-right Labour politicians and even some Tories of the Edward Heath school. Although the Queen would have been required to exercise her prerogative over the appointment of a new prime minister, whether she was aware of the bid to oust Mrs Thatcher at that stage is unknown. In any case, the idea came to nothing: the eruption of the Falklands conflict in April 1982 led to an upsurge in support for the Prime Minister, who cannily chose to be pictured, like a modern Joan of Arc, in combat fatigues. (Cynics have suggested that the war was little more than a media stunt to revive her flagging popularity.)

TROUBLED TIMES

Although the 1980s may have appeared to be by and large a kind of golden age for the House of Windsor, that was just the illusion of cunning 'spin'. Beneath the surface there were massive problems for the dysfunctional family that – in the age of tabloid newspapers and ever-hungry paparazzi – was profoundly shocked to discover it could no longer keep its secrets hidden.

For years the Queen and her husband have lived separate lives: Philip in particular taking several solo trips abroad each year while his royal wife enjoys her own chosen lifestyle. But as long as the Duke of Edinburgh is by her side on formal occasions – and is seen to be supportive – it appears to be an arrangement that suits them both. Prince Philip's view of the monarchy and his own role has changed beyond recognition since he became the consort of the Sovereign, emerging as very much the head of the household and fiercely protective of the royal family's image. Historian Andrew Davies provides a neat summary: 'In 50 years Prince Philip has gone from the arch moderniser to the arch conservative. He's now more royal than the royals themselves.'[12]

Because he leads such an independent existence, inevitably there has been a great deal of often fevered speculation about his private activities. Sarah Bradford writes:

> Since the alleged Pat Kirkwood affair in the mid-1950s, Philip has learned to carry on his flirtations and relationships in circles rich and grand enough to provide protection from the paparazzi and the tabloids . . . The women are always younger than he, usually beautiful and highly aristocratic. They include a princess, a duchess, two countesses, and other titled and untitled ladies, some of them in the society horsy set.[13]

Philip's name has been linked – by John Barratt, Mountbatten's former secretary – with Sasha Abercorn, his uncle's favourite female companion in his later years, as well as Princess Alexandra, only daughter of George, Duke of Kent and Marina, long married to the Hon Angus Ogilvy.[14]

The Duke of Edinburgh's relationship with Prince Charles, which was never close, deteriorated even further after Mountbatten's death: reportedly they even ceased to communicate just before the heir's wedding in 1981.[15] However, the royal family's major problem, in a word, was Diana, whom they expected to change overnight into a royal clone, but she denied them the satisfaction. As one of Charles's advisers said, 'She just seemed to refuse to understand that she was now the Princess of Wales and could not do what she wanted any more.'[16] Not only did she pursue her own interests and insisted on bringing up the boys her way, but she also developed her unique public style, her own special version of being royal – far warmer and more spontaneous than theirs. The Queen, Philip and Charles were bewildered and furious that this often wild girl could steal their thunder with such ease, but even they had to admit that everyone in Britain and abroad seemed to adore her. When the inevitable comparisons were drawn with their own hands-off and stiff royal mode of behaviour, Diana's way won hands down. (Ironically, since her death, the Queen and other royals have begun to adopt certain aspects of her style – because they could see it worked.)

While she was glamorous, slim and chic – like a more modern and appealing Wallis Simpson come back to haunt them – the other senior royal women professed a disdain for self-presentation: after all, they were not movie stars. Yet no matter how much they spent on their clothes they always looked fussy, staid and ill-groomed. Diana looked good in jeans and a baggy T-shirt. When the Queen visited hospitals she smiled remotely, asked formal questions, seemed ill at ease – and *never* touched anyone, even small children, with her pristine white-gloved hands. Diana bounded into AIDS wards or orphanages in deprived areas, sat on the beds, told risqué jokes, hugged, cradled babies, laughed and cried, without losing an iota of respect or dignity. Was there any wonder that organisations and individuals began to clamour for a piece of Diana, while even the Queen herself was increasingly ignored?

Undoubtedly, the Princess of Wales had her emotional and psychological problems, although whether she suffered from them before her marriage or whether it was her royal life that caused or exacerbated them is a moot point: when the Wales's divided into two 'camps', each with their own circle of friends and supporters, each promoted its own answer to that question.

Ever since the breakdown of the marriage, it has been endlessly dissected, as people try to decide who was the villain and who the victim, but relationships are seldom that simple. There is no doubt that it was doomed from the start: as Charles was later to put it, 'A bloody awful mistake.'[17] Although many shades of opinion exist, most commentators plump for one of the two extremes: Charles was cold and callous, only wanting a compliant wife for show while continuing the royal tradition of a clandestine mistress, his wife, meanwhile, being little short of a saint. The other extreme has Diana unhinged and hysterical, totally unfit to be the consort of the heir to the throne, while Charles was a bewildered but essentially caring man, doing his best to help her.

Certainly, even their honeymoon was hardly an idyll, with both newly-weds discovering unwelcome facts about each other. Charles told his biographer Jonathan Dimbleby that he realised Diana was bulimic, while according to members of Charles's staff, even before the end of the honeymoon she chanced upon love letters between her husband and Camilla.[18] However, Charles's supporters deny that this was the case. Countess Pamela Mountbatten of Burma[19] maintains that Charles was not seeing Camilla during the early years of their marriage: 'Absolutely nothing he could say or do would disabuse her of the idea that somewhere she was lurking around in the background, which was an absolute tragedy, because it was untrue.'[20] The implication from Charles's friends and champions is that it was the Princess's behaviour that drove him back to his former lover.

In his ill-advised 1994 television interview with Jonathan Dimbleby, Charles confessed that he had committed adultery with Camilla – an incredible admission, especially for someone in his position – but only after his marriage had broken down beyond repair. (Charles was still married, but separated, when he made this admission; Camilla was also married at the time specified, she and her husband divorcing in 1994.)

Diana became increasingly unhappy and self-destructive. By Christmas 1981 at Sandringham – soon after becoming pregnant with William – she threw herself down the stairs in a cry for help; several more half-hearted 'suicide attempts' were to follow. The Queen, always inclined to avoid emotional situations and never the most understanding of people, moved from initial bewilderment at her daughter-in-law's behaviour to contempt for her lack of self-control and what she saw as self-indulgent emotionalism.

By 1985 Kensington Palace resounded with spectacular, and sometimes violent, rows. There were also increasingly icy, sharp-tongued moments in public, recalling the unpleasant days when Margaret and Snowdon's appearances were often embarrassingly marred by acrimonious exchanges.

Feeling isolated, one of the first people that Diana turned to was her detective, Sergeant Barry Mannakee, a married man in his late 30s. Pouring out her jealousy and rage about what she believed to be the continuing Charles/Camilla liaison, she became increasingly close to him, but although some believe it to have been nothing more than a sometimes flirtatious friendship, according to James Hewitt, Diana told him that Mannakee had been her lover.[21] Certainly, Kitty Kelley states that in 1985 Charles became convinced that the two were having an affair.[22] A year later he walked in on her conversation with Mannakee about her fears on the Camilla situation. A few days later Mannakee was transferred to another unit, and eight months afterwards – in March 1987– he was killed when a car collided with the motorcycle on which he was passenger. Charles was told immediately, but reportedly delayed telling Diana until they were about to step out of a car in front of a crowd of press photographers, knowing she would be distraught – and for once unlikely to take pride of place over photographs of himself.[23]

At around the time of Mannakee's transfer, Diana began her affair with Captain James Hewitt of the Life Guards, whom she met at a reception. A staff officer responsible for royal ceremonial – which is why he mixed in such elevated company – he had been in charge of the Duchess of Windsor's funeral: when he and Diana met he was working on Andrew and Sarah's wedding. As he was a riding instructor, she asked him for lessons, having suffered from a fear of horses since a childhood accident. (This was yet another area in which she felt isolated from royal activities, which mostly centred on the horsey set.) But their private lessons in the indoor school in Knightsbridge Barracks soon became a cover for an illicit relationship, which lasted for three years until he was transferred to Germany. After this she renewed her relationship with one of her old boyfriends, whom she had dated when she was 17, car dealer James Gilbey.

If Hewitt had enjoyed his brief career as royal favourite, his fall from grace was prolonged and spectacular. In October 1994, Anna Pasternak's *Princess in*

Love, telling the story of Diana's affair with James Hewitt – and written with his co-operation – prompted the media to brand him as one of the world's worst 'love rats'. Hewitt later claimed the book was the 'biggest mistake I have ever made in my life'[24] and wrote his own account, *Love and War* (1999), to set the record straight. (The book also covers his experiences in the Gulf War, in which he commanded a tank squadron, earning a Mention in Despatches.) In her 1995 *Panorama* interview, Diana was to disown Hewitt, saying, 'Yes, I was in love with him. But I was very let down.'

CHARLES'S AMBITIONS

Ironically, as Diana struggled to assert her independence, so did her husband. As their marriage crumbled – and perhaps in order to compete with his wife, who was developing her reputation for compassion as the embodiment of humanitarian causes – Charles rekindled his wish to find something useful to do while waiting to become King. Despite the Prince's Trust and his patronage of many other organisations, like previous heirs to the throne, he felt an acute need to make his mark. But there were the usual problems: what issues could he espouse that were innocent of party politics – especially in an increasingly politicised world? Even the well-trodden path of concern for the unemployed – regarded as a safe area since the First World War – was now becoming taboo, since it implied criticism of the Government's policies. Ironically, voicing such concerns now made him a target for Conservative MPs. The Thatcherite MP Norman Tebbitt delivered the cynical put-down: 'I suppose the Prince of Wales feels extra sympathy for those who've got no job because in a way he's got no job...'[25]

Stung by Diana's undoubted sense of vocation where her charities were concerned, Charles showed off his own form of ideology in a series of attacks upon the Government's policies. In a lecture in 1991 he criticised their handling of primary school education.[26] In late 1992, in Paris, he spoke out in support of the French system of farming – at a time when the British Government was engaged in negotiations aimed at reducing the subsidies paid to French farmers by the European Community.[27] Since then Charles has moved on to what appeared to be safer ground, championing environmental issues – as, for example, in his recent warnings about genetically modified crops. But whatever he does attracts criticism from one side or another. As his great-uncle Edward discovered to his cost, being Prince of Wales means being incapable of pleasing everybody – and sometimes nobody at all.

In March 1988, Charles initiated a meeting with Margaret Thatcher to ask for some form of constitutional role, or even a proper job. He suggested that he could be made Prince Regent – co-ruler with his mother – taking on some of her constitutional responsibilities. Remarkably, he appears not to have raised this question with the Queen first, perhaps because he was aware that if Mrs Thatcher advised her to hand over some of her duties, his mother would have had to agree. However, in the event, the Prime Minister rejected all his suggestions, although she did consider Charles for the job of the last British governor of Hong Kong (which was due to be handed back to China in 1997) but in the end it was decided that a more seasoned and experienced politician was needed for such a delicate transition of power.[28]

The fact that Charles went behind the Queen's back in this way illustrates the widening gulf between mother and son, and between Buckingham Palace and St James's Palace. The Prince of Wales had become more and more frustrated at his lack of initiative and the way that Buckingham Palace had the final say over matters that concerned him. This appears to have reached boiling point in an astonishing episode that took place in 1985. During a state visit to Italy with Diana, Prince Charles not only planned to have an audience with the Pope, but also to attend a Mass in the Vatican as a gesture of ecumenical reconciliation. The Government and the Archbishop of Canterbury had been consulted and agreed that, providing he did not take Communion, he was allowed to participate in the service. However, Charles had omitted to consult the Supreme Governor of the Church of England – his mother: when she found out she vetoed the idea, apparently as much because of her son's disregard for protocol as any religious implications. Worse, the Palace arranged for this to be leaked to the press. Charles was forced into the humiliating position of having to cancel his attendance at the Vatican service.[29]

Periodically, the idea had resurfaced that Elizabeth II might be the first monarch effectively to retire, either by abdicating in Charles's favour or, more plausibly, by assigning him her powers as Regent (as during a period of illness). As we have seen, it was Mountbatten who first sowed this seed in the 1970s. Whether the Queen has ever entertained such a notion is debatable – those who know her say that she would never even consider abdication – but it does seem that Charles has wanted her to go while he is still a relatively young man. Now that he had the added glamour of his Princess, besides an heir and spare, there was even a feeling in the country that it might be time for a change. The possibility was comprehensively demolished in 1991, when the Palace issued a statement declaring that abdication, for whatever reason, 'strikes at the root of the Monarchy' and that even the concept of voluntary renunciation of the monarch's duties did not 'fit into the traditions or mystique of the Monarchy as it has evolved in Britain'.[30] In her Christmas message that year, Elizabeth II carefully stressed that she was Queen for life, adding that 'with the love and support of my family, I shall try and help you in the years to come' – a somewhat pointed remark that apparently prompted Charles to stop talking to his mother for a time.[31]

THE *ANNUS HORRIBILIS*

1992 was the year that it all came unstuck. On 23 November, three days after a fire had devastated part of Windsor Castle – widely taken as a symbol of the state of the royal fortunes – the Queen gave a speech that was supposed to mark the happy occasions of her 40th year on the throne and 45th wedding anniversary, in which she uttered the memorable lines: 'The past year is not one I shall look back on with undiluted pleasure. In the words of one of my more sympathetic correspondents, it has turned out to be an *annus horribilis.*' (The 'sympathetic correspondent' was, in fact, her Assistant Private Secretary, Sir Edward Ford.)

The horrible year began with the publication, in January, of photographs of the Duchess of York and Steve Wyatt, the son of a Texas oil baron based in London, on holiday together in Morocco two summers previously – together with the Yorks' two young daughters Beatrice and Eugenie. Although the tabloids had suggested that both Diana and Sarah were involved in adulterous relationships, these had been shrugged off by the Palace as tittle-tattle, even though in both cases they were known by the Palace to be true.

The Queen and the Palace had quickly tired of 'Fergie's' brash style and penchant for publicity – being particularly piqued at the *Hello!* photo shoot. Neither did the way money slipped through the Yorks' hands endear them to Andrew's parents: reportedly they were spending four times their annual income by 1991.[32] Sarah, in turn, was soon fed up with her royal lifestyle, particularly as her husband was away at sea for months on end, a mood that had inevitable consequences. Shortly after the birth of Eugenie in March 1990 she and Wyatt (whom she had met in November 1989, when she was five months' pregnant) had gone off to Morocco together with two-year-old Beatrice, leaving the newborn with a nanny. Other holidays followed in the south of France. Their affair was not distinguished by its discretion, and it was not long before the Queen and Prince Philip knew of it. Particularly embarrassing was the fact that Sarah invited her lover to royal parties – and even, at Wyatt's request, entertained the Iraqi oil minister at Buckingham Palace just a few days after Iraq had invaded Kuwait, precipitating what was to become the Gulf War. The Queen ordered the Duchess to end the relationship, and, taking the hint, Wyatt returned to the States. Unfortunately he left the holiday snaps behind in his London flat, where they were found and sold. It was the publication of these compromising photographs that was the last straw, leading to the formal separation of the Yorks in March.

It seemed as if the family was cursed. Just a month later Princess Anne and Mark Phillips divorced, having been separated for three years, to clear the way for Anne to marry her equerry, Commander Timothy Laurence (after the customary Palace denials of a romance). Princess Margaret may have thought it ironic how little fuss was made about a divorced royal princess marrying a servant, compared to the trauma she suffered during the Townsend affair.

In June came the biggest bombshell so far – the publication of Andrew Morton's book *Diana: Her True Story*, which was serialised in the *Sunday Times*. The book revealed Charles's affair with Camilla Parker Bowles, Diana's bulimia and five 'cry for help' suicide attempts (all of which were blamed on

Charles's adultery, although the evidence suggests that Diana suffered from the eating disorder before her marriage). Although the Palace tried to dismiss the book as contemptuous sensationalism by a journalist known for his republican views, and Diana assured Sir Robert Fellowes (her brother-in-law) that she had nothing to do with it, it soon became apparent that she had co-operated with Morton at least to the extent of sanctioning the co-operation of her friends and family. (Tellingly, Morton – we now know inaccurately – dismissed press stories of her affairs with Hewitt and Gilbey as nothing but gossip.) However, the Princess appears not to have seen the finished product, which therefore had unwelcome consequences: for example, it led to the end of the relationship with Gilbey because certain remarks he made about her were quoted. But it was considered that even her relatively innocent level of co-operation was a serious breach of trust and confidence, not merely with her husband but with the royal family. The media, of course, lapped it up.

In August 1992 more photographs of the Duchess of York graced the world's newspapers – this time showing her topless having her foot kissed by her latest love, John Bryan, on holiday in the south of France. Another Texan (Steve Wyatt had introduced him to the Duchess), he was pictured with her two daughters and bodyguards from the Royal Protection Squad (subsequently moved to other duties) sunbathing nearby. Bryan was a financial expert whom the Yorks had brought in to sort out their perilous money situation, and who after their separation set about marketing the Duchess. The photographs (taken with a telephoto lens) appeared while Sarah and Andrew were staying at Balmoral, precipitating a traumatic breakfast as the Duchess waited for the inevitable royal explosion. Within hours she had packed and left.

If it seemed that disclosures about the private life of the royal family could hardly get more damaging, they only had to wait another four days, when the *Sun* published transcripts of a taped telephone conversation between Diana and her lover James Gilbey – known as the 'Squidgygate' tapes after his pet name for her.[33] The provenance of the tapes (which had been recorded two and a half years before, on New Year's Eve 1989) is examined in more detail below, but the publication – together with the *Sun*'s special phone lines so that readers could listen in to the tapes – was another body blow. Not only was the wife of the heir to the British throne and the darling of the world's media heard in passionate and risqué conversation with her lover, but she also made some less than kind comments about her husband's family. She said of the Queen Mother: 'His grandmother is always looking at me with a strange look in her eyes. It's not hatred, it's sort of interest and pity mixed into one . . . Every time I look up, she's looking at me and then looks away and smiles.' And, talking of her depression at being with the family over Christmas and New Year, 'I was very bad at lunch. And I nearly started blubbing. I just felt really sad and empty, and I thought, "Bloody hell, after all I've done for this fucking family."' Clearly, the days of shy Di were long gone.

THE QUEEN GIVES WAY TO THE TAXMAN

Small wonder that the Windsor Castle fire, on 20 November 1992, seemed to show that the gods were out to get the royal family. The Queen, in Prince Andrew's words, was 'devastated': Windsor was her teenage home during the war, when she dreamt innocent dreams of being married to the man she adored. The day of the conflagration was also her 45th wedding anniversary, but even so, Philip was on a visit to Argentina at the time and could neither celebrate nor console in person.

The fire also launched the Queen into another fraught episode. She assumed that the state would pay for the restoration (the priceless building and its contents not being insured): an estimated bill of £50 million. Although at first the Government agreed to pay, there was a public outcry, the general feeling being summed up by a *Times* columnist, who wrote, 'While the castle stands, it is theirs, but when it burns down, it is ours.' Eventually it was agreed that the bill would largely be paid from the Privy Purse, with income raised by charging admission to Buckingham Palace – the first time it had been open to the public. (After the Windsor restoration was complete another controversy ensued, when it was revealed that the revenue from tours of the Palace – some £14 million a year – was now being allocated to the upkeep of the Royal Collection. MPs complained that, since the state pays for the Palace, any income it generates should go back to the Treasury.)

In the midst of the debate over who was to pay for the restoration of Windsor Castle, there was another blunder. Six days after the fire John Major announced in the Commons that the Queen and Prince of Wales had agreed to pay tax on their private incomes – on a voluntary basis. This was widely seen as a cynical move by the Queen to persuade Parliament to pay for the fire damage. In fact, it had actually been agreed before the fire, but even then it was the result of mounting pressure on the monarch.

In July 1990 Margaret Thatcher had pushed through a substantial increase in the Civil List to the present £7.9 million a year. The Prime Minister had secured the agreement of Opposition leader Neil Kinnock to rush the bill through – and rushed it certainly was. MPs were given only two hours' notice and just 20 minutes were allocated to the debate; some of the increases in allowances for other members of the royal family – in Prince Edward's case a 500 per cent increase to £100,000 a year – were not even announced in the Commons but merely printed after the event in *Hansard*.[34] During that 20-minute debate, however, one Conservative MP had managed to squeeze in a question about the Queen's immunity from income tax, which brought the issue into the public arena. This was fuelled by the researches of Phillip Hall, who for a decade had been slowly piercing the fog of secrecy surrounding the Queen's exemption from tax: his findings were then seized on by the media (for example, becoming the subject of an ITV *World in Action* programme in the summer of 1991), eventually leading to the publication of his book *Royal Fortune* in early 1992. Faced with the prospect of unwelcome light being shed on the Sovereign's tax affairs, in a long-overdue public relations move the Queen decided to volunteer to pay up. At the same time it was announced that she would reimburse, from her Duchy of Lancaster income, the Civil List allowances for Princess Anne, Prince Andrew, Prince Edward, Princess Margaret and Princess Alice, the Duchess of Gloucester.

This was not the end of the *annus horribilis*. Following the publication of Andrew Morton's book, and the Squidgygate tape, the reality that the Wales's marriage was over had to be faced. On 9 December 1992 John Major formally announced the separation. His statement concluded:

> . . . there is no reason why the Princess of Wales should not be crowned Queen in due course. The Prince of Wales's succession as head of the Church of England is also unaffected.

Both remarks – which assumed there would be no divorce – carried far-reaching implications. Could the estranged wife of the King *really* be crowned by his side – or did the royal family just want to keep the Diana-adoring public happy? And, unless both were to remain celibate, could a technically adulterous Charles really become head of the Church of England? The public particularly wanted to know the truth about Morton's allegations that Charles had a mistress, Camilla Parker Bowles . . .

There was not long to wait for an answer. Just over a month after John Major's announcement, on 12 January 1993, it was Charles's turn to squirm as a transcript of a tape of one of *his* private telephone conversations was published.[35] The other half was Camilla Parker Bowles, and it left no doubt that they were more than close friends – indeed, it made Diana's conversation with James Gilbey seem positively circumspect. Of course most private conversations between lovers would seem childish and deeply embarrassing to eavesdroppers, but this one took both qualities to new depths:

Charles: The trouble is, I need you several times a week. All the time.

Camilla: Mmm. So do I. I need you all the week. All the time.

Charles: Oh, God. I'll just live inside your trousers or something. It would be much easier!

Camilla: What are you going to turn into, a pair of knickers? Oh, you're going to come back as a pair of knickers.

Charles: Or, God forbid, a Tampax. Just my luck!

Camilla: You are a complete idiot! Oh, what a wonderful idea.

Charles: My luck to be chucked down a lavatory and go on forever swirling around the top, never going down!

The sorry saga rumbled on and on. In June 1994 Charles was the subject of a television documentary made by Jonathan Dimbleby (who also published his official biography of the Prince the same year). As we have seen, the Prince candidly admits to adultery with Camilla in the programme, while in the biography blaming his parents for his emotional problems and, ultimately, for his disastrous marriage and its consequences.

Virginal she may have been before her marriage, but now Diana seemed to be making up for lost time, her name being linked with yet more men – England Rugby captain Will Carling's wife Julia even threatened to name her in a divorce suit. In October 1994 there were allegations that the Princess was plaguing art dealer Oliver Hoare with nuisance telephone calls, which the police traced to her private telephone line and mobile phone. Diana denied making the calls, and when a former employee of Hoare claimed that he and Diana had had an affair, both denied that, too.

On 5 November 1995 the Princess struck back, with her now-legendary interview for BBC's *Panorama*, in which she spoke – adopting a measured more-in-sorrow-than-in-anger tone of enormous sincerity – of her wish to be the 'Queen of peoples' hearts'. (In retaliation the Queen removed the BBC's traditional exclusive rights to her Christmas broadcast: these days BBC and ITV take it in turns.)

The Queen realised that the situation was now intolerable: her son and his estranged wife were conducting their marital dispute on prime time television. It was better than a soap opera, like the only-too-aptly-named *Coronation Street*. In December – after consulting with John Major, former Prime Minister James Callaghan and the Archbishop of Canterbury – she wrote to Charles and Diana asking them to agree to a divorce. The fairy tale formally ended on 28 August 1996.

At least one member of the royal family knew of a particularly humiliating punishment: after their divorces, both Sarah and Diana lost their HRHs. This was a particular blow to Diana, who suddenly found herself of lower social status than her children. Yet this time the sting was muted: to thousands she was still 'Her Royal Highness', and those who insisted on using the title did not find themselves ostracised; the world had moved on since Wallis.

The events of the 1990s threatened to make a mockery of the monarchy. With tabloid headlines continually screaming, it is easy to forget that behind the tragi-comic soap opera of the Yorks' – and, in particular, the Wales's – divorce, a vitally important element was being overlooked: not merely the dignity of the Crown, but the fundamental principles on which the Government of the United Kingdom is based. Presumably, Charles will one day be King, and in him will be invested all the constitutional powers on which, under the present system, the Government of the country depends. And in due course they will also be invested in his son and heir, the future King William V – or whatever he chooses to call himself.

Many powerful forces were at work during the ignominious and very public disintegration of Charles and Diana's marriage, most obviously the media, certain sections of which treated the whole sorry saga as a blood sport.

(The voluntary news embargoes that kept the 1930s British public ignorant of the imminent abdication crisis are long gone.) Yet the press was not the only culprit: the main players in the unlovely drama were clearly not reluctant to use the press to sway public opinion in their own favour, both Charles and Diana enlisting sympathetic journalists and television reporters to present their case to the public. The Palace, too, put the usual pressure on editors to withhold stories, or organise leaks of more useful information. But it is also clear that there were other, more shadowy, forces at work, and that these events were being manipulated by those who *really* run the country.

THE TAPES

Diana was convinced that not only were her telephone calls being monitored on the orders of the Palace mafia, but also that her rooms were being bugged, at one stage even having them swept for bugs by a security company.[36] While critics dismissed this as evidence of her paranoia – perhaps, at that stage, she was over-suspicious – her fears were soon to prove justified. In the early years of her marriage she had learned quickly how the Palace operates, and knew it was against her: small wonder, then, that she saw sinister adversaries behind virtually everything that happened. Andrew Morton wrote, 'Diana's enemies within are the courtiers who watch and judge her every move.'[37]

There is no doubt that, far from having been picked up accidentally by amateur radio enthusiasts as claimed, both the Diana and Charles telephone conversations were professionally monitored. Under the circumstances, the only likely culprits are the security or intelligence services.

The Diana–Gilbey telephone conversation took place on New Year's Eve 1989, Diana speaking from her room at Sandringham, while Gilbey was in his car near Abingdon in Oxfordshire. The story went that an amateur radio enthusiast, using basic scanning equipment, had chanced upon the conversation, recognised Diana's voice and had the presence of mind to tape it. The circumstances are so unusual that this has been described as a million-to-one chance. But if so, what are the odds of it happening *twice*? The tape was made by retired bank manager Cyril Reenan of Abingdon, being acquired by the *Sun* shortly afterwards. The editor, however, was uncertain about making it public until the woman's voice was conclusively proven to be Diana's, so the tape was locked away in a safe in the *Sun*'s offices. However, about a year later another amateur radio enthusiast, Jane Norgrove from Cowley (less than ten miles from Abingdon), arrived in their offices with a second tape of the *same* conversation, apparently having monitored it just like Reenan.[38]

The *Sun* remained reluctant to publish the story, until the existence of the tape – or tapes – was made public in the American supermarket tabloid the *National Enquirer*. In the meantime, other copies of parts of the conversation had circulated anonymously among the media, which is how the *National Enquirer* got hold of their copy, as did *Daily Mail* journalist Richard Kay (whose tape arrived anonymously through the post). Where these other copies originated has never been explained – but clearly someone desperately wanted the story to get out and was trying to push the *Sun* into publishing the full version.

The odds against the calls being monitored by chance lengthen yet again when it is realised that the Squidgygate and 'Camillagate' tapes, although made public six months apart, were recorded within just 13 days of each other (or at least that was the interval between the two phone conversations). The Charles–Camilla conversation was allegedly recorded in the same coincidental way as the Diana tape, Charles on his mobile phone at the Duke of Westminster's Cheshire mansion, while Camilla Parker Bowles used a landline at her family home in Wiltshire.

Adding to this astounding scenario, in January 1990 – within four weeks of the Diana–Gilbey conversation – it happened yet again. Again the result of a lucky break for an amateur, this time the prize was a telephone conversation between Andrew and Sarah in which she expressed dissatisfaction with their marriage.[39] How can this amazing haul of tapes be due to pure coincidence?

There is also the curious fact that, according to the dates, the calls were intercepted several days after they were made! The Diana–Gilbey conversation clearly took place on New Year's Eve – at one point she asks, 'Are you staying up to see the New Year in?'[40] – but Cyril Reenan recorded it on the evening of 4 January.[41] It also seems that the Charles–Camilla conversation may have been recorded the evening after it actually took place.[42]

Finally, there is a mountain of expert evidence that it was simply impossible for the Diana–Gilbey conversation to have been monitored with the amateur equipment used. Cellnet – clearly alarmed at the implications of calls on their network being monitored so easily – rapidly undertook their own investigation and pronounced that it was impossible for it to have happened as claimed. Author Nigel Blundell had the tape analysed by four British and American experts in voice analysis and surveillance, including one FBI agent experienced in monitoring mobile phone calls on UK networks, in joint operations with the British security forces. The *Sunday Times*, together with other newspapers, also commissioned their own independent expert analyses. All pronounced it technically impossible for the tape to have been intercepted in the way it was alleged, chiefly because mobile networks continually – but undetectably to the user – shift frequency: the scanner would have had to be retuned every few minutes, whereas the Diana–Gilbey tape lasts an uninterrupted 23 minutes. The consensus of these experts is that the call was not picked up from the mobile phone network but from a tap at Diana's end of the line – *at Sandringham*. Nigel Blundell writes:

> Every expert whose advice has been sought has found highly implausible the suggestion that a scanner was used randomly to pluck Princess Diana's conversation from the airwaves. British and American

voice experts, security-service contacts, police and FBI all veer towards
the more controversial theory... that the call was professionally
monitored at her end of the line.[43]

There is also evidence that the tape – particularly Gilbey's end of it – was
professionally cleaned up to improve the quality. The only scenario that fits all
these factors is that the conversation was recorded by a local tap in Sandringham,
then the tape was cleaned up, before being broadcast over the airways
continuously for several days so that it would eventually be picked up by a radio
enthusiast. The only people with the means to do that are the security services.

Considering the amount of worldwide publicity engendered by the very
existence, let alone the content of the tape, it is quite remarkable that there
was not an extensive criminal inquiry into the circumstances of its creation.
Although it suited the authorities to suggest, disingenuously, that a mobile
transmission had been intercepted, once it was known that a land line had
been tapped a very different situation existed.

Theoretically, only the Home Secretary can give authority for the
interception of telephone calls, but it is extremely unlikely that he, or any
other member of the Government, would authorise such activity. Certainly
no member of the Government would have allowed dissemination of the
content. So, who did commission an unlawful tap by the security services?

Undoubtedly, the British security forces – especially MI5 – keep a very
close watch on members of the royal family whose high profile makes them
prime terrorist targets, and because their status adds a potential political gloss
to even innocent friendships (as, for example, when the Duchess of York
entertained the Iraqi minister in Buckingham Palace on the eve of the Gulf
War). This surveillance includes monitoring their telephone conversations:
MI5 even recorded chats between Charles and Diana during their
engagement, when Charles was on a state visit to Australia.[44]

But if the security services were involved, why did they do it? Certainly, ex-
MI6 officer Richard Tomlinson was in no doubt that there were close
connections between his service and the Palace, stating in an affidavit, sworn
connections with the investigation into Diana's death: 'Although contact
between MI6 and the Royal Household was officially only via the Foreign
Office, I learnt while in MI6 that there was an unofficial direct contact
between certain senior and influential MI6 and senior members of the Royal
Household . . .'[45] But why would MI5, MI6 or any other agency consider it
advantageous to ensure that sensitive personal information about the Princess
of Wales should reach the public? It is unlikely that these organisations would
take such an initiative anyway. In the circumstances, the most logical
explanation is that they were acting under the orders of the Palace. But why
should even the most fanatical courtiers want the public to hear these private
and personal conversations?

The true story of the tapes is rather different from the usual tortured and unsatisfactory version. It appears that the instigator of the Camillagate tape was none other than Diana herself. According to Lady Colin Campbell, the author who, through her marriage to the Duke of Argyll, is well connected in royal and aristocratic circles, the Princess of Wales wanted some hard evidence of Charles's affair with Camilla Parker Bowles so she could use it as ammunition in her bid for a legal separation. Accordingly, she arranged for what Lady Campbell describes as 'someone in the security forces' to monitor Charles's mobile phone calls with a sophisticated scanner,[46] finally managing to capture the conversation that became 'Camillagate'. Apparently it was re-broadcast the following evening in the hope that it would be picked up by an amateur radio enthusiast – but when this failed to materialise it was decided that the tape should be sent 'anonymously' to Diana, having allegedly been picked up in this way.

The Squidgydate tape was the Palace's answer to this. Perhaps it was hastily arranged for Diana's line at Sandringham to be tapped, or the line was already routinely monitored by the security services. In any case, the resulting tape was rebroadcast – this time successfully – in the manner intended for the Charles-Camilla conversation.

It seems that Diana was not content to use the tape to bring her husband to heel: in a move designed to whip up public sympathy, she tried to leak the story of his affair to the media. At this stage, senior Palace officials stepped in, coldly informing the Princess that they possessed recordings of compromising telephone conversations she had made from Kensington Palace that revealed, in Morton's words, 'damning evidence of her relationship with the media' – and that the Prime Minister had been informed of what she was up to.[47]

Diana's response was to collaborate with Andrew Morton. Following the favourable reaction to her side of the story, she took the initiative and asked for a separation on her terms, the foremost being – despite her living apart from the Prince of Wales – she would still become Queen when he ascended to the throne. Her solicitors began negotiations with Charles and the royal family's representatives to this end. The push to get the *Sun* to publish the Squidgygate tape in August 1992 was a counter-move by the Palace to redress the balance in the public's perception of the Charles-vs-Diana debate, which briefly reined Diana in. But she still had the upper hand in the separation negotiations, because of her continued popularity – and because she had the Camilla tape.

Significantly, because Diana did not trust the Palace to keep their side of the bargain, part of the deal was that the Prime Minister would make an announcement to the House of Commons to the effect that, despite the separation, she would still be Queen – which is why John Major made such a point of including this otherwise puzzling clause in his Commons statement in December 1992.[48] It appeared that Diana's plan had been brilliantly and devastatingly successful, but the Palace was not finished yet.

Why, then, did the Camillagate tape appear a little more than a month after Major's announcement? Lady Campbell suggests that it was because the public had reacted badly to the idea of Diana becoming Queen now she and Charles lived apart, and that her immediate ambition had shifted: now she wanted to show that her husband was unfit to become King so that, on Elizabeth's death, the crown would pass directly to their son.[49] An alternative scenario is that the situation had simply got out of hand: too many people possessed copies of the tape, and someone decided to make a small fortune out of selling it.

A TRAGIC CATALYST

After Charles and Diana's divorce became final at the end of August 1996, the Princess's name was linked with a few other men, but – tragically – the romance that is best remembered now was her last. Dodi Fayed was the son of the billionaire Egyptian entrepreneur Mohamed Al Fayed, owner of many businesses, most famously Harrod's department store in London and the Ritz Hotel in Paris. Diana and Dodi's whirlwind romance began when, after befriending Mohamed Al Fayed, in July 1997 she and her sons stayed with his family at their villa in St Tropez. Dodi joined them there towards the end of the holiday, and it was then that their affair started. A few days after the end of the break, when Princes William and Harry joined their father at Balmoral for the traditional royal vacation of rain-swept picnics and deer stalking, Diana and Dodi took a short break in Sardinia. At the beginning of August she went to Bosnia to front the campaign against landmines, then on 21 August 1997 she and Fayed enjoyed another ten-day holiday aboard Mohamed Al Fayed's ultra-luxurious yacht, the *Jonikal*, on the Mediterranean.

By now news of the affair between Diana and the son of one of the world's most controversial businessmen was public knowledge: the media was alight with speculation: was this just a casual fling or was it more serious? Was an Egyptian, a man of colour and a *Muslim*, about to become the second husband of the Princess of Wales – not to mention the stepfather to the heir to the British throne? The paparazzi were out in force during the cruise, surrounding the *Jonikal* in speedboats and even hovering in helicopters low over the deck. In many ways the scenario was reminiscent of Edward VIII's cruise on the *Nahlin* 60 years before, but this time the British newspapers were also full of the story.

At the end of the cruise the couple paid a spur-of-the-moment visit to Paris to round off their holiday. Even then there was speculation – which has intensified ever since – that on their return to London Dodi and Diana intended to announce their engagement, once they had broken the news to the two princes. Mohamed Al Fayed maintains that his son told him by telephone of their intention to marry, just a few days before the tragedy in Paris. Despite many denials, there is good evidence that they were indeed planning to wed – most tangibly in the shape of an engagement ring bought from an exclusive Monte Carlo jeweller during the cruise. Friends of Diana stress that she was deeply in love. Their first destination in Paris was the Villa Windsor in the Bois de Bolougne, the former home of the Duke and Duchess of Windsor, now owned by Mohamed Al Fayed. Were they planning to make this their marital home? With her genius for exploiting headlines, Diana would have loved underscoring the historical associations, rubbing the royal family's noses in the fact that another wayward woman whose very existence threatened their future – and another *sans* HRH – was flaunting her unconventional relationship from an alternative court in Paris, and, the cherry on the poisoned cake, from the home of the hated Wallis Simpson . . . It has even been suggested that Diana suspected that she may have been pregnant with Dodi Fayed's child, although there is no conclusive evidence for this.

Of course, the world now knows how the story ended. Not long after midnight, Paris time, on 31 August 1997, while returning from the Ritz to Dodi's apartment off the Champs-Élysée, the Mercedes in which they were travelling ploughed at speed into a pillar in the tunnel under the Place d'Alma on the banks of the Seine. Dodi Fayed and their driver, Henri Paul, the assistant head of security at the Ritz, were killed instantly. Despite initial reports that the Princess of Wales was only slightly injured, she had suffered terrible internal injuries. Although the doctors at the Pitié-Salpêtrière hospital fought to save her, she was declared dead at 4 a.m. The fourth person in the car, their bodyguard Trevor Rees-Jones, suffered appalling facial and head injuries, but went on to make an almost miraculous recovery over the course of several months.

Suddenly the public was galvanised by a sea of emotion and a determination to mark the death of the bright, difficult, stellar princess, each in his or her own way. Cynics have since claimed that the media whipped up the unprecedented wave of grief that swept both the nation and almost the whole world, but anyone who observed at first hand the crowds piling up the mountains of flowers that grew around anywhere associated with the dead Diana knows that for once the reverse was true. The press and television were caught as wrong-footed by the surge of emotion as the royal family, both being compelled by events to endeavour to catch up with the public mood – but one very much swifter than the other. Kensington Palace, her home, was surrounded with tottering walls of flowers and other tributes – poems, cuddly toys, candles and incense, which then spread throughout the whole of Kensington Gardens until on the night before her funeral, virtually every tree was the focus for a curiously atavistic ritual of contemplation, votive lights and of course yet more flowers. Meanwhile, as the BBC announcer continued to intone in a deadly solemn voice, 'This is the BBC from London', like a chilling radio broadcast from the war years, there was not a sign of the royal family among the mourners in the capital. This had not gone unnoticed.

By the middle of the week after Diana and Dodi's deaths, real anger was being expressed among those who stood in line to sign the books of condolence and who came to cry or lay flowers: *why* were the Queen and her family still on holiday in Scotland? *Why* was the only flag in the country not to fly at half mast the one on top of Buckingham Palace? Soon the newspapers caught the mood, headlines begging the Queen to 'show us you care'. A half-hearted announcement from Balmoral explained that the monarch thought it best to keep Diana's now motherless boys in seclusion with their father, but of course that was not the point. By the Thursday anyone who fought their way through the crowds to enter the Palace for whatever reason found themselves the target for hostile questioning. Where was she? Where was the Queen when we needed her most? Suddenly the woman who had famously 'never put a foot wrong' was in real danger of being booed when she did turn up – or worse. What had happened to the 'focus of national unity'?

Balmoral's august walls resounded with raised voices. The Queen was all for a private funeral, while Charles realised that this would be a critical error of judgement and fought to have his ex-wife's power over the people recognised. At last the reluctant monarch, accompanied by Prince Philip, arrived to do a short, uncomfortable walkabout outside the bedecked gates of the Palace: while the media reported the undoubted relief of the majority, only a few noted the loud voice that greeted the Queen, saying, *'About bloody time, too.'* Nor did it go unnoticed that when Philip was asked to put a floral tribute on the heap for a small girl he threw it down casually without looking. Made hypersensitive by raw emotion, the people noticed such things.

Persuaded to talk live on television to the nation in its hour of need, the Queen's original speech was torn apart by Tony Blair's adviser, Alastair Campbell, and reworked until it sounded suitably warm and yet sad, with the phrase '[I speak to you . . .] as a grandmother' and the carefully chosen words about Diana's sterling qualities. Most significantly, however, the Queen admitted that 'lessons have been learned', although in what area was left largely unsaid. Yet as later events proved, and the royal family moved into a new Diana-less era, it became obvious that lessons *had* been learned, albeit few and very reluctantly, about the necessity for the royal image to move with the times and forge a much closer bond with the ordinary people. Stamfordham and George V would not have been impressed that it took the death of a Princess of Wales to shake them up and make them real.

More humiliation was on the way for the senior royals. The brilliantly organised funeral – in just under a week – sparkled sombrely with stars from all over the world, together with many representatives of the charities the Princess had worked for and countless individuals whose lives she had changed for the better. It was not a time to recall her wilfulness, hysteria and self-indulgence: suddenly all that dropped away and the uniquely glamorous and compassionate woman was remembered. But if having to be surrounded by a wall of adoration for the woman who had been the bane of their lives was bad enough for the royals sitting awkwardly among the grief, much worse was to come in the form of Diana's brother, Charles, Earl Spencer, who took the opportunity to swipe at the royal family's coldness compared to the superiority of her 'blood family'. A masterly speech from a heartbroken brother, nevertheless its subtext must have caused even the Queen to shiver as the reaction came rolling through the doors of Westminster Cathedral from the crowds outside – a huge wave of applause, which was even picked up by the congregation inside. The anger of 'Diana week' was still in evidence, and no doubt the Queen would do well never to forget it.

AFTERMATH

The cause of the tragedy was officially blamed on a drunken driver who drove far too fast and lost control, but that was widely dismissed as a cover-up. How could the beautiful Princess be killed in a mere accident? Almost immediately there were claims that the deaths of Diana and Dodi were assassinations designed to look like an accident. The theories have grown ever since, encouraged by an official wall of silence over certain aspects of the affair. Most vociferous is Mohamed Al Fayed, who has very publicly proclaimed his belief that MI6 were responsible, and that they were acting on the orders of Prince Philip, whose motive was to prevent the announcement of Diana and Dodi's engagement. Her marriage to a Muslim would have been unthinkable to the royal family and the British Establishment.

Philip certainly was opposed to the relationship. Ironically, on the morning of Diana and Dodi's death the *Sunday Mirror* went to press with a story based on information from an unnamed friend of the royal family describing the Duke of Edinburgh's views on the matter: 'He's been banging on about his contempt for Dodi and how he is an undesirable stepfather to William and Harry. Diana has been told in no uncertain terms about the consequences should she continue the relationship with the Fayed boy. Options include possible exile, although that would be difficult . . . But now the Royal Family may decide it is time to settle up.' If the *Mirror*'s source is accurate, it is significant that Philip seems to have been aware that Diana and Dodi Fayed planned to marry.

From the outset, we were sceptical that there had been a conspiracy to kill Diana, because of the sheer logistical enormity of the task. How could a car be made to crash at high speed in the middle of a busy capital on a Saturday night in a way that guarantees the death of the intended targets? The difficulty is compounded by the fact that, according to Trevor Rees-Jones, the decision to make the unscheduled visit to Paris was only taken the day before:[50] how could such an elaborate scheme be organised so quickly?

If MI6 or any intelligence or terrorist organisation had wanted to kill Diana and Dodi, there were far easier ways of doing so: a bomb in his apartment (with the finger of blame made to point at a fundamentalist Islamic group opposed to a Muslim marrying a British princess), sabotage of the aircraft taking them back to London, and so on. Whereas previous conspiracy theories surrounding the deaths of famous people – most obviously President Kennedy – had worked from evidence of conspiracy to motive, in the case of Diana the theorists' approach is the reverse: because certain vested interests might want her dead, then her death 'must have' been the result of a conspiracy. While no doubt there were those who did fear the effects of such a marriage on the future of the monarchy and who would stop at nothing to protect the throne, the unromantic truth is that the death of Diana and Dodi Fayed seems to have been just a tragic coincidence.

On the other hand, Mohamed Al Fayed told us that, when the Princess stayed with his family at St Tropez the month before her death, she expressed the fear that her enemies in the Establishment might try to kill her. With his immense financial resources, Al Fayed has assigned his own investigators to the case, and has discovered that an MI6 team was in Paris on the fateful weekend. The identities of some of the pack of paparazzi outside the Ritz have also never been established, suggesting strongly that the couple's movements *were* being monitored.[51]

However, an important piece of information that came our way from a reliable source stopped us in our tracks and made us reconsider. Perhaps, after all, there *was* a connection between the official hostility to the relationship and the deaths in the tunnel at the Place d'Alma. This came from a woman (who for obvious reasons does not want to be named) who was with a Saudi Arabian diplomat in his London apartment on the night that Diana and Dodi Fayed died. At 10 p.m. (11 p.m. Paris time) on 30 August 1997, he took a phone call and had a brief conversation in Arabic. He put down the phone and said to our informant, 'They are going to kill Dodi.' An hour and a half later the fatal crash took place.

On the face of it, this seems to support the assassination theory, yet all the logistical problems remain. However, the fact that certain people were concerned that an attempt was going to be made on Dodi Fayed's life would make sense of some otherwise puzzling details about the affair. First, the diplomat was told that an attempt was going to be made on *Dodi's* life, not the Princess's. This makes sense. If the shadowy protectors of the monarchy had wanted to end the relationship, there was no need to kill Diana, with all the repercussions that would cause. Getting Dodi Fayed out of the way would do the job.

This was not the first time that it has been suggested that a lover of Diana's was killed by the security services. As we have seen, Sergeant Barry Mannakee, whom Diana told James Hewitt was the first lover she had taken after her marriage, was killed in a motorcycle accident in 1987, a few months after he had been transferred to other duties. As early as 1993 it was reported that Diana told several people that she was convinced that Mannakee's death was not an accident.[52] According to Hewitt, she said, 'They killed him. I'm certain they killed him.' When Hewitt pressed her about who 'they' were, Diana said, 'MI5, people in the Palace, somebody who wanted him out of the way.'[53]

(Hewitt's reaction to this was that it was 'not an easy murder to stage, although not an impossible one'.) This has always been explained as Diana's paranoia, brought about by her sense of isolation and the insecurity of her position. However, whether or not Mannakee's death was simply a tragic accident (as his family firmly believe it was), Diana's enemies at the very least let it be thought that there was more to it as a deterrent to others.

James Hewitt has also stated that he was warned off his relationship with Diana several times, some being just 'friendly warnings' and others 'fairly sinister'. In the former category he puts warnings by Diana's private secretary, her bodyguard and a member of the royal family (whom he refuses to name) in person. Questioned about the 'sinister' warnings, Hewitt says, 'One such example is the fact that I was warned that I might meet the same end as Barry Mannakee . . .' He told Diana about this warning, and says, 'She was concerned because she was of the opinion that Barry Mannakee's accident was no accident anyway, and she was concerned for my safety.' He stresses that Diana took the threat against him very seriously.[54]

All this reveals that it was not Diana, but her lovers, who were in the most danger. Undoubtedly she had told Dodi Fayed about what she believed had happened to Mannakee, and about the threats made to Hewitt, and if he believed her – and presumably he did – Dodi would have considered himself a potential target. Therefore, if the word was out in Middle Eastern diplomatic circles that an attempt was going to be made on his life, first, he would have got to know about it and, secondly, would certainly have treated it seriously.

This might explain several oddities in the days before the Paris crash. In his account of the events, Trevor Rees-Jones (who does not subscribe to any of the conspiracy theories) makes it apparent that Dodi was behaving strangely. (Not unexpectedly, considering the physical traumas he experienced, Rees-Jones has no memory of anything that happened after he got in the car at the rear of the Ritz hotel, and therefore can shed no light on the exact circumstances of the crash.) Rees-Jones and a companion, Alexander Wingfield, were members of Mohamed Al Fayed's security staff in London, and had been assigned to the couple's protection on the cruise.

Rees-Jones became frustrated at Dodi's frequent sudden changes of plan – a security man's nightmare. It made it difficult for him and Wingfield to organise routine precautions, such as phoning ahead to a restaurant to co-ordinate their arrival to allow the minimum opportunity for the paparazzi to pounce. Dodi was nervy and seemingly mistrustful of those around him. Of course, given the presence of the paparazzi, and their constant attempts to invade his and Diana's privacy, this is hardly surprising.

What *is* surprising is that – under that sort of pressure – Dodi began withholding information from his security men. The announcement that the couple would be going to Paris was sprung on them, giving them no opportunity to co-ordinate with the control centre in London or the security team at the Paris Ritz.[55] However, it was a different story with the security team in Paris, particularly with Henri Paul, whom Dodi had known for many years and whom he apparently trusted. Rees-Jones records that when their private jet landed in Paris, Paul was there and that 'obviously Dodi had lots of faith in the man, the way he went to speak to him straight off'.[56]

In Paris Dodi's strange behaviour – withholding of information from the security team, but not from the local staff – continued. For example, when asked about their plans for the evening Rees-Jones was simply told that they would be 'going out to a restaurant'.[57] He gives his reaction in *The Bodyguard's Story* (co-written with Moira Johnston):

> 'Where are they going?' Trevor asked René [Fayed's butler], again and again, while the two were dressing, desperately trying to find out what their evening plans were. 'I'd just had it. Zero information was coming from Dodi. I couldn't go knocking on their apartment door saying, "Hey, where are you going tonight?" You can't do anything more. You can't walk up and grab the butler by the scruff of the neck and say, "I need to bloody know." It was so frustrating.' René went in and out of the apartment. If he knew, he never shared it with the bodyguards.[58]

Since it is unlikely that the butler was ignorant of Dodi's plans, the last comment suggests that René was *instructed* not to tell the security men.

After abandoning plans to eat in a fashionable restaurant because the paparazzi were camped outside in force, the couple dined at the Ritz. As they left to return to Dodi's apartment, there was a surprise. He had changed the plan: he and Diana would leave in a car from the rear of the hotel, while the two cars they had arrived in would drive away from the front as a decoy. Dodi asked Henri Paul to drive, rather than any of the Ritz chauffeurs who were on standby. More astonishingly Paul conveyed the message, 'Dodi doesn't want a bodyguard.'[59] Rees-Jones argued with Dodi about this, insisting that at least one security man should accompany them. Finally, Dodi reluctantly agreed that Rees-Jones could come. All this mystified Rees-Jones, who writes:

> *Why* had Dodi insisted upon Henri Paul driving? That mystery can never be solved, but Trevor believes Dodi made the choice because he trusted Paul, as he trusted Philippe [Dourneau, Fayed's regular driver when he was in Paris], who would drive the decoy car at the front. After the tension of the trip, Dodi was trusting an ever-smaller band of people.[60]

Clearly this band did not include his security men. However, Dodi's behaviour is hard to reconcile with his concern about the intrusions of the paparazzi. If he were simply trying to dodge them he would have wanted his security men with him, and presumably one of the professional Ritz drivers.

As it is, it seems as if he were actually trying to ditch his security men – in fact, everyone apart from Henri Paul, apparently the only person he trusted. Rees-Jones also raises the question of why, when asked at the last minute to drive, Paul did not decline on the grounds that he had been drinking (there is controversy about how much he had imbibed, although of course professional security men would never drive a client if they had drunk even the smallest amount). But if he knew that Dodi was anxious about a possible assassination attempt that might have come from anywhere, this may well have overridden the usual rules.

Dodi Fayed was unusually jumpy, which would be explained if, as the information we received suggests, he believed that he was to be the target of an assassination attempt. Is that why Henri Paul took an indirect route to Dodi's flat? (This would be standard procedure for avoiding a possible ambush, but not for evading paparazzi, who would be ready and waiting outside.) Were they even going to Dodi's flat? A glance at the map of Paris suggests they may well have been on their way to the *other* Al Fayed residence – the Villa Windsor in the Bois de Boulogne in an attempt to shake off any pursuers. If they were going to Edward and Wallis' old home, it would answer several important questions about their route and why the security men were told nothing of the plan. Even the unscheduled diversion to Paris, rather than returning directly to London as planned, may have been intended to throw out any plans that had been made to try to kill him there. Does it also explain why Henri Paul was so anxious to outdistance them from the pursuing motorbikes, in case one of them was not carrying paparazzi? Is that why he put his foot down just a little too far? *Was it, in the end, fear of assassination that caused the crash?*

All this is suggestive, but no more. Even five years after the death of Diana, Princess of Wales there are still many unanswered questions. The French authorities are still withholding information that should, if the official version (and our own reconstruction of events) is correct, refute the more extreme conspiracy theories. Doubts have been expressed by Henri Paul's family that the blood sample, which apparently shows that he was far over the legal limit for driving, is really his. They have asked for DNA tests to prove it, but the authorities have refused. Mystery still surrounds the presence of a white Fiat Uno in the Alma tunnel at the time of the crash, although it is now known that it belonged to a press photographer who later died under mysterious circumstances.

Only now, at the time of writing – five years on – are plans being made for an inquest some time within the next year. Strangely, the initiative for the inquest – usually required by law when a British subject dies abroad – seems to lie entirely with the Palace. The reason that no inquest has been held was simply because the coroner to the Royal Household, Dr John Burton, opposed it. In 2002 he was succeeded by Michael Burgess, who has agreed that there *should* be an inquest – providing he presides over it and the jury is made up exclusively of members of the Royal Household.[61]

Mohamed Al Fayed has asked that a public enquiry be held into the circumstances of the deaths of his son, Diana and Henri Paul. Given the questions and uncertainties that remain, this would seem to be the only way to establish the facts – if only to quell the conspiracy theories, which a Palace-controlled inquest is unlikely to do.

For five years the royal family have been slowly regrouping, amid suggestions that there is a deliberate campaign by the Palace to extinguish Diana's memory, perhaps to prepare the public for the marriage of Charles and his now live-in lover, Camilla. It has been a time of sadness, with the deaths of two key players in the story of the House of Windsor: Princess Margaret and the 101-year-old Queen Mother in 2002. With them a whole era seemed to pass, a gilded time of glamour, fun and above all, incontestable privilege. And while the Queen's Golden Jubilee was a rip-roaring success, does she care to remember her promise at the end of 'Diana Week' that 'lessons have been learned'? Will she remember the anger and the pain, the demands that the British figurehead, the focus for national unity, should be present in times of *our* sorrow as well as her own?

EPILOGUE

'WE THE PEOPLE'

The opening words of the American Constitution

Just because Diana is no longer there to show them how it's done, the royal family still have a responsibility to represent the British people of today – a very different breed from the days of the Queen's father, uncle or grandfather. Elizabeth's subjects are more tactile, considerably more emotional, less reverent yet still keen to stand in awe to catch a glimpse of this remote white-gloved old lady, who nevertheless increasingly finds herself criticised for her lack of empathy.

At the opening of the Commonwealth Games in Manchester on 25 July 2002, terminally ill Kirsty Howard, aged six, struggled to present the Queen with the official baton. The Queen smiled and took the baton – and turned away. It was all over in a flash. Viewers watching the ceremony on television flooded newspaper and TV phone lines with their outrage. One woman was quoted in the *Daily Mail* of 26 July, saying: 'I thought the Queen was very cold towards Kirsty. It was as though she thought she shouldn't come into contact with poorly people . . .', while another viewer declared he was 'disgusted' by the Queen's aloofness, saying – somewhat unrealistically – he 'expected her to kneel down and say something to her just like Princess Diana used to do'. Although of course the Queen kneels to no one, and in any case a woman of her years would have difficulty attempting to do so, the point is taken. Was it impossible for her simply to touch the little girl on the cheek or put her arm round her? No dignity would be lost and a great deal of popularity won.

As the success of the Golden Jubilee has shown, the Queen commands enormous respect, but after the scars of 'Diana week', the line is still fine between affection and anger and rebellion. Have lessons really been learned? The royal family will have to address considerably more serious issues than how to be nice to dying children in public if it is to survive, although that would be a good start.

During the last century there have been unprecedented changes as the status of individuals in Britain has moved from subject to near-citizen, in the way we have been governed, in our perception of those who govern us and, perhaps most important of all, in the way we elect those who govern us.

We entered the twentieth century with a Queen Empress and many believing in the 'divine right of kings'. Voting was still restricted to male property owners and the ruling class consisted not only of those who ruled but those who elected the rulers. Warfare involved the whole nation in the melting pot of conflict, helping to erode class divisions, and universal suffrage evolved by demand, allowing every adult to vote for the government of his – or her – choice. A king, no longer divine but only too obviously human, was removed by the scheming of ministers and civil servants. Three-quarters of the way through the century the electorate was even invited to make hugely important economic and constitutional decisions themselves by means of a device called a referendum, on the subject of joining the Common Market.

Yet the fact remains that we are *not* citizens of Britain, but subjects: nominally of the monarch but in reality of her advisers and the largely faceless civil servants who exist to preserve the status quo, and their own standing in it. Mostly this blends seamlessly with the ambitions of the Sovereign, but if the two clash seriously the civil service are unlikely to be the losers. And while governments come and go with each new election, the civil service – and within it, the group we have called the 'Palace mafia' – remain in the same positions of power. Generation after generation of these 'Whitehall mandarins' are allowed to maintain their steely grip on both people and monarch alike largely because Britain has no written constitution – every decision is therefore based on precedent and they are the ones to be consulted on what went before. Although the very lack of written rules is often seen as an advantage, as it only serves the interests of senior civil servants and allows both them and the royal family to ride roughshod over the ordinary Briton, the time is surely long overdue for public accountability.

Ironically, in August 2002 Foreign Secretary Jack Straw, bearing in mind the often wayward machinations of Brussels, called for a written constitution for the European Union. Clearly, the concerns we expressed in earlier chapters about the unconstitutional behaviour that cries out for a written constitution in the UK are also preying on the minds of those self-same mandarins when it comes to the European Union. Suddenly they are anxious that what they have been doing to the people for over a century may now be happening to them. However, for the Government to argue on the one hand for the need for a written constitution for Europe and on the other to reject entirely the prospect of a British constitution being committed to paper is surely indefensible.

The Government itself has already implicitly recognised the move from subject to citizen, in the form of the recently introduced compulsory subject in the National Curriculum for schools. From September 2002 all children will be taught 'citizenship', although the unwritten nature of the constitution of the United Kingdom should surely have made them courses in 'subjectivity'!

Unfortunately, given the vagaries of human nature, no government is ever perfect, but at least a written constitution would give us a solid framework within which to strive for perfect citizenship, perhaps something like the American version, which sets out its stall uncompromisingly with its opening words: 'We the people...' In many respects it has withstood the test of time, of civil war, the upheavals of the Industrial Revolution and despite all the ingrained racism and other problems of tolerance of its people, it remains a statement of attainable near-equality for all people within the American states.

However, few are suggesting that Britain should become a republic, at least not while Elizabeth II is still alive. Successive opinion polls demonstrate that the Queen and her role are treated with affection and respect by the majority of Britons, and the imagination often baulks at the alternative of a President Blair or Thatcher. But if they are to stay, the royal family is in for a rough ride – just how rough, however, is largely up to them. Certainly, there is little craven forelock tugging these days and the media no longer hold back from asking awkward questions of the royal family – if anything, quite the reverse. Yet, while the community as a whole seeks justice and equality, there is no doubt that the chilling Orwellian soundbite 'some are more equal than others' rings as true today as it always did. What equality exists when, while the rest of us struggle to make a living and pay our taxes, just one family – whether it calls itself Windsor or Mountbatten-Windsor – is allowed to decide that it refuses to pay tax? And then, when under pressure and with staggering arrogance, it simply elects to pay just a little tax on a portion of its income?

Where is the equality when *we* would be sent to prison for assisting a grandmother in agony to leave this life with dignity, while the Windsors can despatch a terminally ill relative simply in order to meet the deadline for the morning edition of the *Times*, or to avoid the coronation and other royal celebrations being disrupted by court mourning?

What equality exists when 'Lord Haw Haw' (William Joyce) was executed for broadcasting Nazi propaganda against his country, while certain members of the Windsor family not only provided propaganda for the same cause but also even intelligence and advice – and still received income from the British tax payer for many decades afterwards? To add insult to injury, the evidence of such transgressions is forever hidden in the Windsor Archives, out of our reach.

Since the Second World War many countries have adopted a Freedom of Information Act: surely the citizens of any twenty-first century democracy should have access to information on any subject that concerns them – especially matters of exemption, prerogative and privilege. Although members of the current government and others have proposed that Britain adopts its own such Act, this is opposed by the senior civil service. They doubtless fear that any Freedom of Information Act would expose the true seat of power and its habitual economy with the truth in selecting convenient precedent.

Neither the Palace mafia nor the senior civil service could survive for long in its present form with a Freedom of Information Act, for it would soon identify the otherwise faceless individuals and reveal their true agendas. But if Britain is to have a real hope of being a true twenty-first-century democracy, all this has to happen: openness in government and accountability for the royal family.

In 2002 the Queen's personal popularity may be riding high but the royal finances are under scrutiny as never before. Serious questions are being asked about the cost of maintaining the monarchy, and why the nation should be expected to pay for certain of the privileges enjoyed by the Queen as head of state: the royal yacht *Britannia* has already been decommissioned and not replaced, and the necessity for her to travel in her own personal train is now being queried.

Thanks to the legal privileges she enjoys – such as being able to hide her investments behind the screen of the Bank of England Nominees – the Queen's personal wealth is literally incalculable. There is no information available to enable it to be calculated, although a recent analysis by the *Independent* estimated Elizabeth II's personal fortune to be around £175 million.[1] Of course, the question can fairly be asked why her subjects need to know about her private means, which are quite separate from the Government funds intended to pay for her expenses as head of state. But the distinction is not always clear: for example, although the estates at Balmoral and Sandringham – acquired in Victoria's reign – are said to be the Queen's private property, there is evidence that Victoria and Albert acquired them at least partly with money diverted from the Civil List,[2] in which case surely the state has a claim on them? And when these houses are occupied they are paid for by the taxpayer, on the grounds that wherever the Queen is she is always the head of state.

What of the Royal Collection – the works of art that according to one estimate are worth around £7 *billion*, and which contain three times as many paintings as the National Gallery? In theory the Queen holds all these 'in trust' for the nation; in practice she alone possesses them, while they remain largely unseen by the rest of us (at any one time, less than a half of a per cent of the collection is on public display).[3] There is also the very vexed question of the 'grace and favour' properties, paid for by the state but occupied by members of the royal family and Royal Household. The recent public outcry over the revelation that Prince and Princess Michael of Kent, who carry out virtually no official duties, live in luxury apartments in state-funded Kensington Palace for which they pay 'rent' of £76 per week, raises questions about how far the 'democratisation' of the royal family has really gone.

Finally, there is the issue of to whom the gifts given to the Sovereign and her family on state visits belong – from priceless gemstones from the mines of India and South Africa in the reigns of Victoria, Edward VII and George V, to the extravagant gifts lavished on the Queen and the Prince and Princess of Wales on visits to the oil-rich Middle East. Should they be (as they have been for the most part) regarded as personal gifts or should they be treated as national assets? (A reasonable solution to this question would be that they should belong to whoever paid for the trip.)

The new monarchy must be ready to preside over the change from subject and monarch to citizen and head of state. It must accept that it will pay tax in the same way as every other citizen, deal openly and honestly with issues such as who owns properties and land, the art collections and the jewels. It must separate once and for all the property of the family from that of the state, drawing up and maintaining much better inventories of what is whose. And, having admitted that many of the treasures now locked up inside Windsor Castle or even in the private royal homes such as Balmoral belong to the state, would it be too much to ask to see them from time to time?

But above all in order to survive through the new *glasnost*, the royal family must place its archives within the public domain – without a special constraint of 100 years for royal papers – so that the re-writing of history and the days of concealing both political and financial issues will be over, and the facts cease to be hidden from we, the prople.

Yet even with these changes, as ever, problems may well arise from within the royal family itself. Despite the Diana effect that threatened to eclipse her own popularity, Elizabeth II has proven herself to be a safe pair of hands where the ship of state is concerned, although questions have been raised about the next two heirs. Aside from doubts about his suitability for the role, Charles as King appears unlikely to be content to stand on the political sidelines, potentially becoming a thorn in the side of the Government, while his son has reportedly expressed a desire never to be King. Prince William apparently rarely attends the special lessons on the constitution arranged for him by the Queen, and seems to want an ordinary life without being constantly in the spotlight. He saw what it did to his mother, and in his heart of hearts he must also recognise what Palace machinations can do to destroy the plans of even the best-intentioned royal.

The last time an heir voiced similar opinions it led to the abdication crisis. On the other hand, Prince Harry has now publicly committed himself to continuing his mother's charity work, to become a 'prince of the people's hearts', as the newspapers were quick to dub him. But did this come soley from Harry himself, or can one discern the cynical hand of the Palace in this attempt to get closer to the people – once again? If so, their plan may well backfire, especially if Harry turns out to be *too* like his mother . . . Besides, history has shown only too graphically what happened to 'People's Princes' with a will of their own.

The future of the monarchy will depend on a subtle three-way balance of power – the new generation of royals, the Palace, and of course, the people. If lessons have *not* been learned, the people will be forgotten or, worse, merely patronised. Given the perennial problems and those that are exclusive to the twenty-first century, can the House of Windsor reinvent itself yet again? Have 'lessons been learned' by the royal family, and can the necessary modernisation be made before the next coronation?

NOTES AND REFERENCES

PROLOGUE

1. Ziegler, *King Edward VIII*, p11.
2. Harold Nicolson, who was selected as the official biographer of George V in the early 1950s, was told by the Queen's Private Secretary to withhold 'anything discreditable' about his subject that he might come across in the Royal Archives. (Winter & Kochman, p126).
3. Kelley, p505.
4. A.N. Wilson, pp91–2.

CHAPTER ONE: 'A KINGLY CASTE OF GERMANS'

1. Shaw, p232.
2. The Windsors' immediate antecedents, the House of Saxe-Coburg-Gotha, had borne the family name of Wettin – both taken from Prince Albert when he married Queen Victoria – and prior to that the House of Hanover was the Guelph family.
3. Quoted in Brendon and Whitehead, p18.
4. Spoto, p103.
5. Shaw, p233.
6. Quoted in Emden, p224.
7. Bogdanor, p202.
8. Emden, p224.
9. Prochaska, p157.
10. Ibid., p172.
11. Quoted in Spoto, p167.
12. Quoted in ibid., p169.
13. Brendon and Whitehead, p13.
14. Ibid., p16.

15. Ibid., p19.
16. Quoted in Prochaska, p159.
17. Ibid., p165.
18. Ibid., p163.
19. Quoted in Spoto, p164.
20. James, p64.
21. Ibid., pp64–5.
22. See Kenneth Rose, *Kings, Queens and Courtiers*, p116.
23. Duke of Windsor, *A King's Story*, p126.
24. For more details on this controversy, see www.pharo.com/warofthewindsors.
25. Since 1917, royal status is restricted to the children of the monarch, the children of the sons of the monarch, and the eldest son of the eldest son of the Prince of Wales.
26. Quoted in Spoto, p185.
27. Prochaska, pp170–1.
28. Airlie, p166.
29. Even in 1938, on the eve of the Second World War, 238 MPs – about 35 per cent of the Commons – were either from, or married into, the aristocracy and landed gentry. See Haxey, p165.
30. Duff, *Mother of the Queen*, p257.
31. Brendon and Whitehead, p13.
32. www.royal.gov.uk.
33. Bogdanor, p71.
34. Spoto, p106.
35. Zeigler, *King Edward VIII*, p26.
36. Shaw, pp1–2.
37. Quoted in Brendon and Whitehead, p1.
38. Ibid., p8.

39. Quoted in Spoto, p136.
40. Quoted in Brendon and Whitehead, p8.
41. Quoted in ibid., p13.
42. E.g. Spoto, p8.

CHAPTER TWO: 'THE PEOPLE'S PRINCE'

1. McLeod, p10.
2. Donaldson, *Edward VIII*, p111.
3. Quoted in Spoto, p144.
4 . See Parker, pp80–2.
5. Quoted in Spoto, p144.
6. Donaldson, *Edward VIII*, p49.
7. See Ziegler, *King Edward VIII*, p80.
8. Brendon and Whitehead, p33; Ziegler, *King Edward VIII*, p53.
9. Quoted in Zeigler, *King Edward VIII*, p75.
10. This was the St Clair-Erskine family, today best known as the owners of Rosslyn Chapel near Edinburgh.
11. See the biography *Louis and the Prince* written by his grandson, Geordie Greig.
12. Quoted in Watson, p80.
13. Prochaska, p179.
14. Zeigler, *King Edward VIII*, p111.
15. See Donaldson, *Edward VIII*, p110.
16. Quoted in Zeigler, *King Edward VIII*, p109.
17. Ibid., p183.
18. Quoted in ibid., p111.
19. Airlie, p144.
20. Quoted in McLeod, p67.
21. Quoted in ibid., p68.
22. Quoted in: Brendon & Whitehead, p85; McLeod, p68; Spoto, p178 (each of these sources quotes a different part of the letter).
23. Roberts, *Eminent Churchillians*, p126.
24. Ziegler, *Mountbatten*, p36.
25. Ibid., p21.
26. Quoted in Roberts, *Eminent Churchillians*, p56.
27. Quoted in ibid., p68.
28. Ibid., p55.
29. Hough, *Mountbatten*, p157.
30. Quoted in Ziegler, *Mountbatten*, p55.
31. Ibid., p79.
32. Roberts, *Eminent Churchillians*, p133.
33. Quoted in ibid., p 133.
34. Bryans, p185; Kelley, p46.
35. Quoted in Zeigler, *Mountbatten*, p53.
36. See Hoey, pp91–6; Ziegler, *Mountbatten*, pp52–3.

37. Authors' interview with Madeleine Masson, 27 August 2002.
38. See Shaw, pp253–5.
39. Hoey, p92.
40. Philip Ziegler, introduction to Mountbatten, *The Diaries of Lord Louis Mountbatten: 1920–1922*, p10.
41. Ziegler, *Mountbatten*, p54.
42. Ibid., p55.
43. Quoted in Ziegler, *King Edward VIII*, p124.
44. Donaldson, *Edward VIII*, p81.
45. Spoto, p184.
46. See Donaldson, *Edward VIII*, p84.
47. Duff, *George & Elizabeth*, pp92–3.
48. Bradford, *King George VI*, pp95–6.
49. Quoted in Ziegler, *Mountbatten*, p61.
50. See Hall, pp53–4. Income from the Duchy of Cornwall only goes to the monarch when there is no male heir to take the title of Prince of Wales; if the Law Officers were right about Crown immunity, then only at such times would the profits be exempt from tax.
51. Ibid., p56.
52. Ibid., pp55–7.
53. Ibid., p57.
54. McLeod, p91.
55. A.N. Wilson, p41.
56. Quoted in Kelley, pp17–8.
57. Spoto, p188.
58. Duff, *George and Elizabeth*, p73.
59. Duff, *Mother of the Queen*, p133; *George and Elizabeth*, pp74–5.
60. The first royal wedding to be celebrated since the First World War, the marriage of George and Mary's only daughter to an English aristocrat 15 years her senior took place at Westminster Abbey in February 1922, the first royal union to do so since 1352, establishing another twentieth-century royal 'tradition'.
61. McLeod, p90.
62. Quoted in Spoto, p191.
63. Kelley, p17.
64. E.g. Duff, *Mother of the Queen*, p133.
65. Ibid., p16.
66. Quoted in Duff, *Elizabeth of Glamis*, p61.
67. Quoted in Greig, p196.
68. Ibid., p209.
69. Duff, *George and Elizabeth*, p88.
70. Brendon and Whitehead, p90.
71. James, p93.

72. Quoted in Macleod, p99.
73. Quoted in Zeigler, *King Edward VIII*, p69.
74. Parker, p50.
75. Authors' interview with Madeleine Masson, 27 August 2002.
76. Hoey, p101.
77. See ibid., pp83–6
78. Hough, *Edwina*, p121.
79. Quoted in Hoey, p89.
80. Macwhirter.
81. Channon, p50.
82. Warwick, *George and Marina*, p70.
83. Watson, p87.
84. Quoted in ibid.
85. Hoare, p122.
86. See Thornton, pp402–3.
87. Quoted in Spoto, p195.
88. Costello, *Mask of Treachery*, p466.
89. Shaw, p252.
90. McLeod, p122.
91. Costello, *Mask of Treachery*, p467.
92. Ibid., pp466–7.
93. See Carter, p101.
94. Deacon, *The Greatest Treason*, p89.
95. Watson, p88.
96. Ibid., p89.
97. Quoted in Zeigler, *King Edward VIII*, p200.
98. Quoted in McLeod, p123.
99. Prochaska, p175.
100. Ibid., pp82–3.
101. Ibid., p182.
102. See James, pp72–5.
103. Quoted in Prochaska, p180.
104. Quoted in Duke of Windsor, *A King's Story*, p177.
105. Prochaska, p181.
106. Quoted in Jenkins, p102.
107. Duke of Windsor, *A King's Story*, pp205–6.
108. Ibid., p206.
109. Parker, p52.
110. Kenneth Rose, *King George V*, p390.
111. Ziegler, *King Edward VIII*, p168.
112. Middlemas and Barnes, p976.
113. McLeod, p102.
114. Spoto, pp206–8.
115. Quoted in Ziegler, *King Edward VIII*, p193.
116. Quoted in ibid., p192.
117. Quoted in ibid.
118. McLeod, p103.
119. Quoted in Donaldson, *Edward VIII*, p137.
120. McLeod, p103.
121. Quoted in James, p81.

CHAPTER THREE: 'CHRIST! WHAT'S GOING TO HAPPEN NEXT?'

1. Duke of Windsor, *A King's Story*, p224.
2. Bogdanor, p106.
3. Hall, p68.
4. Marquand, pp629–30.
5. Bogdanor, p108.
6. Ibid., p110.
7. Hall, p66.
8. Bogdanor, p67.
9. Quoted in ibid., p111.
10. Ibid., p107.
11. James, p87.
12. Ibid.
13. Ibid., p85.
14. Ibid., p86.
15. Bogdanor, p111.
16. Hall, p60.
17. The monarch's income can be divided into three categories: amounts given by the state to maintain them as head of state, the best-known example of which is the Civil List; the Privy Purse, which is made up of hereditary revenues built up by successive monarchs since the Middle Ages, the largest part of which comes from the Duchy of Lancaster; and income from personal assets (e.g. investments) owned by the monarch as a private individual.
18. Hall, p61.
19. See ibid., pp64–5.
20. See our *Double Standards* pp27–33
21. See ibid, pp54–5
22. Van Paassen, p165.
23. Ziegler, *Mountbatten*, pp73–4.
24. Newton, p166.
25. Shaw, p233.
26. Kenneth Rose, *King George V*, p387.
27. Duke of Windsor, *A King's Story*, p59.
28. Ziegler, *King Edward VIII*, p183.
29. Watson, p89.
30. Picknett *et al*, p146.
31. Norman Rose, p144.
32. Sarah Wilson.
33. Bogdanor, p68.
34. Bryan and Murphy, p364.
35. Ibid., p501.

36. Parker, p71.
37. Costello, *Ten Days that saved the West*, p497.
38. Newton, pp142–3.
39. Quoted in Bryan and Murphy, p397.
40. Ibid., p399.
41. Quoted in Brendon and Whitehead, p262.
42. Quoted in Kelley, p43.
43. Quoted in Kelley, p108.
44. See Duff, *George and Elizabeth*, p99.
45. Hough, *Edwina*, p118.
46. Authors' interview with Madeleine Masson, 27 August 2002.
47. The Greek monarchy was abolished again in 1923, restored in 1935, driven out by the Nazis in 1941, restored yet again by a plebiscite in 1946, and finally abolished for good in 1973.
48. Duff, *George and Elizabeth*, p100.
49. Quoted in Watson, p94.
50. Spoto, p234.
51. Warwick, *George and Marina*, p137.
52. Kenneth Rose, *Kings, Queens and Courtiers*, p154.
53. Spoto, p242.
54. Warwick, *George and Marina*, p136.
55. Quoted in Higham and Moseley, p76.
56. See ibid., p83.
57. The two royal Hesse families into which Philip's sisters married should not be confused. After the splitting of the original kingdom into two in the sixteenth century, two royal lines, one headed by a Grand Duke and the other by a Landgrave, were commonly referred to as 'of Hesse'. More properly, the name of the former family is Hesse-Darmstadt and the latter Hesse-Cassel. Prince Christopher was a Hesse-Cassel; Lord Mountbatten and the later Duke of Edinburgh were descended from the Hesse-Darmstadts.
58. Higham and Moseley, pp85–6.
59. See Parker, p77.
60. Hough, *Edwina*, pp125–8.
61. Authors' interview with Madeleine Masson, 27 August 2002.
62. Hough, *Edwina*, p128.
63. Spoto, p249.
64. The full text of Rosenberg's report is in Winterbotham, *Secret and Personal*, pp78–81. Significantly, all mention of this report, and de Ropp's dealings with George V and Duke of Kent, was omitted from a later version of Winterbotham's memoirs, *The Nazi Connection*, only Edward VIII's contact with the Nazis (again via Kent and de Ropp) being mentioned in the later edition.
65. This subject is explored in more depth in *Double Standards*, see particularly pp92–3.
66. Quoted in Winterbotham, *Secret and Personal*, p76.
67. Griffiths, pp122–3.
68. Quoted in Winterbotham, *Secret and Personal*, p81.
69. Jenkins, p136.
70. Quoted in ibid., p159.
71. Ibid., p135.
72. Ibid.
73. Ibid., p137.
74. Parker, pp60–1.
75. Vanderbilt and Furness, p291.
76. Quoted in Spoto, p223.
77. Parker, pp63–4.
78. Ziegler, *King Edward VIII*, p224.
79. Duff, *George and Elizabeth*, p91.
80. See pages 120–21.
81. See Duff, *George and Elizabeth*, p101.
82. Spoto, p249.
83. Ibid.
84. Parker, p99.
85. Quoted in Bradford, *Elizabeth*, p49.
86. Quoted in Parker, pp98–9.
87. Spoto, p252.
88. Quoted in ibid.
89. Quoted in ibid., p253.
90. Quoted in ibid., p252.
91. Quoted in Ziegler, *King Edward VIII*, p241.
92. Inglis, pp44–5.

CHAPTER FOUR: 'A KIND OF ENGLISH NATIONAL SOCIALIST'

1. Inglis, p71.
2. Bloch, *The Duke of Windsor's War*, p148.
3. Quoted in ibid.
4. Quoted in Bloch, *The Reign and Abdication of Edward VIII*, p18.
5. Bryan and Murphy, p116.
6. Inglis, p71.
7. Bryan and Murphy, p162–3.
8. Bloch, *The Reign and Abdication of Edward VIII*, pp31–2.
9. Inglis, p125.

10. Young, pp133–4.
11. Channon, p84.
12. Hall, p73.
13. Ibid., p74.
14. Ibid., p73.
15. Bloch, *The Reign and Abdication of Edward VIII*, pp31–2.
16. Bryan and Murphy, p153.
17. Parker, pp101–2.
18. Bryan and Murphy, p154.
19. Quoted in Ziegler, *King Edward VIII*, p208.
20. Parker, p100.
21. Ibid.
22. Quoted in ibid., pp100–1.
23. Quoted in Ziegler, *King Edward VIII*, p268.
24. Speer, p118.
25. Hesse, p22.
26. Young, p133.
27. Parker, p92; see also Middlemas and Barnes, p979.
28. Quoted in Bryan and Murphy, p154.
29. See Spoto, pp273–4.
30. Bryan and Murphy, p165.
31. Ziegler, *King Edward VIII*, p278.
32. Ibid.
33. Quoted in Wheeler-Bennett, p287.
34. Quoted in Parker, p132.
35. A.N. Wilson, p86.
36. Donaldson, *Edward VIII*, p219.
37. Inglis, p236.
38. Picknett *et al.*, p89–90.
39. Bogdanor, p206.
40. Inglis, p75.
41. Bogdanor, p206.
42. Bloch, *The Reign and Abdication of Edward VIII*, p75.
43. Ibid.
44. Inglis, p192.
45. Bogdanor, p208.
46. Quoted in Donaldson, *Edward VIII*, p235-6.
47. Quoted in ibid., p245.
48. Guedalla, p256.
49. See Ziegler, *King Edward VIII*, p299.
50. See Donaldson, *Edward VIII*, pp252–3.
51. Guedalla, p258.
52. Inglis, p267.
53. Duke of Windsor, *A King's Story*, p317
54. Ziegler, *Mountbatten*, p92.
55. Ibid.
56. Bloch, *The Duke of Windsor's War*, p18.
57. Ziegler, *King Edward VIII*, p93.
58. Ibid., p94.
59. Cockburn, p250.
60. Ibid., p252.
61. Bryan and Murphy, p234.
62. Inglis, p301.
63. Quoted in ibid., p301.
64. Quoted in Bloch, *The Reign and Abdication of Edward VIII*, p150.
65. Inglis, p272; Bloch, *The Reign and Abdication of Edward VIII*, p154.
66. Letter from Kenneth de Courcy to Madame S. Blum, 19 December 1978.
67. Donaldson, *Edward VIII*, p286.
68. Letter from Kenneth de Courcy to Madame S. Blum, 19 December 1978.
69. Note written by de Courcy, 20 July 1950, copy in authors' possession.
70. Letter from Kenneth de Courcy to Madame S. Blum, 19 December 1978.
71. Guedalla, p275–6.
72. Bloch, *The Reign and Abdication of Edward VIII*, p202.
73. Duke of Windsor, *A King's Story*, p349.
74. Quoted in Parker, p131.
75. Inglis, p324.
76. Ibid., p333.
77. Bloch, *The Reign and Abdication of Edward VIII*, p214.
78. Duke of Windsor, *A King's Story*, p351.
79. Ibid., pp351–2.
80. Ibid., p352.
81. Quoted in ibid., pp352–3.
82. Kelley, p241.
83. Bloch, *The Reign and Abdication of Edward VIII*, pp189–90, quoting from unpublished parts of Duff Cooper's memoirs.
84. Inglis, p315.
85. Anthony Cox, quoted in Ziegler, *King Edward VIII*, p319.
86. Lacey, p101.
87. See George VI's own account of the events of these days, in Wheeler-Bennett, pp284–7.
88. Nicolson, *Diaries and Letters 1945–62*, p167.
89. See Morrah, *Princess Elizabeth*, p62, and *The Work of the Queen*, p19. Added weight is given to Morrah's statements as he was a writer who was particularly favoured by the royal family in general and Queen Elizabeth in particular (see

Bradford, *Elizabeth*, p332).
90. Thornton, p127.
91. Turner.
92. Ford.
93. Note by de Courcy, 10 December 1936, copy in authors' possession.
94. Letter from Kenneth de Courcy to Madame S. Blum, 19 December 1978.
95. See Bryan and Murphy, p130.
96. Channon, p84.
97. Nicolson, *Diaries and Letters 1930–39.*
98. Bradford, *George VI*, p191.
99. Ibid., p192.
100. Shaw, p261.
101. Inglis, p360.
102. Quoted in ibid.
102. Ziegler, *King Edward VIII*, p268.
104. Quoted in Parker, p140.
105. Ibid., p166.

CHAPTER FIVE: 'THE MOST UNCONSTITUTIONAL ACT'
1. Ziegler, *King Edward VIII*, p397.
2. Mary's title was now Queen Dowager but she was still customarily referred to as Queen Mary.
3. Hall, p75.
4. Quoted in ibid., p77.
5. Ibid., p77.
6. Ibid., p78.
7. Ibid., p80–1.
8. Ibid., p83.
9. See Harlow. The revelations came from correspondence between George VI and Bowes-Lyon that emerged in private hands in 2000.
10. Channon, p130.
11. Brendon & Whitehead, p88.
12. Historian David Cannadine, quoted in ibid., p89. George Formby was the gauche – some might say grotesque – ukelele player and singer who became an unlikely 1930s film star in Britain.
13. Kelley, p27.
14. Ibid.
15. Quoted in Aronson, p103.
16. Brendon & Whitehead, p99.
17. Quoted in Roberts, *Eminent Churchillians*, p9.
18. Quoted in Parker, pp145.
19. Spoto, p294.
20. Quoted in Parker, p145–6.
21. Brendon & Whitehead, pp98.
22. Ziegler, *King Edward VIII*, p379.
23. McLeod, p202.
24. Ibid.
25. Ziegler, *King Edward VIII*, p532.
26. Spoto, p292.
27. Ibid., pp292–3.
28. Quoted in ibid., p295.
29. *Daily Express*, 5 April 2002.
30. Quoted in Bloch, *The Duke of Windsor's War*, p8.
31. Quoted in Kelley, pp18–9.
32. In *Double Standards*, we incorrectly dated the first moves to make Kent the King of Poland to after the Nazi and Soviet invasion of Poland in 1939 and the establishment of the Polish Government in exile under General Sikorski. However, it is apparent that Sikorski was only continuing a move for which the groundwork had been laid in 1937.
33. De Stoeckl, p204.
34. Bethel.
35. Deacon, *The Greatest Treason*, p88.
36. Ibid., p89.
37. Duchess of Windsor, p303.
38. See Parker, pp157.
39. Ziegler, *King Edward VIII*, p393.
40. Heald, pp48–9.
41. Bradford, *Elizabeth*, p84.
42. Ibid., p85.
43. The British peace movement is explored in more depth in our *Double Standards* – see especially pp82–7.
44. Quoted in Aronson, p24.
45. Quoted in ibid., p25.
46. E.g. Brendon and Whitehead, p104.
47. Ibid., p105.
48. Ibid., p107.
49. See Picknett *et al*, pp88–9 and 106–9.
50. Goodchild.
51. Brendon and Whitehead, p105.
52. Ibid.
53. Shepherd, p214.
54. Bogdanor, p68.
55. Quoted in Roberts, *Eminent Churchillians*, p21.
56. Quoted in ibid., p13.
57. Ibid.
58. De Stoeckl, pp212–23.
59. Duff, *George and Elizabeth*, pp153–4.
60. Roberts, *Eminent Churchillians*, p24.
61. Roberts, *The Plot to Betray Poland.*

62. Whiting, p97.
63. De Stoeckl, p226.
64. Aronson, p12.
65. Ziegler, *Mountbatten*, p124.
66. Newton, p142.
67. Quoted Bloch, *The Duke of Windsor's War*, p41.
68. See ibid., pp46–50.
69. Costello, *Mask of Treachery*, p452.
70. Martin Allen, pp168–70.
71. Ibid., pp153–4.
72. Ibid., Appendix.
73. Costello, *Mask of Treachery*, pp452–3.
74. Chisholm and Davie, pp371–2.
75. Aronson, p21.
76. Lamb, p122.
77. See Roberts, *Eminent Churchillians*, pp27–34.
78. James, pp179–84.
79. Channon, p229.
80. Quoted in Aronson, p25.
81. James, p146.
82. Quoted in Roberts, p17.
83. Aronson, p25.
84. Lockhart, vol. 2., 748.
85. When, in 1923, George V had declined to make Lord Curzon Prime Minister, he made it clear that this was a result of the particular circumstances and that he was not creating a constitutional precedent. See Bogdanor, pp75–6.
86. Quoted in Bogdanor, p92.
87. Colville, vol. 1, p141.
88. Quoted in Bogdanor, p102.
89. Costello, *Ten Days that Saved the West*, p47.
90. Brendon & Whitehead, p110.
91. Charmley.

CHAPTER SIX: 'THE END OF MANY HOPES'

1. Quoted in Spoto, p307.
2. Quoted in Greig, p279.
3. Ibid., p278.
4. Kenneth de Courcy, cited in Brendon and Whitehead, p110.
5. See Brendon and Whitehead, p114.
6. E.g. Aronson, p46.
7. Brendon and Whitehead, pp111–2.
8. Aronson, p44.
9. Brendon and Whitehead, pp112–3.
10. Hall, p85.
11. Ibid.

12. Ziegler, *Kind Edward VIII*, p417.
13. *Documents on German Foreign Policy*, vol. 10, p2 and 9.
14. Ibid., pp96–7.
15. Ibid., p188.
16. Ibid., p189.
17. Ibid., p223.
18. Parker, p193.
19. *Documents on German Foreign Policy*, vol. 10, p189.
20. Ibid., p188.
21. Ibid.
22. Parker, p196.
23. See our *Double Standards*, especially pp287–8.
24. *Documents on German Foreign Policy*, vol. 10, p283.
25. Ibid., pp276–7.
26. Ibid., pp290–1.
27. Ibid., pp376–7.
28. Parker, p203.
29. Ibid.
30. Carter, p312.
31. *Documents on German Foreign Policy*, vol. X, pp389–401.
32. Ibid., pp397–8.
33. Parker, p216–7.
34. Ziegler, *King Edward VIII*, pp548–9.
35. Costello, *Mask of Treachery*, pp455–6.
36. Parker, p192.
37. Sarah Wilson.
38. Quoted in Ziegler, *King Edward VIII*, p434.
39. Quoted in ibid.
40. Quoted in ibid., p435.
41. Ibid., p436
42. Note written by de Courcy with observations on Michael Bloch's *Operation Willi*, 10 November 1984.
43. Brendon and Whitehead, p113.
44. Parker, pp191–2.
45. Picknett *et al*, pp120–2.
46. Brendon and Whitehead, p111.
47. Aronson, p46.
48. Quoted in Bradford, *Elizabeth*, p92. Buckingham Palace was hit a further seven times during the Blitz, although the other occasions were during nighttime raids – when the King and Queen were in Windsor.
49. Aronson, p37.
50. Quoted in Parker, p210.
51. Warwick, *George and Marina*, p147.

52. Picknett *et al*, pp309–10.
53. See Bloch, *The Duke of Windsor's War*, pp177–8; Ziegler, *King Edward VIII*, p460.
54. Ziegler, *King Edward VIII*, p460.
55. Aronson, p171.
56. Duff, *Mother of the Queen*, p239.
57. De Stoeckl, pp238–9.
58. Belien.
59. Dear, p118.
60. Belien.
61. Dear, p118–9.
62. Aronson, p27.
63. We are indebted to Charles Destrée for the many discussions about his research, in person and via the internet, and for providing us with an English summary of his unpublished work.
64. Destrée, *From Englandspiel to Great Britain's Game* (unpublished manuscript).
65. Warwick, *George and Marina*, p34.
66. Hatch, pp46–7.
67. Mortimer, p143.
68. Destrée (op. cit.).
69. The Englandspiel affair will be explored in more detail in our next book.
70. De Stoeck, p242.
71. Bethel.
72. Letter from de Courcy to Jeremy Pilcher, 17 July 1989.
73. Bloch, *The Duke of Windsor's War*, p204.
74. Quoted in ibid., p192.
75. See Picknett *et al*, pp311–2.
76. Churchill himself hints at this in his war memoirs, in which he writes, '. . . as a convinced upholder of constitutional monarchy I valued as a signal honour the gracious intimacy which I, as first Minister, was treated [by the King], for which I suppose there has been no precedent since the days of Queen Anne and Marlborough during his years of power.' (Churchill, vol. II, p335)
77. Picknett *et al*, p491.
78. Deacon, *The Greatest Treason*, pp87–8.
79. Lockhart, vol. 1, p356.
80. Roberts, *Eminent Churchillians*, p58.
81. Higham and Moseley, pp90–1.
82. Roberts, *Eminent Churchillians*, p62.
83. Quoted in Ziegler, *Mountbatten*, p138.
84. Roberts, *Eminent Churchillians*, p60.
85. For a detailed discussion of the mysteries and theories about the Dieppe Raid, see www.pharo.com/warofthewindsors.
86. Coates and Coates, pp709–19.
87. Greig, p283.
88. Ibid., p282.
89. Fairbanks, p156.
90. Ibid., p157.
91. De Stoeckl, p245.
92. *The Scotsman*, 27 August 1942.
93. In *Double Standards* (p433), because of discrepancies in the scant accounts of Kent's final movements and particularly Prince Bernhard's claim of a meeting at Balmoral, we suggested that the Duke left the Coppins on 23 August and that a 'missing day' was being covered up. Baroness de Stoeckl's diary entry shows this to be incorrect. However, as Kent would have been in Scotland by the evening of 24 August, there was still sufficient time for the meeting with Bernhard.
94. Since the publication of *Double Standards*, critics of our theory have circulated copies of a memo, dated 25 August 1942, written by the Station Commander of RAF Kaldadarnes in Iceland, giving details of the Duke of Kent's intinerary in Iceland. This, it is claimed, shows that our conclusion that the Iceland trip was a cover story, and that Kent's true destination was elsewhere, is incorrect. However, the memo only shows that arrangements for the Iceland visit were being made by the RAF – since the purpose of a cover story is to mislead as convincingly as possible, the memo's existence has little bearing on the enigma of Kent's death.
95. See *Double Standards*, pp427–35.
96. See ibid., pp434–5.
97. Aronson, p91.
98. We are grateful to Miss P.L. Bowyer Johnson for drawing the latter to our attention.
99. Quoted in Bradford, *Elizabeth*, p99.

CHAPTER SEVEN: 'THE HOUSE OF MOUNTBATTEN NOW REIGNS!'

1. Ziegler, *Mountbatten*, p488.
2. Hoey, pp145–6.
3. James, p269.
4. There was some small comfort for the royals in the fact that the size of Labour's

majority was not an accurate reflection of the actual votes cast: although they had beaten the Conservatives by 12 million to 10 million votes, they had won 203 more seats in the Commons.

5. James, p275.
6. It may also be significant that Dalton seems to have played a major role in causing the failure of the Rudolf Hess plan in 1941 – see Picknett *et al*, p262.
7. Brendon and Whitehead, p115.
8. See Prochaska, pp195–7.
9. James, p313.
10. Aronson, p96.
11. Hall, p85.
12. Hall, pp194–5.
13. Ibid., p195. The Privy Purse kept receiving income from the No Kin Investment Fund until 1983, when it was announced that in future it would be used to support a benevolent fund. However, according to Phillip Hall, writing in 1991, only a quarter of the No Kin revenues had actually transferred to this fund.
14. Parker, p157.
15. Quoted in Thornton, p229.
16. Christopher Warwick, in *Scotland on Sunday*, 25 August 2002
17. Kelley, pp26–7.
18. Quoted in Carter, p165.
19. Wright and Greengrass, p223.
20. Ibid.
21. Costello, *Mask of Treachery*, p459.
22. Thornton p229.
23. Quoted in Costello, *Mask of Treachery*, p448.
24. Ibid.
25. Brendon and Whitehead, p116.
26. Carter, p312.
27. Ibid., p315.
28. Ibid., p316.
29. Ibid., p315.
30. Ibid., p318.
31. In fact, there *were* reasons for suspecting that Blunt was still engaging in espionage during his German trips. A few days after the first of his visits to Brunswick, he passed information to his NVKD handlers that he could only have got from Leo Long, his driver on that occasion. (Carter, p315) Long, a Cambridge Marxist, was one of Blunt's former sources

in London (see Modin, pp219) – apparently unknowingly, although on this basis he *should* have been investigated as a possible Soviet agent. But Wright could never have made this connection, because the Palace refused to allow him to ask the right questions.
32. Ziegler, pp299–300.
33. See, for example, Sarah Bradford, *Elizabeth*, pp103–4.
34. Higham and Moseley, p90.
35. Spoto, p304.
36. Channon, pp286–7.
37. Ziegler, *Mountbatten*, p308.
38. Bradford, *Elizabeth*, p103.
39. Ibid., p112.
40. Kelley, pp48–51.
41. Bradford, *Elizabeth*, pp104–5.
42. Turner.
43. Winter and Kochman, p212.
44. See Lane, pp35–40.
45. Kelley, p63.
46. Spoto, pp317–8.
47. Quoted in Kelley, p76.
48. Bradford pp265–6.
49. Young, p28.
50. Quoted in Bradford, p141.
51. Quoted in Roberts, *Eminent Churchillians*, p71.
52. Quoted in ibid., p74.
53. Quoted in Ziegler, *Mountbatten*, p207.
54. Roberts, *Eminent Churchillians*, p76.
55. Quoted in ibid.
56. See ibid., pp77–8.
57. See Ziegler, *Mountbatten*, pp324–6.
58. Ibid., p344.
59. Although this complex episode is beyond the scope of this book, Andrew Roberts has examined Mountbatten's blunders and misjudgements, and their often terrible effects for millions of people, in *Eminent Churchillians* (1994) – see Chapter 3, 'Lord Mountbatten and the Perils of Adrenalin', especially pp78–132.
60. Hough, *Edwina*, pp181–2. Hough describes Nehru as Edwina's 'first and only great love'.
61. Roberts, p108.
62. Ziegler, *Mountbatten*, p475.
63. Brendon & Whitehead, p121.
64. Ziegler, *Mountbatten*, p488.
65. Bradford, p123.
66. Ziegler, *Mountbatten*, p489.

67. Note by Kenneth de Courcy, 10 March 1951. See also Parker, pp7–12.
68. Ziegler, *King Edward VIII*, p498.
69. Parker, p237.
70. Ziegler, *Mountbatten*, p457.
71. George V – clearly not anticipating that another queen would rule – restricted royal status to the children of monarchs and the children of the sons of monarchs. This meant that Elizabeth's children – including the heir to the throne – would not have royal status.
72. Interviewed by Fiammetta Rocco for the *Independent on Sunday*, 1993.
73. Channel 5 television documentary, *Prince Philip, the Power Behind the Throne* (produced and directed by Jonathan Trace, Tapestry Productions, 2001).
74. Bradford, p177.
75. Ibid.
76. Hoey, p129.
77. Ziegler, *Mountbatten*, pp502–3.
78. Quoted in Hoey p210.
79. Ziegler, *Mountbatten*, p345.
80. Ibid., p52
81. Carter, p355
82. Deacon, *The Greatest Treason*, p91.
83. Quoted in ibid., p169.
84. Ziegler, *Mountbatten*, pp502–3.
85. Deacon, *The Greatest Treason*, p187.
86. Deacon, *The British Connection*, pp74–5 and 135–7.
87. Deacon, *The Greatest Treason*, p2.
88. Ibid., p88
89. Ibid., p169
90. Quoted in ibid., p72.
91. Duff, *Elizabeth of Glamis*, pp133–4.
92. Bradford, p172.
93. Higham and Moseley, p176.

CHAPTER EIGHT: 'THAT GERMAN PRINCELING'

1. Quoted in Kelley, p108.
2. Ibid.
3. Quoted in Bradford, *Elizabeth*, p177.
4. Duff, *Mother of the Queen*, p289.
5. Kelley, p169.
6. Quoted in Ziegler, *Mountbatten*, p501.
7. E.g. *Sunday Telegraph*, 10 January 1982.
8. See Sinclair, p175, for the full text.
9. Bradford, *Elizabeth*, p170.
10. Sinclair, pp175–6.
11. Mortimer, p238.
12. Winter and Kochman, pp120–1.
13. Christopher Wilson, p194.
14. Winter and Kochman, pp126–7.
15. Ibid., p124.
16. *Daily Mail*, 2 April 2002.
17. Quoted in Ziegler, *King Edward VIII*, p538.
18. Quoted in Bradford, *Elizabeth*, p185.
19. Hall, p19.
20. Plans to replace the old vessel were first put forward in 1938 – Mountbatten's suggestion then was that it would be cheapest to buy the German yacht *Grille*, which had been built for Hitler but which he didn't want.
21. Bradford, *Elizabeth*, p244.
22. Kelley, p129.
23. Higham and Moseley, p56.
24. Warwick, *George and Marina*, pp156–7.
25. Picknett et al, pp269–71.
26. Lord Glenconner, quoted in Bradford, *Elizabeth*, p195.
27. Kenneth Rose, *Kings, Queens and Courtiers*, pp189–90.
28. Quoted in Bradford, *Elizabeth*, p213.
29. Higham and Moseley, p240.
30. Quoted in Spoto, p370.
31. Ibid., p371.
32. Quoted in Boothroyd, p50.
33. Quoted in Spoto, p321.
34. Kelley, p152.
35. Quoted in Spoto, p326.
36. Summers and Dorril, p26.
37. Ibid., p25.
38. Ibid.
39. Kelley, pp154–5.
40. Ibid., p159
41. Higham and Moseley, p293.
42. Kelley, p110.
43. See West, pp58–60.
44. Ziegler, *Mountbatten*, pp534–5.
45. Deacon, *The Greatest Treason*, pp187–8.
46. Ziegler, *Mountbatten*, p542.
47. Ibid., p546.
48. Brendon and Whitehead, p147.
49. Ziegler, *Mountbatten*, pp537–8.
50. Ibid., p538.
51. Ibid.
52. Ibid., p535.
53. On the Penkovsky affair, see West, pp86–90, and Wynne.
54. Deacon, *The Greatest Treason*, p187.
55. Ziegler, *Mountbatten*, p568.

56. Hoey, p149.
57. Kennedy, p28.
58. Ibid., p217.
59. Knightley and Kennedy, p254.
60. Kennedy, p217.
61. Quoted in Knightley and Kennedy, p260.
62. Flamini, p275.
63. Summers and Dorril, p212.
64. Ibid., p113.
65. Penrose and Freeman, p407.
66. Higham and Moseley, p292.
67. *Prince Philip, the Power behind the Throne* television documentary (op. cit.).
68. Higham and Moseley, p306.
69. Summers and Dorril, p23.
70. Knightley and Kennedy, p250.
71. Summers and Dorril, p42.
72. Knightley and Kennedy, p255.
73. Ibid., p248.
74. Summers and Dorril, pp240–1.
75. Ibid., p38.
76. Ibid.
77. Keeler and Thompson, pp73–4.
78. Ibid., pp208–9.
79. Deacon, *The Greatest Treason*, p10; Keeler & Thompson, p215.
80. Higham and Moseley, p314.
81. Brendon and Whitehead, p165.
82. There has been considerable evasion on the subject of whether Douglas-Home was told. According to Margaret Thatcher's statement about Blunt in the Commons in November 1979, it was the Home Secretary's decision on whether the Prime Minister was informed, and – astonishingly – neither could recall whether they had in fact discussed Blunt. This may safely be taken as an admission that Douglas-Home was not told. Also at the time of Blunt's public exposure, the Deputy Head of MI6 stated that the decision had been taken not to inform Harold Wilson. On the other hand, the next two Prime Ministers, Edward Heath (who came into office after Blunt had retired) and James Callaghan, have both stated that they *were* informed.
83. *Daily Mirror*, 12 November 1981.
84. Quoted in ibid.
85. Carter, pp1–2.
86. Ibid., p4.
87. Quoted in Penrose and Freeman, p3.
88. Costello, *Mask of Treachery*, p52.
89. Wilfred Blunt also became an art historian and Curator of the Watts Gallery in Surrey. Christopher Blunt was a successful merchant banker.
90. Carter, p309.
91. Modin, p161.
92. Ibid., pp108–9.
93. Ibid., p112
94. Ibid., pp159–60
95. Ibid., p197

CHAPTER NINE: 'IN SPITE OF EVERYTHING, HE WAS A GREAT MAN'

1. See Prochaska, p205.
2. Bradford, *Elizabeth*, p324.
3. At least technically: George I was already divorced when he came to the throne, and George IV had his marriage to a Catholic quietly annulled before his accession.
4. Warwick, p157.
5. Ibid.
6. Quoted in Roberts, *Eminent Churchillians*, p128.
7. Ziegler, *Mountbatten*, p701.
8. Quoted in Roberts, *Eminent Churchillians*, p81.
9. Quoted in ibid.
10. Quoted in Deacon, *The Greatest Treason*, p186.
11. Authors' interview with Madeleine Masson, 27 August 2002.
12. Quoted in Kelley, p171.
13. Roberts, *Eminent Churchillians*, p134.
14. Quoted in ibid.
15. Ziegler, *Mountbatten*, p509.
16. Bradford, *Elizabeth*, p327.
17. Ibid., p396
18. Quoted in Kelley, p168.
19. Blundell, pp36–7.
20. Hoey, p129.
21. Kelley, p169.
22. Ziegler, *Mountbatten*, p677.
23. Ibid., p678
24. Leigh, p157.
25. Ziegler, *Mountbatten*, p658.
26. Quoted in Roberts, *Eminent Churchillians*, p134.
27. Quoted in Ziegler, *Mountbatten*, p660.
28. Ziegler, *Mountbatten*, p660, citing Cecil King's article in *Encounter*, September 1981.

29. West, pp169–70.
30. Leigh, p159.
31. Ibid., p158
32. Ziegler, *Mountbatten*, p661.
33. Ibid.
34. Ibid., p660.
35. *Sunday Times*, 22 March 1987.
36. Quoted in Higham and Moseley, p354.
37. Bradford, *Elizabeth*, p352.
38. See pp46–8.
39. Quoted in Bradford, *Elizabeth*, p360.
40. *Independent* Special Investigation, 30 May 2002, p4.
41. Ibid.
42. Hall, pp19–20.
43. Bradford, *Elizabeth*, pp362–3.
44. Ibid., p363.
45. *Daily Mail*, 27 July 1989.
46. See Bradford, *Elizabeth*, pp360–8.
47. *Independent* Special Investigation, 30 May 2002, p5.
48. Morton, *Theirs is the Kingdom*, pp85–6.
49. 'Secrets of the Palace', Channel 4 television documentary (Dual Purpose Productions, produced by David Batty, directed by Callum Macrae), 2002.
50. Hoey, p87.
51. See ibid., pp86–91
52. Bradford, *Elizabeth*, p398.
53. Higham and Moseley, p381.
54. Bradford, *Elizabeth*, p327.
55. Ibid., p397.
56. Kelley, p214.
57. Bradford, *Elizabeth*, p398.
58. Quoted in Kelley, p215.
59. Ibid.
60. Bradford, *Elizabeth*, p426.
61. Ibid, pp426–7.
62. Spoto, p402.
63. Bradford, *Elizabeth*, p397.
64. Quoted in Ziegler, *Mountbatten*, p679.
65. Bradford, *Elizabeth*, p412.
66. Thornton, p324.
67. Ibid., p330.
68. Quoted in Ziegler, *Mountbatten*, p680.
69. See Bradford, *Elizabeth*, pp415–6.
70. Quoted in Spoto, p389.
71. Bradford, *Elizabeth*, p416.
72. Parker, p335.
73. Letters from Maître Suzanne Blum to Kenneth de Courcy, 24 March and 5 April 1979, copies in authors' possession.
74. Letter from Maître Suzanne Blum to Kenneth de Courcy, 24 March 1979.
75. See Thornton, p354.
76. See Spoto, pp380–381; Bradford, *Elizabeth*, p404.
77. Quoted in Hoey, p.146.
78. Phillip Hall, interviewed on BBC's *Newsnight*, 16 April 1985.
79. Lane, pp39–40.
80. Ibid., p37.
81. Lacey, p301.
82. Bradford, *Elizabeth*, p421.
83. Quoted in Spoto, p400.
84. A.N. Wilson, p56.
85. Bradford, *Elizabeth*, p428.
86. Ibid, p421.
87. Spoto, pp397–8.
88. See Bryans, *Blackmail and Whitewash*.
89. Deacon, *The Greatest Treason*, p7.
90. Ibid., pp195–6.
91. Ibid., p196.
92. Ibid., p197, quoting *Sunday News* editor Frank Doherty, *Now* magazine, September 1989.
93. Bryans, p104.
94. Ziegler, *Mountbatten*, p692.
95. Kelley, p250.
96. Blundell, p36.

CHAPTER TEN: 'AFTER ALL I'VE DONE FOR THIS F——ING FAMILY'

1. See Bradford, *Elizabeth*, p436.
2. Dimbleby, p282.
3. See Spoto, p404 and Kelley, pp267–8.
4. Quoted in Bradford, *Elizabeth*, p437.
5. Morton, *Diana: Her True Story*, p81.
6. Bradford, *Elizabeth*, p429.
7. Quoted in Kelley, p284.
8. Bradford, *Elizabeth*, p381.
9. Ibid.
10. A.N. Wilson, pp25–6.
11. Ibid., p25
12. *Prince Philip, the Power Behind the Throne* television documentary (op. cit.).
13. Bradford, *Elizabeth*, p400.
14. Kelley, p424-5.
15. *Prince Philip, the Power Behind the Throne* television documentary (op. cit.).
16. Quoted in Spoto, p416.
17. Ibid., p412.
18. Ibid.
19. Because Mountbatten had only daughters, he obtained a 'special remainder' in order that his title, for one generation, could be

inherited by a female.
20. *Daily Mail*, 24 May 2002.
21. Hewitt, pp49–50.
22. Kelley, p339.
23. Holden, *Charles* (1998 edition), pp203–4.
24. Hewitt, p163.
25. Holden, *Charles* (1988 edition), pp208.
26. See Bradford, *Elizabeth*, pp460–1.
27. See A.N. Wilson, pp47–50.
28. Holden, *Charles* (1988 edition), pp208–11.
29. Bradford, *Elizabeth*, pp458–60.
30. Quoted in Spoto, p429.
31. A.N. Wilson, p57.
32. Kelley, p385.
33. For a transcript of the tape, see Dempster and Evans, pp240–64.
34. Bradford, *Elizabeth*, p465.
35. For a transcript, see Dempster and Evans, pp231–9.
36. Blundell, p125.
37. Morton, *Diana: Her True Story*, p134.
38. Blundell, p127.
39. Morton, *Diana: Her True Story*, pp166–7.
40. Dempster and Evans, p248.
41. Blundell, p129.
42. The conversation is said to have been recorded during the evening of 18 December 1989, but during it Camilla Parker Bowles refers to it being her son Tom's birthday the next day – and his birthday is 18 December.
43. Blundell, p117.
44. See Spoto, p408.
45. Affadavit for the official French enquiry into the death of Diana, Princess of Wales, Dodi Fayed and Henri Paul, made by Richard Tomlinson, 12 May 1999. (Copy in authors' possession.)
46. Campbell, p155.
47. Morton, *Diana: Her True Story*, p167.
48. Campbell, p165.
49. Ibid., pp165–6.
50. Rees-Jones and Johnston, p73.
51. Authors' interview with Mohamed Al Fayed, London, 30 August 2002.
52. See Kelley, pp347–8.
53. Hewitt, p50.
54. Videotaped interview with James Hewitt, supplied to authors by Mohamed Al Fayed.
55. Rees-Jones and Johnston, p73.
56. Ibid., p75.
57. Ibid., p76.
58. Ibid., p78.
59. Ibid., p83.
60. Ibid., p85.
61. Reported in the *Sunday Express*, 9 June 2002.

EPILOGUE: 'WE THE PEOPLE'
1. *Independent* Special Investigation, 31 May 2002, p8.
2. See Hall, pp11–4.
3. *Secrets of the Palace* television documentary (op. cit.).

BIBLIOGRAPHY

Entries are for editions cited in the text. Where this is not the first edition, details of the original publication (where known) are given in brackets.

Airlie, Mabell, Countess of (ed. Jennifer Ellis), *Thatched with Gold*, Hutchinson, London, 1962

Allen, Martin, *Hidden Agenda: How the Duke of Windsor Betrayed the Allies*, Macmillan, London, 2000

Allen, Peter, *The Crown and the Swastika: Hitler, Hess and the Duke of Windsor*, Robert Hale, London, 1993

Aronson, Theo, *The Royal Family at War*, John Murray, London, 1993

Bagehot, Walter, *The English Constitution*, updated edition, H.S. King & Co., London, 1872 (Chapman & Hall, London, 1867)

Belien, Paul, 'Princess Liliane of Belgium' (obituary), *The Independent*, 11 June 2002

Bethel, Nicholas, 'When Kent nearly went to Poland', *Sunday Times*, 3 November 1972

Bloch, Michael, *The Duke of Windsor's War*, Weidenfeld & Nicolson, London, 1982
    Operation Willi: The Plot to Kidnap the Duke of Windsor, July 1940, Weidenfeld & Nicolson, London, 1984
    The Reign and Abdication of Edward VIII, Black Swan, London, 1991 (Bantam Press, London, 1990)

Blundell, Nigel, *Windsor v. Windsor*, Blake, London, 1995

Bogdanor, Vernon, *The Monarchy and the Constitution*, Clarendon Press, Oxford, 1995

Bolitho, Hector, *King Edward VIII – Duke of Windsor*, revised edition, Peter Owen, London, 1954 (*King Edward VIII: His Life and Reign*, Eyre & Spottiswoode, London, 1937)

Boothroyd, Basil, *Philip: An Informal Biography*, Longman, London, 1971

Bradford, Sarah, *King George VI*, Weidenfeld & Nicolson, London, 1989
    Elizabeth: A Biography of Her Majesty the Queen, Heinemann, London, 1996

Brendon, Piers and Phillip Whitehead, *The Windsors: A Dynasty Revealed*, revised edition, Pimlico, London, 2000 (Hodder & Stoughton, London, 1994)

Bryan III, J., and Charles J.V. Murphy, *The Windsor Story*, Granada, London, 1979

Bryans, Robin, *Blackmail and Whitewash*, Honeyford Press, London, 1996

Buchan, John, *The Marquis of Montrose*, Thomas Nelson & Sons, London, 1913

Cadogan, Sir Alexander (ed. David Dilkes), *The Diaries of Sir Alexander Cadogan, O.M. 1938–1945*, Cassell, London, 1971

Campbell, Lady Colin, *The Royal Marriages: Private Lives of the Queen and Her Children*, Smith Gryphon, London, 1993

Carter, Miranda, *Anthony Blunt: His Lives*, Macmillan, London, 2001

Channon, Sir Henry (ed. Robert Rhodes James), *Chips: The Diaries of Sir Henry Channon*, Weidenfeld & Nicolson, London, 1967

Charmley, John, 'The King of Appeasers', *Sunday Telegraph*, 8 December 1996

Chisholm, Anne and Michael Davie, *Beaverbrook: A Life*, Hutchinson, London, 1992

Churchill, Winston S., *The Second World War*, 6 vols., Cassell & Co., London, 1948–54

Clarke, William, *The Lost Fortune of the Tsars*, Weidenfeld & Nicolson, London, 1994

Coates, W.P. and Zelda, *A History of Anglo-Soviet Relations*, Lawrence & Wishart, London, 1943

Cockburn, Claud, *In Time of Trouble*, Rupert Hart-Davis, London, 1956

Colville, John, *The Fringes of Power: Downing Street Diaries 1939–1945*, 2 vols., Sceptre, London, 1986 (Hodder & Stoughton, London, 1985)

Costello, John, *Mask of Treachery*, William Morrow & Co., New York, 1988
Ten Days that Saved the West, Bantam Press, London, 1991

Deacon, Richard, *The British Connection: Russia's Manipulation of British Individuals and Institutions*, Hamish Hamilton, London, 1979
The Greatest Treason: The Bizarre Story of Hollis, Liddell and Mountbatten, revised edition, Century, London, 1990 (Century, London, 1989)

Dear, I.C.B. (ed.), *The Oxford Companion to the Second World War*, Oxford University Press, Oxford, 1995

Dempster, Nigel and Peter Evans, *Behind Palace Doors*, Orion, London, 1993

De Stoeckl, Baroness (ed. George Kinnard), *Not All Vanity*, John Murray, London, 1950

Dimbleby, Jonathan, *The Prince of Wales: A Biography*, Little, Brown & Co, London, 1994

Documents on German Foreign Policy 1918–1945, Series D, 13 volumes, HMSO, London, 1949–64

Donaldson, Frances, *Edward VIII*, Weidenfeld & Nicolson, London, 1974
King George VI and Queen Elizabeth, Wiedenfeld & Nicolson, London, 1977

Duff, David, *Mother of the Queen: The Life Story of Her Majesty Queen Elizabeth the Queen Mother*, Frederick Muller, London, 1965
Elizabeth of Glamis: The Story of the Queen Mother, revised edition, Magnum Books, London, 1977 (Frederick Muller, London, 1973)
George and Elizabeth: A Royal Marriage, Collins, London, 1983

Emden, Paul H., *Behind the Throne*, Hodder & Stoughton, London, 1934

Fairbanks, Jr., Douglas, *A Hell of a War*, Robson Books, London, 1995

Ford, Richard, 'Queen Mother Files will cover the Abdication Crisis', *The Times*, 20 May 2002

Frankland, Noble, *Prince Henry, Duke of Gloucester*, Weidenfeld & Nicolson, London, 1980

Goodchild, Sophie, 'Queen Mother Hoped for Peace with Hitler', *Independent on Sunday*, 5 March 2000

Greig, Geordie, *Louis and the Prince: A Story of Politics, Intrigue and Royal Friendship*, Hodder & Stoughton, London, 1999

Griffiths, Richard, *Fellow Travellers of the Right: British Enthusiasts for Nazi Germany 1933–39*, Constable, London, 1980

Guedalla, Phillip, *The Hundredth Year*, Doubleday, Doran & Co., New York, 1939

Hall, Phillip, *Royal Fortune: Tax, Money and the Monarchy*, Bloomsbury, London, 1992

Harlow, John, 'How George VI tried to Dodge the Taxman', *Sunday Times*, 2 April 2000

Hatch, Alden, *H.R.H. Prince Bernhard of the Netherlands*, George G. Harrap & Co., London, 1962

Haxey, Simon, *Tory MP*, Victor Gollancz, London, 1939

Heald, Tim, *The Duke: A Portrait of Prince Philip*, Hodder & Stoughton, London, 1991

Hesse, Fritz, *Hitler and the English*, Allan Wingate, London, 1954 (*Das Spiel um Deutschland*, Munich, 1953)

Hewitt, James, *Love and War*, Blake, London, 1999

Higham, Charles, *Wallis: Secret Lives of the Duchess of Windsor*, Sidgwick & Jackson, London, 1988

Higham, Charles and Roy Moseley, *Elizabeth and Philip: The Untold Story of the Queen of England and her Prince*, Doubleday, New York, 1991

Hilton, James, *HRH: The Story of Prince Philip, Duke of Edinburgh*, Little, Brown & Co., Toronto, 1956

Hitler, Adolf, *Mein Kampf*, Hurst & Blackett, London, 1939 (Munich, 1925 & 1927)
(ed. Taylor Telford), *Hitler's Secret Book*, Grove Press, New York, 1961

Hoare, Philip, *Noël Coward: A Biography*, Sinclair-Stevenson, London, 1995

Hoey, Brian, *Mountbatten: The Private Story*, Sidgwick & Jackson, London, 1994

Holden, Anthony, *Charles: A Biography*, Weidenfeld & Nicolson, London, 1988
The Tarnished Crown, Bantam Press, London, 1993
Charles: A Biography, Bantam Press, 1998

Hough, Richard, *Mountbatten: Hero of Our Time*, Weidenfeld & Nicolson, London, 1980
Edwina: Countess Mountbatten of Burma, Sphere Books, London, 1985 (Weidenfeld & Nicolson, London, 1983)

Howard, Patrick, *George VI: A New Biography*, Hutchinson, London, 1987

Independent, 'Special Investigation: The Queen's Finances', *The Independent*, 30 and 31 May 2002

Inglis, Brian, *Abdication*, Hodder & Stoughton, London, 1966

James, Robert Rhodes, *A Spirit Undaunted: The Political Role of George VI*, Abacus, London, 1999 (Little, Brown, London, 1998)

Jenkins, Roy, *Baldwin*, Collins, London, 1988 (first edition 1987)

Judd, Dennis, *Prince Philip: A Biography*, Michael Joseph, London, 1980

Keay, Douglas, *Elizabeth II: Portrait of a Monarch*, Century, London, 1991

Keeler, Christine with Douglas Thompson, *The Truth at Last: My Story*, updated edition, Pan Books, London, 2002 (Sidgwick & Jackson, London, 2001)

Kennedy, Ludovic, *The Trial of Stephen Ward*, Victor Gollancz, London, 1987 (first edition 1964)

Kelley, Kitty, *The Royals*, Warner Books, New York, 1997

King, Stella, *Princess Marina: Her Life and Times*, Cassell & Co., London, 1969

Knightley, Phillip and Caroline Kennedy, *An Affair of State: The* Profumo *Case and the Framing of Stephen Ward*, Jonathan Cape, London, 1987

Lacey, Robert, *Majesty: Elizabeth II and the House of Windsor*, Hutchinson, London, 1977

Lamb, Richard, *The Ghosts of Peace 1935–1945*, Michael Russell, Salisbury, 1987

Lane, Peter, *Princess Michael of Kent*, Fontana, London, 1986 (Robert Hale, London, 1986)

Leigh, David, *The Wilson Plot: The Intelligence Services and the Discrediting of a Prime Minister*, Heinemann, London, 1988

Liversidge, Douglas, *The Queen Mother*, Arthur Baker, London, 1977

Lockhart, Sir Robert Bruce, (ed. Kenneth Young), *The Diaries of Sir Robert Bruce Lockhart*, 2 vols., Macmillan, London, 1973 and 1980

Longford, Elizabeth, *Elizabeth R: A Biography*, Weidenfeld & Nicolson, London, 1983
  The Royal House of Windsor, revised edition, Weidenfeld & Nicolson, London, 1984 (first edition 1974)

Mackenzie, Compton, *The Windsor Tapestry, being a Study of the Life, Heritage and Abdication of H.R.H. The Duke of Windsor, K.G.*, The Book Club, London, 1939 (first edition 1938)

Macwhirter, Robin, 'The Tragedy at Eagle's Rock', *The Scotsman*, 24 August 1985

Marquand, David, *Ramsay Macdonald*, Richard Cohen Books, London, 1997

McLeod, Kirsty, *Battle Royal: Edward VIII & George VI, Brother against Brother*, Constable, London, 1999

Middlemas, Keith and John Barnes, *Baldwin: A Biography*, Weidenfeld & Nicolson, London, 1969

Modin, Yuri, *My Five Cambridge Friends*, Headline, London, 1995

Morgan, Janet, *Edwina Mountbatten: A Life of Her Own*, HarperCollins, London, 1991

Morrah, Dermot, *Princess Elizabeth: The Illustrated Story of Twenty-one Years in the Life of the Heir Presumptive*, Odham Books, London, 1947
  The Work of the Queen, William Kimber, London, 1958

Mortimer, Penelope, *Queen Elizabeth: A Life of the Queen Mother*, Viking, London, 1986

Morton, Andrew, *Theirs is the Kingdom: The Wealth of the Windsors*, Michael O'Mara, London, 1989
  Diana: Her True Story, updated edition, Michael O'Mara Books, London, 1993 (first edition 1992)

Mountbatten of Burma, Earl, (ed. Philip Ziegler), *The Diaries of Lord Louis Mountbatten 1920–1922: Tours with the Prince of Wales*, Collins, London, 1987
  (ed. Philip Ziegler), *Personal Diary of Admiral the Lord Mountbatten*, Collins, London, 1988
  (ed. Philip Zeigler) *From Shore to Shore: The Tour Diaries of Earl Mountbatten of Burma, 1953–1979*, Collins, London, 1989

Newton, Scott, P*rofits of Peace: The Political Economy of Anglo-German Appeasement*, Clarendon Press, Oxford, 1996

Nicolson, Harold, *King George the Fifth: His Life and Reign*, Constable & Co., London, 1952

(ed. Nigel Nicolson), *Diaries and Letters 1930–1939*, Collins, London, 1966

(ed. Nigel Nicolson), *Diaries and Letters 1939–1945*, Collins, London, 1967

(ed. Nigel Nicolson), *Diaries and Letters 1945–1962*, Collins, London, 1968

Parker, John, *King of Fools*, Futura, London, 1988 (Macdonald & Co., London, 1988)

Pasternak, Anna, *Princess in Love*, Bloomsbury, London, 1994

Penrose, Barrie and Simon Freeman, *Conspiracy of Silence: The Secret Life of Anthony Blunt*, Grafton Books, London, 1986

Picknett, Lynn, Clive Prince and Stephen Prior with Robert Brydon, *Double Standards: The Rudolf Hess Cover-Up*, updated edition, Time Warner Books, London, 2002 (Little, Brown & Co., London, 2001)

Poolman, Kenneth, *HMS Kelly: The Story of Mountbatten's Warship*, New English Library, London, 1980 (William Kimber & Co., London, 1954)

Pope-Hennessy, James, *Queen Mary, 1867–1953*, George Allen & Unwin, London, 1959

Prochaska, Frank, *The Republic of Britain, 1760–2000*, Penguin, London, 2001 (Allen Lane, London, 2000)

Rees-Jones, Trevor, with Moira Johnston, *The Bodyguard's Story: Diana, the Crash and the Sole Survivor*, Little, Brown & Co., London, 2000

Roberts, Andrew, *Eminent Churchillians*, Weidenfeld & Nicolson, London, 1994

'The Plot to Betray Poland', *Sunday Telegraph Review*, 8 August 1999

Rose, Kenneth, *King George V*, Weidenfeld & Nicolson, London, 1983

Kings, Queens and Courtiers, Weidenfeld & Nicolson, London, 1985

Rose, Norman, *The Cliveden Set: Portrait of an Exclusive Fraternity*, Jonathan Cape, London, 2000

Schellenberg, Walter, *The Schellenberg Memoirs*, André Deutsch, London, 1956

Shaw, Karl, *Royal Babylon: The Alarming History of European Royalty*, Virgin, London, 1999

Shepherd, Robert, *A Class Divided: Appeasement and the Road to Munich, 1938*, Macmillan, London, 1988

Shirer, William L., *The Rise and Fall of the Third Reich*, Secker & Warburg, London, 1960

Sinclair, David, *Queen and Country: The Life of Elizabeth the Queen Mother*, Fontana, London, 1980 (J.M. Dent & Sons, London, 1979)

Speer, Albert, *Inside the Third Reich*, Sphere Books, London, 1971 (*Erinnerungen*, Propyläen Verlag, Berlin, 1969)

Spoto, Donald, *Dynasty: The Turbulent Saga of the Royal Family from Victoria to Diana*, Simon & Schuster, London, 1995

Summers, Anthony and Stephen Dorril, *Honeytrap: The Secret Worlds of Stephen Ward*, Weidenfeld & Nicolson, London, 1987

Terraine, John, *The Life and Times of Lord Mountbatten*, Hutchinson & Co., London, 1968

Thornton, Michael, *Royal Feud: The Queen Mother and the Duchess of Windsor*, Pan Books, London, 1986 (Michael Joseph, London, 1985)

Turner, Graham, 'Bertie, the Centre of Her World', *Daily Telegraph*, 6 July 1999

Vanderbilt, Gloria and Thelma, Lady Furness, *Double Exposure: A Twin Autobiography*, Frederick Muller, London, 1959

Van der Kiste, John, *George V's Children*, Alan Sutton, Stroud, 1991

Van Paassen, Pierre, *Days of Our Years*, Hillman-Curl, New York, 1939

Warwick, Christopher, *Princess Margaret*, Weidenfeld & Nicolson, London, 1983
  George and Marina, Duke and Duchess of Kent, Weidenfeld & Nicolson, London, 1988
  Princess Margaret – A Life of Contrasts, André Deutsch, London, 2000

Watson, Sophia, *Marina: The Story of a Princess*, Weidenfeld & Nicolson, London, 1994

West, Nigel, *A Matter of Trust: MI5 1945–72*, Weidenfeld & Nicolson, London, 1982

Wheeler-Bennett, John W., *King George VI: His Life and Reign*, Macmilland & Co., London, 1958

Whiting, Audrey, *The Kents*, Hutchinson, London, 1985

Wilson, A.N., *The Rise and Fall of the House of Windsor*, Sinclair-Stevenson, London, 1993

Wilson, Christopher, *Dancing with the Devil: The Windsors and Jimmy Donahue*, HarperCollins, London, 2000

Wilson, Sarah, 'Wartime Papers Reveal Grave Concerns over Edward's views', *The Scotsman*, 4 December 1996

Windsor, Duchess of, *The Heart Has Its Reasons: The Memoirs of the Duchess of Windsor*, Michael Joseph, London, 1956

Windsor, H.R.H. The Duke of, *A King's Story: The Memoirs of H.R.H. The Duke of Windsor, K.G.*, The Reprint Society, London, 1953 (Cassell & Co., London, 1951)
  The Crown and the People 1902–1953, Cassell & Co., London, 1953

Winter, Gordon and Wendy Kochman, *Secrets of the Royals*, Robson Books, London, 1990

Winterbotham, F.W., *Secret and Personal*, William Kimber, London, 1969
  The Nazi Connection, Weidenfeld & Nicolson, London, 1978

Wright, Peter with Paul Greengrass, *Spycatcher: The Candid Autobiography of a Senior Intelligence Officer*, Viking, New York, 1987

Wynne, Greville, *The Man from Moscow: The Story of Wynne and Penkovsky*, Hutchinson, London, 1967

Young, Kenneth, *Stanley Baldwin*, Weidenfeld & Nicolson, London, 1976

Ziegler, Philip, *Mountbatten: The Official Biography*, Guild Publishing, London, 1985 (William Collins & Sons, London, 1985)
  King Edward VIII: The Official Biography, Collins, London, 1990

INDEX

Abdication crisis, 30, 33, 80, 96, 100–1, 107–9, 111, 113–32
Abercorn, Alexandra Anastasia ('Sacha'), Duchess of, 55, 266
Abercorn, James, Duke of, 266
Aberconway, Lord, 152, 170
Adeane, Edward, 272
Adeane, Sir Michael, 196, 198, 202, 228, 237, 247, 266, 272
Adler, Larry, 207, 232
Airlie, Mabell, Countess of, 20, 39
Albert of Saxe-Coburg-Gotha, Prince, 10, 13, 14, 21, 222, 231, 311, 313
Albert Victor, Duke of Clarence, 28, 29, 226
Alexander of Battenberg, Prince, 40–1
Alexander III, Tsar, 43
Alexander, Sir Ulick, 122
Alexandra, Queen, 28, 82
Alexandra of Kent, Princess, 83, 285
Alexandra of Greece, Princess, 203
Al Fayed, Mohamed, 299, 302, 303, 304, 306
Alice, Duchess of Gloucester, 83–4, 293
Alice of Battenberg, Princess, 82, 84
Allen, George, 118, 122
Allen, Martin, 154–5
Allen, Peter, 154
Andrew, Duke of York, 223, 265, 271, 281–2, 284, 287, 293
Andrew of Greece, Prince, 82, 84, 85
Anglo-German Fellowship, 78-9
Anne, Princess Royal, 214, 223, 227, 253, 270–1, 282, 290, 293
Anne, Queen, 13, 179
Anne-Marie von Bismarck, Princess, 107
Argyll, Duke of, 21
Aronson, Theo, 171
Arthur, King, 11, 20
Asquith, Anthony, 244
Asquith, Herbert, 17
Astaire, Fred, 56

Astor, Lord, 240, 245
Astrid of Belgium, Princess, 274
Atatürk, Kemal, 110
Attlee, Clement, 121, 130, 156, 190, 209, 211
Aung San, U, 210

Bagehot, Walter, 22, 25, 26
Baldwin, Stanley, 59–61, 63–4, 68, 92–3, 100–1, 105, 107–8, 110–3, 115–22, 124–6, 128–32, 146
Balfour, Arthur, 19
Bank of England Nominees, 266
Baring, Helen 'Poppy', 46
Barnes, John, 63
Baron (Baron Nahum), 207, 215, 231, 232, 233, 245
Barratt, John, 280, 285, 267
Barrett, Vickie, 242
Battine, Cecil, 20
Beatrice, Princess, 290
Beauchamp, Anthony, 245
Beaverbrook, Lord, 112–3, 118, 127, 183, 155, 204, 215
Bedaux, Charles, 139, 143, 154–5, 217
Beigbeder y Atenzia, Juan, 162–3
Bennett, Captain Geoffrey, 219
Benning, Osla, 204
Bermejillo, Javier 'Tiger', 163, 165, 167
Bernal, John Desmond, 218
Bernhard of the Netherlands, Prince, 172–4, 232, 320
Bernhardt, Sarah, 28
Bertholdt of Baden, Landgrave, 87
Bertil of Sweden, Prince, 185
Bevin, Ernest, 190
Bill, Charlotte, 30, 33–4
Birkett, Norman, 109
Blair, Tony, 310
Bloch, Michael, 117, 169
Blum, Maître Suzanne, 129, 269
Blundell, Nigel, 296, 257
Blunt, A.W.F., Bishop of Bradford, 121
Blunt, Anthony, 9, 57–8, 165,

195–203, 218, 219–20, 237, 239,
  244, 246–51, 274–5, 276, 323
Blunt, Hilda, 249
Blunt, Rev. Stanley, 249–50
Bogdanor, Vernon, 15, 69
Boiset, Max, 206
Bonar Law, Andrew, 59, 85
Bowes-Lyon, Sir David, 48, 57, 128,
  136–7, 171, 190, 240
Boyle, Andrew, 249, 275
Brabourne, Dowager Lady, 276
Brabourne, John, 216
Brabourne, Lord, 130
Bracken, Brendan, 255
Bradford, Sarah, 224, 256, 267, 283,
  284, 285
Brendon, Piers, 137, 161, 197
British Empire, 12, 72–3, 79, 190–2
British Union of Fascists, 74, 79, 83,
  123
Brooke, Field Marshall Alan, 208–9
Brooke, Henry, 246, 248
Brooks, Yvonne, 246
Brown, Frances, 246
Brownlow, Peregrine, 118
Brunswick, Duke of, 198
Bryan, John, 291
Bryan III, J., 102
Bryans, Robin, 249, 274, 276
Buccleuch, 7th Duke of, 84
Buccleuch, 8th Duke of, 229
Buchan, John (Lord Tweedsmuir), 128
Bullitt, William C., 147
Burgess, Guy, 195, 218, 246, 250
Burgess, Michael, 306
Burton, Dr Julian, 306
Butler, R.A. ('Rab'), 130, 227, 237
Byng, Douglas, 56

Cadogan, Major William, 35
Caetini, Prince, 94
Caine, Michael, 253
Caldecote, Lord, 168
Callaghan, James, 246, 294, 323

Cambridge, Marquess of, 13
Cameron, James, 205
'Camillagate' tape, 293, 295-8
Campbell, Alastair, 301
Campbell, Lady Colin, 297–8
Campbell-Geddes, Margaret, 144
Carl Gustav of Sweden, 257
Carling, Julia, 294
Carling, Will, 294
Carter, Miranda, 165, 201
Carter, Pip Youngman, 207
Cartland, Barbara, 278
Cassel, Sir Ernest, 53
Cecile of Greece, Princess, 87
Chakrabongse, Prince Chula, 57
Chamberlain, Neville, 71, 92, 125,
  135, 141, 146–7, 149–50, 152,
  155–7
Channon, Sir Henry 'Chips', 55, 62,
  82, 103, 130, 156, 203–4
Chaplin, Charlie, 54
Charles, Prince of Wales, 10, 48, 208,
  215, 222, 227, 269, 270, 278, 311;
  and Camilla Parker Bowles, 27, 28,
  267–8, 280, 281, 286–7, 290–1,
  293–4, 307; finances, 47, 262–3;
  birth, 214; and Mountbatten,
  256–7, 267–8, 277; investiture,
  261-2; relationship with father, 267;
  search for role, 272–4, 288–9;
  marries Diana, 279–81; breakdown
  of marriage, 286–7, 293–4, 299;
  and 'Camillagate' tape, 293, 295–8;
  future, 312
Charlotte, Queen, 198
Charlton, Warwick, 232, 244
Charmley, John, 159
Charteris, Sir Martin, 266
Chisholm, Janet, 239
Chisholm, Roderick, 239
Christian IX of Denmark, 82
Christian of Schleswig-Holstein, Prince,
  17
Christiansen, Arthur, 207, 215

Christopher of Hanover, Prince, 230
Christopher of Hesse-Cassel, Prince, 84, 87, 205
Churchill, Randolph, 113
Churchill, Winston, 14, 41, 137, 188, 164, 183, 211, 220, 283, 234, 245; in General Strike, 61, 62; warns against Nazi Germany, 75, 92; admires Mussolini, 78; in Abdication crisis, 118–20, 122–6, 128; and Duke of Windsor, 121, 134, 143, 163, 166–7, 168, 179, 213; opposes Munich Agreement, 150; becomes Prime Minister (1940), 156–8; and George VI, 159–60, 179; wartime leadership, 169, 189, 191; attempts to oust, 176, 178–9, 187; uses Hess plot, 177, 179–80; and Mountbatten, 182, 208, 216, 222; loses 1945 election, 190; and Elizabeth II, 227, 237; death and funeral, 252
Cilcennin, Lord, 236
Civil List, 70–1, 72, 103, 135–6, 192, 227, 292–3, 311, 315; 'crisis', 263–5
Civil Service, 25, 309, 311
Cockburn, Claud, 117
Coke, Lady, 36
Coke, Sir John, 120–1, 213
Coleridge, Samuel Taylor, 20
Colville, John, 157, 209
Colville, Richard, 233
Commonwealth, British, 192, 227
Communist Party, British, 59, 123, 217
Constantine I of Greece, 82, 84
Constantine II of Greece, 257, 258
constitution, British, principles of, 19, 21–7; need for written, 309–10
constitution, US, 310
Cook, Peter, 253
Cooper, A. Duff, 117, 124, 200, 202
Cooper, Lady Diana, 81
Corbitt, Frederick, 161

Cordet, Hélène, 206
Cornwall, Duchy of, 47, 109, 134, 136, 262, 314
Costello, John, 154
Coward, Noël, 54, 56, 181, 187
Crabbe, Lionel 'Buster', 234–6, 239
Crawford, Marion, 188
Crown immunity, 47, 71
Cudlipp, Hugh, 258–60
Cumberland, Duke of, 13–4
Cunard, Lady Emerald, 83
Cunningham, Sir Charles, 247
Curzon, Lord, 59, 319
Curzon, Lady Alexandra, 79

Daladier, Edouard, 149
Dalkeith, Earl of, 229
Dalton, Hugh, 190
Davidson. Colin, 123–4
Davies, Andrew, 285
Davis, Admiral William, 235
Dawson, Lord, 97–9
Dawson, Geoffrey, 112, 114, 118, 127–8
Deacon, Richard, 143, 180, 219, 235, 275, 276
de Courcy, Kenneth, 79–80, 96, 98, 119–21, 128–9, 169, 177, 213, 269
De Geer, 174
Delamere, Mary, Lady, 88
Denning, Lord, 241–6, 247
de Ropp, Baron William, 89–90, 148, 316
Destrée, Charles, 172, 173, 174
de Stoeckl, Baroness Agnes, 142–3, 151–3, 171, 175, 320
de Stoeckl, Baron Alexander, 142
de Tajo, Count Nava, 78, 197
Diana, Princess of Wales, 10, 28, 21, 45, 141, 215, 262, 277, 278, 289, 290, 311, 312; impact on royal family, 278–9, 308; background, 279; marries Charles, 279–81; birth of children, 281; public persona,

285–6; breakdown of marriage, 286–7, 293; affairs, 287–8; and *Diana: Her True Story*, 290–1; and 'Squidgygate' tape, 291, 293, 295–8; *Panorama* interview, 294; divorce, 294; and 'Camillagate' tape, 297–8; and Dodi Fayed, 299–300; death and reactions, 300–1; circumstances of death, 302–7

Dieppe Raid, 182–3, 184, 209, 215
Dimbleby, Jonathan, 286, 293
Doherty, Frank, 276
Donaldson, Frances, 34
Dorman-Smith, Sir Reginald, 210
Dorril, Stephen, 246
Douglas, Lewis, 205
Douglas-Home, Sir Alec, 247, 248, 323
Douglas-Home, Robin, 271
Dourneau, Philippe, 305
Dudley Ward, Winifred ('Freda'), 36, 39, 43, 46, 58, 82–3, 95, 160
Duff, David, 49, 50, 96, 171
Duke of Edinburgh Award Scheme, 234

Eddowes, Michael, 240
Eden, Anthony, 43, 107, 137, 230, 236–7, 253
Edward VII, 14, 15, 18, 24, 26–7, 28, 46, 53, 71, 272, 311
Edward, Duke of Kent, 83
Edward, Duke of Windsor:
  As Prince Edward (1894–1910): birth and upbringing 30, 32–3; personality 33–4; education 34, 35; possible infertility, 34
  As Prince of Wales (1910–1936): 7, 8, 38, 65, 66, 70, 272, 273, 299; on his German ancestry 14, 76; investiture 27; and working class 31, 32, 38–9, 45, 52, 62–3; character, 33–4, 36; social life, 35, 40, 45–6, 55, 63; in First World War, 35–6; affairs, 36, 46; and Freda Dudley Ward, 36, 46, 95; finances and tax affairs, 36–7, 46–8, 263; political views and ambitions, 38–9, 76–7, 78–9; his view of his role, 39–40, 62–3, 97; depressions, 39–40, 45, 46; Empire tours, 40, 43, 44–5, 46; and Mountbatten, 44, 45, 53, 75, 87; rejects Elizabeth Bowes-Lyon, 49–50, 137; rumoured homosexuality 56, 57; and Prince George, 57, 58; and General Strike 61–2; Baldwin's concerns about, 63, 101; and George V's illness (1928), 63–64; and Nazi Germany, 75, 78, 89; view of USSR, 80, 92; rift with father, 81, 95; affair with Marina, 82; meets Wallis Simpson, 93; considers abdicating, 97, 129; and death of George V, 97–9
  As Edward VIII (1936): 9–10, 33, 137, 150, 156, 160, 205, 227, 228, 229; abdication 9, 30, 33, 80, 100–1, 107–9, 111, 113– 32, 147; and Nazis, 75, 104–6, 108, 200–2; and de Courcy, 80; at funeral of George V, 99; political ideas and actions, 101–4, 106–7, 115–6; character, 102; finances, 103–4; opponents, 110–2, 119; South Wales tour, 115–6
  As Duke of Windsor (1936–1972): 33, 34, 49, 76, 102, 129, 135, 188, 251, 299, 306; on abandoning of Tsar, 19; pro-Nazi views, 75, 78; and Mosley, 79; and de Courcy, 80, 120; later views on abdication, 100–1; wedding, 117, 138–9; opposes war, 131, 148; political ambitions, 133–4; financial settlement, 134–5; and HRH issue, 139–40; German tour, 143, 194; war service in France, 153–4, 162;

passes information to Germans, 154–5; contacts with Nazis in Lisbon, 162–8, 197; Nazi plans to restore to throne, 168, 170, 177; in Bahamas, 170–1; and Hess plan, 177–8; cover-up of Nazi contacts, 193, 195, 213; correspondence with Nazi leaders, 198, 200–2; refused post-war public role, 213; settles in France, 213–4; at funeral of George VI, 221; and death of Queen Mary, 225–6; and Elizabeth's coronation, 227; meetings with Elizabeth II, 253–4; death and funeral, 268–9

Edward, Count of Wessex (Prince Edward), 223, 265, 282, 292, 293
Eisenhower, Dwight D., 167
Elizabeth I, 11
Elizabeth II:
  As Princess Elizabeth (1926–52): 22, 97, 188; birth, 52; considered as successor to Edward VIII, 126; finances, 136, 192; meets Philip, 144–5; on VE Day, 191; courtship by Philip, 203–5; Commonwealth declaration, 205–6; engagement and marriage, 207–8; married life, 214
  As Queen (1952–): 10, 21, 27, 82, 84, 132, 145, 218, 226, 234, 245, 268, 279, 282; Golden Jubilee, 11, 26, 307, 308; style of reign, 11, 227–8, 283, 312; powers and prerogatives, 22–3, 25; financial/tax affairs, 72, 135, 227, 263–6, 292–3, 312; and Anthony Blunt, 195–6, 202, 248; accedes throne, 220–1; and Mountbatten(-Windsor) name, 222–3; coronation, 227; and Margaret/Townsend affair, 228–230; and Philip's role/status, 237–47; and Suez crisis, 236, 238; appoints Macmillan, 237; appoints Douglas-Home, 247; decline in popularity

(1960s), 252–3; consents to Harewood divorce, 253; and Charles's education, 256; and coup plan, 258, 259; *Royal Family* TV documentary, 261; and Duke of Windsor, 253, 254, 268; Duchess of Windsor's funeral, 270; and Anne's marriage, 270; and Kents' marriage, 271; and sacking of Whitlam, 273; abdication in favour of Charles?, 273–4, 289; Silver Jubilee, 274; and death of Mountbatten, 277; and Thatcher, 283–4; and breakdown of Charles's marriage, 285–6, 287, 294; and Charles's role, 288–9; *annus horribilis*, 289–90, 292; and Duchess of York, 290; and death of Diana, 300–1; rise in popularity 310
Elizabeth, Queen, the Queen Mother:
  As Lady Elizabeth Bowes-Lyon (1900–23): background, 48; courtship and marriage to Duke of York, 48–51; considered as bride for Prince of Wales, 49–50, 82
  As Duchess of York (1923–36): married life, 50–1; births of daughters, 52; emotional support for husband, 52–3; on Edwina Mountbatten, 81; and Marina, 83–4; and Abdication crisis, 121, 127–8, 130
  As Queen Elizabeth (1936–52): papers on withheld, 9, 27, 205; hostility to Edward and Wallis, 50, 134; and Churchill, 126, 147, 156; Hitler on, 132; character, 137–8; and Duke and Duchess of Windsor, 95, 139–41, 213; wartime role, 146, 160–1, 169, 191, 192; attitude to war, 147, 150; character, 147; US visit, 151; and bombing of Palace, 161, 169; and resignation of Hardinge, 190; and suppression of wartime documents, 193–4; and engagment of Princess Elizabeth,

203–5, 206; and Mountbatten, 214
As Queen Mother(1952–2002): 9, 10,
17, 21, 49, 127, 190, 245, 249,
268, 273, 277; on her marriage, 50;
and Duke and Duchess of Windsor,
140–1; possible pregnancy, 224;
title, 225–6; death, 226, 307;
influence on Elizabeth II, 227; and
Margaret/Townsend affair, 228–9;
and Margaret's marriage, 231; and
Mountbatten, 231, 256, 267; and
Prince Philip, 231; on death of
Edwina, 240; and Duchess of
Windsor, 253, 269–70; finances,
265; and Charles's marriage, 278–9;
Diana on, 291
Elizabeth of Greece, Princess, 84
Elliott, Walter, 99
Englandspiel, 174
Esher, Lord, 15, 16, 18
Espírito Santa Silva, Ricardo, 163, 166
Eugenie, Princess, 290

Fairbanks, Jr., Douglas, 54, 185, 187,
245, 253
Fayed, Dodi, 299–300, 302–7
Fellowes, Jane (née Spencer), 279
Fellowes, Sir Robert, 279, 291
Fermoy, Ruth, Lady, 278, 279
FitzAlan, Lord, 113
Ford, Sir Edward, 220, 290
Formby, George, 137, 318
Fox, Angela, 140
Fox, Edward, 140
Franco, General Francisco, 164, 257
Franz of Teck, Prince, 30
Frederick II, Emperor, 197
Freeman, Simon, 249
Frost, David, 253
Furness, Thelma, Lady, 94

Gable, Clark, 137
General Strike, 61–2
George I, 13

George II, 53
George III, 13, 20, 24, 30, 198
George IV, 24, 28
George V:
As Duke of York (1892–1910): 15;
mistresses, 28, 29; marriage and
children, 29–30, 37
As King (1910–36): 16, 26, 34, 35,
37, 48, 49, 50, 53, 57, 75, 102,
110, 137, 138, 191, 222, 301, 311,
313; Nazis's influence on, 8, 89–93,
148; and House of Windsor, 11, 12,
14, 16–17; and Stamfordham, 15,
66; attitude to First World War, 17;
abandons Tsar, 19–20; and
democratisation of royal family,
20–1, 27, 32; tests constitutional
powers, 24, 77; character 29–30;
relations with Edward, 39, 45, 58,
63, 81, 89, 95, 96, 97; reprimands
Elizabeth Bowes-Lyon, 51; kept
informed of subversive movements,
59; appoints Baldwin Prime
Minister, 59; and first Labour
government, 60; and General Strike,
60–1; illness (1928), 64; creates
National Government, 66–70;
finances, 70–72; opposes war with
Germany, 76, 146, 155; opposes
communism, 78; anti-Semitism, 81;
orders rescue of Greek royal family,
84–5; and Mountbatten libel case,
88; and formation of 1935
government, 92–3; on Edward's
succession, 97; euthanasia of, 97–9,
225; funeral, 99; will, 134; Blunt
illegitimate son of?, 249–51
George VI
As Prince Albert (1895–1920): 44;
birth and upbringing, 30, 32–3, 37;
character, 32–3; in Navy, 34, 37;
affairs, 46, 48
As Duke of York(1920–36): 7, 55;
courtship and marriage to Elizabeth,

48–51; married life, 51–2, 54; expands public role, 52–3; proposed as Governor-General of Canada, 72; and Freemasonry, 111; and Abdication crisis, 113–4, 118, 126–7, 130–2
As King (1936–52): 7, 33, 132, 172, 173, 227, 231; opposes Jewish emigration from Germany, 81, 150–1; and Freemasonry, 112; dislike of Churchill, 126; accession, 131; character, 133, 137–8, 191–2; and Duke of Windsor 134–5, 138–40; finances 134–7, 192–3; style of reign, 137–8; opposes war with Germany, 145–7; and Munich Agreement, 149–50; visits USA, 151–2; briefed by Kent, 148, 153; and resignation of Hore-Belisha, 155–6; opposes Churchill as Prime Minister, 156–8; Churchill and, 159–60, 179; wartime role, 160–1, 191; Nazi plans to force to flee, 168–9; and bombing of Palace, 169–70; and Hess plan, 177–8, 193; and Mountbatten, 182, 189, 215; and alliance with USSR, 183; and 1945 Labour government, 190; post-war anxieties, 190–1; and Anthony Blunt, 198, 202, 203, 248, 250; and Princess Elizabeth's engagement, 203–5, 206; South Africa tour, 205–6; ill health, 208; and Indian independence, 212; and Prince Philip, 215; death and funeral, 220–1, 225; and choice of husband for Margaret 228–9
George II of the Hellenes 171–2, 204–5
George, Duke of Kent:
  As Prince George (1902–34): 53, 63, 88; birth, 30; character, 32, 38, 45–6, 55–6, 82; education, 38; naval career, 38, 55; bisexual affairs,

54, 56–8, 203; drug addiction, 58; political views, 77–8; public role, 77; courtship of Marina, 82, 83; and Mountbattens, 82
  As Duke of Kent (1934–42): 99, 189, 218, 251, 253–4, 271, 285; and Hess plan, 7; as 'forgotten royal', 7–9; proposed as Governor-General of Australia, 72; as royals' contact with Nazis, 8, 91–92, 93; marries Marina, 83–4; and Anglo-German co-operation, 84, 89, 92; and Mountbatten, 87, 117, 182; possible successor to Edward VIII, 126–7, 130, 132, 137, 142; visits Windsors, 139; Empire broadcast, 142; political views, 142; as future King of Poland, 142–3, 147–8, 151, 172, 318; attempts to avert war, 147–50, 152–3; becomes Grand Master of Freemasons, 153; visits Portugal, 162; and Philip of Hesse-Cassel, 166, 193, 197–8, 200–1; and exiled royals, 171, 174, 184; mystery of death, 183–8, 320; suppression of papers, 194–5

George Donatus of Hesse, Grand Duke, 87, 144
Getty, Paul, 245
Ghandi, Mahatma, 102, 212
Gilbey, James, 287, 291, 293, 295–7
Giles, Frank, 34
Goddard, Theodore, 109
Goebbels, Josef, 171
Goodman, Lord, 242
Gordon, John, 215
Gore, John, 29
Göring, Hermann, 87, 143, 170, 173, 200
Gottfried of Hohenlohe-Langenburg, Prince, 86–7
Green, Mrs, 33
Greig, Geordie, 37, 160

Greig, Sir Louis, 37, 46, 51, 159–60, 184, 186
Griffith-Jones, Mervyn, 242
Grigg. John, 133, 137, 150
Guedalla, Phillip, 101, 115
Gustav V of Sweden, 257

Haakon VII of Norway, 77, 171
Habsburg dynasty, 17
Hahn, Kurt, 86, 234
Halifax, Lord, 131, 137, 147, 150, 152, 155–7, 179
Hall, Phillip, 47, 67, 135, 292, 264, 271
Halsey, Rear-Admiral Sir Lionel, 45, 110
Hamilton, Duke of, 176
Hamilton, General Sir Ian, 62, 124
Hamilton, Nigel, 42
Hamilton, Willie, 284
Hanover, House of, 12, 13–4, 20–1, 223, 313
Hansell, Henry, 38
Hardcastle, Ephraim, 226
Hardinge. Sir Alexander, 108, 111, 113–6, 131–2, 137, 146, 150, 156, 168–9, 190
Harewood, Earl of, 253
Harmsworth, Esmond, 113, 116, 118
Hauke, Julie, 41
Hawke, Mr Justice, 114
Heath, Edward, 260, 266, 284, 323
Heffer, Simon, 254
Helen Vladimirovna, Grand Duchess, 82
Helena, Princess, 17
Henry V, 11
Henry, Duke of Gloucester, 30, 32, 38, 55, 63, 72, 81, 99, 130, 154, 265
Henry ('Harry'), Prince, 281, 302, 312
Henry of Prussia, Prince, 17
Heseltine, William, 261
Hess. Ilse, 143
Hess, Rudolf, 7, 8, 9, 73, 80, 89, 90, 91, 93, 143, 165, 170, 176–80, 183, 186–7, 193–4, 200, 229
Hesse, Fritz, 106, 107
Hesse-Cassel family, 316
Hesse-Darmstadt family, 40–1, 144, 208, 316
Hewitt, James, 287–8, 294, 303–4
Hicks, David, 255–6
Higham, Charles, 181
Himmler, Heinrich, 87
Hirohito, Emperor, 46
Hitler, Adolf, 7, 9, 18, 73–4, 76, 78, 81, 87, 89, 90–91, 92, 93, 103, 105–7, 108, 119, 131–2, 143–5, 148–9, 151–6, 164, 166, 169–70, 172–3, 175–6, 179–80, 194–5, 197, 200
Hitler Youth, 86, 230, 234
Hoare, Oliver, 294
Hoare, Sir Samuel, 93, 179
Hobson, Valerie, 240
Ho Chi Minh, 210
Hoey, Brian, 54, 216, 266
Hollis, Roger, 96, 246–7
Hore-Belisha, Leslie, 124, 155
Hough, Richard, 42, 54, 88
Howard, Kirsty, 308
Hurd, Douglas, 180
Hutchinson, Leslie 'Hutch', 88

Imperial Policy Group, 79–80, 92, 119–20, 180
Inglis, Brian, 101, 102, 116, 122
Inland Revenue, 47–8, 135–6, 263
IRA, Provisional, 276
Ivanov, Lieutenant-Colonel Yevgeny, 240–1, 243, 244

Jack, Andrew, 186
'Jack the Ripper', 28
'Jack the Stripper', 246
James II, 132
James, Sir Robert Rhodes, 69–70, 156
Jameson, Derek, 235

Jenkins, Roy, 92
Jenks. Sir Maurice, 111
John, Prince, 30, 226
John, Caspar, 254
Johnston, Moira, 305
Joyce, William, 310
Juan Carlos of Spain, 257
Juliana of the Netherlands, 173–4, 273
Justice, James Robertson, 207

Kagan, Lord, 259
Karl Adolf of Hesse-Cassel, 87
Kay, Richard, 296
Kaye, Danny, 228, 245, 253
Keeler, Christine, 240–3, 244, 246–7
Kelley, Kitty, 194, 205, 222, 287
Kemsley, Lord, 113
Kennedy, John F., 302
Kennedy, Joseph, 161
Kennedy, Ludovic, 241
Keppel, Alice, 28, 46
Keppel, George, 28
Keppel. Sonia, 28
Kerr, Sir John, 272–3
Kerr-Smiley, Maud, 36
Khrushchev, Nikita, 234, 238
King, Cecil Harmsworth, 244, 258–60
Kinnock, Neil, 292
Kinross, Lord, 78
Kirkwood, Pat, 215, 288
KGB, 58
Knatchbull, Amanda, 268, 274
Knatchbull, Nicholas, 276
Knatchbull, Timothy, 276

Lambe, Charles, 117
Lancaster, Duchy of, 71, 72, 104, 134, 193, 293, 315
Langtry, Lillie, 28
Lansbury, George, 60
Lascelles, Sir Alan ('Tommy'), 63, 64, 101, 110, 137, 190, 198, 220, 222, 228, 229
Lascelles, Henry, Viscount, 21, 49

Laurence, Commander Tim, 282, 290
Lawrence, Gertrude, 56
Lazzolo, Vasco, 207, 232, 245
Legh, Sir Piers, 192
Leigh, David, 259
Leopold III of the Belgians, 172–3, 274
Letellier, Yola, 54
Leveson-Gower, Lady Rosemary, 36
Llewellyn, Roddy, 271
Lloyd George, David, 19, 20, 27, 29, 68, 74, 118, 283, 164–5, 178
Locarno, Treaty of, 106
Lockhart, Robert Bruce, 156
Logue, Lionel, 53, 191
Long, Leo, 198, 321
Lonsdale, Gordon, 239
Loren, Sophia, 245
Loughborough, Sheila, Lady, 48
Louis of Battenberg, Prince – see Milford Haven, Louis
Louis II of Hesse, Grand Duke 40–1
Louise, Princess, 21
Ludwig of Hesse-Darmstadt, Prince, 144

MacDonald, Ramsay, 18, 60, 65, 66–70, 71, 92
McGirl, Francis, 276
Mackenzie, Compton, 101
Maclean, Donald, 246
McLeod, Iain, 207
McLeod, Kirsty, 33, 49
McMahon, Thomas, 276
Macmillan, Harold, 237, 241, 247
Macwhirter, Robin, 55
Major, John, 292, 293, 294, 298
Mangold, Tom, 246
Mannakee, Sergeant Barry, 287, 303, 304
Mansfield, Earl of, 79, 119
Margaret, Princess, 52, 136, 188, 191, 192, 204, 205, 228–31, 244, 245, 265, 271, 287, 290, 307
Margaret of Hesse-Cassel, 201

Margarita of Greece, Princess, 86, 87
Marina, Duchess of Kent (Princess of Greece), 56, 82–4, 89, 91, 139, 142–3, 147–9, 152–3, 170–1, 173–4, 188, 204–5, 228, 244, 245, 253–4, 285
Markham, Beryl,   63
Markham, Mansfield, 63
Marlborough, Duke of, 179
Marples, Ernest, 244
Marshall, Sir Archibald, 242
Martin, Arthur, 244
Mary, Princess Royal, 21, 30, 32, 49, 53, 82, 83, 138, 220, 226, 253, 314
Mary, Queen:
  As Princess Victoria Mary of Teck (1867–1892): background, 11, 13, 14, 30; friendship with Hilda Masters, 249
  As Duchess of York (1892–1910): marriage and family, 29–31, 37; character 30–1
  As Queen Mary (1910–36): 19, 20, 27, 32, 36, 39, 46, 66, 76; and York's marriage, 49, 50; on Hitler, 81; and Marina, 83; and Mountbatten libel case, 88; and China Dossier, 96, 97; and death of George V, 98–9
  As Queen Dowager (1936–53): 149, 172, 191, 224, 226, 253, 279; disapproves of Wallis Simpson, 107; and abdication of Edward VIII, 112, 119–21, 126, 128; and Duke and Duchess of Windsor, 134, 139, 213; as matriarch, 137; opposes war with Germany, 146; and Churchill, 158, 160; letters to Duke of Brunswick, 198; and marriage of Elizabeth and Philip, 205; and death of George VI, 220; and House of Mountbatten, 222; death, 225–6; and Blunt family 249–50
Mary Adelaide of Teck, Princess, 30

Masson, Madeleine, 44, 54, 82, 88, 255
Max von Baden, Prince, 86
Maxwell, Paul, 275
Menzies, Sir Stewart, 80, 176–7
Metcalfe, Edward 'Fruity', 46, 79, 138, 162
MI5, 9, 25, 58, 96, 195–6, 198, 199, 202, 205, 217, 297
MI6, 25, 80, 90, 176, 297, 302, 303
Michael of Kent, Prince, 83, 271, 311
Michael of Kent, Princess (née Marie-Christine von Reibnitz), 140, 205, 271–2, 311
Middlemas, Keith, 63
Milford Haven, David, Marquess of, 43, 204, 207, 228, 229, 232, 233, 245
Milford Haven, George, Marquess of, 43, 54, 86, 94, 144, 152
Milford Haven, Louis, Marquess of (Prince Louis of Battenberg), 13, 41–2, 43
Milford Haven, Nadeja ('Nada'), Marchioness of, 43, 54, 55, 86, 87, 94, 152, 181
Mills, Florence, 56
Modin, Yuri, 248, 250
Monckton, Walter, 109, 112, 113, 114–5, 118, 122, 127, 129, 141, 143, 147, 155, 236
Monkman, Phyllis, 46
Montgomery, Field Marshall Bernard, 208
Montgomery, Monsignor Hugh, 246
Montgomery, Peter, 246
Moore, Bobby, 253
Moray, Lady, 49
Morgan, Janet, 88
Morrah, Dermot, 126, 317–8
Morshead, Owen, 195, 197–8, 201, 250
Mortimer, Penelope, 224
Morton, Andrew, 280, 290–1, 295,

298, 266
Moseley, Roy, 181
Mosley, Diana, 79
Mosley, Sir Oswald, 74, 79, 103, 145–6
Mountbatten, Edwina, Countess (née Ashley), 44, 53–5, 75, 78–9, 82, 87–8, 109, 117, 144, 182, 211–2, 217, 223–4, 239–40, 255, 275
Mountbatten of Burma, Louis, Earl (Lord Louis Mountbatten/Prince Louis of Battenberg), 13, 82, 86, 170, 228, 232, 244, 261, 265, 280, 281, 285; and Duke of Kent, 8, 82, 87, 117, 143, 185, 189; on abandoning of Tsar, 19; and Edward, Prince of Wales, 40, 42, 44, 44–5, 46, 87; family background, 40–1; change of family name, 41–2; character, 42–3, 55, 254–5, 257; bisexuality, 43–4, 57, 217–8, 238, 256–7; courts and marries Edwina, 44, 53–4; and Peter Murphy, 44, 216–7; left-wing views, 44, 181, 209; extramarital relationships, 54–5; naval career, 75; and Anthony Blunt, 58, 203, 247, 274–5; and Prince Philip, 84, 144–5; and Edwina's libel action, 87–8, 109; promoted to Admiralty, 117; and Abdication crisis, 117–8, 138; and Windsors' wedding, 117, 138; ambition to be King of Rhineland-Westfalen, 143; war service on destroyers, 153, 181–2; and Hess plan, 180; contacts in Nazi Germany, 181, 189; as Chief of Combined Operations, 182–3; and Dieppe Raid, 183; and cover-up of royal wartime secrets, 194; as Supreme Commander of SEAC, 203, 208–10; and marriage of Philip and Elizabeth, 203–6, 207–8, 212; and Thursday Club, 207; influence over Elizabeth II, 208, 214–5, 223–4, 231, 238; and post-war settlements in South East Asia, 209–10, 216; post-war ambitions, 210; becomes Earl, 210–1; and Indian independence, 211–2; and Labour government, 212, 213; as Soviet agent, 218–20, 234; and 'House of Mountbatten', 221, 222–3, 267, 270–1; as First Sea Lord, 234; and Crabbe affair, 234–6, and Suez crisis, 236–7, 238, 239; as Chief of Defence Staff, 237–8; pro-Soviet views, 238; and Penkovsky affair, 238; retires, 254; and rewriting of history, 254, 255–6, 260; influence on Charles, 256–7, 267–8, 273–4; and European royalty, 257; and 'coup' plot, 257–61; and Duke and Duchess of Windsor, 268–9; and Prince Michael's marriage, 271; encourages Queen to abdicate, 273; death, 275–7; funeral, 278
Mountbatten, Pamela (later Pamela Hicks), 211, 214, 221
Mountbatten, Patricia, Countess of, 216, 275–6, 286
Mountbatten-Windsor name, 256, 270–1, 310
Mount Temple, Lord (Wilfred Ashley), 53, 78
Muggeridge, Malcolm, 252
Munich Agreement, 149–51
Murphy, Charles J.V., 102
Murphy, James Jeremiah ('Peter'), 44, 58, 181, 143, 211, 212, 216–8, 220, 239, 240
Mussolini, Benito, 64. 78, 87, 93, 103, 125, 131, 144, 148–9, 166, 197

Nasser, Gamel Abdel, 236
Nehru, Jawaharlal, 211, 240
Nicholas I, Tsar, 82

Nicholas II, Tsar, 14, 18, 19, 41, 43
Nicholas of Greece, Prince, 82, 215
Nicolson, Harold, 34, 130, 313
Niven, David, 253
Nixon, Richard, 257
NKVD, 58, 195
No Kin Investment Fund, 104, 192–3, 321
Norfolk, Duke of, 113
Norgrove, Jane, 295
Northcliffe, Lord, 258

Ogilvy, Angus, 285
Olga of Greece, Princess, 83
Otto von Bismarck, Prince, 107
Oursler, Fulton, 170

Parker, John, 107, 169
Parker, Michael, 204, 215, 221, 232, 233, 245
Parker Bowles, Andrew, 268
Parker Bowles, Camilla (née Shand), 27, 28, 29, 267–8, 280, 281, 286–7, 290, 293–4, 296–8, 307
Pasternak, Anna, 287
Paul of Yugoslavia, Prince, 83, 148
Paul, Henri, 300, 305, 306
Peacock, Sir Edward, 68
Pembroke, Earl of, 281
Penkovsky, Oleg, 238–9, 240
Penrose, Barrie, 249
Peter II of Yugoslavia, 171
Philby, Harold 'Kim', 207, 250
Philip, Prince, Duke of Edinburgh:
    224, 228, 234, 258, 261, 268, 301;
    family, 82; childhood and education,
    84–6; sisters' marriages, 84, 87, 144,
    204–5; and Mountbatten, 87; meets
    Elizabeth, 144–5; courtship and
    engagement, 203–4, 205–6;
    bachelor life, 204; change of name
    and titles, 206, 233; social life,
    206–7, 215, 232–3; rumoured
    infidelities, 206, 232, 285; marriage,

207–8; naval career, 214; and
    accession of Elizabeth, 221; and
    Mounbatten name, 222; public role,
    231–2, 233–4; 1956 world tour,
    233; and Profumo/Ward affair,
    243–5, 258; relations with Charles,
    257, 267, 285; and Civil List crisis,
    263–4; and Anne's marriage, 270;
    and Charles's marriage, 280; and
    Edward, 282; lives separate life to
    Elizabeth, 285, 292; character, 285;
    and Diana, 285; and Duchess of
    York's affair, 290; on Dodi Fayed,
    302
Philip of Hesse-Cassel, Prince, 84, 87,
    144, 148–9, 152, 165–7, 178, 189,
    193, 197–8, 201
Phillips, Gina, 55
Phillips, Harold 'Bunny', 55, 266
Phillips, Mark, 282, 290, 270, 271
Phillips, Peter, 270, 271
Phillips, Zara, 270, 271
'Phoenix', 199–203, 247, 249, 258
Pilcher, Jeremy, 177
Pilcher, Lieutenant-Colonel William S.,
    177
Plurenden, Lord, 259
Poklewska, Zoia, 142–3, 151, 171
Poklewski, Alik, 142, 171
Pollitt, Harry, 217
Portland, Duke of, 186
Poussin, Nicholas, 195, 250
Powell, Enoch, 276
Preston, Kiki Whitney, 58
Primo de Rivera, Don Miguel, 165–7
Prince's Trust, 288, 272
Prochaska, Frank, 38
Profumo, John, 207, 240–1, 243, 244,
    245, 247, 253, 258
Public Record Office, 8, 9, 10, 47,
    194–5

Raffray, Mary, 109
Reenan, Cyril, 295–6

Rees-Jones, Trevor, 300, 302, 304–5
Reith, Lord, 161, 255
Ricardo, Ronna, 241–2
Rice-Davies, Marilyn ('Mandy'), 241–2
Roberts, Andrew, 42, 151, 155, 209, 256
Robeson, Paul, 88, 109
Robyns, Gwen, 255–6
Romsey, Lord, 280
Roosevelt, Franklin D., 108, 151, 171, 184, 211
Rose, Kenneth, 83
Rose, Patricia, 235
Rosebery, Lord, 15
Rosenberg, Alfred, 89–93, 94, 148
Rothermere, Lord, 74, 113, 116, 258
Rothschild, Baron, 138
Royal Archives, 143, 180, 187, 193–4, 197–8, 201, 250, 269, 310
Royal Collection, 194, 292, 311
Royal family – see Windsor, House of
Royal Victorian Order, 53, 68, 138, 195, 202, 248
Runciman, Lord, 149
Runciman, Sir Steven, 56
Russian Revolution, 14, 17, 18, 59, 61, 93

Salazar, Antonio, 162
Salisbury, Lord, 113, 128
Samuel, Sir Herbert, 68
Sarah, Duchess of York (née Sarah Ferguson): 281–2, 284, 287, 290, 291, 294, 297
Saxe-Coburg-Gotha, Charles, Duke of, 105, 143
Saxe-Coburg-Gotha, House of, 11, 12, 14, 222, 223, 313
Scanlon, Major Martin F., 108
Schellenberg, Walter, 165–6
Shaw, Bobbie, 246
Shaw, Karl, 27
Sheffield, Davina, 274
Sikorski, General Wladyslaw, 172, 175,

187, 318
Simmons, Jeffrey, 8
Simpson, Ernest, 36, 94, 107, 108, 109, 110, 111, 112
Sinatra, Frank, 245
Sinclair, Sir Archibald, 121, 130, 186
Sinclair, Major-General Sir John, 235
Smuts, Jan, 205
Snowden, Ethel, 59
Snowden, Philip, 59
Snowdon, Lord (Antony Armstrong-Jones), 230–1, 245, 287, 262
Soames, Sir Christopher, 268
Soekarno, Dr Ahmed, 210
Somerville, Sir Robert, 193
Sophia of Hanover, 206
Sophie of Greece, Princess, 84, 87
Spaatz, General Carl A., 184, 185
Special Office, 80
Special Operations Executive (SOE), 174
Speer, Albert, 106, 107, 155
Spencer, Charles, 9th Earl, 301
Spencer, Earl Winfield, 94
Spencer, John, 8th Earl, 279
Spencer, Lady Sarah, 278
Spoto, Donald, 83, 140, 268
'Squidgygate' tape, 291, 293, 295–8
Stalin, Josef, 79, 145, 175, 180, 183, 216
Stamfordham, Lord (Sir Arthur Bigge), 14–5, 16, 18, 19, 20, 22, 26, 27, 31, 32, 35, 36, 38, 39, 40, 46, 52, 58, 59, 62, 65, 66, 123, 156, 228, 272, 301
Stark, Koo, 281
Stead, W.T., 28
Stephenson, Francis, 120
Stephenson, Sir William, 171
Strachey, John, 117
Straight, Michael, 247
Strathmore, Lady, 49
Strathmore and Kinghorne, Earl of, 48
Straw, Jack, 309

Stuart, House of, 13
Stuart, James, 49
Suez crisis, 233, 236–7, 238, 239
Summers, Anthony, 246
Suñer, Serano, 164
Sutherland, Duke of, 36
Szapáry, Countess Marianne, 272

Tailford, Hannah, 246
Taylor, Elizabeth, 245
Taylor, Mitzi, 232
Tebbit, Norman, 288
Templer, Field Marshall Sir Gerald, 43
Thatcher, Margaret, 275, 283–4,
    288–9, 292, 310, 323
Théodora of Greece, Princess, 86, 87
Thin, Dr Jean, 268
Thomas, Godfrey, 40, 62, 111
Thornton, Michael, 49, 141, 268
Thornton, Sir Henry, 59
Thorpe, Jeremy, 231
Thursday Club, 207, 215, 232, 240,
    243, 245
Tomlinson, Richard, 297
Törring-Jettenbach, Charles, Count zu,
    94, 91, 148
Townsend, Group Captain Peter,
    228–30
Turner, Clare Forbes, 267
Turner, Graham, 127

Uriburu, Jose Evaristo, 56–7
Ustinov, Peter, 207

Vanderbilt, Gloria, 86
Vanderbilt, Gloria Morgan, 86–7, 94
van der Post, Laurens, 273
Verkaik, Robert, 263
Versailles, Treaty of, 73, 74, 106
Victoria, Princess, 83
Victoria, Princess Royal, 197
Victoria, Queen, 10, 12, 13–4, 15, 16,
    17, 18, 21, 22, 24, 26, 28, 29, 41,
    60, 71, 83, 107, 135, 197, 198,
    222, 249, 311, 313
Victoria Alberta of Hesse, Prince, 41
von Hoesch, Leopold, 104
von Huynigen-Heune, Baron Oswald,
    166, 187
von Papen, Franz, 200
von Ribbentrop, Joachim, 89, 100,
    105–6, 107, 108, 131–2, 144, 162,
    168
von Reibnitz, Baron Günther, 205,
    271–2
von Stohrer, Eberhard, 162, 164
Wallace, Anna, 274
Wallis, Duchess of Windsor:
    As Wallis Simpson: 36, 99, 103; 'China
    Dossier' on, 9, 96–7, 120–1, 130;
    background, 93–4; affair with Prince
    of Wales begins, 94–6; sexuality, 96;
    allegations of Nazi contact, 96; and
    Edward VII's abdication, 100–1,
    113, 115–8, 121, 125, 129–30,
    132; as security risk, 107–9; divorce,
    109, 112–4, 119–20
    As Duchess of Windsor: 33, 70, 102,
    120, 134, 153, 213, 225, 226, 254,
    286, 287, 299, 306; feud with
    Queen Elizabeth 50; wedding 117,
    138–9; and HRH issue, 139–40,
    163, 213; German tour, 143; in war,
    162–3, 165–8; and Edward's
    restoration, 169; on Hess affair, 178;
    settles in France, 213; and Queen
    Mother, 253, 269–70; and
    death/funeral of Duke, 268–9;
    Mountbatten's pressure on, 269;
    death, 271
Ward, Stephen, 207, 232, 240–7, 258
Warwick, Christopher, 56, 83
Watson, Sophia, 58
Watt, Donald Cameron, 194
Watts-Ditchfield, John, Bishop of
    Chelmsford, 16, 18, 20
Webber, Andrew Lloyd, 282
Wellesley, Lady Jane, 267

Wells, H.G., 11, 12, 14, 17
Wenner-Gren, Axel, 170
Wernher, Sir Harold, 55, 152, 170, 266
Wernher, Lady Zia, 55, 152, 170, 266
West, Nigel, 259
Westminster, Statute of, 72
Wharton, Bryan, 246
Wheeler-Bennett, John, 138, 156–7
Whitehead, Phillip, 137, 161, 197
Whitlam, Gough, 273
Whitney, Gertrude Vanderbilt, 86
Wiedemann, Fritz, 156
Wigram, Sir Clive (later Lord), 15–6, 51, 59, 66, 70, 95, 99, 102, 110–1, 137
Wilde, Oscar, 28
Wilhelm II, Kaiser, 12, 17, 173, 197, 198, 230
Wilhelmina of the Netherlands, 171–4, 273
William IV, 28
William, Prince, 281, 287, 294, 302, 312
William George I of the Hellenes, 82
Williams, Marcia, 260
Wilson, A.N., 10, 49, 112, 283
Wilson, Harold, 247, 248, 252, 253, 257, 258, 259, 260, 263–4, 323
Wilson, Woodrow, 40
Windsor, House of: 8, 10, 20, 40, 42, 61, 142, 283, 284, 308; control over public information concerning 9–10, 312; origins (1917), 11, 12–4, 16; German roots of, 13–4, 20–1; constitutional powers, 22–5; and tax, 46–8, 71–2, 264, 265, 292–3; and Mountbatten(-Windsor) name, 222–3; and the people, 309–10; cost of, 311–12; future of, 312; sources of revenue, 315
Wingfield, Alexander, 304
Winter, Gordon, 225–6
Winterbotham, Squadron Leader Frederick, 90–1, 92, 316
Wise, A.R., 119
Wolfgang of Hesse-Cassel, Prince, 197
Woodward, Clifford, Canon of Southwark, 16, 20
Wright, Cobina, 204
Wright, Peter, 196, 198–9, 202, 248–9, 259
Württemburg, Alexander, Duke of, 30
Württemburg, Charles Alexander, Duke of, 108
Wyatt, Steve, 290, 291
Wynne, Greville, 239
Young, George Kennedy, 260

Zetland, Marquess of, 119
Ziegler, Philip, 9, 27, 39, 43, 44, 77, 88, 96, 117, 153, 168, 197, 216, 235, 252, 254
Zog of Albania, King, 171
Zuckerman, Sir Solly, 258, 261